LITERARY
HOUSTON

"Papa used to tell me that when he was a boy in Harris County, the bad fellers would come in to Houston and yell out: 'Hoopie! Born in the canebrake. Suckled by a she-bear. The farther up the creek they get, the worse they are, and I come from the head of it.'"

J. Frank Dobie, in Carl Lindahl,
American Folktales from the Collections of the Library of Congress.

Q: Lastly, when you were growing up as a teenager you were planning to move to Texas?
Ringo: Yeah. I was trying to immigrate to Houston, Texas, because Lightnin' Hopkins, the blues player, lived there. I'm still into the blues and Lightnin' is still my hero. I was working in a factory at the time and so was my friend, and we were looking for factory jobs. We had no real qualifications for anything else.

Ringo Starr, interviewed in *Goldmine* magazine

LITERARY HOUSTON

Edited by David Theis

TCU Press • Fort Worth, Texas

For Susanne

Copyright © 2010 by TCU Press
Introduction and headnotes copyright © 2010 by David Theis

Library of Congress Cataloging-in-Publication Data

Literary Houston / edited by David Theis.
    p. cm.
  ISBN 978-0-87565-419-5 (cloth : alk. paper)
  1. Houston (Tex.)—Literary collections. 2. American literature—Texas—Houston. I. Theis,
David, 1951–
  PS559.H68L58 2009
  810.809764'1411—dc22

                                    2010008267

TCU Press
P. O. Box 298300
Fort Worth, Texas 76129
817.257.7822
http://www.prs.tcu.edu

To order books: 800.826.8911

Cover art: *Waiting To Fly* by Lynden St. Victor

CONTENTS

INTRODUCTION

MAYBE IT'S THE FATE OF EVERY CITY EXCEPT New York and a handful of others to feel undervalued when it comes to literature. That's certainly the case with Houston.

We've got a renowned creative writing program at the University of Houston, complete with a first-class faculty. And for years Houston school kids have been studying creative writing in their classrooms under the Writers in the Schools Program. (Many of the kids write truly amazing things.) The adult citizenry has been taking creative writing classes (even novel writing classes) at Inprint Houston, Rice Continuing Education, and other locations for ages.

So, the complaint has gone, where are the Houston books? Why are the "all things local" shelves in our bookstores stocked mainly with picture books? Where is the great Houston novel, the one that explains the city *Chinatown* style?

Once, when discussing a version of that question during an interview, a Rice architecture professor lamented, "Do our crimes lack poetry?" He followed this with "What this city needs is a civic awakening!" Of self-consciousness, one presumes. Of seeing Houston as a real city, and not simply an economic zone where you go to make your first million before moving on to less humid and topographically deprived pastures.

The architecture professor was speaking off-the-cuff. If there's any genre in which Houston is well represented, it's in crime writing.

But, if the letter of the architect's comment doesn't stand up to strict scrutiny, the meaning behind it does register with Houstonians who care about such things. It's the kind of conversation you hear at parties where writers and professors gather to buck ourselves up. "I never would have believed there would be so little writing about Houston, after we've had the writing program here for twenty years."

Of course, the point of this anthology is to demonstrate that there has been a fair amount of writing about Houston through the years; that, despite our insecurities, the world has in fact noticed us. Architecture critic Ada Huxtable of *The New York Times* even declared Houston "*the* city of the second half of the twentieth century." Still, the insecurity is there, whether you find it tiresome or amusing. It's fueled, in part, by the demonstrable fact that we haven't paid much attention to the city ourselves. That is, very little in Houston has been declared sacred, or even worthy of protection. Because of the city's lack of historic preservation, all of our cherished places, even most of our neighborhoods, are subject to the wrecking ball. This has led essayist Phillip Lopate, among others, to declare Houston "an amnesiac city." And, presumably, amnesiacs don't have many stories to tell.

Is there a relationship between this lack of connection to place and the fact that the most acclaimed of native Houstonian writers have generally fixed their gaze well outside the city limits? Donald Barthelme's fictions mostly exist in a world of his own creation, and when they're tethered to a place, it's usually New York. Vassar Miller's poems are addressed more to God and eternity than to the Bayou City, which in "Pilgrim Perplexed" she describes as "the marshes of monotony/or the flatlands of finitude/ (the designation is indifferent,/because the geography is undistinguished)—." William Goyen grew up in the Woodland Heights but his imagination was nourished by his ancestral East Texas homeland, not the (to him) drab city.

Larry McMurtry is the exception. He came to Houston to study at Rice University, and in his pre-*Lonesome Dove* novels, including *Terms of Endearment, Moving On,* and *All My Friends Are Going to be Strangers,* he came closer to claiming the city as his imaginative property than any other writer to date.

Finally, though, when people say "there's nothing written about Houston," I think they're referring to the fact that there is no Great Houston Novel, not even in McMurtry's case. Maybe that's because his Houston books, as opposed to his novels of the nineteenth century, finally don't have enough blood in them.

There is a violence, whether by the wrecking ball or the revolver or the shady deal, to the city, which for many years was known as "the murder capital of the country," that probably has to be addressed in an ultimate novel of Houston.

But if there is no mythic Great Houston Novel, there are plenty of great Houston stories. In fact, if this project has taught me anything about the city, it's that Houston is a city of stories. This claim sounds fatuous: "There are eight million stories in the Naked City," as the old television series had it. But in fact people don't come to Houston simply to live, to enjoy the fruits of their labors. People come here to strive; to fly to the moon and to create empires of various kinds and to build both fortresses against cancer and temples to surrealism. So the results are often dramatic.

That's why many of the pieces here are in fact narratives, as opposed to meditations. On its face, Robert Caro's account of LBJ's tenure as a local high school debate teacher doesn't promise much excitement. But because the future president was a driven man, and a driving teacher, the short excerpt from *Path to Power* is downright intense. Walter Cronkite's memoir about his cub reporter days at the *Houston Press* is more genial, but still tells an absorbing, *Front Page*-style story. And so on.

To be more specific, several of these real-life stories describe famous people at early points in their lives or careers: the boyhood of Howard Hughes in John Keats' rendering; Willie Nelson's impoverished year in Pasadena spent writing songs, disc jockeying, and honky-tonking from Joe Nick Patoski's *Willie Nelson: an Epic Life*; Barbara Jordan's introduction to political life in *Barbara Jordan: a Self-Portrait*; these are all stories of ambitious people who were on the road to glory.

None of them stuck around, because Houston is not the place where you enjoy your rewards; it's where you earn them. If Houston were an easier place to live (and it never has been—see the excerpt from Stephen L. Hardin's *Texian Macabre*), with a better climate and the occasional hill, beach, or pedestrian-friendly neighborhood, it might be a more cosseting place to live. Houstonians might see a little more envy in out-of-towners' eyes when we tell them where we're from.

But would the city have the "mighty sense of purpose" that Jan Morris found here, and which compelled her much more than did the constant talk by her hosts that she just had to visit the "damned Alley Theater?" Maybe not.

***

Still, we'd like to have both. The vitality and the nuturing. And not only so that we can finally be "world class." The city isn't as brash as it used to be. Perhaps it glorifies the individual a little less. Houston was severely chastened by both the oil bust of the 1980s and by the fall of Enron. And, despite the fact that some Houstonians now feel we were a little too generous in our collective response to Katrina (described in part in the excerpt from Jed Horne's *Breach of Faith*), that surreal and sublime episode from our recent history may have reinforced many citizens' growing hunger for a more communal life, one where the private yard doesn't *always* have to substitute for the public park.

***

It seems to me these days that Houston is growing into itself. For years it's been the joke—and the truth—here that, when you're having a particularly fine experience; when you feel really comfortable in a restaurant or at an event, you feel compelled to say, "This is so great. I feel like I'm not in Houston."

You hear this refrain much less often these days; I know that I don't think it anymore, except when I'm in a particularly self-mocking mood. On the rare occasion when people still trot out the cliché, I want to say, *Open your eyes. This is what Houston is like.*

Part I

Biography and Memoir

Obviously, any book about a city is mostly going to be about that city's inhabitants. And so it is here. The biography and memoir section of *Literary Houston* has more entries than any other. But it may well be that, in the case of Houston, the stories about the city's people have to carry even more weight than they do elsewhere.

If that is true, it's not necessarily because Houstonians are per capita more interesting than Dallasites or San Antonians. Instead it's because Houston has so few physical markers of its past. Most cities, perhaps every city, tear down beloved buildings. New York lost Penn Station. Austin knocked down the Armadillo World Headquarters for no good reason.

But does any city really compare to Houston in this regard? Since we have by far the weakest historic preservation laws of any major American city, probably not.

So we have to rely largely on our people for our identity. And, in the cases of the memoirs and biographies I've excerpted here, the people don't disappoint. But, not many of the people portrayed here are really lifelong Houstonians. Howard Hughes grew up here, but left at an early age, and only came back to be fêted after his around the world flight of 1938. Barbara Jordan represented her native Fifth Ward in Congress, but after she left public office she moved to Austin and stayed there. Walter Cronkite graduated from the old San Jacinto High School, and he came back for his fiftieth class reunion, but he never lived in Houston again after he took a job at the *Kansas City Star*. Townes Van Zandt was in his late teens when his family moved to Houston. After he lived here for several years, and started a family, he essentially took up the musician's itinerant life.

James Thomas Jackson, after years of being the only black writer in Houston, as far as he knew, moved out of the city in the mid-sixties, looking for a more racially accepting place. And Willie Nelson was really just passing through. He lived in Pasadena during 1959, then moved on. LBJ spent a year here, teaching high school debate, of all things. And the shipwrecked would-be conquistador Álvar Núñez Cabeza de Vaca certainly got out of here as fast as he could, back in the 1530s.

It may seem a reach to include stories from early in the lives of these people, for whom Houston apparently was just a way station. But, in each case the Houston chapter is either important, or quite revealing. In many cases Houston is where these well-known people found out who they were, and what they were capable of, so their Houston stories are not without drama.

Others from this section were more or less lifelong residents. Lightnin' Hopkins, Dominique de Menil, and Felix Tijerina came here early in their adulthood and stayed the rest of their lives, leaving indelible marks on the city. River Oaks socialite *cum* anti-communist crusader Joanne Herring is perhaps the most deeply Houston person profiled here.

A father and son team, Albert L. Guerard and Albert J. Guerard, wrote two of the most evocative pieces in this section. Both are largely describing the long-gone world of Houston in the 1910s and '20s, though Albert L. (the father) has a brilliant description of the architecture of Rice Institute, where he taught French. But his son Albert J.'s imaginative conjuring of the world of his childhood is for me perhaps the most moving selection in the entire book. It's always difficult truly to summon the past and make it live again. In Houston this almost never happens. But the younger Guerard, who was after all an accomplished novelist, does so quite beautifully.

There are plenty of memorable Houstonians whose fame never spread beyond their own front door. Newspaper columnist Sig Byrd was a master of giving such people their due attention and his bemused respect, as he does here in the case of "Monsoor" Brown, who as a dancer was apparently quite "lagoon."

Finally, current Houston journalists Lisa Gray and Robb Walsh have a pair of profiles—Gray of art-world renegade Jim Harithas and Walsh of Mexican immigrant-turned-restaurateur Hugo Ortega.

ÁLVAR NÚÑEZ CABEZA DE VACA

Most of Álvar Núñez Cabeza de Vaca's (ca. 1490-ca. 1556) Houston-area saga takes place, of course, on Galveston, where he was held captive by the Karankawa after his party shipwrecked in 1528. He remained in the Galveston area for around eight years. But as he explains here, during much of that time he was given the freedom to travel through the region up to "forty leagues" in order to trade with other Native American peoples. Here is a brief description of how he and the indigenous people lived, taken from the account he wrote for the king of Spain.

From *La Relación*: How the Christians Left the Isle of Misfortune

MY SICKNESS PREVENTED ME FROM FOLLOWING or seeing [other Spaniards who had escaped from Galveston]. I had to remain with those same Indians of the island for more than one year, and as they made me work so much and treated me so badly I determined to flee and go to those who live in the woods on the mainland, and who are called those from [of] Charruco.

I could no longer stand the life I was compelled to lead. Among many other troubles I had to pull the eatable roots out of the water and from among the canes where they were buried in the ground, and from this my fingers had become so tender that the mere touch of a straw caused them to bleed. The reeds would cut me in many places, because many were broken and I had to go in among them with the clothing I had on, of which I have told. This is why I went to work and joined the other Indians. Among these I improved my condition a little by becoming a trader, doing the best in it I could, and they gave me food and treated me well.

They entreated me to go about from one part to another to get the things they needed, as on account of constant warfare there is neither travel nor barter in the land. So, trading along with my wares I penetrated inland as far as I cared to go and along the coast as much as forty or fifty leagues. My stock consisted mainly of pieces of seashells and cockles, and shells with which they cut a fruit which is like a bean, used by them for healing and in their dances and feasts. This is of greatest value among them, besides shell-beads and other objects. These things I carried inland, and in exchange brought back hides and red ochre with which they rub and dye their faces and hair; flint for arrow points, glue and hard canes wherewith to make them, and tassels made of the hair of deer, which they dye red. This trade suited me well because it gave me liberty to go wherever I pleased; I was not bound to do anything and no longer a slave. Wherever I went they treated me well, and gave me to eat for the sake of my wares. My principal object in doing it, however, was to find out in what manner I might get further away. I became well known among them; they rejoiced greatly when seeing me and I would bring them what they needed, and those who did not know me would desire and endeavor to meet me for the sake of my fame.

My sufferings, while trading thus, it would take long to tell; danger, hunger, storms, and frost overtaking me often in the open field and alone, and from which through the mercy of God, Our Lord, I escaped. For this reason I did not go out trading in winter, it being the time when the Indians themselves remain in their huts and abodes, unable to go out or assist each other.

Nearly six years I spent thus in the country, alone among them and naked, as they all were themselves. ★

JOHN KEATS

John Keats [1921–2000] began writing nonfiction after World War II. He published six books and for years taught magazine writing at Syracuse University. His two biographies covered very dissimilar subjects, Howard Hughes and Dorothy Parker.

From *Howard Hughes*: Sonny

HIS FAMILY CALLED HIM SONNY OR JUNIOR. To the rest of Houston he was Young Howard or Little Howard. He was six feet, three inches tall, but he would never be Big Howard. Big Howard was his father, who was now dead. There was a question in Houston business circles as to what Little Howard would do when he came of age, because the lives of a great many people were predicated on the success of the Hughes Tool Company, in which the boy had inherited a majority interest. It was an immediate question, because Young Howard did not wish to wait. Not yet nineteen, he had come into a Texas courtroom, asking Judge Montieth, an old friend of the family, to declare him a responsible adult. If the judge should sign such a declaration, nothing could prevent Little Howard from voting his stock as he wished. The family view of the matter was that Sonny's request should be refused. The family held all the rest of the stock.

The boy came into the courtroom carrying himself with that slight stoop that so often is the attempted apology of the excessively tall, or which in his case might have represented an adolescent fear of being conspicuous. To many people he seemed somewhat hard of hearing and terribly shy. He had attended seven schools and was the distinguished graduate of none. He was trained for no trade. He liked to tinker with mechanical contraptions, to drive fast cars, fly airplanes, and had spoken of wanting to play the saxophone in a jazz band.

One of his father's business associates knew the boy as "this thing, a sort of nocturnal varmint type, six feet tall and a hundred and four pounds, sitting up in bed in a hotel room, playing the saxophone. No tune, just blowing." Sonny seldom smiled; the melancholy cast of his features was enhanced by his somber clothes. Despite his fidgeting, there seemed an old world courtliness about him, a sort of understated politeness perfectly matched to his soft Texas drawl. All he wanted, he told the judge, was something he was going to get anyway. He just wanted it three years early. Judge Montieth said he would take the matter under advisement until he could learn what there was to be known about the spindly orphan who wanted to be called a man.

The evidence was sketchy; not all of it favorable. But one fact was immediately, brilliantly obvious: There was little in the boy's life that could be called average or normal. Even the date of his birth seemed singular. Howard Robard Hughes was born on Christmas Eve, 1905. His mother was a dark-eyed beauty of French descent; his father was a Harvard lawyer who dressed like a dandy, practiced no law, lived on his wits and his luck, and spent what he had whenever he could get it. Big Howard had spent the years between his Harvard graduation and his marriage at the age of thirty-six chasing the ends of rainbows across the Texas plains, sometimes finding them and sometimes not—an activity that often had him sitting down at a dinner table in evening clothes, but just as often required his sweating in Levis and rough boots as a day laborer at an oil rig while he accumulated enough money for another, hopefully more fortunate, gamble. He was a wildcatter and a speculator in oil leases, wheeling and dealing his way through an oil boom. In the year of his marriage, good luck attended him: He bought and sold leases on land that actually proved to have oil under it. So he took his bride and $50,000 to Europe for a honeymoon, returning several months older and exactly $50,000 poorer. To spend such a sum so quickly in that simpler time required a certain ingenuity. But Big Howard's ingenuity at all manner of activities was most remarkable, as no few of his business associates rather bitterly observed.

When the son arrived, Mr. and Mrs. Hughes were living in a small frame house that stood at 1402 Crawford Street, next to Fire House Station Eight in downtown Houston. It was a rented house on a dirt street, but it was the first home the young couple had known in two years of peripatetic marriage. Sonny was born at home, and he was to be their only child.

By the time the boy was three, two facts about him had already attracted adult attention. First, the firemen who played cards at Station Eight remarked that he was an unusually quiet and lonely child. The world of 1908 believed that children should be seen not heard, and judging by this standard one of the firemen said that Little Howard was "just about the nicest kid who ever came to visit us." Second, the boy's interest in machinery of all sorts was rather more than merely noticeable. His view of the world around him was such that, as his mother said, "I think he thought a puppy dog was a machine of some sort." At the age of three he was already taking pictures with a box camera given him by his indulgent father.

Big Howard's indulgence of his son was to burgeon as the means came more to hand, and, in 1908, it seemed that the family was on its way to stable wealth. Big Howard was something of an inspired tinker, and he brought this talent to bear upon a problem.

The problem was that the oil drills of 1908 were incapable of penetrating the truck rock shale of southwest Texas, beneath which, geologists said, lay enormous deposits of oil. So far, it had been only the easy oil, lying close to the surface, that had been reached. Understandably, many oilmen were frantically trying to devise a drill bit that could cut deep through rock. Big Howard came across a promising idea for something called a roller bit. The trouble was it didn't work. It looked as if it should, but for some reason it didn't. Big Howard, laboring with pencil and paper on the dining-room table of his rented house, came up with a revolutionary drill bit that had 166 cutting edges, and he worked out a method of keeping the bit constantly lubricated as it tore at rock hundreds of feet below the surface. He took the plans almost as far away from Texas oilfields as he could possibly get—to a tool shop in Massachusetts. A pilot model was made, and Big Howard promptly covered it with patents in his own name. Then, together with his partner in the leasing business, Walter B. Sharp, Big Howard established the Sharp-Hughes Tool Company for the manufacture of roller bits. The partners refused to sell their devices, preferring the far more lucrative scheme of renting them for short periods to drilling companies. A bit sold was a bit gone, but a bit could be leased to a company at a fee of $30,000 per well, dry hole or gusher, and then be leased again.

Development of the bit and production of the first models took place in a small workshop during the three years the Hughes family lived on Crawford Street. So quickly was the invention accepted by drilling companies that in 1908 the partners were building a factory on a seventy-acre site east of Houston. The same year they moved their families to substantial houses in Houston's most fashionable part of town.

Moving from the familiar to the unknown was no doubt as much of a shock to Young Howard as it always is to any child, but he was to find certain compensations. Instead of his friends the firemen he now had a playmate—Dudley Sharp, the son of his father's partner. There was also a workshop behind the Hughes house. Here the boy was allowed to amuse himself for hours on end with bits of wire and metal, inventing those curious objects to which only a child's imagination can give meaning, but which, in that imagination, are just as real as the inventions of the father. The boy had the freedom of the workshop on one condition: that he keep it spotless. Big Howard came often to inspect it, and an oil smear, or a tool out of place would mean exile from the workshop for a week.

The picture that emerges of Young Howard at this time is that of an only child, tall and thin for his age, sometimes playing with his one friend, but spending many more lonely hours puttering by himself in the dim quiet of a room that smelled of oiled metal. He was the observer from a distance of the teas, the garden parties, and the lawn dances which his mother, the descendant of Huguenots and the granddaughter of a Confederate general, staged for the delectation of Houston's society.

Another picture emerges from these years: that of a boy creeping like a snail unwillingly to school. Sonny was first enrolled in a kindergarten kept in Christ Church Episcopal Cathedral in downtown Houston. Next came a private elementary school, Professor Prosso's Academy, then South End Junior High School—a public school. The boy took very little interest in any of them. An aunt, Mrs. F. R. Lummis, said "I wouldn't say he was studious, except in the courses he was interested in." He did well in arithmetic and seemed bored by everything else.

Between the ages of ten and thirteen, Sonny's principal energies were spent in the workshop, where his inventions were no longer precisely childlike. He built and operated a ham radio set. He asked his father for a motorcycle, but Big Howard said no. Days later, Sonny was scooting down Houston streets on a motorcycle. He had built it himself, devising a power plant for his bicycle out of a storage battery and a self-starter motor taken from one of his father's automobiles. Big Howard, whose own great hobby was speed and who fancied himself an amateur racing car driver, was too pleased with his only son to punish him. He said Sonny could keep the battery and the starter.

It was during these same gawky, gangling years when the boy was crossing the threshold of puberty that he discovered the witchery of the night. He had known its solitudes while sitting up late at his ham set talking with wireless operators aboard inbound Gulf freighters, but the first time the world became aware of his predilection occurred on a Boy Scout expedition to the San Jacinto battleground. The Scoutmaster heard strange moans coming from a tent in the pre-dawn hours. In the tent, under a blanket, there was Sonny playing his saxophone. The boy's punishment—which may not have seemed a punishment to him—was to stand guard the rest of the night. In the morning he was made Troop Bugler, and later his mother was to wonder if Sonny could not invent a muffler for his bugle.

It was Big Howard's wish that his son attend Harvard, just as he had and his father before him. Fearing that a Texas education would hardly prepare a boy for admission, the father took Sonny out of South End Junior High and packed him off to the Fessenden School in Newton, Massachusetts. Fessenden remembers Howard Hughes as awkward, shy, lonely and homesick for Houston and his tool shop. The boy, well dressed, good-mannered and remote, kept his monastic room immaculate, made no real friends, sat in silence at the rear of the class and underwent stammering agonies of embarrassment when called upon to recite.

The most massive experience in Sonny's life at Fessenden occurred in the spring of his fourteenth year, when Big Howard came to visit and took him to the Harvard-Yale boat races. If Harvard won, his father said, then he would buy Sonny anything that Sonny wanted.

Harvard did win, and the delighted father wondered what his boy would ask. He probably suspected it would be a sailing canoe, inasmuch as the boy had been talking about little else since Big Howard had arrived. But it seemed that Sonny had seen a flying boat moored on the river. It interested him more than the races had and had driven sailing canoes out of his mind. More than anything else, he wanted a ride in that seaplane.

In 1920 flying was hardly one of the least dangerous forms of amusement, albeit the most glamorous. In those days, youth wanted wings, and perhaps those who felt the pull of flight most strongly were boys who had been too young for the recent war, but whose special heroes had been the well-publicized young duelists in goggles and leather who had fought for possession of the French skies. In any event, Sonny had named his choice, and his father had given his word.

The flying boat roared heavily downriver, gathering speed until it fell lightly upward into the vacuum created over its cambered wings. It swung through the air on a flight that might have seemed hours long to the father waiting below, but which would have been only an inadequate instant to an excited boy. During the flight, Sonny shouted incessant questions to the pilot, and by the time the craft splashed down, he had an elementary grasp of the mechanical principles of flight.

On his return to Houston that summer, Sonny discovered that a barnstorming pilot was selling flying lessons. Without telling his parents, he enrolled in what was apparently the first course of instruction that he had ever really wanted to take. He paid for the lessons out of his allowance, and he kept his experience and his new knowledge secret. That summer, flying, tinkering with his father's new Locomobiles and Stanley Steamer racing cars, and operating his ham radio in the midwatches of the night commanded the major part of Sonny's attention. Little else impressed him. He lurked in corners at the debutante parties he was made to attend. He took more interest in the automobiles parked outside the club than in the girls who arrived in them.

At this time of the boy's life, the father was spending increasing amounts of time and money on parties, automobile racing, and travel. One of Big

Howard's amusements was to charter a railroad car, fill it with friends, and roll to and fro between California and New York. He dressed his beautiful wife in high fashion, maintained a yacht, cut an elegant figure, and was one of the most popular men in Houston. He spent so freely that his executives protested his cash withdrawals from what was now, since the death of his partner, the Hughes Tool Company. (Widow Sharp had inherited her husband's half of the concern; was advised by bankers to sell it. She did, but the purchaser, alarmed by Big Howard's lavish spending, feared the company would collapse, and he sold his interest to Hughes.) Perhaps to show his executives exactly how much attention he would pay to their advice, he then withdrew $75,000 in cash from the firm. There seemed to be no limit to the earning potential of Hughes Tool so long as men would hunt oil. Big Howard held the patents to the best drilling bit in the world. He had bought out his closest competitor, who marketed a very similar bit, and already a majority of United States oil prospectors were leasing Hughes bits. So many men were drilling in California that Big Howard opened a branch of Hughes Tool Company in Los Angeles. He began to spend longer periods of time away from Houston, tending to his California business and cultivating a growing circle of Hollywood friends. If this fortunate man suffered from any disappointment, it might have been the realization that his son would never go to Harvard. He took the boy with him to California in the fall of 1921, and instead of returning him to Fessenden, enrolled him in the Thacher School at Ojai, California. According to one California educator, Thacher was not unduly challenging.

In the spring term of that school year, when Sonny was sixteen, Mrs. Hughes entered a Houston hospital and died on the operating table.

To Sonny, the news was as abrupt as it was unexpected. The effect that any mother has on any boy's life is always a matter of conjecture, but the opinion of friends and relatives of the Hughes family was that Sonny had always been more his father's boy than his mother's. After the mother's death he was wholly in his father's hands, and after a conventional period of mourning, Big Howard introduced Sonny to a pace and style of life that might best be described as existentialism-with-money.

Soon after the mourning band disappeared from Big Howard's arm, Hollywood actresses appeared on it. He began to give parties lavish even by Hollywood standards, and proudly brought his sixteen-year-old son into a tinsel world compounded of hotel suites, games of chance, evening clothes, Prohibition whisky, and flash money; a world largely nocturnal and generously populated by breathtakingly beautiful women. Such a world and such a life constituted an education of a sort; it served as a kind of finishing school for a basically introverted boy who was never to complete a formal education.

The principal lesson that such a world would teach might be that wealth was one means to satisfaction of one's whims. Here was Big Howard, a glittering figure, one of the best-dressed men in America, singularly popular, doing what he pleased, a freewheeling spender in what would become the tradition of the Texas oil man, the frequent companion of Mae Murray, an actress known to the nation as "the girl with the bee-stung lips." It might have seemed to Sonny that there was a direct relationship between his father's purchases of jewels from Tiffany's and Cartier's and the friendship of Miss Murray and of sundry other young ladies upon whom these baubles were bestowed; another relationship between his father's open-handed generosity and the willingness of people to serve him. Money certainly made possible Sonny's own pursuit of pleasure at the golf courses and behind the wheels of fast cars. It made possible additional flying lessons—and California flyers said that Sonny enrolled in three different flying schools, one after another, always as a beginner, never telling his instructors he had flown before, carefully dissembling his knowledge. Pilots wondered why. Was it because the boy wished to check each instructor's theory of flight against the others? Was it that a lonely boy, attending the only kind of school that he really seemed to enjoy, badly wanted the praise that his instructors were quick to give?

Meantime, the money poured in. Rumor had it that the Hughes Tool Company was then worth between seventeen and eighty million dollars; that Sonny, when he turned seventeen, had an allowance of $5,000 a month; that Big Howard would draw $10,000 a month for himself from the company, and if he had anything left in his pockets at the end of the month, would give it to the first man he met. And money made further education possible. After Sonny had spent an undistinguished year at Thacher, Big Howard made an anonymous donation to scholarship funds at the California Institute of Technology, in return for which the institute allowed Sonny, not yet of college age, to take special courses to prepare him for entrance to Rice Institute. The following year, Sonny earned fair grades at Rice—except for his course in mathematics in which he received the highest possible mark.

There was every evidence that the boy had a mind as intricate as his father's. The apparent problem was that Sonny was unwilling to apply it to that which bored him. Given his fortunate circumstances, there might have seemed to him no reason why he should. Yet beneath that shyness and apparent apathy, there was a streak of stubbornness and a smoldering spirit of revolt that the adults of Sonny's acquaintance seemed not to have suspected. But boys confide to one another, seldom to adults, and Sonny's one close friend, Dudley Sharp, had this to say: "He seemed to have an absolute mania for proving himself. He didn't want to stay in Houston in his father's shadow. I think he even disliked bearing his father's name. He wanted to get out and find something he wanted to do. He didn't know exactly what, but nothing was going to stop him." ★

Albert L. Guerard

Albert Leon Guerard [1880–1959] was one of the leading literary critics in France, but he left his home country and moved to the U. S. in order to persuade the parents of his Protestant American girlfriend to let her marry him. Once here, he embarked on a memorable career. He remained one of France's most respected men of letters, and for many years served as a cultural liaison between his two countries. The excerpt from his autobiography, *Personal Equation*, tell of his years teaching at Rice during that institution's earliest years, of his affection for Houston of the 1910s and '20s, and of his dismay at the racism of those years.

From *Personal Equation*: Houston and the Rice Institute

In 1906, I knew nothing of Williams College; in 1907, nothing of Stanford University; in 1913, nothing of the Rice Institute. My career has been a happy series of leaps in the dark. I trust that the next leap, which cannot be long deferred, will prove no less fortunate.

At his request, I went to San Francisco to meet the president of the Rice Institute, which had just been opened in Houston, Texas. I found Dr. Edgar Odell Lovett a most impressive and suave gentleman, a very Grand Duke among educators. The interview was extremely pleasant, but inconclusive. Dr. Lovett wanted first of all a teacher of Spanish; but, although I am very fond of sonorous Castilian, my mastery of the language was—and remains—limited to reading. And I was not nimble enough to keep, as he suggested, one jump ahead of my students. So I dismissed the matter from my mind; and the invitation from Houston came, if not as a shock, at any rate as a great surprise.

My wife and I both loved Stanford, work and people, climate and spirit. But man does not live by climate alone; nor, to be grossly materialistic, will the spirit of Rabelais and Ulrich von Hutten meet one's grocery bill. In Babu English, "the wind of freedom butters no parsnip." Stanford was then in its second Stone Age. Making the buildings safe for academic democracy [after the 1906 earthquake] had been an expensive enterprise. I had just been promoted to associate professor, without increase in salary: a Barmecide feast. In some classical comedy, a master asks his valet: "How much am I paying you?"

"Nothing, my Lord."

"Very well: I double your wages."

The Rice Institute did offer to double my salary. . . . To use a formula familiar to all ministers of the Gospel, "I felt it my duty to accept a wider field of usefulness." But not without misgivings.

Of Houston, I knew nothing at all, not even the local pronunciation of the name, Hewston. An encyclopedia, hastily consulted, told me that it was "built on a bluff": a perplexing statement. Friends who had been in Texas informed me that Houston was an inland settlement, on a bayou, "somewhere back of Galveston." The word "bayou" evoked torpid waters infested with alligators. Galveston was decidedly on the map, because a tidal wave had done its best to wipe it off. I was in Brighton when it occurred, and heard a sermon on "the daily benefits of God": "Such catastrophes never happen on the Sussex coast." I thought the reasoning rather tribal.

My ignorance, although excusable, was not so shameful as it would be now. Those were the days when the Ship Channel was barely out of the utopian stage; when Jesse Jones and Will Clayton were rising young businessmen, and not statesmen of international stature; when, to the general public, Colonel House was not even an enigma wrapped in a mystery. I saw Houston turn in a decade from a slumberous semitropical town into a dynamic metropolis, wrestling with historic New Orleans for the scepter of the Gulf. Oil and transportation worked the miracle. When Marshal Foch [Supreme Commander of the Allied Armies in World War I] went through Houston (December 7, 1921), I, as master of ceremonies, asked him: "Have you heard the noise of seventeen railroads meeting the sea? No? You are going to hear it now." And, inevitably, the president of the chamber of commerce did give the marshal a most impassioned amplification of Houston's famous slogan.

What first struck me in Houston was the absolute, the miraculous flatness of its site. A suburb known as Houston Heights, because it was a good eight feet higher than the center of the city; and the Country Club was voted delightfully picturesque, because it contained depressions of at least six feet. The prairie encircling Houston was as illimitable as the sea; and like the sea, it possessed a horizontal majesty more impressive than the hillocks of a crumpled landscape. Over that immensity, the sky was enormous. Nature was boldly simplified, reduced to a single line, stark, functional, yet smiling; for the sky was gay with lazily drifting white clouds, as it seldom is in California. If the humid heat of late summer was oppressive, the nights were luminous and soft, balmy with the steady and gentle breezes from the Gulf, fifty miles away.

Houston, which had barely passed the hundred thousand mark, sprawled indefinitely over the prairie. Only Main Street was fully paved, in rather uneven bricks. As the level area was hard to drain, and as the rainstorms were of tropical frequency and violence, the streets were lined with deep open ditches; every house had its little bridge of shaking planks, soon decayed in the hot moist atmosphere. After a cloudburst, cars could be seen bogged in all the side streets, axle deep in gumbo mud.

Houston at that time was purely southern. . . . I was unspoilt by literary prejudices. I had never indulged in those nostalgic vision of the Old South which move so strangely the natives of Keokuk, Iowa. Faulkner's nightmare country was still terra incognita: We did not know what delectable horrors we were missing. I had glanced at *Uncle Tom's Cabin*, but purely in the light of a campaign document; by 1913, only a few episodes survived as semihumorous bits of folklore. O. Henry's story, "A Municipal Report," had struck me as a very fine piece of work, a perfect epitome of his smart, journalistic, yet very genuine art, all complete with wisecracks, atmosphere, humor, pathos, and trick ending. It happened that for the first few weeks of our Houston life, we boarded a house where the odor of aristocratic decay was faint but undeniable. It created a curious association in my mind between crystal candlesticks and cockroaches. Like all growing cities, Houston had blighted areas which had been the haunts of elegant society. Certain streets lined with once-proud mansions, their pillars askew, their white paint blistered and peeling, their lawns a weed patch, seemed a perfect setting for mournful tales of shabby-gentility. With a Hollywood sense of atmosphere (although Hollywood was but an infant then), Nature draped the live oaks with the ragged gray lace of Spanish moss, a Baudelarian growth which brings beauty and death.

But it would have taken a more determined sentimentalist than I am to linger in that sweet melancholy twilight. The essential fact was that Houston was conscious of a new day, and facing it with eager joy. I imagine we caught Houston at its delightful and evanescent best, when southern grace and leisureliness still held in check the bustle and ruthlessness of the competitive market. Old families were growing rich again: but those who lagged behind in that race for wealth were still honored members of the best society. Genealogies—all our friends had delightful albums with ingenious little windows—counted for more than bankbooks. A very dear lady boasted (but the term is too coarse for such a true gentlewoman) that she belonged to "one of the First Families in Louisiana": First Families in Louisiana were transported, for the good of the country; and Manon Lescaut, with a little better luck, might have founded one.

All this was Old Southern rather than purely Texan. For the original Texans were not aristocrats, but adventurers: sea pirates and land pirates. There were still faint traces of the heroic old days. The watchman at our bank—a particularly mild-looking citizen, with a shy and kindly smile—was reputed to be quicker on the draw than any man in Texas. The Unwritten Law was almost the only one which commanded universal respect: the Ten Commandments and the Constitution of the United States trailed a long way behind. A gentleman shot another gentleman dead through a door at the Rice Hotel. He was on the wrong floor, and apologized. But as the affair was between gentlemen, and there was a lady in the case, the jury promptly returned a negative verdict.

The Rice Institute was part of the new day for Houston; and it was welcomed with almost as much enthusiasm as the Ship Channel and the Humble Oil Field. There was a neat mystery story about the Rice bequest. William Marsh Rice died leaving a great deal of his property to his lawyer; but—

through some ghost writer, no doubt—he also signed checks after his death. This unusual procedure aroused suspicion; and it was hinted that Rice had been poisoned by his valet at the instigation of the lawyer. This learned gentleman managed to save his neck, but not his legacy; and for many years, he kept up his practice in the West, the shield of widows and orphans. He must have been a very good criminal lawyer.

So the money went, as originally intended, to the Rice Institute. The name had been selected by the founder; no one knew exactly what he meant by it—probably a trade school. This uncertainty was embarrassing at times. I was asked, "How many inmates has the Rice Institute?"—a misconception justified by the fact that the great wrought-iron gates were kept severely closed at all times. When my colleague Colonel Blayney went through Indo-China, a French official told him: "We are waiting with impatience the publications of the Rice Institute; for the rice crop is a matter of life and death in this country." Dr. Lovett added the comprehensive subtitle: "A University of Liberal and Technical Learning Dedicated to the Advancement of Letters, Science, and Art." He wanted to make it an institute in almost every sense of the term: on the broad foundation of a good college, a graduate school of technology, a research center, and also an Athenaeum, a place where visiting or resident lecturers could, without loss of self respect, address an intelligent general public.

Dr. Lovett, being an astronomer, had a lofty ideal. *Tout bien ou rien*: nothing but the best is good enough. He did not fully succeed: Men have a regrettable way of being human, and the limits of even a generous endowment are soon reached, when prices begin to soar. There was in him the flaw which, according to Aristotle, often is the excess of a virtue. Lofty in thought and speech, he was also lofty in bearing, with the scrupulous courtesy of a royal personage. He could be frigid. Dr. Cook, the highly imaginative arctic explorer, exclaimed after meeting him: "At last, I have discovered the North Pole!" The folklike quality of [Stanford president] David Starr Jordan was not in him; and his exquisite taste would not permit him even to attempt that which was repellant to his nature. He was aloof and lonely. Universally respected, he was also genuinely beloved; but no one would presume to let him know. I am now breaking the reticence of many years only because he and I are academic ghosts.

In architecture also, it was Lovett's desire to set a standard. He could do so with a clear conscience. Stanford, I noted, had to go through the ordeal of a second Stone Age; but in the spacious early days of Rice, the income was adequate both for decent salaries and for elaborate buildings. The object of the architectural perfection was not conspicuous waste: the high standard was a discipline, a costly but effective lesson. The school, in that easygoing southland, was to be faultlessly attired, like Lovett himself. The lesson was taken to heart. I left Rice twelve years after its opening: the careless youngsters had taken no liberties with its beautiful walls.

The designing had been entrusted to Cram, Goodhue, and Ferguson. That famous partnership was dissolved before construction was well under way; Cram remained in sole charge, with W. W. Watkins as his very able local representative. From the aesthetic point of view, the institute raised many problems. Cram was an artist, which is the supreme way of being a functionalist: I am not sure that the converse is true. He believed in poetry, music, painting, statuary: the beauty that exists for its own sake, on its own merits, not as a byproduct, or as a premium for efficiency. The Rice Institute is a work of art, that is to say a luxury: like Solomon's Temple, the Parthenon, the Pantheon, the Sainte-Chapelle, and the Taj Mahal. Cram refused to consider a university as a factory for the "processing" of young minds.

When I first beheld the institute, I was struck by the perfection of its color scheme. It has the same quality as that of the Grand Canyon; in description, it might seem brilliantly bizarre; in reality, it is a tapestry, rich but subdued. White marble framing the great archway, tinted marbles for the columns and the ornamental slabs, stand out without violent contrast against a background of tawny brick, which on certain days has a salmon tinge. At all hours, but especially in the evening, the walls absorb the light and make it a part of their own texture: Cram had drafted the sun as his co-decorator. To me, the effect was not gorgeous, but friendly: The buildings offered themselves as a bouquet of welcome.

It had, manifestly, a style, which was not that of the sheds at the turning basin. Cram loved Gothic, but could use it with the freedom of a master; but he had felt that it would not be suitable to Houston's subtropical climate. There was no local tradition, either Colonial or Spanish: Houston had never been a Mexican city. Connoisseurs would tell you that the whole had a Venetian, or more accurately, Dalmatian character, with a tinge of the Byzantine and hints of the Persian. Of course, it was absurd to erect a Dalmatian monument in the Texas Prairie, and the Rice Institute had no desire to foster a Byzantine turn of mind, especially with Persian overtones. But this orthodox objection was valid only for the erudite, who could trace the details to their distant source. For Cram himself, the work was not a pastiche, but a free creation in a chosen key.

I lived for nine years in and with the Rice Institute, and Cram's symphony in brick and marble was to me a constant source of joy.

Houston society might have "taken up" the Rice faculty, with all the patronizing that the ugly phrase implies. What did happen was very different. The Rice trustees were among the leaders in the city; and it seemed to them that trustees and professors, associated in a great new venture, might very naturally be friends. We were not lionized; a very pleasant circle widened itself to admit new members. They were not overawed by our alleged learning any more than we were by their alleged wealth. I felt myself transported back to my Utopia, the eighteenth century, the age when sociability was the supreme art. In such a world, shabbiness is a sin, but not so deadly as vulgar display; dullness is a crime, but more venial than the brilliancy that demands the spotlight. No topic is barred—I talked socialism and racial equality without being tarred and feathered; but pedants must leave their erudition in the cloakroom, cranks their pet nostrum, prophets their righteous anger. Within the charmed circle, the first rule is courtesy, which means, not etiquette, but kindliness. That circle, I knew, was not the whole of life; beyond it were found the deeper concerns and the higher values: work, fight, and solitude. But a man whose inner life is austere is entitled to his modicum of luxury. And there is no luxury that can compare with good company. There certainly is none that is so hard to find.

On a partisan basis, my Houston friends and I were on opposite sides of the barricade. The most formidable [barricade] was the race question. I came to Houston in 1913 with very definite convictions; I left in 1924, with my convictions confirmed. The verdict was all the clearer in my mind because it was untainted with any animus. The people whom I condemned were my friends.

I knew, not only how charming they were, but how good . . . race prejudice is not a wreath on the tomb of the Lost Cause: it is a curse. Even if it did not affect the material interests of both races, it would inflict upon both incalculable harm. It is not good for a ruling caste to pin its whole faith to an idol which is, at bottom, a lie. It corrupts politics; it paralyzes thought.

Even if the Negroes were as well paid, as decently treated, as the white proletariat is in many parts of the world, the fundamental injustice would still rankle the soul. We are told that they are happy and thoughtless; that religion, love and song are comforts which no Jim Crow law can take away from them; that if it were not for northern agitators, they would be perfectly satisfied with the southern way of life. [But] even if only a few were sensitive to the stigma imposed upon them, inflicting it would still be a crime. If there were but a single Negro tortured in the Devil's Island of our contemptuous prejudice, we should not cease from mental fight. To acquiesce in such an evil is degrading.

But it is too easy to declare that the Negroes do not suffer, because they are carefree and childish. There must be in thousands of hearts moments of nameless despair and revolt. Resentment seldom flares into violence, not merely because the oppressed are cowed into submission, but above all because they are truer Christians than we are. Religion is not merely an escape into a less cruel world; in this world, it strengthens their patience, and makes it more difficult for them to hate. But their meekness cannot be our excuse; and our oppression is none the less cruel, when it uses invisible chains, and a whip that spares the body and lashes the spirit.

After a decade in the South, it was not the South I blamed most for the blight. There were historical extenuating circumstances. It is impossible for the patient to cure his own disease, when he cherishes it with pride. What I could not, and can not, condone is the apathy of the country as a whole. We accept with resignation, and even with relief, that we have morally lost the Civil War. We even attempt to persuade ourselves that slavery had nothing to do with the conflict, and that Lincoln became the Emancipator by sheer accident. The unsolved problem weighs on our soul. We refuse to acknowledge remorse; but our sense of guilt is there, and makes a mockery of our crusading attitudes. Eloquent voices are urging a return to religion: but no religion is worthy of the name, if it places an arrogant idol above brotherhood and love. We are the self-appointed champions of liberty; but there is no genuine liberty without equality of status. Among the competing "ways of life," that one will deserve to win that evolves the most generous solution of the race problem. In that contest for moral leadership, we have lost our lead. We could regain it, if only we believed in our own principles. ★

ALBERT J. GUERARD

Albert Joseph Guerard [1914–2000] was born in Houston in 1914, while his father, Albert Leon Guerard, taught at Rice. The younger Guerard went on to have a very distinguished career as a writer and teacher. He taught creative writing at Harvard and Stanford for decades, and John Updike, Robert Bly, John Hawkes, and Alice Hoffman were among his students. Hoffman described Guerard as "the greatest teacher of creative writing in the twentieth century." He was also the author of nine novels, six books of criticism, and a memoir, *The Touch of Time: Myth, Memory and the Self*, from which this very evocative excerpt is taken.

From *The Touch of Time: Myth, Memory and the Self*: The View from the Persimmon Tree: Houston 1924–1972

ONE REASON I ACCEPTED AN INVITATION TO a comparative literature conference in Tallahassee in February of 1972 was so I could stop off in Houston on the way back for the first time in thirty-one years. To the dismay of the other speakers, all closer to the *crise de quarante*, I argued that certain literary journeys into the interior reflected, really, the crisis of early middle age. Thomas Mann, Joseph Conrad, Andre Gide, et al. The crisis may involve, I said, "the resurgence of Oedipal anxieties, or a first genuine realization of the inevitability of death, or a disgust with security and routine." All this, I could fatuously suppose, was behind me.

After Tallahassee then (where my Jungian speculations were amiably taken to task), a warm night in New Orleans, crab sandwich and Chablis at midnight, a café open to the street across from Preservation Hall. And in the morning chicory and beignets at the Café du Monde (near where, my father's diary says, I had enjoyed an "ice" in June 1924). A dozen oysters on the half shell. Then the flight to Houston, and the deathly stillness of Saturday afternoon, streets and vast parking lots empty, the skyscrapers empty too. One great towering slab of glass mirrored half a skyline as clearly as in a film, but a film without soundtrack or people. (The skyscraper monument to Niels Esperson nearby, erected by his widow, has ornamental urns above the main entrance with its Corinthian columns, and chimes patterned after Westminster Abbey's: a mausoleum to honor real estate and oil.)

My first impression was that almost nothing had changed in thirty-one, or even forty-eight years. We had left Houston reluctantly in 1924 because there had been so much sickness in the family, which was blamed on the abominable climate. We returned for four days in September 1925, which my father's diary records as the "most perfect visit we had anywhere." And I returned with my wife on our honeymoon in 1941, and stayed in a hotel near Rice. We looked down from our fifth- or sixth-floor room on a vast flat savannah of green, broken only, three or four miles east, by the cluster of downtown buildings. A modern city, less southern now. Yet the opaque white globes of the street lamps, singularly old-fashioned, were unchanged from my childhood when I thought of them as peppermint in taste and cool to the touch. We had stiff drinks in the pillared mansion of a family friend, the architect William Ward Watkin, whose daughters I had loved centuries before in Paris, then rushed to San Antonio in the dusk and the flat Texas night, seeing on the way only a gasoline attendant and one bewildered jackrabbit.

And that was all until February 1972, when I spent not quite twenty-four hours in Houston. I stayed in the once incomparable Rice Hotel, still a noble pile. Its roof garden had seemed to me, at eight and nine, a place of ultimate luxury, remote as New York's Waldorf Astoria. But the hotel was a place of mystery, too: because one man had killed another man there, shooting through a door, killing the wrong man as it happened, but had gone free because of the "unwritten law," a sinister phrase indeed. William Marsh Rice himself had been murdered by his valet.

The Rice Hotel of 1972 was peaceful enough, and cheerful too. The lobby was thronged with rosy-cheeked, smiling youngsters in expensive ranch attire and an aura of confidence straight out of the fifties. They had come for the

Livestock Show and Rodeo. Outside, though, I seemed to be the only person who walked in a city that lives in cars. A few Mexicans stood near shop windows, a few blacks. A silent scatter of overaged cowboys leaned against the wall of a bank, staring with scorched eyes. Here was the Buffalo Bayou of our childhood song, now an oily pool of scum at the foot of Main: "Bye Buffalo Bayou, Bye, Buffalo Bayou: They made a Ship Channel of You." But did they still exist, the two great romantic places of my ninth year, the Majestic Theater and the Brazos Hotel? The Majestic, with its blue-starred ceiling and deep-upholstered luxury, its great organ and marble lobby, where my mother held her hands over my eyes during the erotic portions of *Three Weeks*, silky embracings on a tiger-skin divan.

The Majestic, I am sure, has long since given way to some soulless sky-scraper. Still, it is an act of piety to inquire. I find the theater in the yellow pages and walk quickly to the listed address, only a block from where I had remembered it, expecting some smaller new theater. But there it is—a shock as of a cold inrush of breath—there, but half-demolished. A great bulldozer and wrecking ball, larger than I have ever seen, wait in weekend idleness. Much of the fine Greek Revival façade still stands and a single nymph dances on the frieze, though all is rubble behind. Forever will she be fair. A distinct impression, this: that the Majestic (which had descended to skinflicks in its last years) had awaited my return, beyond any reasonable expectation of longevity; but now could be demolished. *Requiescat in pace*, Majestic, and the old Civic Auditorium too, where I heard Paderewski play and saw Anna Pavlova dance ("Why aren't your legs white like that, mother?" asking too loud, scandalizing everyone near us). The Civic Auditorium where my mother blunderingly concluded a 1917 war preparedness speech with a plea for the "elimination of thrift."

The Brazos Dinner at the Brazos Court was a great treat in the 1920s. It had an old southern elegance and a higher lobby ceiling than the Rice, a marble floor, gleaming silver, and courtly black waiters. But a treat most of all because my violin teacher played there with a string quartet on Sundays: dinner music under the palms. It gave me prestige to go up to the bandstand and speak to him between numbers: a fox-faced nervous little man, vaguely Central

European, as estranged (I now think) as Thomas Sutpen's French architect in Faulkner's *Absalom, Absalom!* Yes, a less commercial place than the Rice, redolent of plantation grace. I look in vain for it on Main Street, then walk to the spotless desolation of the new Civic Center, the vast parking lots empty except for one black attendant, and the strangling freeways beyond. And then another moment of real vertigo. A last modest five-story building with rusting fire escapes stands at the very edge of this nothingness—half-effaced lettering: BRAZOS HOTEL.

I approach it with trepidation, finding a boarded-up liquor store and tiny barber shop also closed, an empty shop advertising passport photos in thirty minutes, a "Kitty's Lounge" with a Coca-Cola sign. Across the street the Martin Seed Co., 1897, has sunk into a final repose, so too the Stelzig Saddlery Company. The hotel's name is lettered in the marble floor of the main entrance. But everything is too dingy and too small inside, the lobby is full of bad Grand Rapids bedroom furniture, price-tagged or marked as sold. A sign at the reception desk: "All accounts must be settled in advance." The kindly clerk confirms that the hotel is closing, will soon be destroyed.

I describe those dinners and my violin teacher scraping away under the palms. Where was the dining room, the Brazos Court?

"And I remembered it as out on Main Street."

"No, the old Brazos used to be over there, about a half a mile. They tore it down in 1927 to make way for the station."

"Was there a hotel like that, really elegant, a few blocks from the Rice on Main?"

"You must have gone to the Bristol."

I go out again into the late afternoon heat, wander quite alone in the rubble. Depressing, depressing, that I had only fantasized dinner at the Brazos. It is not until my return to California, with explorations in the library and in my father's diary, that my faith in the past returns. For there I learn that we did dine at the Brazos Court from time to time. Also that a Brazos was demolished in 1931, not 1927, to make way for the station. Here, says the WPA guide, socialites once dined. The obituary in the *Houston Press*: "Farewell Brazos, old friend.

Your day has come at last . . . . The heels of many famous ones have clicked across the white floor of your lobby . . . . Sarah Bernhardt's hand fluttered across the pages of your register . . . the great heavy fist of John L. Sullivan made an ink smudge for your record . . . 'Gentleman Jim' Corbett wrote his name in a bank clerk's script."

It is time, in the deepening afternoon, to seek out our neighborhood, our house. Now my vertigo comes not from spatial distortion but from the fact that so much, at a first glance, seems almost unchanged. It is still the rural neighborhood of the 1920s. The houses are the same, and the ditches to carry off wild rains, where we would fish for crawfish, not the langoustines of starred French restaurants, but as native as the shiny cockroaches. The reddish bark of our pine tree, easily broken off, could be rubbed on the sidewalk to shape small boats that could then be sailed in the ditches—off to the Bayou, the Gulf, the North Pole!

Caroline Boulevard with its green strip, only a block from our house, belonged to the rich. But now all is sickeningly altered, as seen through another person's glasses, or on a television badly tuned: shimmering, blurred. Here is the noble Will Clayton home with its sally port where I can almost see a brown Pierce-Arrow touring car, its headlamps joined to the fenders in a lovely curve. Imagine riding in that car! (In 1959 I was tempted to buy a 1935 Pierce-Arrow that had been in storage for many years: "almost new"!)

Somewhere remain scraps of the Clayton Pierce-Arrow, pinches of sacred dust. The house itself has become the "Clayton Museum for Genealogy." Across from it, on the vacant lot where we buried our pets, is a modern clinic. My father's diary records a beloved rabbit's demise: "May 3, 1924. Pushkia killed by dogs, aet. 4. R.I.P."; and our own two dogs needlessly sacrificed at the time of a rabies scare.

The vertigo diminishes, but returns more severely as I approach our house cautiously, on the very strips of pavement, but broken now, propelling my wagon, left knee inside it, where I first conceived itineraries circling the globe. I knew the area was now black and that our house had been converted into four apartments, yet was unprepared for the immense magnolia tree, higher than the roof, and the black man and woman sitting under it, and the minute child playing near the front steps. They answer me courteously, but with no desire to go into details. I am an interloper who in a few minutes will be gone, never to return.

Strange: I seem to have repressed all images, memories of the inside of the house, though I notice external changes, and that our sleeping porch has been boarded up. Across Oakdale the house gives no sign, touches no chord, where lived bachelors Julian Huxley, the English biologist, and Griffith Evans, the mathematician, both in their mid-twenties, and the genius William James Sidis, a seventeen-year-old teaching assistant, later a suicide. He would pump us up in a swing that hung from the pine tree, counting in many languages, and once produced overnight, after borrowing a dictionary, a five-thousand-word essay in Esperanto on the transfer of civilization through Atlantis. Later, he spent years classifying streetcar transfers by scientific methods, but could not a find a publisher.

The house next to ours on Austin, where my best white friend lived, had apparently become a brothel. Two jaunty black girls in hot pants arrived as I watched, to be welcomed by a motherly smile. Moments later a seedy white customer pulled up in a decrepit small truck. Professor Tsanoff's house was now The Eagle Café, promising soul food and beer. I look at the comer where the terrifying horse "Buddy," later my favorite, fell. But look in vain, near a new funeral parlor, for the persimmon tree I climbed under the guidance of my good black friend (Henry? what a betrayal to have lost his name!) and, turning to look down, experienced a deep vertigo, a disruption of the visible world. My feet jammed against two branches, a third across my chest, looking down in a quite new way: the familiar sidewalk and street only fifteen feet below taking on a glittering strangeness.

And so it seemed to me that February: dizzying alteration of the known. For the two spatial worlds were oddly superimposed: 1924 and 1972. I refused to test my feeling that I could, by simply taking off my glasses, correct the distortion, remove some of the wild overgrowth, repair the broken windows, take down that sign on a house three doors from ours: "Unfit for Human Habitation." As the stage suddenly darkens and the wilderness of a century blurs the outlines of the castle behind which the ballet princess lies asleep, so the Houston I could not quite remember was only half-hidden by shrubbery and by the decayed houses at which I stared. I could not, for the moment, imagine the inside of our house. I would have to go back to California, and to my father's books and diary, and to other books, to find my way inside.

It was only later, back in California, that I exposed memory to the test of the written word. History's savage reduction of chaotic experience or brute happiness to a paragraph, a sentence, a line! "A. J. operated (tonsils) 8.30. Takes it very well." Thus the diary for January 3, 1922, with no reference to the scary malevolent witch's head that hung over me (wearing a nurse's cap) at the moment of waking from ether, and associated for years, as she returned in dreams, with the ether's sickly aftertaste. For February 1, 1923, my father simply denies my existence, erases me, since he records that my sister heard Paderewski. But I too was there! I can even describe our place in the balcony, about the twelfth row, and my delight when (in an ultimate encore) Paderewski played "Turkey in the Straw" with two fingers. Might as well say I hadn't seen Pavlova of the preternaturally white legs, or Gloria Swanson in *Three Weeks!*

But sociology, [such as] the competent *Houston: The Bayou City* [an "urban biography" by David McComb], can momentarily recapture the past. For two of its most minor facts are almost as effective for me as Marcel's madeleine dipped in tea or Vinteuil's sonata. The Galveston interurban "utilized fifty-four seat cars," was powered by electricity, "painted Pullman green and capable of moving fifty-five to sixty miles per hour . . ." I had not thought of our Galveston trip for years, though a lover of interurbans. Now the bleak landscape returns, flat as the French Camargue, and the sway of the cars, the mysterious surge of power. Galveston, dinner at the Galvez Hotel, a walk along the seawall, gulls and the glittering sea: January 1, 1920. Another trip to Galveston, or at least down the Bayou some way, on Miss Ima Hogg's yacht in 1924, permitted us to see the immense white hulls of transports built during the First World War but left unfinished because of the Armistice. Their concrete hulls, an anomaly, lean heavily toward shore, deeply embedded in mud. In McComb's book I read: "In 1921 three uncompleted hulls and five wooden vessels could be seen rotting where they had been left on the bayou." A flat sentence, which in no way accounts for the emotion I feel at these words. And wooden not concrete. Turning on a hunch to the end of Faulkner's *Wild Palms*, I discover why I have always found his pages so deeply moving. For the prisoner Wilbourne sees such a ship from his cell and, aware of the couple living on the ship, surviving, more fully values the free life he is about to lose: "... saw, beyond the flat one-story border of the river and toward the sea, the concrete hull of one of the emergency ships built in 1918 and never finished, the hull, the hulk: It had never moved, the ways rotted out from under it years ago, leaving it sitting on a mudflat beside the bright glitter of the river's mouth with a thin line of drying garments across the after well deck."

Again I look at our Houston house as from across the street, from two thousand miles, and try to imagine myself inside. Of the downstairs I see only the rabbit Pushkia, redivivus, a lovely buff against the snowy tablecloth, about to overturn the sugar bowl. Our sleeping porch, stretching the width of the house and open on three sides to the sky, in 1972 is boarded up to create some more practical room. Next to it on the second story, at the front of the house (facing me, that is) was the nursery, a large bright room, one of the best in the house, a place of warmth and security.

It is hard to hold the nursery in mind. Next to it is the bathroom where my sister and I, soaped all over, played in the bath, assuming new names—I "Slithery," she "Blithery." Opaque memories, opaque as soapy water, as a cloud of steam ... "Don't you remember," my sister asks, "the wallpaper of our bathroom—blue sea gulls with waves underneath and cross-hatched with lines to represent tiles?" I do remember the sleeping porch well: the wind in the pines, distant storms with flashes and rolling thunder, sudden beating rain. The whole family slept on the porch, one large double bed, single beds for my sister and me. On Sunday mornings we would all pile into the one big bed for a romp. Only a few sounds reach me after fifty-five years, over the wind in the pines. One was a sinister sound. For many years my father suffered from nervous fatigue, depressions, and the possibility of breakdown. His *crise de quarante*, if it was that, lasted many years. Occasionally he would slam and lock the door to his study and, as I understood it, "smash the furniture," throw chairs and small tables and books against the wall. There would be long silences, as I held my breath, imagining quite clearly my father red in the face and biting his tongue at a corner of his mouth, trying to suppress his rage. Silence, then, like a clap of thunder, a first chair flung against the wall, silence again, once more the wild shatterings.

What frustration, what deep sense of failure, what feeling that the big decisions of his life had been a mistake? As I think about it now, that furniture so frequently smashed against the wall was remarkably durable.

A romantic sound was that of "old Methuselah," an oil well some miles away that gushed and roared for a week, a mysterious murmur by the time it reached us. The satisfaction of waking in the bright morning to know old Methuselah was still alive! Most thrilling of all, though, was the wail of the "Katy Flyer" deep in the night, crack train of the Missouri, Kansas, and Texas. I had been on great trains. I knew well the breathtaking crescendo approach, at night, of a train speeding in the other direction as one lay trembling in his berth—the wild roar and the ten or so sucking sounds clearly punctuating each flying car. Yet nothing was so romantic as this train, the Katy Flyer, departing from the other end of Houston: a long, long banshee wail, a sound that traveled both toward me and rushingly away.

And we would leave it all, by train, provisionally we thought, for the summer only, in June 1922. However, my father's summer session teaching in Los Angeles would ultimately take us, three years later, to California for good. Luckily, a true Texas patriot, I did not know it then. So few days in my life can have been richer, more exciting than June 13, 1922, in that eighth year of my life. "Very hot. House cleaning (cellar, yard, garage). Downtown. Leave 5.30 in Clayton's car. Dinner Brazos Court. Movies 'School Days' at Iris. Leave 10.50 Sunset Limited." So I did ride after all in the great Clayton Pierce-Arrow, driven not by Mr. Clayton but by a chauffeur who suddenly appears on my page, military cap and moustache. I see the shining brass instruments, the handles, the headlights that blend back into the fenders, a different and more feminine curve when seen from inside the car. I watch the skillful shifting of gears as we glide down Oakdale and onto Main. Then the Brazos Court of the marble floor and immaculate tables, the flowers, the black waiter smiling, the palms, the grapefruit. And yes, corn on the cob held by silver spits!

And then, so late at night, not to go home but to board the Sunset Limited! We wait, then hear the distant wail, the humming of the rails, a small secret light snaking oddly in the dark, then a piercing beam. And the train bearing down on us, the grinding dinosaur engine, now the cars gliding, the squeal and crunch of brakes; the dark sleeping cars with their numbers slowing, slowing, stopped. Drippings and a great rush of steam. We find our car. And here, flourishing his stool as a Brazos waiter with his white napkin, is the smiling porter to welcome us: a powerful and knowing man, a king. He leads us, tiptoeing, finger on his lips, past the washroom with its curtain just revealing the basins (one tiny spigot for the teeth only, incredible luxury), past gleaming mahogany walls and the sumptuous closed door of the drawing room. Then the real sleeping car, with a smell as familiar as the Paris Metro's, the stiff green curtains concealing the sleepers who got on at New Orleans: a place of dimmed lights and two whirring fans. A cough, a sharp snore; strangers turn in their berths. And the comic business of trying to undress while sitting down. No excitement, no bliss of Proust's was comparable to mine as I lay by my father—or was it my mother—in the lower berth. My sister and I would trade off this privilege all the way: the early morning pleasure of peeping out to look at the plains, a lonely station, a ranch. I would have missed, sometime during the night, San Antonio.

For the next morning we woke to the solitudes of West Texas, which we would be traveling much of the day. Do I see the wonderful dining car, a vase of flowers for each table, through my own eyes truly, or through those of Stephen Crane's embarrassed bridegroom on his way to Yellow Sky? Sometime during the trip I wrote a "book"—title page, contents, illustrations, all—which I then wanted my father to pay for. He gave me a singularly humorless sermon on the importance of distinguishing between real life and playacting, fact and fantasy. An unhappy moment. But most of that long day I spent on the observation car platform, staring at the receding desert and timing the small white posts that marked each receding mile (not knowing it was my life that was receding, carried westward at sixty miles an hour, Houston behind us, myself behind) as I computed the train's speed, marking off the miles against the second hand of my watch. ★

ROBERT A. CARO

Robert Caro has twice won both the Pulitzer Prize, and the National Book Critic Circle Award for Best Nonfiction Book of the Year. In his four-volume biography of Lyndon Baines Johnson (volume four is due in 2012), Caro has been accused of being too hard on the late president. But in fact Caro performs truly exhaustive research, and then looks at his subject in detail that goes far beyond the call of duty. Consider the following story, in which young Lyndon coaches a Houston high school debate team for a year. Another biographer might give that episode a sentence, but Caro uses it to paint an unforgettable portrait of a driven man.

From *The Path to Power: The Years of Lyndon Johnson, Volume I*: A Very Unusual Ability

HOUSTON MUST HAVE LOOKED HUGE TO Lyndon Johnson as he drove toward it across the flat Gulf plains in his battered little car; from miles away, the setbacks of its skyscrapers, thirty stories high and more, cut right angles out of the blue Gulf sky; the long lines of factory smokestacks before them belched out plumes of smoke like banners announcing a new age for Texas, and the last miles before he reached the city were covered with forests of oil derricks. With its population closing in on 300,000, Houston dwarfed the cities of his youth; the high school in which he was to teach, with its 1,800 students, was twice as large as his college (and its faculty had more advanced degrees than the San Marcos faculty). But if he felt intimidated or unsure, he gave no sign of it; while informing Lyndon that he would not only be teaching public speaking but coaching the debating team, his new principal mentioned that the team had never won the city championship, and Lyndon announced that it would win this year—and would win the state championship as well!

Public speaking at Sam Houston High School had been taught by a mild-mannered gentleman whose classes were rigidly decorous. On the first day with Lyndon Johnson, every student had to stand up in front of the class and "make noises" for ten seconds. Any noises, Johnson said: "Ow, ow, ow," or "Roaw, roaw, roaw"—just any noises at all. The next day, it was thirty seconds, and the noises had to be animal noises: roar like a lion, quack like a duck. "You were sort of encouraged to be silly," recalls one of his students. "He was trying to get people to feel comfortable on the podium, to make the whole thing such a game that no one would feel embarrassed. He'd do it with smiling and laughter to make you feel at ease. 'Everybody's going to do it, so don't worry about it—just have fun.' And we did. Even the shy kids did. There was a feeling that we're all comrades, we're all going to be doing these silly things, so we were all together in it. And everyone would laugh." Then came speeches—first, thirty seconds, "very short, and on so limited a topic that you wouldn't be scared." Then a minute, and then five minutes. Speeches no longer extemporaneous but prepared, and prepared thoroughly. "I have a memory of an *enormous* number of assignments," says one student. "And he was terribly strict about you doing them." Says another: "We had to do more reading for Mr. Johnson's course than all the rest of my courses combined. You really had to *know* your stuff." Then came the heckling. "No kidding—heckling," one student says. If the heckling wasn't fierce enough, the teacher would join in. Students could try to pick holes in a speaker's arguments, or simply insult him, or shout nonsense to try to drown him out. "The idea of that was so you could keep your head clear and think logically of the arguments, no matter how much pressure you were under," a student says. Always the teacher was picking out flaws, not only in arguments but in appearance. "Mr. Johnson wanted you to stand straight, but not stiff, to move your eyes around, no silly gestures but make some gestures to show you're alive. And he'd shout at you, 'C'mon, Gene, stand up! Stop slouching! Who're you talking to, Gene—the ceiling? Look at the audience! C'mon, Gene, look at them!' Boy, he wanted you *perfect*."

In general, his students didn't resent the shouting or the insistence on perfection. One of them—William Goode, later a renowned sociologist—says this was partly *because* of the insistence: "He made you feel important just because he's nagging at you so much. He's throwing his whole self into improving you." Partly it was because the students could see that he was working himself as hard as he was working them. When they handed in written assignments, the assignments were handed back the following day, always. And they were handed back with their margins filled with comments. For some months, another teacher, Byron Parker, roomed in the same house as Johnson. He remembers that sometimes when he went to sleep, Johnson would be sitting at a little desk piled high with his students' papers, and sometimes when he woke up the next morning, Johnson would still be sitting there, correcting the last of the papers; he had not slept that night. "He did that job as if his life depended on it," William Goode says. His classes were "very exciting, and everybody thought so. He wasn't a sitdown teacher—he strode back and forth and harangued. He was overpowering as hell."

Out of his public-speaking classes, the new teacher had to select a debating team. The two youths he chose were both, in those Depression years, delivery boys, but there the similarity ended. Luther E. Jones, seventeen (known as "L. E."), was tall, handsome, brilliant, but stiff and aloof—"smart as hell, but cold as hell," a student says. "And so reserved, I remember thinking, 'How the hell is he going to get up on a stage and sell himself?'" Gene Latimer, a short, stocky, sixteen-year-old whose hair never stayed combed, was, this student says, "an Irish charmer, with a cocky, wonderful smile, and a marvelous gift of gab." But he was rebellious, insolent, notorious for not doing his assignments, always in some kind of mischief. "They were not the ones people expected Mr. Johnson to pick," a student says.

But Mr. Johnson was a reader of men. "At first he is not my favorite teacher," Latimer says.

> He impinges too much on my hours of leisure. . . . In practice he has no reticence in cutting me off in the middle of a sentence to comment on its inadequacy, and to make pointed suggestions for improvement.

Soon, the rebellious, independent Irish boy who had never willingly obeyed any teacher was waiting anxiously for an expression of approval in this teacher's eyes.

In competition he sits at the back of the auditorium and has an unsettling habit of frowning and ruefully shaking his head just when I think I am on the right track. But once in a while he opens his mouth in amazement at how clearly I am making a point. He sits up very straight and looks around in wonderment at the audience to make sure they're not missing this. And it is then he makes me think I have just personally thought of, and am in the process of enunciating, an improvement on the Sermon on the Mount.

Johnson had somehow seen in Gene Latimer—as he had in Willard Deason, another man not easily led—someone who would accept his leadership, totally and unquestioningly. Latimer would work for Johnson off and on for much of his life as, in the words of another Johnson staff member, "his slave—his totally willing slave." In his oral history Latimer says of Johnson: "He [is] the best friend I shall ever have."

Having picked his men, he trained them. No one at Sam Houston High had ever witnessed training like this. Day after day, teachers passing the auditorium late in the afternoon—hours after classes had been dismissed—would hear voices and, looking in, would see Jones or Latimer (or Margaret Epley and Evelyn Lee, the two women debaters) or one of the "declaimers," five or six students who had lost out for the debate team but represented the school in declamation contests, up on the stage, practicing. And seated in the audience, commenting on their delivery, was their coach. Delivery was only part of what he was teaching. William Goode, one of the declaimers, says: "He picked out your suit for contests, [or] how much lipstick and what dress you wore. Nothing was too small. Everything had to be perfect . . . It was a total enveloping process." And the work in the auditorium was only part of the work. Day after day, the debating team polished its delivery; night after night, it polished its arguments. The topic for the Interscholastic League Debates—the state championships—was: "Resolved: That the Jury System Should Be Abolished." In the evenings, Johnson and his debaters read everything they could find on the jury system. But, other teachers noticed, the debaters didn't seem to mind the work their coach loaded on them. "He worked the life out of them, but they would do anything for him," one says.

Then the schedule of practice debates began. No one in Texas had ever seen a schedule like this. In informal, "no-decision" contests, the Sam Houston High School team faced every team in Houston that would debate them. Then the team left Houston: writing letters to scores of high schools, arranging without any assistance all the complicated logistics involved, the new debating coach had, in his first year as coach, arranged a tour—hundreds of miles long—of a magnitude beyond any ever before scheduled by a Texas high school debating team.

The time spent driving those hundreds of miles could not be wasted; as they drove, Lyndon Johnson's debaters practiced. The debates themselves were learning experiences: a telling point or anecdote used by another school had to be incorporated into their own presentation. They debated one school on their way west from Houston, and a week or two later—on their way back, they debated the same school again—and its coach heard the Sam Houston High team using the very arguments his team had used on them in the first debate.

Nonetheless, the trip was fun. A certain barrier between the coach and his team, between the teacher and his students, was never lowered. "Lyndon was always the teacher, and I was the pupil," L. E. Jones says. "He was always in a position of command, and he acted like that." But they *were* pupils, and they understood and accepted that. And as long as that understanding existed in the Model A roadster, there could exist also laughter. Assured of his position, Johnson may not have been more relaxed, but he was more jovial. He regaled the four debaters with stories—most of them about politics ("He talked about Welly Hopkins incessantly, about the campaign he had won for Welly Hopkins; he was proud of himself"). They were so fascinated by his stories that they would remember some of them in detail forty-five years later. The hundreds of miles sped by—and not just because of the speed at which Johnson drove. "Though we practice even as we drive, we also sing and joke with the Chief leading," Latimer recalls. "With the Chief leading the singing and the joking. And these are days to cherish and remember."

And the trip—and the whole debating season—was fun because they and the women's teams won. The school newspaper ran their pictures—on a page which contained a drawing of a crowing cock and the words: " 'Nuff said."

During the two weeks before the state championships were to be held in Austin, preparations intensified. With the school caught up in the excitement, whole classes researched the jury system and its alternatives to find new material, and Johnson scheduled still more practice debates. "In Austin," Latimer recalls, "it is evident that a few other teams had been practicing, too." Epley and Lee were defeated in one of a series of elimination debates, but Latimer and Jones advanced to the finals. After sixty-seven consecutive victories, one more would give Sam Houston High the state championship Johnson had promised.

For that final, debate, Johnson's team drew the affirmative. "I just almost cried," Johnson was to recall. "We had no trouble on the side that it shouldn't be abolished. But when we had the affirmative," although his boys had always managed to win anyway, "we always had trouble." Waiting for the judges' verdict, the two young men and their coach thought they had won again. Johnson was to remember for the rest of his life the suspense as the judges announced their votes. "They drew it out, and they said affirmative and that brought smiles and then negative and then they waited a long time and it was negative and we lost it by one vote, 3-2." Latimer looked first for his coach. "The look on [his] face is one of disbelief, and my worst reaction is that in some ways we have let him down." But that look passed quickly. "He tells us that we have done well and he comforts us," Latimer says. And Latimer and Jones never knew that when he was done comforting them, their coach went behind the stage and vomited.

Despite the defeat which ended their months of effort, the debaters were still heroes—and so was their coach. Accepting the trophies the team had won, Moyes, after praising Jones and Latimer, had said that credit for their victories "is due to the splendid work in all lines of public speaking done by Lyndon B. Johnson, who is making a great record in his first year as a teacher in a Houston school." Now, at a banquet on May 23 in the Lamar Hotel attended not only by faculty and students from Sam Houston High but also by delegations from Houston's four other high schools, and by the city's business and political leaders, the principal repeated his praise of the young teacher, which was echoed by a parade of other speakers, including one who had been invited at Johnson's request, Welly Hopkins. The following day, at a meeting of the Houston School Board—a meeting at which many teachers' salaries were again lowered—Johnson's salary was raised by $100 as he was rehired for the next year.

Students tried to change their course schedules so that they could attend "Mr. Johnson's speech class"; in his first year at Sam Houston High, enrollment increased from 60 to 110. "He was a handsome guy—a tall, lean, handsome, attractive guy who was full of excitement," one student says. "And he was always up there leading assemblies—he was a charismatic figure at that school." As for the feelings of the faculty, a reporter was talking to a mathematics teacher, Ruth Daugherty, one day when he saw "a tall and strikingly handsome young man" rushing down a corridor during a break between class periods, towering "above the milling students." He recalls Miss Daugherty saying: "That man is going to be a big success someday. He'll be ahead of everybody. Nobody can keep up with him." ★

THOMAS KRENECK

Thomas Kreneck is an associate library director at Texas A&M, Corpus Christi, and a member of the Texas State Historical Association. He is co-editor of *Collecting Texas: Essays on Texana Collectors and the Creation of Research Libraries*. *Mexican-American Odyssey* is his most important literary creation, and it also the most in-depth examination of Mexican-American life in Houston yet published.

Kreneck's subject, Felix Tijerina, was a famed and beloved restaurateur and a LULAC activist. As Kreneck tells it, Tijerina played as large a role as anyone in bringing Mexican-Americans into the Houston mainstream. This excerpt describes his early days in the city, working on Produce Row, and entering the restaurant business.

From *Mexican-American Odyssey*: La Immigración

SITUATIONALLY, PRODUCE ROW SERVED AS an introduction to city life. Trucks and automobiles continuously pulled in and out of its parking spaces to deposit or pick up merchandise. A rough set of street peddlers with horse-drawn wagons of fruits and vegetables also lined the curbs, often competing with the wholesale houses. Frucht's operation stood within sight of the south end of the Main Street Viaduct that arched Buffalo and White Oak bayous; the viaduct served as the major thoroughfare connecting the city's north side with downtown. Houston had been founded in the immediate area, and this locale was still a center of activity. The electric streetcars that ran along Main brought passengers to the corner of Commerce Avenue, adding to the number of pedestrians. The sidewalks of Produce Row, elevated from the brick street along the entire two blocks between Main and Milam, accommodated people of all ranks and colors. Individuals with ethnic names like Desel, Boettcher, Dissen, Schoenmann, Schneider, Japhet, Kuhn, La Rocca, Levy, Liebermann, Meyers, and Morales owned the other wholesale houses on Commerce. Produce Row provided a spectrum of business people, middle-class Houstonians, and laborers. Such constant association with older men, Tijerina would tell his younger sisters, was one way by which he gained knowledge about business and life in general.

Produce Row also brought Tijerina into contact with young men of Houston's Mexican community who would soon form his circle of close friends. William Aguilar, two years his junior, was on a break from his own job as a clerk in a downtown hardware store when he and Tijerina first met. He stopped by the produce house where Tijerina worked and picked up a piece of fruit for a snack. Tijerina would not allow him to pay; they began to chat, and Aguilar may have been the first of his generation in Houston to experience the charm that would become Tijerina's trademark.

Tijerina found a better job at a Mexican restaurant on Main Street. By the early 1920s, many young Mexican men worked as cooks, dishwashers, waiters, and busboys in Houston's hotels and cafés. Restaurant work was often the best many recent arrivals could expect, especially without speaking English fluently. Due to the underemployment among Mexican workers in the city, even during boom times, such jobs came at a premium. As a result, these men had constructed an informal network through which they placed friends and relatives in these establishments. An older friend named Doroteo Piña, whom Tijerina knew from Sugar Land, apparently worked as a waiter at the Original Mexican Restaurant at 1109 Main, and he arranged for Tijerina to secure employment there as a busboy. This move proved to be seminal in Tijerina's life.

When Tijerina came to Houston he was no longer Feliberto. Somewhere in his mental move from the fields of Sugar Land Industries to the Bayou City, Tijerina took a small but significant step on the road to urban acculturation in the United States. He had abbreviated his name to Felix.

As a commercial port, Houston, Texas, in the 1920s was a place of new beginnings; most sectors of the city accommodated outsiders. Since the nineteenth century, Houston had been absorbing people of many different ethnic backgrounds—Irish, Germans, Italians, Greeks, Asians, Jews, a large black population, and numerous others. In return, it required a certain conformity. Feliberto was a name that was no doubt too foreign and cumbersome for a fast-paced English-speaking city. Even the most accepting, non-Hispanic residents in those days would have appreciated (perhaps helped to bestow) a shorter name to pronounce.

At the same time, many dominant members of Houston society were not so tolerant, and disliked, or at least "suspicioned" Mexicans of the working class. The town had an anti-Mexican prejudice as a legacy from the nineteenth century and the Battle of San Jacinto, which had been fought only several miles away.

***

She [his future wife Janie] waitressed nightly at the restaurant of Tomas Corrales at 1905 Congress, hoping to supplement her meager wages with tips.

Felix was a regular customer, and Janie was bright and attractive. They talked and, over the next year or two, began to see one another on a regular basis. They would usually meet at dances held by the Roseland Steppers, perhaps the most popular young persons' club in the *colonia* during the 1920s. Commonly called the "Rolling Steppers," it was a group of fun-loving young Mexican men that came together to sponsor dances in halls from downtown Houston to Magnolia Park where young people could enjoy the music of *orquestras*. Felix looked every inch the dapper urban man, with skimmer, bow tie, white shirt, slacks, and plaid socks; he was, no doubt, a far cry from the country boy who had come to Houston to work on Produce Row. He had also become popular with hundreds of Mexican and Anglo Houstonians.

The Congress Avenue area helped Felix to move beyond the confines of his working-class world. Specifically, he came into contact with Houston's Mexican business owners and professionals, a group that one local Spanish-language publication in 1928 called, "*el esfuerzo mexicano en Houston*" (the Mexican initiative in Houston). These individuals, mainly in their late twenties and thirties, were represented by men like José Sarabia (originally from Guanajuato), grocer Gonzalo Mancillas (from Nuevo León) druggists Alejandro Canales and Juan José Ruiz (from San Antonio, Texas, and Veracruz, respectively), jeweler

Fernando Salas A. (from Chihuahua), several young Mexican doctors from northern or western states in Mexico who had set up practice in Houston, and a host of lesser figures who worked for themselves, mainly catering to the Mexican trade.

These prominent men among Houston's *mexicanos en el extranjero* (Mexicans abroad) chaired the *comités* that held the Mexican Independence Day celebrations, important community events in Hispanic Houston during the 1920s. They often interceded with Anglo Houston authorities on behalf of their compatriots and were universally admired in *la colonia*. As Mexicans, they reminded the members of their community to be proud of their heritage, but as entrepreneurs, they entreated other Mexicans to emulate the business practices of successful Anglo Houstonians. One 1928 editorial in Sarabia's *Gaceta mexicana* put it succinctly: "*un negocio, en manos gringos florece*" because "*el gringo se pone a trabajar con los hombros, dedicandose a el en cuerpo y alma* (a business, in Anglo hands, flourishes because the Anglo works like a man possessed, as he commits himself to his work body and soul).

Though not a member yet of this elite group, Felix, by his subsequent actions, indicated that he either listened to or shared its admonitions. By the late 1920s, he all but managed Caldwell's restaurant and, because of his competent, genial manner, received encouragement from Anglos and Mexicans alike to open a place of his own.

Felix fell in with Antonio Reynaga, one of the several restaurant owners among the Congress Avenue *esfuerzo mexicano*. Reynaga owned the Iris Café and Bakery, a thriving business at 1819–21 Congress. Originally from Monterrey, he was a tall man who reportedly had business interests in Mexico and always seemed to have extra cash to invest. On May 30, 1929, Reynaga and Felix signed a document of co-partnership for "establishing, running and maintaining a 'Mexican restaurant,'" and calling for each to invest fifteen hundred dollars in the venture. They agreed to call their new establishment the Mexican Inn.

Reynaga's role was not only that of investor, but also as purchaser of supplies for the business, since he already operated the Iris Café and they felt he could obtain commodities more cheaply because he could buy them in quantity. From the start, they agreed that Felix would control and manage the inside operations of the Mexican Inn, such as planning the menu, supervising the employees, and overseeing all other parts of the daily operations. He also would "devote all of his time, attention, skill and energy for the purpose of promoting" the business. They were to share profits and losses equally.

The Mexican Inn had one large dining room, similar to the Original Mexican Restaurant just a block north [on Main]. When he began to take out ads, Felix advertised that he served "Mexican Dishes Exclusively." Also, like Caldwell's café, Felix's food was designed for Anglo tastes and was therefore not highly spiced. Although he was influenced in many ways by Houston's Mexican entrepreneurs and by his Mexican background, Felix's Main Street location meant that, from the start, he followed the lead of George Caldwell and wanted to tap the Anglo market. Reynaga, Corrales, and others in their barrio locations would continue to deal solely with the Mexican trade. Of the more than two dozen Mexican-owned cafés in Houston, the Mexican Inn was the only one outside *a mexicano* neighborhood. When the Mexican Inn started operation, it was one of only three Mexican restaurants on Main Street; the other two included the Caldwells' and the Spanish-American Garden (in the euphemism of the time), also owned by an Anglo.

Barely twenty-four, Felix had made the leap from restaurant employee to restaurant owner. Within seven years of his moving to Houston he had transcended the status of a faceless laborer to become the "Señor Tijerina" of the Houston press. He had evolved from an urban *obrero* to entrepreneur, a man able to promote his efforts in a major Anglo Houston newspaper.

Felix Tijerina's personal growth had been a process of accommodation that had drawn upon his Mexican background and associations as well as upon his new, non-Mexican surroundings and had transformed him into an urban man. This transformation had witnessed the dilution of Tijerina's specific sense of Mexicanness and the emergence of a bicultural Mexican American identity geared to life in the city. Distinct from, yet deeply influenced by the 1920's *esfuerzo mexicano* in Houston, Tijerina's efforts clearly illustrated the interconnection between the Immigrant Generation and the cohort that would come into its own during the 1930s, the group in which Felix would play a prominent role. ★

WALTER CRONKITE

Walter Cronkite [1916–2009] grew up in Houston, and attended San Jacinto High School (now the Houston Community College Central campus). He studied journalism at the University of Texas, and today his so-familiar voice speaks from beyond the grave in commercials touting the glories of his old school.

In this excerpt from his 1996 memoir, Cronkite remembers his beginnings as a working print reporter—and in the process spins a yarn that recalls *The Front Page*, and the demanding but good old days of competitive print journalism.

From *A Reporter's Life*

THE *HOUSTON PRESS* RECRUITED ME FROM the Austin bureau to come to work for it in Houston. I had a feeling that I had reached the pinnacle of journalistic success. I had a desk in the city room just like the big fellows, and I was dragging down fifteen dollars a week.

With a portion of my first check I went out and bought a Kaywoodie pipe on which I had long had my eye. I still have the old relic today, although the habit, which at one time kept a fire stoked just beyond my nose from rising to retiring, has long been abandoned. Now I only fall off the tobacco wagon when another sailor lights up on a long cruise. The pipe went more as a concession to public opinion than to prolong my life. As the antitobacco campaign took hold, more letter writers complained that I was setting a bad example by lighting my pipe at the end of each news broadcast. I finally took the hint. That first Kaywoodie, however, served me well as the new boy on the *Press* staff. It gave me a sense that I somehow looked like a writer.

Whatever I looked like, I got the usual freshman assignments. I did obituaries. I was the church editor and wrote the whole weekly church page—a feature, the digest of a couple of sermons, and the notices of extraordinary ecclesiastical events. And I was privileged to review the lesser movies to which our theater editor chose not to go.

The movie passes, the occasional sports passes, and the police badge with "Press" embossed upon it assured me the social success I had not quite achieved in my high school years. Girls who at that time had preferred the company of football players finally began to recognize my virtues.

Flashing the press badge not only got you free passage on the city buses, but if done ostentatiously enough, I imagined, won you the admiration of your fellow riders. Sitting on the bus and watching others reading my story or stories of the day was one of life's great pleasures.

The year on the *Press* was a learning time. Perhaps my first lesson came at the end of my first week, when I put in an expense account for a dollar or two. Carefully itemized were several phone calls at a nickel each. "What are these doing on here?" city editor Roy Roussel demanded as he waved the account under my nose. "Don't you know how to make a phone call? Harold, show the kid how to make a phone call!" So Harold took me downstairs to the lobby pay phone and showed me. He had two straight pins inserted into the underside of his coat lapel. He removed them and stuck one pin in one of the pair of twisted wires leading into the phone box, and one into the other. Holding them together, he made the connection. The telephone company got wise to this a short time later and, always the spoilsports, put all the wires in impenetrable cables. It must have nearly broken Scripps-Howard.

I learned, too, the serious lessons of daily journalism. The need for accuracy, for instance. We competed in the afternoon with the Houston *Chronicle*, and we each published several editions a day. At press time each paper had a copy boy standing by the loading dock of the opposition to grab several copies literally hot, or at least warm, off the press. He then ran the eight blocks to his paper to breathlessly drop copies on the desks of the key editors.

Roy Roussel spread the *Chronicle* out on his desk and stood over it, flipping the pages, exclaiming when he thought we had bested them, frowning when the shoe was on the other foot—frowning until his heavy, graying brows almost covered his eyes.

Then, if there was hope of catching up in the next edition, he'd get the reporter on the phone or in front of his desk for a hurried conference. The cry from the city desk had a different tenor, though, when Roussel found what he thought might be an error. The call penetrated the clatter of the city room.

"Cronkite!"

The barely-innocent-until-proved-guilty hastened to the dock.

"The *Chronicle* spells this guy's name S-m-*y*-t-h. We've got it *i*-t-h. Which is it?"

Or: "*The Chronicle* says it was at 1412, we say 1414 Westheimer. Who's right?"

He was a stickler for that kind of accuracy, but most editors were in those days. They understood a fundamental truth about newspapers and how the public perceived them. One mistake—"y" or "i," "1412" or "1414"—standing alone didn't make that much difference perhaps. But for each such mistake there was a given number of readers who recognized the error and whose trust in the paper was diminished thereby. And each of them probably told their friends, and the circle of doubt grew.

Regrettably, there isn't that sort of accuracy today. There can't be, and that may be a contributing factor to the distrust in which a portion of our population holds the press. There can't be because competitive newspapering is dead. Only in a few and diminishing number of American cities are there newspapers going head-to-head, edition by edition. Elsewhere, no matter how devoted to accuracy the editors may be (and most of them are), they have no mechanism with which to monitor the accuracy of their reporters. The Roussels of today don't have the luxury of spreading the competition out on their desks and checking item by item. Clearly the transitory broadcast competition is a useless resource for fine-tuning a printed report. The result is a generation of reporters who have escaped the discipline of accuracy and have left the rest of us with newspapers just a little less reliable, in this regard at least, than they used to be.

There was a frightening day when Roussel called me to his desk and there was no *Chronicle* spread out in front of him. The matter concerned the previous day's bank clearings, for which I was responsible.

We carried a little two-line item on the front page of each day's final edition under a standard head: "Bank Clearings." The item simply said: "Today's Houston bank clearings were"—for instance—"$13,726,359.27."

"You had the bank clearings wrong yesterday," the city editor said. The brows were hanging very low, the strong jaw was clenched.

"You said 27 cents. It was 17—17! What happened?"

A ten-cent mistake on a multimillion-dollar number? Surely he was kidding. His countenance warned me that I had that assumption wrong too. I returned to my desk in a blue funk of despondency—afraid that perhaps I was not going to make it in this profession I had chosen.

My mood was not alleviated by the older reporters' comments:

"Kid, you're in the soup now."

"How you going to fix this one, kid?"

"Have you thought about getting out of town?"

The whole thing bore heavily on me as I dropped into the *Press* Lunch for the end-of-the-day beer. Paul Hochuli, clever writer and local columnist, greeted me.

"Where's your bodyguard, kid?"

My frustration—and my innocence—burst forth.

"What's this all about? A ten-cent error on a three-million-dollar number! What's the big deal?"

Paul and the others around him looked at me in amazement—an amazement that quickly turned to pity.

"Kid, don't you know why we print those bank clearings? Do you think anybody really cares about *bank* clearings? Kid, the numbers racket pays off on the last five numbers of that figure. They paid off yesterday on a bad number—and they don't much like the idea that somebody might be tampering with their numbers."

The next few weeks were a fear-filled time. I know what it is like to be a marked man. If there had been a witness protection program available, I would have applied. Every car that paused alongside my jalopy at a stoplight was filled with hoods casing me for the hit. Kid Cronkite was about to die at an even earlier age than Billy the Kid.

There was one genuine brush with the underworld in Houston. Our ace police reporter was one Harry McCormack. Harry was straight out of Ben Hecht and Charlie MacArthur's classic story of Chicago newspapering, *The Front Page*. He was from the same mold as their hero, Hildy Johnson.

Harry looked a little like Bogart, a ruggedly good-looking tough guy. The felt hat was cocked back on his head whether he was outside or inside, its band showing signs of wear at the point where he jammed in his press card when out on a story. A cigarette frequently dangled from the corner of his mouth.

I was the "second man" at police headquarters, when needed, and every afternoon after the home edition had gone to bed I stood by in case anything broke for the last two editions. So I did my best to imitate the great Harry McCormack. I mastered the art of picking up one of the then-standard upright telephones. To show that you were a member of the press, you grabbed it from the desk in a sweeping motion that catapulted the earpiece from its cradle. With the left hand you casually retrieved the hurtling earpiece in midflight and proclaimed: "McCormack." (This was not terribly effective if your name was Cronkite.)

This was at a time when a lot of the day's news was reported and called in by so-called leg men in the field and composed by so-called rewrite men at the office. My imagination was never quite up to matching Mac's use of the phonetic alphabet for spelling proper names for rewrite. It was an art form in itself. Mac could spell the name "Smith" so that every letter was represented by a different dirty word—and frequently the entire name would end up in a pornographic acrostic of soaring imagination.

He lives in my memory—hurrying into the headquarters pressroom, snatching up the *Press's* private line, shouting to our switchboard operator: "Give me the desk, baby," and dictating the latest details of the hottest running story.

Mac was helpful to his cub protégé, but he didn't have much time in his busy life for the social conventions—or what passes in a police environment for social conventions. So I was mightily flattered the afternoon he suggested a beer after I got off.

I imagined I would be with my hero at the best table in the police head-quarters' hangout, Ed's Good Eats Grill. But it was not to be.

"I'll pick you up in front at five-thirty," Mac advised. In his car we started on a route away from downtown.

"We're going to a little speak I know out by the ship channel," Mac advised. "Now listen, kid, and listen real careful. I'm going to meet somebody out there. I want you to not say a darned word . . . no matter what. Just sit there and listen and enjoy yourself. Got that?"

So ours was a business date—news business or monkey business. Frequently there is a close kinship. On a back street behind the channel we pulled up at a small frame building on whose flyspecked show window you could hardly make out the fading letters of a sign that had once said "Grocery."

Mac parked behind the building and we went in a back door. Four linoleum-covered tables, two of them occupied by some laboring types in over-alls. A hefty woman of indeterminate age and almost indeterminate sex greeted Mac as we pulled up a couple of old kitchen chairs. Without our asking, she put a couple of drinks, without ice, in front of us. Rotgut—genuine, straight-from-the-bathtub rotgut. Mac contained his enthusiasm, just touching his drink to his lips.

I was pleased to perform my monkey-see, monkey-do act. We sat there a long time, perhaps a half hour. Very little conversation, Mac frequently check-ing his watch. And then a fellow walked in, through the door that led to the grocery. He had on a felt hat and the blue overalls that were virtually a uniform in this part of the world.

Mac waved a greeting and the newcomer pulled up a chair at our table. Mac and he exchanged a few words. A brief discussion of the weather and other inanities, and the guy left. We followed within a few minutes.

"Well, how about that?" Mac asked.

"About what?"

"How about Ray there?"

"Ray who?" I asked.

"You didn't recognize Ray? You didn't recognize Ray Hamilton? You didn't recognize Ray!"

Mac's voice was rising. A hint of apoplexy maybe.

Well, let's put this in context. The year was 1935. One of the biggest stories gripping the nation's attention in that prewar depression time had been the depredations and flight of a trio of desperadoes, Clyde Barrow and his cigar-smoking partner, Bonnie Parker, and their occasional sidekick, Ray Hamilton. They roamed the Southwest robbing banks and other targets, murdering lawmen who stood in their way and virtually thumbing their nose at the authorities, who seemed hopelessly inept in tracking them down.

But on a May day in 1934, in the bayou country of Louisiana, a carefully arranged police ambush caught Bonnie and Clyde. They were shot in a fusillade of fire worthy of Gettysburg. Hamilton was not with them, and the hunt for him over the next months narrowed to a small corner of southeastern Texas and Louisiana—roughly between Houston and New Orleans.

From out of those headlines Ray Hamilton had stopped in to see Harry McCormack in a sleepy ship channel speakeasy. And I hadn't even recognized the fugitive whose picture was in every paper in the land almost every day. McCormack was incredulous—and that may be an understatement.

"All right, kid. But here's what you've got to do: You don't ever, ever mention that you saw me with Hamilton here tonight. Ever! It'll go hard on both of us if you do. We've been consorting out here with a criminal. We could be in real trouble. So you don't ever say a word! Unless I need you to. I could need you to say that I met with Hamilton tonight. I'll tell you if I do. But otherwise, not a damn word!"

Naïveté played only a small part in my bewilderment. Nero Wolfe couldn't have imagined the deep plot that McCormack of the *Press* was spinning.

It began to unfold a few days later. Mac told the desk he was leaving headquarters to meet some anonymous informant at a designated street corner in the Houston Heights area. Shortly thereafter the desk got a call from police saying they had received an alarm that a man who looked like McCormack had apparently been forced into a car at gunpoint in the Heights. They had no leads.

Mac was missing for twenty-four hours until a farmer a few miles outside Houston found a car in his fields. In it was Mac, bound hand and foot, his mouth taped. As the farmer untaped him, Mac's first words were: "Don't touch the windshield, don't touch the windshield."

When the sheriff's deputies arrived, Mac told them he had been kidnapped by Ray Hamilton and, to prove his story, pointed out that Hamilton had left his fingerprints on the windshield. Mac's tale was that Hamilton had kidnapped him because he wanted somebody to record his true story—the usual invented saga of the underprivileged Robin Hood. The story was spread across the front pages of the Houston *Press* for several days thereafter. It was, of course, a sensation, and Harry McCormack was the journalist hero of the hour.

Mac stuck with the fiction, even to me, that he had had no part in framing his "abduction." But clearly my role was to be his witness should the story break down for whatever reason and the need arise to establish that he had a relationship with Hamilton. Mac was probably better prepared in his own mind to admit to consorting with a criminal than to having his story doubted. It never came to that, and my testimony, thank goodness, was not needed. It was just weeks after Mac's coup that Hamilton was caught and executed.

In 1967 a hit movie was made of the Clyde Barrow-Bonnie Parker legend, and Parker was played by Faye Dunaway. Hollywood exercised the full extent of its literary license with that casting. Parker was no beauty by anybody's standards. Shortly after the film's release I was introduced to Miss Dunaway at a small party. She was stunning. I palpitated, and I couldn't wait to get a chance to tell her of my personal acquaintance with Ray Hamilton. She was overwhelmingly underimpressed. But then I was married anyway.

The newspaper competition was hot, heavy and healthy in Houston, and in our daily effort to beat each other, there were no holds barred. We resorted to all the dirty tricks ever devised in the game.

There was the day that screaming sirens brought Bill Collyer, my *Chronicle* opposition, and me to the open window of the police pressroom. We watched as two ambulances approaching on different streets met at the corner in a horrendous collision. From the back of one the gurney, with a patient aboard, flew out and went rolling at considerable speed halfway down the block before upending as it hit the curb. One of the ambulances smashed into a storefront. The other turned over. It was a dandy wreck.

As Collyer and I grabbed phones to our offices, he said: "Hey, don't say you saw this thing. If you do, you'll end up in court as a witness the rest of your life."

The advice seemed well taken, and I took it. My story was strictly a routine third-person report. Collyer's first-person, eyewitness report was spread all over the *Chronicle's* front page.

Newspaper competition led to a little practice called picture snatching. The idea was to get a picture of the victim by whatever wiles one could employ. Families were frequently reluctant to loan out photographs of loved ones at their time of bereavement, and, perhaps having given a photograph to one paper, they had none to spare or they weren't inclined to let their last picture out of the house.

In Houston this was a particular problem for us on the *Press*. The *Chronicle* was the old-line, conservative paper. We were more flamboyant newcomers and owned by a distant—and *northern*—chain.

I was rather honored to get the picture-snatching assignment from time to time. I assumed that this was in recognition of my resourcefulness, but, upon later reflection, I'm afraid that the attributes from which my city editor was profiting were youthful innocence, a certain touch of diplomatic blarney, and a willingness to engage in larceny in the splendid cause of the people's right to know.

I was remarkably successful, partly because I reached the home of the victim faster than the opposition man from the *Chronicle*. This was achieved through breakneck driving that would rival the kind seen in one of—*any* of—today's television films.

My success was also achieved, usually, by convincing the grieving that a picture in the *Press* was just as prestigious as one in the *Chronicle* or the morning *Post*.

But sometimes other methods were called for, and it was an imaginative use of these that caused my downfall. A young lady had died in an automobile crash with a prominent married citizen whose wife she did not happen to be. Upon arrival at her modest cottage home in one of the city's poorer sections, I found no one there. In keeping with the law-abiding nature of the times, the front door was unlocked. Through the screen door I could see on the mantel a picture of a young woman. If I left it there, the man from the *Chronicle* would surely filch it. Defensive journalism was called for. So I filched it and a delighted city desk made over the home edition to splash it on the front page.

There was just one little hitch. I had gone to the wrong address. The picture was of a next-door neighbor. Surprisingly, I was not arrested or fired for the incident. I deserved both. ★

SIG BYRD

For columnist Sig Byrd [1909–1987], the Houston of the 1940s and '50s was a setting for the Human Comedy. Writing his "Stroller" column for the old *Houston Press* daily, Byrd got to know all manner of dreamers, dingbats, con artists, ventriloquists, and lost souls. And he brought them to life in what was probably the most literary—and lively—prose style ever to enliven a Houston daily. *Sig Byrd's Houston*, the collection of his columns from which this excerpt is taken, is the one Houston book that readers simply fall in love with. It's a great pity that it is long since out of print.

From *Sig Byrd's Houston*: Catfish Reef

THE CLOSEST ANY CAT ON CATFISH REEF [Milam Street, between Prairie and Preston] ever came to getting the world by the short hair was when Gafftop Powell got on the television, with the George Washington that he would end up on the West Coast. But Gafftop never even made it out of town. He got smoked like a champ, and now he's back, putting a high gloss on stomps at Nelson's photo, recording, and shoeshine parlor.

Evenings, Gafftop still slaves as an eccentric dancer at the Club de Lisa, in the Bloody Fifth Ward, where the cats say he is very lagoon in the shake-dance number.

The other day he found a ring on the floor under his shoeshine chair. He put the ring in his jeans, fast, before somebody income-taxed him out of it, and went on watching Monsoor Brown's one-man show.

Monsoor is a bright man, fat as lard. Weighs about three-fifty. Wears an eyebrow mustache, tan beret, cowboy boots; trousers, jacket, and vest that never match; a black silk shirt, and, outside his clothes, a leather girdle. His pockets are always loaded with junk: screwdrivers, pliers, wrenches, pencils, pens, sticks, bottles, and assorted small hardware. He wears a rosary around his neck and always carries a French harp in the breast pocket of his coat. Totes a small zipper bag when he goes to town, and among the stuff in the bag is an item of his own invention, a combination screwdriver, tire tool, stabbing chill, and billy.

If you ever saw Monsoor in the street, you'd look right at him and not believe your eyes. Listen to him talk, and you'd disbelieve your ears.

Just now Monsoor was performing what he called his Hangover Number, a pantomime routine that he does in a bent position with a collapsible beaver hat sitting on his back, and a bottle opener suspended from a string held in his teeth.

Everybody gave Monsoor a warm hand when he finished. Everybody, that is, except Gafftop and Red. Red was temporarily in charge of the place. Shamrock had left him in charge while he went over to Travis Street to buy four yards of dress material for one of his donie-gals. Martin Nelson had previously left Sham in charge while he went out to one of his rent houses on Washington Avenue to investigate a report that a penniless commercial artist who was living in the house rent free was painting strange murals on the wallpaper and the windowshades. Red is a Negro boy, and it's not his hair that's red. It's his eyes. Always bloodshot.

As the applause died away, Monsoor turned to the zipper bag sitting on one end of the long platform where the shoeshine chairs stood, opened the bag, and took out a bottle of scrap iron. He uncorked it and began working on it.

Red disapproved. He urged Monsoor to take his bottle elsewhere, but since he weighed less than a third as much as Monsoor, Red lost the argument.

"Monsoor," said Gafftop Powell, who is as spare as Red and a span lower, up and down, "don't shuck me, now. How is you listed in the human race?"

Monsoor's fat, tan cheeks wrinkled into a happy grin. "A question I often ask myself. Am I man, or monkey, or both? A phantom, a figment? Oh, that this-too-solid flesh would melt, resolve itself into an ectoplasm, and fade! Or, like I told the gentleman from Homicide, putting my hand in my pocket like this, I said, 'How could I have shot that man, when I never took the gun out of my pocket? If I shot the man, where's the hole?'"

Answering his own question, he tapped the side of his head significantly, then tilted the bottle again.

"Monsoor," said Red, "I wish you was long-gone. Sham, he gona clown me when he come back. How come you don't go to the teaser and hit the pad and knock you a nod?"

Monsoor set the bottle down beside the zipper bag and opened the bag again. He took out his invention, the combination tire tool, screwdriver, chill, and billy, made of three-quarter-inch pipe and spring steel. The pipe acts as a scabbard and club, and when Monsoor withdrew the needle-sharp weapon from the pipe, Red back-pedaled.

"Get me a glass, Red," commanded Monsoor, grinning. "I won't drink out of the bottle no more."

Reluctantly Red fetched a water glass, but Monsoor didn't pour. He sat down on the platform where he had put the whisky bottle, overturning a bottle of tan liquid shoe polish, which spilled and began soaking into the seat of his enormous trousers.

"That feels cooling," said Monsoor, drawing the French harp from his pocket. "What is the scientific basis for that, *mon ami*?"

"Ain't no scientific basis," said Red. "Just water and shoe wax. You done spilled four bits' worth of polish."

"Doc Carver would know the answer to that," mused Monsoor. "Last time I was at Tuskegee, I called on Doc Carver. That man was a monkey with a peanut. I asked Doc if he had anything to say for the record, and he said, 'Carry me back to ol' Virginny.'"

"Monsoor," begged Red, "don't blow your harp in here. I'd rather you drank that hoosh than played."

But Monsoor paid no heed. He started blowing the harp, playing "Carry Me Back to Old Virginny." He had a technique, a certain style. Even Gafftop Powell was impressed.

Monsoor inserted one end of the French harp into the water glass, blew into the other, and sang the words at the same time. The glass gave the music and his rich baritone voice an unusual tone, a peculiar mellow resonance. But the words to the song were unfamiliar to everybody. They went something like this:

"Carry me back to ol' Virginny, but Mary, don't you go out on that big date . . . Tell him the same thing . . . Tell him it's gona rain where the birds warble sweet in the spring-time . . ."

A small crowd had gathered in the shine parlor, spilling out onto the sidewalk. Monsoor played and sang on and on—"Tipperary," "Sonny Boy," "Old Black Joe," and "Casey Jones." Interpolating his own words, singing, sobbing, talking into the harp, keeping the crowd fascinated. Playing and singing for the joy of it, never thinking he might pass his compeller and collect the price of a square scarf, with pork chops.

"Monsoor," said Red at last, "you got to go now. Mr. Nelson finds you here, I ain't no more slave."

I wonder, Gafftop Powell wondered, what he got that I ain't. Besides four stomachs. And that chill he totes in the bag. I wonder how many rags Mr. Marv will give me for this-here ring in my jeans. Maybe enough to buy me a second-hand buster and drive to California . . .

"Look a-here!" Somebody in the doorway said, "I sees the law-hawk a-coming!"

The concert ended as though on schedule. Unhurriedly, Monsoor put away his weapon and the French harp. He poured the water glass half full of whisky and drank it down like ice water, smacked his lips, and said, "Red, you take life too seriously. You ought to worry less and listen to music more. The world is getting too complicated; folks is getting too smart. They're getting so smart that their blood is flowing in the River Nile and the River Shannon, into the waters of the Rio Grande and the Mississippi. Tote that barge! Lift that bale! Their blood is flowing in Buffalo Bayou and the Bayou La Teche, where they make that jambalaya gumbo. So I'll say good-by, Red, me gotta go pole that pirogue down the bayou."

Monsoor closed the zipper bag on his terrible invention and the bottle of scrap iron and heaved himself toward the door. The crowd melted away. By the time the law-hawk drew abreast of Nelson's and looked in, the place was quiet, almost empty.

"Red," said Gafftop Powell, "I got to see a cat down the cut."

"What's shaking?" asked Red.

"Don't interrogate me none," said Gafftop, and went out.

He skated down the Reef to Marv Bernhard's Milam Jewelry Store and went in, the ring in his fist, the fist in his pocket.

"What's shaking, Jack?" Mr. Bernhard asked.

"Could you let me have two till Sue gets through?" replied Gafftop.

"Don't shuck me that," said the jeweler. "What have you got?"

Gafftop took the ring out of his pocket and had a good look at it for the first time. It was a lagoon-looking band with rocks and rocks. Large size. Mr. Bernhard took the ring, put a loupe to the right lens of his glasses, and peered at the ring.

***

Marv Bernhard was a bookmaker in our town for fourteen years before he went into the jewelry business four years ago.

Even yet, the Vice Squad dicks are always cruising past his place and peering in from their cars.

All they see is the little hole-in-the-wall store filled with jewelry, a few notions and novelties, sometimes a customer, and Marv himself. Marv looks remarkably like Groucho Marx, even to the cigar, except that the retired bookmaker's mustache is real and he has an artificial right leg.

When Marv was a boy, his father ran a lumberyard in Hattiesburg, Mississippi. One day when Marv was seven he was riding on the tail of a one-horse wagon, driven by one of his father's deliverymen. The horse ran away, and Marv was thrown out.

A doctor set the boy's broken leg, but blood poisoning set in, and the leg was amputated at a hospital in Mobile.

"A horse handicapped me for life," says Mr. Bernhard, who is a somewhat embittered, yet affable man. "So I spent my life handicapping horses. That is, until the reformers outran me."

***

Now, peering through his loupe at Gafftop Powell's ring, Mr. Marv looked exactly like an old-time jeweler. You would never guess that he was the emeritus dean of bookmakers in our town.

Watching the jeweler, Gafftop broke out in a cold sweat. He felt exactly the way he had the time he stood in an office, still blinded by the hot, dazzling lights, waiting for the nod from the Hollywood press agent who had slaved him for the eccentric dance turn on the television.

That Hollywood cat had influence. He had discovered Gafftop through a mutual acquaintance, a musician, and he had promised Gafftop at least a pass at the corner of Hollywood and Vine. On Catfish Reef, such dreams are as rare as bubbles in flat beer.

As soon as the cat from Hollywood looked at him, Gafftop knew the dream had run out.

Now Mr. Bernhard looked up, and the only difference was that the jeweler's heart was plugged in. "This," he said, holding out the ring, "is one hundred per cent fertilizer."

"Well, I ain't gona lose my cool over it," said Gafftop, taking the ring. "I found it on the floor at the gloss house."

"You might win the favors of an idle fun-gal on an off-night with that," said Mr. Bernhard. "But in cash money, I wouldn't give you a rough for it."

"I ought to have knowed," said Gafftop, looking down at the circlet of rhinestones. "These-here rocks is too big. Too fat, like that Monsoor. Do you rebop, Mr. Marv?"

"I rebop," said the jeweler. "When the easy rocks come too big, or the big rocks too easy, they won't get you two. Look, I'll show you the difference."

From his wallet Mr. Bernhard took an envelope, from the envelope a pill of lovely blue ice, the kind that doesn't defrost, even from its own red, white, and blue fire.

"Lagoo-oo-*oon!*" said Gafftop, his eyes as big and round and white as hundred-watt light globes. ★

Barbara Jordan and Shelby Hearon

Barbara Jordan [1936–1996] served in Congress from 1972 to 1979, and was twice keynote speaker at Democratic national conventions. She electrified the nation with her call for the impeachment of Richard Nixon during the Watergate hearings. After she left elected office she taught ethics at the LBJ School of Public Affairs at the University of Texas. In 1973 she was diagnosed with MS, and in 1996 she died from complications of pneumonia

Co-author Shelby Hearon has published sixteen books, mostly novels. She has won an NEA grant, a Guggenheim fellowship, and has twice won the Texas Institute of Letters Award.

From *Barbara Jordan: A Self-Portrait*: White World

AFTER I GOT MY LAW DEGREE I REALLY wanted to stay in Boston. It was the whole integration thing; that was just it. I thought: The air is freer up here. I'll stay and not go back to Texas. I had that idea in my head. I thought: The opportunities must be greater up here and I won't have all the hangups with segregation. I'll just stay. Having said that, I took the Massachusetts bar exam. While I made these decisions and studied for the exam, I served as a housemother at one of the dorms.

Having decided I wanted to stay, the next step was that I should look for a job. Which I did. I went to a couple of insurance companies. I didn't go to any lawyers because I didn't know any except Ed Brooke, and I had one meeting with him in which he did not seem interested in advancing my future.

I could have gotten a job at John Hancock Insurance Company as one of the hundreds of lawyers they have doing various claims and things. But when the personnel person said that I could have a job and took me down the hall to show me the office I could have, it was one of a row of little cubbyholes all divided by plywood. So I thanked him very much and left. This required some reconsideration. I thought: Now, look—true the air is freer up here, true the opportunities are probably greater, but nobody in Boston, Massachusetts, is interested in the advancement of Barbara Jordan. They don't know you. They don't even know your name. I decided: Maybe it makes more sense to go home where people will be interested in helping you.

So at that point I called my mother and said: "I'm coming home." And she said: "Thank God." She said: "I've been praying every night that you would decide to come home. When I got down on my knees I knew that you couldn't really stay up there." "Well," I told her, "I didn't know I had all that working against me when I was doing my best to stay."

So I got organized and came back home. On my return from Boston to Texas my father purchased a Simca for me, a light-green Simca, a little car. The understanding between us was that he would pay on the note until I could afford to do it myself. So I was driving this little Simca around and one day my father said to me: "Okay, now you've got the law degree from Boston University. What next?"

And I asked myself: "What next?" I said: "You're a lawyer. The first order of business is that you ought to pass the Texas bar, because it doesn't help at all if you are not licensed to practice in Texas." I took a bar review course for the bar exam, and the administering officials and I had a little dispute as to whether I was a resident of Massachusetts, as I had taken that bar exam, or whether I was a resident of Texas. But when I was called before these gentlemen to talk about my residency, I just told them I had never intended to stay in Boston. That it was a matter of formality to take the bar exam in the state in which you had graduated from law school. I told them: "I have always been a Texan."

The Texas bar exam was a three-day affair. And after the second day, when I really felt I was doing well on it, I got a call from the dorm in Boston saying I had passed the Massachusetts bar. So I announced this to all my friends who had assembled in the motel on East Eleventh Street in Austin, where we were staying while taking the bar. I told them: "Well, now, folks, I'll have you know there is one in your midst who is already a lawyer." And that required our having to go out and celebrate my passing the Massachusetts bar when we should have been studying for the third day of exams. I said: "This makes me a Boston lawyer."

I passed the Texas bar also, and the question still was: "What next?" I thought: I'll just have some cards printed up saying BARBARA JORDAN, ATTORNEY AT LAW. And I'll hand them out at Good Hope and to anybody who'll take them. Then, if anybody calls wanting me to do something, I'll do it.

I was still at my family's house at that time when I started handing out my lawyer's cards. And then people did start asking me to do things for them as an attorney, so that I was working out of the dining room at Campbell Street and driving the little Simca to the courthouse. But my problem had not been solved. I had passed two bar exams, but did not have that much to do really. I asked myself: "What does one do after work with one's free time?"

The campaign of John Kennedy for President and Lyndon Johnson for Vice President was under way. I was interested in their getting elected, so I went down to the Harris County Democratic Headquarters and offered my services. I asked: "Is there anything I can do to be of assistance in getting John Kennedy and Lyndon Johnson elected President and Vice President of the United States?" And the people there said, "Well, what do you want to do?" "I'll do anything," I told them. "I've got lots of time."

I started then to help with the development of a block-worker program for the forty black and predominantly black precincts in Harris County. There was a lady named Versie Shelton and a man named John Butler who designed the program, which was headed by Chris Dixie, a labor lawyer and liberal Democrat. We four keyed the whole operation so that there would be one block worker per twenty houses in these forty precincts. That campaign, our block-worker efforts, was eminently successful. Of the forty boxes in those precincts we worked, there was a turnout of some eighty per cent of the vote. It was the most successful get-out-the-vote that anybody could recall in Harris County.

I continued to work with Chris Dixie and Versie Shelton and John Butler. We went from church to school to meetinghouse, everywhere we were invited, selling the block-worker program. Then one night Versie Shelton could not attend one of the meetings in Fifth Ward to give the speech which she always gave, the presentation, so I substituted for her. After that speech Chris Dixie and John Butler decided that it was a waste of time for me to lick stamps and address envelopes and be an all-around generalist. They decided that I ought to be put on the speechmaking circuit for the Harris County Democrats.

And that's what I did. I spoke primarily to black groups, political groups, civic organizations, clubs, and churches. Any group could call who needed a speaker, and I would go. I was not restricted to black groups, but of course all of the whites were of a liberal bent. If you called the Harris County Democrats requesting a speaker, you were naturally a liberal.

By the time the Kennedy-Johnson campaign ended successfully, I had really been bitten by the political bug. My interest, which had been latent, was sparked. I think it had always been there, but that I did not focus on it before because there were certain things I had to get out of the way before I could concentrate on any political effort. I recall I had been keenly interested in the Stevenson-Eisenhower contest, but that my interest had been unfocused. Now that I was thinking in terms of myself, I couldn't turn politics loose.

So I continued to speak: to any group who wanted me, on any topic they requested. If they wanted somebody to talk about flowers, I'd be the one out there to talk about flowers. And there were numerous requests. I was getting my name in the paper often at this point, as there was the novelty of my being a black woman lawyer, and graduating from a law school in Boston, and sounding different. That got attention.

After the presidential race I remained active with the Harris County Democrats and we began to screen candidates for local offices. By that time I had left Campbell Street and was settled in my office on Lyons Avenue, when one day Chris Dixie said to me that I ought to run for the Texas House of Representatives when that election came up again in 1962. Dixie was the one I worked with most closely on this whole political scene, so when he broached that matter I paid attention.

I said: "Well, Chris, I make enough money to eat and buy my clothes, and gasoline for my little Simca, but I certainly don't make enough money to run a political race." I told him that. I said: "I don't have enough money." But he said: "Don't worry about that. The filing fee is five hundred dollars and I'll lend you the money for a filing fee. You can pay me back." So, all right, Chris loaned me the five hundred dollars. Five crisp new one-hundred-dollar bills. And I liked that.

I thought: I've got to get serious about this. I've been talking politics, and wanting to get into it, and here I am. I asked myself: "Do you really understand the way Texas state government functions?" The answer being no, I went out and got a state government textbook and read it. I read all about the various funds, the special funds, when the legislature met, and how often—the rules of the game. Or what I thought at that point were the rules of the game in the state of Texas.

I don't remember in which era of Texas government it was, but some governor talked about *retrenchment* and *reform*, and I liked the sound of those words. I thought: Now here, these are two nice, fine words. I thought about them, and I decided: "That will be my campaign theme. Retrenchment and reform." And I began to work them into my campaign speeches after I had announced for the House of Representatives.

There were twelve state representatives coming from Harris County, all running at large, so that we all had to canvass the whole county. The Harris County Democrats advanced their slate of candidates for the state legislature, and I was one of these, and each of us had as an opponent a conservative, backed by other groups. My opponent in the race was Willis Whatley, a lawyer also.

We were all presented to a big gathering of liberal Democrats from Harris County, twelve of us, including me and Bob Eckhardt. Each candidate was presented and said a few words, and I was the tenth candidate to get up and give a speech. I gave them my Retrenchment and Reform, and talked about all the good things I was going to do in Texas state government if I got elected, the textbook type of concerns, such as how I was going to break up the University Fund, and change the state budgeting procedures. I talked a lot about welfare, and how we had the obligation to take care of people who couldn't take care of themselves. I thought it all sounded wonderful.

At the conclusion of my speech the audience stood up and applauded. That was the first standing ovation I had ever received, and it occurred to me right then that the question was: Why are all these people standing? They hadn't stood for others. I needed to know whether they were standing because I was the only black, or the only woman, or sounded different, or had said such fantastic things about state reform. I didn't know what had really turned them on, what had given them the spark. And I needed to know so that I could keep doing it throughout my campaign. There they were, all on their feet just cheering and cheering. And after that response the last two speakers, whoever they were, Places Eleven and Twelve, were just wiped out.

From that time on, as we moved along the campaign trail, the standing joke was: "Let's get there early so we can get on the program before Barbara Jordan." That was when I first started to hear that.

Meanwhile Hobart Taylor, Sr., had contributed twenty-five dollars to my campaign to let me know he was behind me. And Chris Dixie continued to keep me pumped up. They set me up to go around to the Houston *Post* and the *Chronicle* and ask for their endorsements, which of course I did not get. But Chris continued to say: "You're great. You're going to win." He had compiled all the figures: "You're going to get ninety per cent of the black vote, thirty per cent of the white vote. There's no way you can lose."

On occasions when I would be at the same meetings with my opponent, Willis Whatley, I would listen to him and I would say to myself: "Anybody in his right mind will vote for me against this fellow." I would think: Because I've got a better case to present. I'd look at him and I'd just shake my head, thinking: You ought to just forget it, Willis, and go back to the practice of law.

***

So one fine day Election Day came. And I cast my vote at seven o'clock in the morning. The polling place was filled by seven o'clock there in Fifth Ward, and I got reports that it was that way at all the black boxes in the city.

The Atlanta Life Insurance Company had let me have a headquarters downtown in their building on Prairie Street, free for the campaign. And people were pouring in there for the returns. As the first returns showed up on the television, I, of course, was behind. But Chris kept telling me: "Just wait until after ten o'clock when the black boxes come in." But they came in and I still hadn't won. Reality entered. I got forty-six thousand votes, and Willis Whatley got sixty-five thousand. And that was that.

I asked myself: "What happened?" It was all supposed to work out. Bob Eckhardt won. Now, Eckhardt was an incumbent; but Whatley was not. Others were not. And I got the feeling that everybody won on the slate endorsed by the Harris County Democrats but me.

I asked; "How could everybody else do so well? How could the other liberals make it and not me?" I did well in the black areas, but I didn't do well anywhere else. The feeling I had was that I had been used to get black people to vote. And that nobody else on the ticket brought that kind of strength to me in return. Those fine people, I thought, all the Harris County Democrats, they had me come to teas and coffees in their areas in the southwest part of town, and the people would come to hear me and be very polite. But they didn't give me their votes. The votes were just not there from these fine white people. That was very puzzling to me, and disturbing. I spent a lot of time trying to figure out what did happen in that race.

***

Chris Dixie was not bothered. He said: "That was your first race, and even though a lot of people voted for you, and you got around a lot, there were a lot of people who didn't know you and didn't know who you were. You have to give some weight to your being a newcomer." But a professor at Rice University who came into my campaign headquarters during that first race had said to me: "You know it's going to be hard for you to win a seat in the Texas Legislature. You've got too much going against you: You're black, you're a woman, and you're large. People don't really like that image." "Well," I told him, "I can't do anything about the first two elements." But I had tucked that away, as something to remember. At that time I did not feel those were factors to overcome. I felt that the *black* and the *woman* stuff were just side issues, and that people were going to ignore that. Now, that was naïveté on my part, but it seemed to me that no one would care at all about such factors, that those were extraneous issues, that they were neutral.

After the primary I continued to go around and speak and meet people and testify before committees in the Texas Legislature on pending educational bills that would benefit blacks. All that whole bit in order to get my name well-known. One day I went to Austin to testify, and when I sat up in the House gallery and looked down at Willis Whatley at his desk, I thought, "I ought to be in his place. I deserve it."

Then it was time to run again in 1964, and I hoped things would be different. This time there was another seat where the incumbent was more vulnerable than Willis Whatley, so I thought: I'll try for that place instead. But John Ray Harrison—a white who had been part of that original slate of twelve candidates, and I guess had also lost—wanted to run for that better seat.

One day he called me into his office and explained that it would make better sense for me to go again for the same place, Place Ten, against the same opponent that I had before. He made me feel that it was the thing to do, so I agreed to that. But I remember thinking after I left him that Harrison had sold me a bill of goods, and that I had made a mistake in not saying: "I'm going against this guy who is more vulnerable." I knew that, and I took a deep breath and said to myself: "Well, you made a mistake."

Willis Whatley, now the incumbent, had his big billboards all over the county, and his conservative groups behind him. So we had a repeat performance.

When I saw that the second race was an extension of the first and that Whatley had won, and that John Ray Harrison had also won, but I had not, I didn't go to the campaign headquarters. Instead, I just got in my car and drove around most of election night. The question was: "Is a seat at the state legislature worth continuing to try for?" I got a few thousand more votes the second time out, but the basic facts were the same. I asked myself: "Am I just butting my head against something that's absolutely impossible to pull off?" I drove around in the car, listening to the returns while I asked myself: "Why are you doing this?"

After I got home and had gone to bed, my campaign manager and campaign coordinator came to my house asking: "Where have you been? The people are all waiting for you at headquarters." I said: "I've been driving around." And when Chris called to say, "Well, we've got the analysis for you,"

I snapped at him, "I've got the analysis for you: I didn't win." And went back to bed.

I had to decide by myself whether I was going to stick it out a little longer, and thinking that if I did I certainly wouldn't do it in concert with anybody else. I couldn't let anyone else get in my head and make decisions any more. I wasn't going to go their teas if they were not voting for me at the polls.

The first order of business was to decide: Is politics worth staying in for me?

***

Meanwhile, my family and my friends out there started in on the refrain that if I was not going to be winning, I ought to want to get married. And I remembered what the Rice professor said, and realized that different standards were applied to men like John Ray Harrison and Willis Whatley than were going to be applied to me. At that time, I finally admitted that fact.

Public expectations were different for a white man than for a black woman. Where a man was concerned, the public perception was that he was supposed to get out there and lead and do and make decisions and the rest of it; and no one said to him that he needed to care for the babies, or iron the curtains, or clean the johns. That was not expected of him. What was expected was that he'd marry a woman to do it for him. And why not?

The public believed that a woman had to have, over and above and beyond other aspirations, a home and family. That was what every normal woman was supposed to want. And any woman who didn't want that was considered something a little abnormal. People didn't expect a woman to make rough decisions. She was the ward of her man; she was always to be available at her husband's side no matter where he had to go or what he had to do. She must always be prepared to turn and kiss his puckered lips.

Now, I thought it unfortunate that the public perceived such a neat little box for us, and that in most cases we felt that the box was right. I thought: The question you have to decide, Barbara Jordan, is whether you're going to fly in the face of what everybody expects out there because you've got your eye someplace else, or whether you can bring the public along to understand that there are some women for whom other expectations are possible.

I realized that my friends out there thought that marriage was the most important thing there was, and that they all wanted to guarantee that they got the right man and the right home. I ticked them off in my head, all the people I went to school with—Rose Mary and Bennie and the Justices—and I thought: "Now they've already done that and they expect me to do that." My mother wanted me to be married, and my father wanted me to be married, and so did everybody else. But they also wanted me to be successful. I decided I would tell them: "Down the road a piece." In those years I always said, "Down the road a piece. Just let me get it all organized, and then we'll see."

***

But I made the decision, and it was a fairly conscious one, that I couldn't have it both ways. And that politics was the most important thing to me. I reasoned that this political thing was so total in terms of focus that, if I formed an attachment over here, this total commitment would become less than total. And I didn't want that. I did not want anything to take away from the singleness of my focus at that time.

I had learned that five crisp one-hundred dollar bills and talking about doing away with the University Fund was not the way to win. And, as I learned back in the Elks Oratorical Contest, I did not like losing. I intended to devote my full attention to figuring out the way to succeed. And the first thing I knew was not to let anybody else get inside my head. It was not to let anybody else make the decisions again. ★

JAMES THOMAS JACKSON

James Thomas Jackson [1925–1985] grew up in Houston, but chafed at the restrictions and humiliations imposed on him by racism and poverty. But, as his writing makes clear, he retained an optimism and nobility of spirit, qualities he was determined to express through his writing. The following piece tells the story of his relationship with a fellow idealist, and a man of the theater, Ned Bobkoff. Bobkoff appears to have been the first person to take Jackson's aspirations seriously.

As this memoir recounts, after Jackson's experiences with Bobkoff he was inspired to leave Houston and seek his literary fortunes elsewhere. He wound up in Los Angeles in 1965 and became part of a literary workshop conducted by Budd Schulberg. He was also befriended by long-time Houston writer David Westheimer, who wrote the introduction to the University of North Texas Press' collection of Jackson's work, *Waiting in Line at the Drugstore*.

From *Waiting in Line at the Drugstore*: Ned Bobkoff and Me

FOR ALMOST TEN YEARS, IN MY HOMETOWN of Houston, Texas, I was the only black writer I really knew.

Struggling, unpublished, hustling construction jobs, I was determined to one day get my work published. After trying every gambit a fledging writer would try—after submitting manuscripts, getting rejection slips back by the boxcar, posting them on a 4′×4′ plyboard on my wall—I thought I'd try yet another tack. I started paying attention to a young man, who happened to be Jewish, who was writing and putting on plays like a horse trot, in a small theater in Houston called The Hamlet.

My new friend was Ned Bobkoff and I took to him like a duck to water. Mostly because he was an underdog like me. But more than that, because he was putting on avant-garde plays in the Richmond Avenue neighborhood, which always—especially in my formative years—had been staunchly secessionist, which fairly reeked with antebellum mores, regardless of the changing times. I thought Ned Bobkoff was either brave, foolhardy, or the most intense idealist that Houston had ever known. He was probably all three, and enjoyed every minute of it. In some ways we were two of a kind.

At this point I had written darn near every type of writing around: chapters for my novel, sixteen short stories, essays, a book of poetry, news and feature articles for two of Houston's black newspapers. I had tried the local yearly creative writer's contest for three years running. And had lost out each time. (I'm black, my experiences are black, and I incorporate them in my writings within the scope of a black-white world. But *that's* no guarantee that I'm supposed to make it.)

Worst of all, I was no spring chicken. Hell, I was nearing forty. One should have made it by then, our elders had taught us. My friends and associates were *eagerly* looking forward to my success. So was I. My father—alive then—was wondering what I was putting down, for I was always seeming to him like a down-and-outer; he was forever admonishing me to "get a decent job" and "settle down." But I was living alone and making my own hustles, so I didn't have to listen to that mess every day.

But I had always felt that I was cut out to be a writer. As a youth I had read to the blind, the bedridden, the moribund in our ghettos. (Mostly I read them the Bible, our mainstay; readers were few, to say the least.) Writing was lonely, but I was tuned in to words and her winged creatures fluttering and screeching past my window in pondered great books—creatures that would fill my life with meaning. I knew that the study of writing would be a long and lonely crusade, but I could live with that. My biggest hassle was in keeping a steady job and a roof over my head. I never liked writing in the gutter.

***

It was the marvelous "Naked City" that inspired me to write a TV play. That series was too much! The voluble intensity of Paul Burke was just what I wanted an actor to do. I knew I had stories like that in my mind. And I worked at it like a dog. I also knew that Houston's *cultured* mores wouldn't let blacks enter their theaters for play viewing just like that, without a hassle. "Sorry" this and "sorry" that and "no night for nigras to see this play" were standard excuses. (It would be such a big help to see a good play every now and then.)

Yet every week, when I bought a *Houston Post*, I could read something about Ned's theater. I followed him religiously for over a year. I kept viewing "Naked City," and getting moved. Then I tried my hand. It was a great idea, I thought: an ex-GI transplanted from the South, and a good cop who more and more understands the dude. But it got too long . . . and too strong! Then the teleplay became a play. Acts I, II, III. . . .

I worked into the Texas summer nights. Sweating profusely in the one room of my Louisiana friend's apartment upstairs. Working my behind off as Hurricane Carla besieged us for three days while live power lines swirled about our downstairs porch lintels. It didn't matter. I was in heat, in love with my writing. I pounded away on my monthly rental Underwood and my play was born, by God!

Then it was done.
But who could I give it to?
There was only one person handy. . . .

II—I was working with an independent contractor, installing kitchen cabinets into new apartments. I had only recently gotten the job as a helper, and was hoping that it would stretch out long enough for me to make some financial waves. My paycheck wasn't magnificent, but it made for a living. Ned Bobkoff's Hamlet theater was around the corner and a few blocks down Richmond Avenue from my job. After getting a hot sandwich from the segregated eatery, I decided to get my play into his hands. (I had it tucked between my t-shirt and my outer shirt.) It was with trepidation that I approached Ned's living quarters, down a brief sidewalk adjacent to The Hamlet. Me, my play, my grease-stained cheeseburger and all.

Ned's father answered the door. A Houston taxi driver, he looked about what I thought a Jewish father would look like: a little gray around the ears, baldish, not too short. He had that no-nonsense "I'm-used-to-meeting-people" look. And that spoke reams.

"I'm a writer," I stammered out, feeling foolish and looking like the working man I was, soiled clothes and all. (I felt like an idiot. A fledging writer could try a stunt like this in the East or on the West Coast; but this was Houston and therefore Home, and I was a nobody, even to my parents.) "I know I don't *look* like a writer"—not having the faintest idea what a writer looked like. "But I am a writer and I want Ned Bobkoff to look at this play of mine." With that I thrust the manilla envelope in his hand and started to walk away.

"Hey! Wait a minute! . . . What is it, Dad?" It was Ned, even shorter than I, his face more bronze than his father's, with a smile of surprise a mile wide.

"He says he doesn't *look* like a writer," the father mimicked, making me feel even more like an idiot. "But he gave me this script to give to you."

"Well, let me see it," Ned said eagerly, surprising me for some reason, taking the envelope from his father and pulling the bulky script out. I was fidgety.

"Come in, come in," Ned said, glancing at my name and address on the top page and at my opening narrative.

"I can't," I stammered furiously. "I've only got thirty minutes for my lunch break. Just read it when you get a chance. My phone number is at the top there. I'm at home nights. I've just got to go."

And I moved out smartly, walking a block down the street. Then I ripped open my sandwich bag and began to gobble my sandwich. Out of their view, I was just another black nonentity, eating my lunch as though I had no cultural value whatever, no sense of decorum. Just another nigger hurriedly masticating his food so he could get back on that white man's job. In the meantime I was smiling to myself because I had put my masterwork in the hands of a writer-director to read when he got the chance. I didn't give a damn if he took all year. I had broken a barrier in Houston, some "gentleman's agreement," with a last-ditch determination to get a reading at *home*. I chomped on in relish. No cheeseburger ever tasted so good.

III—It was nearly three weeks later that I found a free day to go to The Hamlet and talk with Ned about my piece. We sat in his comfortable home. Although he went at my play with hammer and tongs, his criticisms were helpful. (God, did this man know theater!)

His theater-in-the-round staging wouldn't seat too many people. (Just enough to pay the rent, I'd say.) But Ned was happy with striving to attain his goal. His father carried much of the financial load for both the theater and the home. A huge keg of dark beer was the main concession, which patrons bought throughout a performance, contributing to the "survival" kitty. I thought Ned was a stone genie, the way he gathered his actors and actresses to perform his plays. Most of them—black and white—were struggling like him to keep the wolf of starvation from their doors. Ned was a showman. Writers had things to say. The Third World was here already and he was engrossed in it.

Events moved swiftly after that meeting. My cabinet-helper job had played out, and I had been recommended to a new contractor-builder who had just finished a sixteen-unit, studio-type one-bedroom; I was due to start cleaning them up soon. But first I was aroused by a loud knocking on my door from a *Post* writer, Charlotte Phelan: "All right, Jackson, come on out of there!"

Believe it or not, I was ready to chicken out. The idea of suddenly becoming a celebrity in Houston was scary. But I wasn't so ungallant that I'd keep a lady journalist waiting. So I chested up and went out that door.

I sat in the front seat of her car, trying to seem aloof, and oblivious to passing, curious blacks who lived in my neighborhood. "All right," she said. "How long have you been writing? Is this your first play?" All business, this woman. I felt uncomfortable, simply because she *was* white, and we were in my ghetto. And a patrolling white policeman—even on a bright spring morning—could read all sorts of things into that union.

"How long? I don't know. Forever, it seems. Since I was eighteen and in the army air force. Writing letters to my comrades' folks and girlfriends. I got so good at it that I began to charge them for it . . . especially when they came to me at oddball hours of the day or night—even when I was on pass or at the USO. The money wasn't much; but they paid willingly. They thought my writing was more imaginative and colorful than theirs. Who knows? I was there, we all had oodles of time, and deep within, I was happy to do it."

And it just all poured out. About keeping a daily diary on the Liberty ship, going to Italy. About being a feature writer for our mimeographed battalion newspaper, and covering a disabled B-25 bomber that was threatening to crash. I took a jeep from the motor pool without permission and picked up each crew member as he bailed out; I put men and parachutes in the jeep as we jogged and jumped over the Italian field. The special interview with the pilot, who made a safe (but scary) landing after all, saved my bacon (for stealing the jeep).

About being stationed in Austria. "You think the Peace Corps is new?" I told her. "We had our own Peace Corps. A Negro's face goes before him, and it took plenty of kindness, patience, and understanding for him to make friends. Those people in those little hamlets way back there behind those hills would take one look at us and disappear.

"But we would go back in there Thanksgiving or Christmas and pitch a party for them. We gave them tobacco, snuff, goodies, food, necessities. Wherever there is a Negro, there's a Peace Corps."

On and on, spilling my guts, letting all those repressed memories hang out. Repressed because many black people—especially women—did not want to hear of the black soldier's exploits overseas. And the southern white man for damn sure did not want to hear it at all. No wonder I was paranoiac! My society had clamped a strong lid over my talent, and I had failed to break its bonds.

Charlotte Phelan looked at me with an expression not usual to reporters—a look more in awe than anything.

"I suppose this could go on?" she said. "That there's more? These things happened to you?"

I looked at her squarely and said, "Yes. It certainly could. There are too many stories about black people that look like they will never be told. That's why there's a need for writers like me. . . .

"It looks like here I am. Everybody says, 'You've got great potential,' and pats you on the back. But you've got to start somewhere, but how?

"Day after day, year after year, there's old James, still on a job like this. Those people around that neighborhood where I live, where I grew up—my friends— they want me to succeed.

"They don't want you as a failure . . . I may give in sometimes, but I don't give up."

Then came the photographer. On the third day of my cleanup job, he walked in the apartment room amidst my swirl of dust. "I want you to do as you do every day," he said with perfect ease. That was easy. I just grabbed my broom and continued sweeping—though not as vigorously as I usually did, out of respect for his lens. He took several pictures. Then just as suddenly as he had come, he was gone—"Thank you very much, Mr. Jackson." All of sudden I was a *Mister*.

In his wake were the puzzled white contractors and laborers gawking at me as if to say: "Who in hell is he? What was *that* all about?" I was beginning to enjoy the notoriety. After all, it wasn't *how* a writer got started; it was the fact that he got started at all!

Of course, as a double safety, I displayed more vigor than usual—though not too much; this was still a job that paid by the hour, and I had to make it stretch as much as possible.

IV—The whole thing was beautiful. Charlotte Phelan sure let it all hang out. The photographer got the real me: broom and all. Only the title bugged me: "DREAMER." I hated that. It was the damndest truth, but I still hated it. Yet it was there, my photograph was there, and my life's dream was there, exposed for all of Houston's readers. I was both elated and morose. I didn't want to make waves through this kind of media. Not really. Literary blacks weren't always in abundance and how would any of them react to my being singled out to represent our race? (That inferiority feeling again.) But who can pick his entree for success? Be glad, stupid, I told myself. You're in: a nonentity no more.

***

When I arrived at The Hamlet that night, I was late. Outside the closed doors of the inside corridor, I heard snatches of dialogue. They sounded so familiar yet theatrical. Then it dawned on me that those were my words, my thoughts.

"That's the very reason you're in this trouble today," said my character, Jean, on stage. "Getting mixed up in somebody else's problems, and with a woman who's not even your own race. What's so killing about it, she wasn't nothing but a street woman! That's what all your smooth words did for you. All your knowledge, all your education, all your books. In the end (she points to Dusty's jail cell), this is all you wind up with!"

(Dusty stands and stares at her, seeming a little shocked. He gestures in seeming resignation.)

"And don't tell me that old psychology stuff about 'Nobody understands me,'" Jean continued. "Phooey! I've heard that gawk so much I could vomit. You're not a baby. You know right from wrong. You should have stayed in your place."

"God Almighty!" said Dusty, smiling through it all. "Why are women so beautiful when they're angry?" He paused. "I knew you were feminine all along. I like that . . . Got doggit, I sure do!"

Then he turned serious. "Don't kid yourself. People understand me. I've gone to a lot of trouble to *make* people understand me. Don't forget: I'm a Southerner and white folks used to use us for playthings when I was a boy. They might bring one of us into a white-filled room, and we, or I, would sing at their commands, strain those incredibly stratospheric notes of *The Star Spangled Banner*. And do you know what? None of them ever asked us to sing *The Negro National Anthem!* No, no. Not once!"

***

I tiptoed through the aisle in semidarkness to a seat near one of Ned's paying customers. Ned was in the middle rear, to my left, standing, in that intensity that so easily enveloped him, signaling cues. Save for the sporadic noises of cars on Richmond Avenue, the tempo and sound of the actors held us in rapt subservience. Of course, I was more moved than most, I thought. Ned put on only one act from my play, but it was one of the meatier ones and his kids really put their hearts into it. God Almighty, I was moved!

***

VII—Ned helped me pack my bags. I had already learned to travel light. The bulk of my stuff was books, notebooks, manuscripts. My clothes were in threes: underwear, pants, shirts, socks, handkerchiefs. Two coat jackets and one topcoat without lining.

Ned took me to the Greyhound terminal in his battered old car in the middle of the night. He helped me with my ticket money. We drank coffee while waiting for my bus, and talked about our futures.

Ned was going to try again after he had gotten himself together. We would keep in touch through his father. I was going to Temple, Texas, my birthplace; my sister was there and I would hustle work until I'd decided where to go next. Fortunately, I had a beautiful cousin, Robert Lee, who remembered my potential and saw to it that I came on up to Los Angeles. From there I went on to Budd Schulberg's Watts Writer's Workshop and to some degree of fame that I doubt I'd ever have acquired had I stayed down home. (Two of the pieces that had lost out in Houston's creative writing contest won stature. One appeared in an anthology, *From the Ashes—Voices of Watts*. The other was presented to millions in the NBC documentary, *The Seven Angry Voices of Watts*. It was my voice that the nation heard, and my face that it saw.)

It was cold outside the bus station. February. To me it was like a winter day from one of O. Henry's stories. Two *significant* failures drinking coffee that seemed laced with a stimulant of knowing which mistakes *not* to make again. The biggest thing I had in my favor was a backlog of experiences that would become stories of many dimensions. Ned plotted confidence, too. Hurt and disappointment were etched in his voice, but they weren't killing him.

Four a.m. The bus was sparsely loaded. I sat near the rear. Leaving Houston—possibly forever. I didn't sleep.

But I didn't have any compunction about sneaking away like a thief in the night. I didn't owe this city anything. My only debt was to my young upstart Jewish white friend, who had reaffirmed the dignity that had always been in me anyway; who had taught me that though we came from two houses, two ways, we both could win. And that was cool enough. Swell.

The winter outside my bus window, kissing the cedar posts, the Austrian pines, the cyclone fences, both chilled and warmed me. It felt good, challenging. I was going to forty and I was turned on. All my roads were new, my compass was pointing due North—Freedom, by God!

How many, bless God, how many aging dreamers could have such luck? How do people get married? Or friends meet? Or cross rivers, ford streams without the hand that comes suddenly out of nowhere?

That, all of that, and God knows how much more, swept across my mind as the Greyhound whisked me farther and farther away from where I had been to where I was going. Now. That was where it was. Now. ★

DOMINIQUE BROWNING

After leaving *Texas Monthly*, Dominique Browning was editor-in-chief of *House and Garden*. Her memoir, *Slow Love* will be published in 2010. With this in-depth accounting of the de Menil family saga, she found a truly great subject, and she did it full justice. The article appeared in *Texas Monthly* in 1983, four years before the Menil Collection opened.

From "What I Admire, I Must Possess"

PART I

The Eye

"WHAT I ADMIRE, I MUST POSSESS," SAYS Dominique de Menil, talking about how her collection came to be. "I call myself covetous. I have an enormous appetite for whatever turns me on." As she talks, she caresses a nineteenth-century black Wedgwood inkstand, points to a striking red and mauve oil by Max Ernst, strokes the highly polished surface of an old and beautifully crafted zebrawood writing table. Her long white hair is pulled low in a bun at her neck; her clothing, of fine, soft wools and silks, is simple. At 75 years old, Mrs. de Menil is an attractive woman with startling blue eyes and delicately chiseled features. Her wedding diamonds are loose on her finger nowadays; a recent bout with pneumonia has left her looking fragile. Every once in a while a terrible cough rattles through her, and she clearly hates that sign of human frailty.

Unlike most wealthy people, she is fundamentally an intellectual, and most of the time her mind is faraway from the quotidian details of life. She is ethereal. In Houston in the fifties and sixties, she showed up at fancy art openings in the same black strapless gown time after time, wearing mismatched shoes, one green, one blue, because their mates had been abandoned in a closet in some other city. She wore her mink coat inside out because she liked the warmth of the fur against her skin. She would invite people to dinner, then greet them blankly at the door, asking, "May I help you?" and send them away with an invitation for another evening. She could be as absent-minded as she was alert, as abrupt as she was gracious, as close as she was generous. When bored, she would drop her chin to her chest and take a nap in the middle of a dinner or a concert or a lecture. "She could sleep standing up," says one friend. "She was from another world."

There is a portrait of the young Dominique de Menil painted by surrealist Max Ernst around 1934. The painting shows just her head, in three-quarter profile. Her short blond hair waves around her ears, her skin is pale and unlined, her eyes are focused on the distance, and an enigmatic smile plays about her small mouth. The head floats on a strange orange, red, and deep blue background, and ambiguous curled shapes hover around it; they look like edges of seashells or shards of crockery.

At the time the portrait was painted, Dominique de Menil was in her midtwenties and newly married. She and John lived in an apartment in Paris. They were by no means art collectors; they were simply trying to decorate a large, empty wall in their dining room when a friend suggested that they ask Max Ernst to paint a mural for them. "We were told he did wonderful birds," she recalls. "When I saw the kinds of birds this fellow did, I hated them. But since he was expecting something from us, we suggested he paint a portrait of me."

Mrs. de Menil sat for Ernst several times in his studio and later went to see the results. "I did not like the painting at all," she says. "I thought I looked very stiff." She left instructions for it to be delivered; when many months passed and the portrait did not arrive, she wasn't sorry.

Dominique de Menil was born Dominique Schlumberger in 1908 in Paris, the second of three girls. To avoid having to become citizens of Germany after the Franco-Prussian War in 1871, her family had immigrated to France from their home in the border province of Alsace, where they had made a fortune in the textile industry. Her father, Conrad Schlumberger, was a physics professor at the Paris School of Mines; her uncle Marcel was a mechanical engineer.

Dominique's father was obsessed with an invention that he worked on in every spare moment: a device that could identify minerals by their degree of resistance to electrical current and that he later refined to identify fluids, such as water and oil, by the amount of spontaneous electricity they generated. His experiments were fully launched after World War I, when his father decided to finance them with the money he had made by selling his shares of the family textile business in Alsace. In 1927 Conrad and Marcel went into business selling the services of the measuring device to drilling companies.

Until the late thirties, the family held an exclusive patent on Conrad's invention, a sonde that could be suspended by cables in a borehole to send up electronic, sonic, or nuclear analyses of the makeup of the hole. They were in a position like that of the Hughes Tool Company with its famous drill bit—anytime anyone drilled an oil well anywhere in the world, the Schlumberger company was called in. Within ten years of its founding, it was a huge global concern, and the Schlumbergers were on their way to accumulating another great fortune. Schlumberger now gets plenty of competition from Halliburton (which, with the help of Standard Oil, broke the monopoly in 1938) and Dresser Industries, among many others, but the process of well-logging is still called "running a Slumberjay" in the oil fields, no matter whose equipment is being used.

The Schlumbergers were sophisticated, educated, and hardworking people. Dominique received an advanced degree in mathematics from the Sorbonne. She rode her horse in the Bois de Boulogne every morning and vacationed every summer at the family chateau in northern France. But her parents did not spend money lavishly. "We had no fine rugs, no antiques, no rare books, no great art in our home," she says. "Spending money was frowned upon. We entertained only once or twice a year, and that was only for family. My parents were very strict, puritanical Protestants."

It was not until her marriage in 1931 to Jean Menu de Menil and her conversion to his Catholicism that Dominique began to leave behind the restrictions of her parents' values. John de Menil (he changed his name to "John" and dropped all his names between "John" and "de Menil" when they took American citizenship in 1962) was an ambitious, charming, and driven young man who, having twice failed to pass his baccalaureate exams, decided to make a career for himself in banking. John's father was a career army officer, the bearer of the title of baron thanks to Napoleon's having conferred it on the family in 1813, but a man of very modest means. John, determined to make his own way in the world, for years resisted going to work for his wife's family. But when Conrad Schlumberger died in 1936, he joined the company.

The young de Menils had moved into an apartment near the Schlumberger offices when one day, out of the blue, the portrait by Max Ernst was delivered to their door. As it happened, Ernst had sent his wife to the framer with the painting; she had left it there without supplying the name or address of its owner. The framer had hung it in his window, and there it stayed for years, until the parish priest, whom Dominique de Menil had visited only once, recognized her face in the painting and arranged for it be sent to her. Mrs. de Menil had unfortunately not grown any fonder of the portrait during its absence, so she wrapped it in brown paper and stuck it on top of an armoire.

She forgot to take it along when she and her family evacuated Paris at the start of World War II, so there it was when the Nazis burst in to ransack the house, looking for valuable drilling information. John de Menil had joined the Resistance and gone to Rumania, where he was sabotaging railroads and destroying Schlumberger equipment to keep it from failing into Nazi hands. He worked his way east through the Orient and finally took a steamer to South America. Mrs. de Menil and her three young children escaped from Europe on a steamer out of Spain to Cuba and then New York, where the family was reunited. From there they took a train to Houston, where Schlumberger had opened an office in 1935. The de Menils bought a saltbox house on the edge of the city, and John went to work supervising South American operations for Schlumberger. The Ernst portrait remained in the old apartment in Paris.

It was not until the late forties, when she returned to Paris to retrieve her belongings, that Dominique de Menil found the portrait once again. It was still on top of the wardrobe, wrapped in brown paper. In the years since she had seen it, she had learned a great deal about art. Two mentors—a Dominican priest in France named Marie-Alain Couturier and an Egyptian-born New York art dealer named Alexandre Iolas—had tutored the de Menils in the wonders of modern art and persuaded them to begin buying some of it, including works by Ernst. Mrs. de Menil was beginning to feel the Eye developing within her; she could judge a painting, appreciate it, feel its magic. Now, when she opened the package containing her portrait, her breath was taken away by the beauty of the painting's colors and the originality of its composition. She suddenly realized, staring at the canvas—and she relates this with the fervor one might use to describe a religious awakening—"how much my eyes had been opened."

It remained only for her to want to have as much as she wanted to see, and for that, Texas was responsible. "I would never have started collecting so much art if I had not moved to Houston," she explains in heavily accented, graceful English. "When I arrived in Texas there was not much you could call art. Houston was a provincial, dormant place, much like Strasbourg, Basel, Alsace. There were no galleries to speak of, no dealers worth the name, and the museum . . ." she trails off helplessly. "That is why I started buying; that is why I developed this physical need to acquire."

***

John de Menil took over the leadership of the [Contemporary Arts Museum] board in 1950, and immediately exerted his influence. He put on one-man shows that featured non-Houston artists, like Lyonel Feininger and Christian Bérard. A few of the [museum's] founding members resigned in protest; one-man shows were a big risk and therefore a luxury, particularly when they gave short shrift to the local talent. The de Menils plunged ahead with the most ambitious show Houston had ever seen: an exhibition of the paintings and drawings of Vincent van Gogh, which at the time had been shown in New York, Chicago, and Paris alone. And the hit parade went on: Calder came to Houston to install his works in an exhibit with paintings by Joan Miró; Ernst came to Houston and made a drawing for the pamphlet that was to accompany his show. Another founding member resigned in protest. In 1953 the *New York Times* noted cryptically, "There is a schism within the CAM, based on many factors: personality clashes, fear of domination by an individual, differing philosophies of professionalism versus cooperative endeavor."

The de Menils pressed on: now it was time for the CAM to hire a professional, full-time director. The Museum of Fine Arts didn't even have a full-time director. It took three years and the resignation of a few more board members, but in 1955 the de Menils got their way—a director, chosen by them, her salary guaranteed by them, with the money and the freedom to put on shows the likes of which Houston would never see again.

Jermayne MacAgy came from the California Palace of the Legion of Honor, where she had been the youngest museum director in the country; she was known for her unusual and provocative installations. She immediately staged shows featuring surrealists, which inspired several Houston collectors to invest heavily in that period. She showed fifteen of the fuzzy, multicolored rectangles by Mark Rothko, who had up to then been shown solo only once, in Chicago. She put on an exhibition of contemporary portraiture and another called "Collage International: From Picasso to the Present." In all her shows she placed works on high pedestals, hung them in windows cut out of mysterious walls that rose up out of nowhere, hung others at ground level. On a minuscule budget of $20,000 a year she created a staggering 29 shows during her four years as director and brought the little museum to national attention.

But that didn't win her the friendship of the CAM board, in whose eyes she was too completely her own woman—or perhaps the de Menils', but certainly not anyone else's. "The problem in Houston was that everyone wanted to run the association," Mrs. de Menil recalls. "The board would appoint a chairman for each show, and MacAgy would do all the work without credit. And she was constantly fighting to keep inferior works out of her shows, not always with success. Sometimes I would spot some terrible thing and ask her what it was doing there. She would tell me about Mr. So-and-so who had threatened to withdraw all his support if she didn't indulge him. There were too many people in Houston who thought of themselves as great curators."

MacAgy's crowning success was the inaugural exhibit in 1959 for the cavernous Cullinan Hall at the Museum of Fine Arts, designed by Mies van der Rohe and donated by Nina Cullinan with the stipulation that modern art be exhibited there occasionally. Brought in as a guest curator, MacAgy put on a show called "Totems Not Taboo." She gathered up more than two hundred rare tribal works and placed them on pedestals, some close to the ground, some soaring up into the hall; these were lined up along a balcony and staircases that were also covered with works. Tropical plants were everywhere. Still more works were placed on small islands of gravel. The staid museum was showing a little of the de Menil touch.

Just as the show opened, the Contemporary Arts Association announced that it would not renew MacAgy's contract because of lack of funding. The statement was a marvel of thinly veiled diplomacy; in fact, MacAgy was being fired by those directors who were tired of the domination of the CAM by the de Menils and their like-minded friends. The de Menils were less upset than might have been expected; they had other plans for MacAgy. As Mrs. de Menil says, "In those days, we figured that since the CAM was such a difficult place, why not use St. Thomas?" Jermayne MacAgy was soon ensconced as the chairman of the art department. For years to follow, the shows held there outshone those at the CAM.

In the meantime, the de Menils had begun to turn their attention to the institution that had eluded them upon their arrival in Houston, the Museum of Fine Arts (MFA). With the completion of Cullinan Hall, there was an opportunity to give modernism its due at the conservative museum. John de Menil had a seat on the board when it undertook the task of finding a director who could handle Mies' intimidating open space. When he heard that James Johnson Sweeney had resigned his post as director of the Guggenheim Museum in New York, John de Menil picked up the phone, and within a short time Sweeney was settled in Houston.

Well, almost settled there. Sweeney seemed to prefer spending time in New York or Paris or at his house in Ireland and therefore wasn't in Houston as much as some thought a museum director should be. But the de Menils were Sweeney's champions. They supported his extravagant expenditures in the name of quality, even when it meant he had to send to Manhattan to have his catalogs printed or his shirts laundered. Sweeney was in a hurry to move the MFA "out of the provincial ranks," as Edward Mayo, registrar at the museum, puts it, and he brought in works by Picasso, Miró, Fernand Léger, Piet Mondrian, Georges Braque, and John Tinguely. But—fatal flaw—he could not bring himself to court the guardian families of culture.

The de Menils were in step with Sweeney; his ambitions matched theirs exactly, and so did his tastes. There began to be grumbling, just like the earlier grumbling at the Contemporary Arts Association, about how much control the de Menils were gaining, though as always the exercise of their power was accompanied by great generosity. During Sweeney's tenure, they donated some of the museum's most important gifts: a Calder mobile, a classical bronze figure of an emperor, and Jackson Pollock's *Painting Number 6*. Other patrons continued to give—or at least tried to. And that was what cost Sweeney his job.

Museum policy had always been to accept gifts, some of questionable value, from the Blaffer family. In 1967 Sarah Campbell Blaffer presented the museum with a Fragonard, and Sweeney refused it, saying it was a fake. Blaffer, furious and insulted, took back her painting, and the Blaffer family turned their attention to the college of *their* choice, the University of Houston. Sweeney was fired.

With Sweeney went the de Menils. Clearly the next director, Philippe de Montebello, was not one of "their" people. He had the temerity to tell a reporter that one of the de Menils' gifts, abstract orbs designed by Italian sculptor Lucio Fontana, could stay at the South Garden entrance because they made "good receptacles for chewing-gum wrappers." The de Menils gave their last gift, Claes Oldenburg's *Giant Soft Fan*, to the MFA the year of Sweeney's departure. From then on they would give some money, service on the board, and nothing else.

St. Thomas was left as the place in which the de Menils had the most at stake—the most to gain in terms of control and the most to lose in terms of how much time, money, thought, work, and love they bad invested in it. They were not competing with other patrons for control of a board; in fact, they could not even sit on the board, since it was composed only of the fathers. But the board seemed completely receptive to its patrons.

In the late fifties, hiring Jermayne MacAgy was asking a lot of the Basilian Fathers, as she was a controversial figure in the city. Her first show in Philip Johnson's gallery at St. Thomas, lit by candles for the opening, was a ravishing display of surrealist paintings by Yves Tanguy, Rufino Tamayo, Ernst, René Magritte, Mark Tobey, Léger, and others, which she had grouped with medieval sculptures.

"Two days later," Mrs. de Menil says, "a nut walked into the office of the president and said, 'Father, you must take the show down. It is communistic.' This man, a Houston citizen of the highest order, said so many crazy things. It was unbelievable—hammers and sickles hidden in the paintings, things like that." The de Menils and the fathers protected MacAgy from such lunacy, and within St. Thomas she was becoming the object of near-adoration. But in 1964, while she was working on a show to be called "Out of This World," she suffered an insulin attack (she was diabetic) and died of it. "I felt as if the floor had opened up under my feet," says Dominique de Menil. "I finished her shows and tried to keep things going, and that was when I was led to my career—the installation of shows. MacAgy had never let me see how she was doing things; she always wanted the openings to be a surprise. I had to learn all the little tricks of installing, and there are plenty of them, for myself." Mrs. de Menil took over the art department herself.

The de Menils became more deeply involved at St. Thomas than they had been anywhere else. They underwrote salaries, set up a fund for "faculty improvement," and began pushing to hire more professors in the social sciences. More and more talented students were attracted to the school, and new buildings were added to the mall. Philip Johnson began designing a chapel, and Mark Rothko was commissioned to paint fourteen large, meditative canvases for it. At the end of every year the de Menils wrote a check to cover the school's deficit. They hired St. Thomas graduates to work for them. They started a media department and screened trendy films in the student center, joking about what the nuns might think of the latest Andy Warhol picture.

The art department was truly their domain; it grew all out of proportion to the rest of the school. People muttered that its budget was bigger than that of the entire university. Mrs. de Menil started an art collection for St. Thomas and donated many fine pieces; her standards for it were so unbending that when Jane Blaffer Owen tried to donate a tapestry, history repeated itself. Mrs. de Menil refused the gift on the grounds that it was not of a high enough quality, and Mrs. Owen wrote an angry letter. "If a child brings a gutter flower to its mother, and tells her it is an orchid, should the mother throw the flower away because it isn't?" she asked. Mrs. de Menil apologized, but as far as the tapestry was concerned, she was unmoved.

The de Menils started an extensive art library, and Dominique de Menil put on remarkable shows, publishing detailed catalogs with each. She often wrote lucid, straightforward introductions to guide visitors through the difficult works. She even taught an art history course, pausing now and then to leaf through a large dictionary looking for a word in English or pulling out of her handbag some priceless object to share with her students.

John de Menil, for his part, had decided that St. Thomas had to become a world-class institution. It had everything going for it: a home in a booming city, lots of money, land, and contacts. There was only one hitch, and that was the Catholicism. Though the de Menils were themselves devout, they were also fervent ecumenicalists, if that was not an impossible paradox. They believed excellence at an academic institution could be achieved only if it was open to the study of all faiths. John de Menil urged Father Patrick Braden, the university's president, to put in place a board of laymen that would have the authority to elect St. Thomas' presidents. But ecumenicalism was not the critical issue to the de Menils. Liberalism was.

***

The de Menils were Radical Chic long before it was considered chic in Houston. If anything, it was a complicated feat. While on one hand they were giving dazzling dinner parties for the likes of Magritte, Warhol, Oldenburg, Ernst, Rossellini, Jean-Luc Godard and Norman Mailer, on the other hand they were trying earnestly to get their friends to begin to appreciate modernism. They started a print club, offering at cost—$5 to $200—works by Roy Lichtenstein, Ernst, Robert Rauschenberg, and Warhol to their friends. They organized a group of twelve wealthy Houstonians (including Bank of Texas chairman George Butler, tobacco and real estate magnate Henry J. N. Taub, and Lloyd Bentsen, then with Lincoln Consolidated holding company) to participate in a partnership called Art Investments at $10,000 a share.

As general partners, the de Menils used the money to buy nine works of art, which were distributed to members' homes and rotated every three months. "I know that some people kept their art hidden in a closet during their three months," says Aaron Farrel. People called from Dallas and San Antonio and even New York to find out how to start such a club, but no one else had the de Menils.

Editors and scholars and curators were enlisted all over the world to research arcane subjects for exhibitions, catalogs, and books. One, called *The Image of the Black in Western Art,* is a lavishly illustrated series that has been labored over by scholars, photographers, writers, editors, and translators for fifteen years; two volumes have been published, and another will appear in 1984.

The image series is an indication of a second great passion of the de Menils that grew along with their passion for art after they came to Houston and found its expression in similar ways: the history and the rights of blacks. As early as the mid-forties, Mrs. de Menil was giving luncheons to which she invited black businessmen, educators, and religious leaders along with her society friends; through the fifties and sixties many a dinner party erupted into arguments, some ending in fistfights, over "the race question." The de Menils gave, with no fanfare, to the campaigns of liberals and blacks running for the then all white and segregationist school board. Over the years they supported liberal candidates for other local offices, most notably mayors Fred Hofheinz and Kathy Whitmire. They gave generously to the American Civil Liberties Union and to Amnesty International. They set up funds to put black students through college and graduate school. They supported black radicals, such as Jeferree James and Lee Otis Johnson.

When Johnson complained to Mrs. de Menil that the police regularly tried to frame him by lying about his activities, she hired a "witness" (whom he later married) to follow him around.

In 1971 Mrs. de Menil installed a show in the Rice Museum called "Some American History." It was a collaborative effort, masterminded by artist Larry Rivers and meant to show scenes of black life in America by several different artists. Rivers himself created the set piece of the show, *Lynching*: four life-size plywood cutouts of black men stuck onto coffinlike boxes and dangled by heavy rope nooses. Sprawled beneath them on a bed, legs spread, was a construction of a very pink and blond heavy-breasted woman in black stockings, black garters, and pointy spike-heeled shoes. At the glittering opening of the show, Rivers walked around tape-recording the (mostly white) audience's reactions.

They were not altogether pleasant. "I really objected to that show, blacks being hung, Aunt Jemima with a machine gun, slave ships," says Jane Blaffer Owen. "The de Menils were sympathetic with the poor blacks, but so were we. I was a Southerner, but my family fought the KKK. My daddy's family had slaves, but he was kind and wonderful to them. That show was terrible."

If rich white folks were suspicious of the black-power sympathies of the de Menils, so too, at first, were black radicals. One in particular, Mickey Leland, a 25-year-old who had dropped out of the Texas Southern School of Pharmacy to help run a black minister's campaign for a seat on the school board, was taken completely by surprise when the de Menils began to befriend him in 1969. The de Menils had decided to open an art gallery in the Fifth Ward. They asked Leland to be a liaison between them and the ward leaders, who were incredulous of the whole idea.

They rented an abandoned, run-down movie theater, once the grand Deluxe Theatre, where Leland had gone as a boy. (In his mother's generation in Houston, Leland recalls, black people were allowed to sit in the balcony of any picture show. In his generation, they weren't even allowed to go into the same houses as whites.) The de Menils hired a painter named Peter Bradley to be the show's curator. He gutted the interior of the Deluxe Theatre, put in new floors, walls, and lighting, and in three weeks turned it into a gallery. Bradley asked nineteen artists, among them painters Kenneth Noland and Larry Poons and sculptors Michael Steiner and Richard Hunt, to contribute work, with the proviso that they need not use it to make explicit political statements.

The Deluxe Show was an enormous success. People poured in from all over town; certainly it was the first time that most of River Oaks had ventured into the Fifth Ward. It was held over for months, and then the space was turned into a museum that stayed open for several years, to which the de Menils lent dozens of African objects, masks, and sculptures.

After the Deluxe Show, Mickey Leland's relationship with the de Menils took on a new intimacy. Leland was exactly the sort of man John de Menil prized in his retinue; he was young and bright and cut an extremely dashing figure with the ladies. He would be a leader no matter what he did. Finding the young Mickey Leland was, in terms of the de Menil Eye, not too unlike spotting the unknown Max Ernst.

John de Menil began to counsel Leland on the course his life. He urged him to finish school and donated $50,000 to Texas Southern for a program in clinical pharmacy so that his protégé could study it. Whenever the de Menils entertained someone who might someday be useful to Leland, they asked him to join them. When Leland needed a new car, they bought him one. When he decided, finally, to run for the Legislature in 1972, they were at his side with money and campaign advice. They were his Pygmalions.

"I was a rough and crude personality, and they polished me," Leland says. "People tend to think in terms of what the de Menils have done financially; that's not right. What the de Menils did for me was to turn me into a sophisticated human being who happened to make a career in politics. They did not know what I would end up doing, and they helped dozens and dozens of people the same way."

When Leland became depressed about George McGovern's candidacy in 1972 and disillusioned about his own future in politics, John de Menil offered to send him on a trip to think things over. Leland suggested California. No, said de Menil, that wasn't far enough. Leland suggested China. John de Menil sent him to Africa. The two set off together and went first to Los Angeles, then to New York, then to Paris. From there Leland went off on his own; he spent three months traveling all over Africa. When he returned, John de Menil was in the hospital, dying of cancer. He lived to see Leland win his seat in the Texas House but died during his first year in office.

***

[John's] funeral became the occasion for a reunion of the entire de Menil circle—the people from the worlds of art, business, politics, religion, science, architecture, and education whom the de Menils had collected about themselves with as much urgency as they collected art.

[St. Anne's Catholic church] was jammed with mourners. In the front pews sat the family and their closest friends. Behind them sat the rich and powerful of Houston, New York, Los Angeles and Paris. Behind them were ranked the local members of the Black Panthers, in full uniform, holding their berets, and behind them were hundreds of friends and admirers from all over the world.

Six months before he died, John de Menil sent a memo to his children and his closest friends explaining, down to the minutest detail, how he wanted his funeral to proceed. And so, in accordance with his wishes, his son François, Mickey Leland, and several other people, found themselves, one hot summer day, driving to the Ross Mortuary on Lyons Avenue in the Fifth Ward to meet the proprietor, Burnett Ross.

"When Mr. Ross saw us walk in," Leland recalls, "he thought he had landed himself some big pigeons, and he started showing us his top-of-the-line pink tufted satin caskets with brass designs and things like that." The group explained that Mr. de Menil wanted a simple wooden box; Ross was unable to find one (his clientele did not share Mr. de Menil's simple tastes), so they had to troop out to his warehouse. They put rope handles on a pine coffin they found there and asked Ross to come around to the de Menils' River Oaks home.

Back on San Felipe Road, John de Menil, rich oil executive, had been lying in state in his bedroom, wrapped only in a sheet, in the old peasant tradition. On the day of the funeral, his body was carried to St. Anne's in a tan Volkswagen bus that had been used to carry de Menil art back and forth across Houston.

When everyone was seated and the music started, there was an audible gasp from the congregation. John de Menil had had quadraphonic speakers installed in the sanctuary, and they were blaring Bob Dylan songs—"Girl From the North Country" and "Blowin' in the Wind"—so loudly that you would have sworn Dylan himself was in the choir loft. The funeral ceremony was then recited by a black Baptist preacher, a rabbi, and several lay readers including a Muslim who read from the Koran. A Lebanese Catholic priest performed a requiem mass—a fitting end to John de Menil's lifelong devotion to ecumenicalism.

It was pitch-black outside when the church doors opened, disorienting at six-thirty on a summer evening. Suddenly the sky was rent by a violent streak of lightning, which lit up an enormous bank of clouds hanging low in the sky. Roberto Rossellini, the film director, turned to his companion and said, "So speak the prophets. The funeral is attended by the gods." ★

GEORGE CRILE

George Crile [1945–2006] covered some great stories at CBS News—the disintegration of the USSR, the Vietnam War (he was sued by General Westmoreland)—but it's doubtful that he ever had a more colorful, or simply amazing story than the one he told in the 2003 book *Charlie Wilson's War*. A good deal of the book's giddy appeal comes from its depiction of Charlie Wilson's muse in all things Afghan, River Oaks socialite Joanne Herring. You simply couldn't make Herring up; luckily, Crile didn't have to. He just had to write sentences like, "A curious romance began, with much talk of Christ, anti-Communism, and Zia ul-Haq."

From *Charlie Wilson's War*: A Texas Bombshell

YEARS LATER, AS HE TRIED TO EXPLAIN HOW it all happened, how the CIA ended up with a billion dollars a year to kill Russian soldiers in Afghanistan, Avrakotos would offer a curious explanation. "It began with a Texas woman, one of Wilson's contributors. She's the one who got him interested."

Joanne Herring was a glamorous and exotic figure out of the oil-rich world of Texas in the 1970s and '80s. At the time nobody imagined that, in addition to her role as a social lioness and hostess to the powerful, she was simultaneously responsible for setting in motion a process that would profoundly impact the outcome of the Afghan war. When almost everyone had written off the Afghans as a lost cause, she saw potential for greatness in the most unlikely characters. In the pivotal first years of the jihad, she became both matchmaker and muse to Pakistan's Muslim fundamentalist military dictator, Zia ul-Haq, as well as to the scandal-prone Charlie Wilson.

Most of the women Charlie was seeing in those days—and there were many—were half Herring's age. But Joanne Herring was a woman of extraordinary resources who knew how to mesmerize a man on many levels—not the least of which was her ability to sweep this congressman from the Bible Belt into her dazzling world of black-tie dinners, movie stars, countesses, Saudi princes, and big-time Republican oil magnates. Invariably, when reporters wrote features about Joanne Herring, they invoked Scarlett O'Hara. The comparisons are found in clips from the *Washington Post*, *People* magazine, and *Lifestyles of the Rich and Famous*. Few modern women can trigger such a comparison. But to appreciate her full impact, it helps to add Zsa Zsa Gabor, Dolly Parton, and even a bit of Arianna Huffington.

Something about Texas and its oil heritage seems to permit its citizens to reinvent their histories and to carry out their lives as if they were part of an ongoing theatrical experience. As Herring tells it, she was born on the Fourth of July, a direct descendant of George Washington's sister; her great-uncle had died at the Alamo; and there were suggestions of old family money and an ancestral home modeled after Mount Vernon. Hers was a family whose history embodied all the virtues of the American experience, Texan style. "You see, I'm descended from Washington, and all my life I've been told that by my family. It's kind of nice to know who you are down through the years, and I feel I know all my people who came before me."

But Joanne's story was nothing compared to that of so many other high-rolling Texans, like her best friend from high school, Sandra Hovas, who would become another link in Wilson's introduction to Afghanistan. As a buxom teenager, Hovas was known affectionately as "Buckets." But as a young woman in the 1960s, she began to reinvent herself, and her friends soon went along with calling her Sandy, then Sandra, and then Saundra. When she met and fell under the influence of Baron Ricky di Portanova, a dashing young Italian who had moved to Houston to claim his share of the Cullen oil fortune, Saundra became Allisandra. When she married the baron, Buckets was reborn as Baroness di Portanova.

To the uninitiated, Joanne and the baroness appeared to be typical social butterflies, but they actually shared a conspiratorial past. As young debutantes, both had been inducted into the Minutewomen, an offshoot of the ultraright, paramilitary Minutemen. While other debutantes across the country were tittering and talking about boys, Joanne and Buckets were sitting at high tea listening to "patriotic women who cared about their country. They opened my eyes to the conspiracy that threatened our way of life," remembers Joanne. By the time the two girls were eighteen they had become part of a semisecret national organization of right-wing patriots so convinced of the possibility of a Communist takeover that they were organizing for guerrilla warfare. And like all good Texas girls, Joanne and Buckets had learned to ride and shoot from the earliest age.

"It is difficult talking about this now," says Herring. "You can easily be thought of as a nut or a nutty hawk." Nevertheless, she remains deeply proud of her involvement in the arch-conservative organization. That's where she acquired a "sense of obligation to act like a lady," which included a commitment to fight Communism. "I decided back then that I would dedicate my life to making the free-enterprise society survive for my children."

One would never have imagined such ambitions by reading about Joanne in the Houston society columns of the 1960s and '70s. Her Roman Toga party was so lavish and theatrical that *Life* magazine covered it, and everyone in Houston who counted was invited. Slave girls were auctioned off. Christians were burned to the accompaniment of fireworks. And to lend authenticity, ten-year-old black Boy Scouts, playing the role of Nubian slaves, moved about the gathering of Roman-clad socialites, filling the crystal goblets with wine.

By the 1970s, she was entertaining all of Houston daily with her own immensely popular television talk show. When she married a rich oilman, Bob Herring, who ran the largest natural gas company in the country, she began traveling with him through Arab lands. They met and befriended kings, sheikhs, and chiefs of intelligence. Arab oilmen have a special connection with Texas. Texans have drilled their oil and sold them machinery, and they have invariably visited Texas and watched cowboy movies. And when they met Joanne Herring, they all tended to turn to Jell-O.

Houston was a boomtown back then, and when kings and foreign leaders asked to visit, the State Department found it helpful to enlist the ever enthusiastic Herring to entertain. Her parties were always magnificently overdone.

For the king of Sweden, there was a sheikh's-tent discotheque, complete with zebra-rugs, stuffed tigers, and belly dancers. She so charmed Ferdinand and Imelda Marcos that when she and her husband visited the Philippines, the Marcoses reciprocated by meeting them with a brass band and an honor guard. Herring soon added Anwar Sadat, King Hussein, Princess Grace, the Shah of Iran, and Adnan Khashoggi to her list of intimate new friends, all of whom were extravagantly entertained at the Herrings' twenty-two-room River Oaks mansion.

In the midst of this heady swirl, Joanne departed for Paris to produce and narrate a "documentary" on the life of the Marquis de Lafayette, entitled *A Thirst for Glory, a Struggle for Freedom*. During 1976 she kept herself busy at Versailles directing thirty French aristocrats in the roles of eighteenth-century French nobles. She was a novelty, and the Parisian café society loved this Texas bombshell who talked of nothing but politics and the origins of freedom. There were even whispers of a romance between her and the elegant chief of the French intelligence service, the count de Marenches.

Until then, Herring had thought she was fully sensitized to the Communist threat. But the count opened her eyes to a new dimension when he took out maps and carefully described the "master plan" being carried out against the West: "'In every government and agency—even in the airports—there was infiltration,'" she recalls him saying. De Marenches explained that he had played a critical role in stopping the student riots in Paris in 1968. He was a center post in what Herring now describes as a worldwide network of people ready to sacrifice "everything: their lives, their fortunes, and their sacred honor, just like the Founding Fathers."

It can be said that Ms. Herring's future fixation on fighting the Russians in Afghanistan originated in Paris when de Marenches arranged for her and her husband to meet one of the key players in his network, the brilliant Pakistani ambassador to Washington and eventual foreign minister Sahabza Yaqub Khan. At the end of the 1970s, Pakistan was a poor country and out of favor in Washington. Trying to build friendships, Yaqub Khan proposed that Bob Herring become Pakistan's honorary consul in Houston. Herring declined but suggested his wife instead. Thus began Joanne's love affair with Pakistan and certainly one of most bizarre diplomatic appointments ever made by a funda-mentalist Muslim country.

Ordinarily, an honorary consul is not expected to do much more than get drunken sailors out of jail, ship dead citizens home, and generally show the flag. But Joanne Herring acted as if she had been made a full-fledged ambassador or minister of trade. She was suddenly organizing benefits, even one in which all of her designer friends—Pierre Cardin, Oscar de la Renta, Emilio Pucci—were shanghaied into coming up with designs for Pakistani craftsmen to use as pat-terns. She plunged into Pakistani villages on fact-finding missions, giving the poverty-stricken Muslims inspirational talks on capitalism and inspiring hope with her idea that each village could get rich selling beautifully made dresses and rugs designed by her famous friends.

There was no precedent for an American woman playing such a role on be-half of the Pakistani government, so Pakistan honored Herring with the official status of "honorary man"; she was addressed as "sir." Back in the United States, she managed to put the out-of-favor Pakistan diplomats in the limelight, in-cluding them at elegant black-tie dinners with the likes of Henry Kissinger and Nelson Rockefeller.

It was all going very well until the military seized power and hung Presi-dent Zulfikar Ali Bhutto, perhaps best known today as the father of Benazir Bhutto. President Jimmy Carter led the charge in condemning the new dicta-tor, Mohammad Zia ul-Haq, accusing him of killing democracy in Pakistan as well as of building an Islamic atomic bomb. Carter cut off all military and economic assistance, declaring Pakistan unworthy of further U.S. aid.

When "Pakistan" became a dirty word in Washington, another honorary consul might have lost heart. Herring, however, reacted differently. The count de Marenches had recently confided in her that there were only seven men stand-ing between the free world and Communism. Zia, he said, was one of them. So that year she set off for Pakistan, prepared to find virtue in the maligned dictator Zia ul-Haq. In Islamabad, Zia quickly won her heart. He invited her to dinner at his simple military headquarters, explaining that he would never move into Bhutto's palace as long as his people were starving. The unexpected surprise of this visit was the astonishing impact Herring had on Zia. He was a fundamentalist Muslim and she a born-again Christian, yet by all accounts, their bond grew so strong that, for a time, she is said to have been Zia's most trusted American adviser, a development that Foreign Minister Yaqub Khan found alarming. "She absolutely had his ear, it was terrible," he said.

It was all the more unusual given that Zia was in the process of reimposing fundamentalist restrictions on women. But he was so spellbound by Herring, and took her so seriously, that to the utter dismay of his entire foreign office, he made her Pakistan's roving ambassador to the world and even awarded her his country's highest civilian honor, the title of *Quaid-e-Azam*, or "Great Leader." Charlie Wilson says that Zia would leave cabinet meetings just to take Joanne's calls. "There was no affair with Zia," Wilson recalls, "but it's impossible to deal with Joanne and not deal with her on a sexual basis. No matter who you are, you take those phone calls."

When the Russians invaded Afghanistan in 1979, Zia's relationship with the United States could not have been worse; nor could he have been closer to his honorary consul, who took the novel position with the dictator that the invasion was a great blessing in disguise. "At last there were Russians crossing the border," she told him. "Before, they were just using nicknames like FMLN or FSMLN. But now they were Russians, and I knew there was a possibility to do something."

That kind of bravado was typical of Joanne Herring, who, at age forty-eight, was accustomed to seizing and holding center stage and refusing to let anything get her down. She had married two men, raised two boys, and worked five days a week for twelve hours a day on her television talk show. She was one of the social dragons of Houston and a tireless promoter of Pakistan. But the year after the invasion, for the first time in her life, she felt defeated. She found that no one seemed to want to hear about Zia or Pakistan, much less about Afghanistan. It seemed that life was passing her by, and she felt alone. After a long struggle, her husband had died of cancer, and Joanne turned to her church in Houston, where she remembers sobbing at the altar, in a state of complete despair. "I never thought I would laugh again," she says. "I thought my life was over."

Joanne Herring remembers those dark days with a shudder, but mainly she remembers how Charlie Wilson arrived to save her life. They had met two years before at one of her River Oaks parties, after he had passed an important piece of oil and gas legislation that her husband had thought impossible. Joanne collected powerful men, and as she told him about the virtues of Pakistan, she locked eyes with the handsome congressman. Wilson left with the distinct impression that Joanne Herring had been flirting with him. So he was delighted when she called him one day out of the blue, in the midst of her depression.

It is said that hypochondriacs make the best nurses, and if Charlie Wilson was responsible for lifting Joanne Herring from her depression back in 1981, then it was because he knew where she was coming from. Very few were aware of the depths of Charlie Wilson's frequent depressions—the insomnia, the alcoholism, the asthma, the trips to the doctor, the constant loneliness. He disguised it well. No matter what his inner mood, whenever the public door opened, the darkness disappeared, replaced by the bigger-than-life, can-do Texan.

For Joanne Herring, that overflowing energy was like a miracle cure. "Charlie taught me to laugh again and made my life really wonderful," she said. A curious romance began, with much talk of Christ, anti-Communism, and Zia ul-Haq. As the weeks passed, she found her spirits returning. "Everyone else's eyes would glaze over when I would talk about the Afghans, but Charlie was interested in these things."

As the romance bloomed, Herring found herself reborn as a ferocious champion of Zia and the Afghans, and she became convinced that Wilson was the one who could save the day. "I really gave Zia a story on Charlie," she recalls, "because I was scared someone could do an investigation of Charlie and write him off. I told Zia, 'This is the man who can really do it for you.' You see, they were very frightened of America." Joanne also began to use all of her wiles to pull Wilson into the Afghan war. "I knew that if he was serious about something, he went all out. I'd say to Charlie, 'You are powerful, you are wonderful, just think what you can do.' It had to be a sort of brainwashing," she explained. "But it was very easy, because Charlie thought in those terms too. You can raise that spirit in a Texan. It's there."

Wilson, now fully under Herring's sway, quickly accepted her invitation to River Oaks to meet the man who she said would explain it all. "You will adore this man," she told Wilson. "There have been eighteen books written about him. He has been decorated by every country in the world. To give you an idea, he was the first man in the Belgian Congo after the bloodbath, he married eleven Jewish girls to get them out of Nazi Germany and said he didn't have one honeymoon. Every time there has been a disaster in the world, Charles Fawcett was there. You will never meet anybody like him."

For those who don't know her, there are times when Joanne Herring sounds quite detached from reality. But the stories she told about Fawcett turn out to be largely true, including her account of how he had recently lured her into Afghanistan. She explained that six months earlier, she had been at home in River Oaks when a message from Afghanistan came in "via the underground." It was from her friend Charles Fawcett, a note scribbled with crayons on the back of a child's notebook: "Come immediately. Bring film equipment. The world doesn't know what's going on here."

It was hard for the congressman not to be impressed as he listened to Joanne described how she had left immediately for Islamabad and then crossed into the war zone with Fawcett. "All this had to be very secretive," she whispered conspiratorially. "Zia sent his planes and helicopters with us to the border. He even sent troops to areas where they were not supposed to go. You see, the least little thing could have created a Russian invasion. Zia kept telling me that the Russians wanted nothing more than for his troops to cross over so that they could justify an invasion.

"They dressed me like a man. I had a bodyguard who was seven feet tall with a handlebar mustache and an Enfield rifle." At one point, Joanne told Wilson, this giant moved her about in a barrel to hide her. "It was so cold that all the men gave me their blankets. But it was like sleeping under a dead hippo. I was so cold, it was horrible, but it was the most exciting thing in my life."

As she told this story to Wilson, she played on themes she knew would move his Texas spirit. She described how these primitive tribesmen would bow to Mecca in prayer five times a day. She emphasized how few weapons they had and described how the Afghans treated their guns like library books—as soon as one warrior crossed the border, he would turn in his gun, handing it over to another man going off to face death. "It was so humbling," she went on. "Nothing ever affected me like seeing those twenty thousand men raising their guns and shouting to fight to the last drop of their blood."

When Joanne introduced Wilson to Fawcett, she was operating on the powerful conviction that they had two things in common: an impulse to stand up for the underdog, mixed with a thirst for glamour and adventure.

Charles Fernley Fawcett is an immensely likable man and, as Joanne had hoped, he immediately charmed Wilson with tales of nonstop swashbuckling, adventure, and good deeds. As Wilson learned, Fawcett had begun life as an orphan of sorts, watched over very loosely by an uncle from the well-heeled Fernley-Fawcett family of South Carolina. By fifteen, Fawcett says, he had commenced an affair with his best friend's mother; "a wonderful woman," he recalled warmly. "If that's child molestation, I would wish this curse on every young boy." But this mother of his dreams cut off the relationship, and at six-teen the handsome, powerful young man, already an all-state football player, escaped on a tramp steamer bound for the great fleshpots of the world.

The young Fawcett was one of those gifted all-purpose talents. He had a commanding voice; a strong, beautiful body, which he bared for sculptors; an artistic talent, which made him a gifted sketcher; and a musical ear, which allowed him to play the trumpet well enough to go backstage one night and get a few tips from Louis Armstrong: "What you do, my boy, is you pick up the trumpet thusly, and you put it to your lips thusly, and then you blow, boy, blow."

One day, after watching a professional wrestling match, he went backstage and asked the wrestler to show him some moves. For the next year he traveled through the back-alley theaters of Eastern Europe playing the role of the hon-est American boy heroically fighting underhanded opponents. "It got to the point that I didn't care that the villain always pinned me," Fawcett remembers, "because I was clean, and the others were dirty and the audience was always for me. So much so that they sometimes would storm the ring trying to get the other guy."

Fawcett still has scrapbooks, news clippings, and book entries that docu-ment an otherwise unbelievable life: an ambulance driver in France at the out-break of World War II; an RAF pilot during the Battle of Britain, scrambling to his Hurricane to take on Messerschmitts over London; and even a tour as a member of the French Foreign Legion. At the end of the war, Fawcett came down with tuberculosis and was discharged from the legion. He was reduced to playing "Taps" at funerals and digging up graves to identify Nazi victims until an old friend rescued him with an offer of a bit part in a movie. Over the next two decades Fawcett reinvented himself as an actor, appearing in over a hundred B-grade movies, many of them in Italy. He was a star of sorts, but always cast in the role of the villain. He performed his own stunts, leaping out of buildings, brawling with Buster Crabbe, and riding horses off cliffs. He may have been a second-tier player during the day, but at night, in the words of the gossip columnists, he was "the king of Rome" and "the mayor of the Via Veneto." Warren Beatty remembers him as the centerpiece of the Dolce Vita of the city, loved and adored by everyone.

It was there that Fawcett met Baron Ricky di Portanova, who would later marry Joanne's childhood friend Buckets. At that time, di Portanova didn't advertise his title; he was penniless and relied on his deep voice to scratch out a living dubbing films into English. He and Fawcett shared a tiny apartment off the Via Veneto. Whoever had a woman for the night got the bed. The toilet was down the hall.

Had it not been for Joanne Herring, di Portanova might have remained impoverished. His mother was a Cullen but she was mentally impaired and had virtually no contact with her family or its fortune. Joanne convinced di Portanova to return to the United States and sue for his share of the family fortune. When the suit was finally settled, di Portanova received, under dictates of the Texas Trust Act, a reported million dollars a month in income. His life was transformed. Overnight, he became a centerpiece of Houston's high society. The exotic, international jet-setter, Baron di Portanova, so flamboyantly rich and extravagant that he tried to buy the famous "21" Club restaurant in New York as a birthday present for Buckets.

Like many men who come into fortunes late in life, the baron romanticized his penniless days in Rome with his old friends. And twenty years later, alarmed when he discovered that Fawcett was in bad health and had run out of money, he insisted that his old roommate come immediately to Houston to supervise the construction of his mansion's vast new swimming pool wing. Fawcett accepted the plane ticket and the appointments with Houston's best doctors, and moved in with the baron and the baroness, quickly becoming a prominent, much-loved extra man in Houston's roaring '70s society. But somehow he didn't feel right about living in this lap of luxury. To begin with, all was not well in the baron's house.

The year before, di Portanova's loyal valet had been mysteriously shot and killed while carrying a platter of cold partridges in to lunch. The baron insisted that he, not the valet, had been the real target, No evidence ever surfaced to warrant such thoughts, but di Portanova's paranoia was now so intense that his household was rife with rumors of rival kinsmen plotting against him. When the entire swimming-pool wing burned to the ground, once again the baron suspected foul play. It was all too much for Fawcett, who found himself irrationally guilt stricken, convinced that somehow he could have prevented the disaster.

In truth, the old adventurer had grown restless in the baron's house—too long without a cause and feeling decadent. So when the Soviets invaded Afghanistan, the sixty-year-old Fawcett announced to his devoted friend, Joanne Herring, that he intended to leave Houston for the mountains of Afghanistan to pass on to the Afghan resistance tactics he had learned in the Foreign Legion.

No amount of cajoling from the baron and baroness could change Fawcett's mind, so they gave in and threw him an elegant going-away dinner in the wine cellar of Houston's finest restaurant. Joanne Herring saw him off at the airport the next morning, and six months later, after receiving his scribbled note, she was in Afghanistan with a camera crew to help Fawcett rally the conscience of the world.

Wilson was entranced by Fawcett, whom he considered a Renaissance romantic. "He loves beauty, he loves war, and he loves killing bad guys," Wilson remembered. As far as Wilson was concerned, Fawcett was a hero, an American who "had killed fascists in Spain, shot down Messerschmitts over London, and had been in the Hindu Kush shooting Russians. How could I say no to a guy like that?"

But it was not so easy to be flattering about Fawcett's film. He had chosen Joanne to serve as his blond interviewer and persuaded Orson Welles, an old friend from the Via Veneto, to be the narrator. The baron threw himself into promoting the effort with a lavish black-tie dinner for the Houston premiere. The setting he chose was the newly reconstructed wing of his mansion, built around a giant Grecian swimming pool with oversized chandeliers.

As the lights went down, a lone mujahid warrior was seen on the back of a rearing stallion. An Afghan with a great white beard, bearing a startling resemblance to Fawcett, ran up to the mounted horseman and asked, "Commander, where are you going?" In the background, music straight out of an Errol Flynn adventure rose up. "I'm going to fight the Russians," the mujahid warrior growled. "But, Commander, how can you fight the infidel without weapons?" Onto the screen flashed the film's title: "Courage Is our Weapon."

Joanne Herring watched with mixed reactions. "Fawcett couldn't bear to cut any of it," she says. She acknowledges that the film is something less than sophisticated, particularly during her interviewing segments. "Here the Afghans were, telling me how the Russians had stuck a bayonet into a pregnant woman's stomach, and I'm trying to understand their language, and smiling, always smiling, because I'm trying to encourage them to speak English."

When the lights came on after the two-hour documentary, the baron tapped his champagne glass and stood to offer a toast. "Theeees," he said, gesturing to his lavish swimming-pool annex with the great chandeliers, "theees is not reality." Pointing theatrically to the projector, Fawcett, and Herring, he continued: "Theees movie, theees eeez reality."

Wilson was delighted to be included in the baron's social circle. "I had never met any of those people before," recalls Wilson. "It's the kind of fantasy world that every Texan has always heard about and found exciting." But Wilson, the great anti-Communist, had to cope with the fact that Fawcett and Joanne had gone into the war zone. They had actually taken risks to do something about the Communists. He didn't quite know what to say when Joanne insisted that the CIA was playing a fake game in Afghanistan, that the U.S. consul she had met at the frontier was a kind of apologist for the Russians, and that brave men were dying because of congressional neglect. It didn't matter that he had made a telephone call to double the covert-aid budget for the mujahideen. A few million dollars more was a meaningless gesture, she said. Joanne Herring wanted Wilson to become the mujahideen's true champion. Wilson's manhood, she implied softly, was on the line. ★

JOE NICK PATOSKI

Joe Nick Patoski has been one of the leading chroniclers of the Texas music scene since the 1970s. He has published six books, including biographies of Stevie Ray Vaughn and Selena, and has contributed chapters to four other books. Among many other endeavors, he also hosts a radio program on Austin's KGSR. For eighteen years he was a staff writer at *Texas Monthly*.

In his 2008 biography of Willie Nelson (winner of the TCU Texas Book Award), he tells the little known story of how Nelson came to write some of his greatest songs while making the lonesome drive home to Pasadena, where he and his family lived, from the honky-tonks where he was barely scraping out a living.

From *Willie Nelson: An Epic Life*: Houston, 1959

WITH MARTHA AND THE KIDS STAYING AT her mother's in Waco, Willie decided Houston, the biggest city in Texas (pop. 932,680) was worth the 19.9 cents a gallon expense to check out the scene he'd sampled with Johnny Bush a few years earlier.

Wide open, the physical layout of "America's Industrial Frontier" and "World's Greatest Petro-Chemical Center" was perched on the edge of Galveston Bay, fifty miles from the Gulf of Mexico. Houston's hot, humid, buggy, and muggy climate was one ingredient in a strange gumbo that also included poverty, cheap guns, stoved-up passion, and redneck sensibilities fermented in alcohol; when cooked together, they fostered Houston's reputation as Murder City, USA.

Houston was Texas, all right, but in many respects, more Southern than Fort Worth, Abbott, San Antonio, even. It was the blackest city in Texas, with African-Americans comprising more than a quarter of the population with almost as many Mexicans as San Antonio. Since the end of World War II, Houston had become a magnet for thousands of Cajuns and Creoles from southwest Louisiana and southeastern Texas as well.

Big Houston was big fun, and big business. The galaxy of homegrown country stars included Floyd Tillman, George Jones, Benny Barnes, Smilin' Jerry Jericho, Claude Gray, Sonny Burns, James O'Gwynn, Link Davis, Ted Daffan, Leon Payne, Leon Pappy Selph, and Eddie Noack. Two significant country music record companies were based in Houston—Starday Records, formed by Pappy Daily and Jack Starnes, which launched the career of George Jones, and Daily's D Records, created in the wake of Starday's move to Nashville. While dance halls, honky-tonks, and icehouses were the scene's underpinnings, its showcases were in Houston's recording studios, especially Bill Quinn's Gold Star Studio in southeast Houston.

Harry Choates recorded his Cajun classic, "Jole Blon," at Gold Star. George Jones cut a string of early hits there, beginning with "Why, Baby, Why," and the Big Bopper did his rock and roll chart topper "Chantilly Lace" at Gold Star. The bluesman Lightnin' Hopkins recorded most of his early material with Quinn, and conductor Leopold Stokowski was bringing in the Houston Symphony Orchestra to take advantage of the studio's superior acoustics.

"Quinn was always trying to get you a good sound," said Frankie Miller, who cut his biggest hit, "Blackland Farmer," at Gold Star Studio. "He wanted to get it right."

So did Willie Nelson, which is why he went to Houston.

In the spring of 1959, he showed up one afternoon at 11410 Hempstead Highway on the northwest fringe of Houston to check out the Esquire Ballroom, the spacious dance hall owned by Raymond Proske, where the house band led by Larry Butler was rehearsing new material. A waitress informed Larry that a man wanted to talk to him. After rehearsal Larry sat down at a table and drank a beer with the out-of-town musician who wanted to play some compositions for Larry. Larry was game. Willie played him four compositions— "Mr. Record Man," "Crazy," "Night Life," and "Funny How Time Slips Away."

Those are good songs, Larry told him.

"Ten bucks apiece," Willie said. Larry could have the songs, publishing and everything, for $10 each. He needed the money. Larry leaned across the table. "Don't do that," he said. "They're worth more than ten bucks. If you need money, I'll loan it to you. You can pay me back by joining my band and working at the club here."

Larry fronted Willie $50, and Willie became one of Larry Butler's Sunset Playboys, the house band at the Esquire. Larry went one step further. Musicians worked for union scale in Houston. As bandleader, Larry made $25 a night and the other musicians made $15. When owner Raymond Proske said he couldn't afford Willie, Larry offered to add him to the band by splitting his leader's pay with him, as long as he showed up and did his part.

Larry Butler gave Willie hope, letting him showcase his own songs during the band's sets and closing out the evening with Willie's original "The Party's Over." Frankie Miller, who'd played with Willie at the Cowtown Hoedown, was surprised to run into him at the Esquire, "playing guitar, paying his dues," when Miller passed through, promoting his single. In addition to working with Larry, Willie was playing gigs with Denny Burke, with Curley Fox and Texas Ruby, the husband-and-wife fiddling-singing duo who brought country music to Houston television, and with anyone who needed a guitarist who could sing and write songs.

The gig at the Esquire and other pickup work convinced Willie that Houston was for him. With Larry Butler's help, he moved Martha, Lana, young Susie, and baby Billy into a tiny rent house in the shadows of Houston's oil and chemical refineries clustered around the Houston Ship Channel in Pasadena. He scored a shift at KRCT 650 AM in Pasadena, the Houston-area country music radio station owned by Leroy Gloger; the job didn't pay much, but he used the airtime to plug upcoming gigs.

Instead of playing for scale as a sideman, which was $12 to $15 a night, he was able to get up to $25 from front men such as Smiling Jerry Jericho, for whom Johnny Bush was playing, in exchange for free mentions on the radio. Guitarist Lucky Carlisle frequently called on Willie to play rhythm for him, but he didn't think Willie's media status merited a higher salary.

When Lucky called, Willie asked, "What's the pay?"

"The usual, scale."

"I don't like to get out much these days for less than twenty-five," Willie replied, trying to up the ante.

"I bet you stay home a lot," Lucky said.

"Come to think of it, you're right," Willie said, wrapping up the negotiation. "I'll be there."

Paul Buskirk, Willie's mentor and friend, offered a third job to Willie, which would fit in with his plan to make a living writing, singing, and playing music. Paul had moved from Dallas to Houston to open Buskirk Music Studios at 108 East Bird in Pasadena while picking up work on the side whenever he could. He thought Willie would make a good guitar teacher. Willie hesitated. He'd taught Sunday school, but he'd never taught music. "C'mon, brother," Paul Buskirk cajoled, pooh-poohing Willie's complaint. "Teaching music isn't hard. Just buy a beginner's book and teach what you learn from that." Willie did just that, reading a lesson a night from the Mel Bay book of beginning guitar and the next day imparting what he had learned. "It's really where Willie learned to play guitar," said Freddy Powers, Paul's friend. Between Paul's teachings and Willie's book learning, he figured out chords and styling that would have otherwise gone unappreciated.

Willie didn't know it, but his own songwriting was improving too. Houston was an inspirational setting for some of his best songs. The struggle to provide for Martha and three kids was more of a challenge than ever, but it offered plenty of material for sad songs. The long, lonely commutes on the Hempstead Highway, the Gulf Freeway, and Eastex Freeway provided close to an hour's worth of quality time to think and create every night. If a lyric came to him, he wouldn't necessarily write it down until he'd reached his destination. "If I forgot the words," he would later say, "they weren't very memorable in the first place."

The twinkling lights and pungent odors of oil and chemical refineries, paper mills, and factories turned private thoughts into poetry as he reviewed the day, the night, and the people he encountered, the family he was trying to support, his wife, the other women who were attracted to him, the slices of life that crossed his mind. The songs flowed like never before. "Night Life," "Crazy," "Mr. Record Man," "I Gotta Get Drunk."

He showed his stuff to his sister on a visit to Fort Worth. "That's the first time I remember ever seeing a tape recorder," Bobbie said. "He had this little tape recorder. On his way up, he had written three songs. He was so excited. One of them was 'In God's Eyes,' one was 'It's Not for Me to Understand,' and one was 'Family Bible,'" the song he'd played for Mae Axton two years before.

His musicianship continued to improve. Paul Buskirk was turning him on to more Django Reinhardt. They discussed singing and vocal styles, agreeing Floyd Tillman was as much of a crooner as Frank Sinatra was. And when Willie found himself behind on the bills, Paul bought some of his songs.

Selling songs was nothing new to Willie. Despite his three jobs, he was so broke, he didn't have a pot to piss in. Finding someone willing to pay for something that he made up was validation in his eyes. If one he sold ever became a hit and made the buyer all the money, there were more where that came from. "I knew my songs were good," Willie said.

Buskirk paid $100 for the rights to "Night Life" and $50 for "Family Bible." Willie had been enjoying a beer and barbecue with him in a Pasadena bar when he sang "Family Bible" and told him, "This is one you'll like. I'll sell it to you." Selling a song was more honorable than borrowing money, in his mind.

Buskirk led to a second buyer. Claude Gray was a spindly six foot five honky-tonk singer from Henderson, in East Texas, who worked as a DJ in nearby Kilgore before moving to Houston to sell Plymouths and Dodges for a living after he'd gotten out of the navy. The same year Willie came to Houston, Claude quit selling cars when he scored another disk jockey job at a radio station in Meridian, Mississippi.

Claude returned to Houston, though, for several recording sessions at Bill Quinn's studio, paid for by D Records and Pappy Daily. Paul Buskirk put together a studio band for Claude and between sessions sent several songs over for Claude to consider covering. They were "Night Life," "The Party's Over," and "Family Bible." Claude knew Willie from the Esquire Ballroom up north of Houston and followed Buskirk's suggestions by recording them all.

D Records released 45 rpm singles of Claude Gray singing "My Party's Over," slightly changing the song title, and "Family Bible." Claude Gray paid $100 for a piece of "Family Bible" and another $100 for the musicians and studio time to cut that tune as well as "Night Life," "The Party's Over," and

"Leave Alone." In exchange for the session work, Gary shared ownership of "Family Bible" with Buskirk, who backed up Gray on the recordings, and Walt Breeland, a friend of Paul's who was a business agent for the Drivers and Helpers Union and an aspiring singer with a Jim Reeves voice, who was looking for songs. Claude signed a napkin, promising to buy "Night Life" if his version was released as a single. "Willie wanted it released," Claude said. "He would give me half the writer's [royalties]. But Pappy didn't think it was country enough."

Pappy Daily's D Records was one of the main reasons Willie had come to Houston. He was signed to the label, and if he was closer to the home office, maybe he would get more attention from D Records and Glad Music, the record label and publishing company owned by Pappy Daily.

D Records was the big dog of country music in Houston, a critical piece of the vertically integrated country-music empire Pappy was trying to build out of his H. W. Daily one-stop record wholesaler. With all the elements working, he could take what he learned with his previous label, Starday, and make his new start-up competitive with any Nashville label short of Decca and RCA.

Willie's first single for D Records, the surprisingly upbeat "Man with the Blues," done honky-tonk style, b/w "The Storm Has Just Begun," one of the first songs he'd ever written, were released on both D Records and Betty Records in 1959 after the sides were recorded in Fort Worth.

In Houston, Willie managed to do two more sessions for D Records at Bill Quinn's Gold Star. "What a Way to Live" and "Misery Mansion" were recorded on March 11, 1960, with the backing of Paul Buskirk on guitar, Ozzie Middleton on pedal steel, Dean Reynolds on bass, Al Hagy on drums, and Clyde Brewer and Darold Raley on fiddles. Both songs were head and shoulders above his D sessions in Fort Worth, a reflection of the musicianship behind him, the recording facility, and Willie's developing talents. He sang the vocal of "What a Way to Live" like a spirited blues, in contrast with the melodramatic sound of the backing band, and tackled "Misery Mansion" like a traditional country beer-rhymes-with-tear weeper. They were fine, though unspectacular, tunes.

A few weeks later, Willie and Paul Buskirk, Al Hagy, and Dean Reynolds returned to Gold Star, along with pianist Bob Whitford, steel guitarist Herb

Remington, and vibraphonist-saxophonist Dick Shannon, to do two more originals. Something had happened between the two sessions.

"Rainy Day Blues" was a classic Texas shuffle, a popular dance rhythm that had been played with equal exuberance by white country players and black rhythm and blues artists since the 1930s. The music, projected over sad honky-tonk lyrics, showed Willie had chops as a guitarist.

"Night Life" was from another realm. Mature, deep, and thoughtful, the slow, yearning blues had been put together in his head during long drives across Houston. At Gold Star, he was surrounded by musicians who could articulate his musical thoughts. He sang the words with confident phrasing that had never been heard on any previous recording he'd done. Paul Buskirk's and Willie's guitar leads were straight out of the T-Bone Walker playbook, while Dick Shannon's bluesy saxophone was pure Texas tenor, with his vibe work adding subtle jazz atmospherics. If not for Herb Remington's low-note hokum on his steel guitar and his Hawaiian flourishes, the song could have passed for race music. No matter what style the music was or how personally Willie sang it, the lyrics were a commentary just about anybody could relate to:

> When the evenin' sun goes down
> You will find me hangin' round
> Oh, the night life, it ain't no good life
> But it's my life . . .
> Life is just another scene
> In this world of broken dreams
> Oh, the night life, it ain't no good life
> But it's my life.

"It was a level above what we had been doing," Willie said of the session.

Pappy Daily hated the song. He refused to release the song as the A-side of a single because it was neither country nor commercial as far as he was concerned. If Willie wanted to write blues he should be doing it for Don Robey over at Duke-Peacock Records, the nigger music company down on Erastus Street in the bloody Fifth Ward, Houston.

Willie thought Pappy was full of shit. "Night Life" was a great song and he knew it. So did Paul Buskirk. He knew a groove when he heard one, and he knew Willie was about to blow his top out of frustration. If Pappy wouldn't release it, Willie would, and did, with Paul's help. "Night Life" was released on a small Houston label, Rx ("Prescription for Happy Times"), under the name of Paul Buskirk and His Little Men featuring Hugh Nelson. The single was mastered at Bill Holford's ACA Studios. A few copies were pressed and passed around as demos in the hope somebody would hear it. But only a handful of disc jockeys, including Uncle Hank Craig on XEG, played the single.

If "Night Life" wasn't his ticket to recognition, selling "Family Bible" to Claude Gray sure helped. Claude's single, also on D Records, began climbing the charts in the early weeks of 1960, eventually nudging into the Top 10, topping out at number 7 on the national country singles chart compiled by *Billboard* magazine. Whatever royalties he'd lost by signing his rights away were balanced by the word getting around that this Willie Nelson fella knew how to write songs. "When it went into the Top Ten, I thought, goddamn. I'd sold it for fifty dollars," Willie said. But he didn't regret it. "I just thought I would write more. I would have just as soon got fifty here, a hundred there, because it was cash in hand, and I knew plenty of guys who recorded their songs and still didn't make a quarter."

***

He might have written a hit single, but he didn't have much to show for it. His gig on the radio had ended when he was fired for showing up late one too many times after way too many nights out late, so he sought out Charlie Brown, the country singer from way back in West whose daughter Faye Dell had once been the light of his life. Charlie had a nightly gig at a club on Canal Street in a rough part of Houston down by the port. "I'm broke," Willie said when he found Charlie. "I've got my family with me, I need some work."

"Tell you what I'm going to do," Charlie said. "I'll give you some money. You get you something to eat, and come back and sit in, you can make a few dollars."

Willie followed Charlie's advice and stuck around for the next few nights. By the end of the week, the club owner took Charlie Brown aside. "Charlie, you're going to have to fire that guy sitting in," he told him. "He cain't sing worth a lick."

Willie had heard it all. He couldn't sing. He couldn't play. He was hard to follow. He couldn't keep a beat. He tried not to take it personally. "You know, I always thought I could sing pretty good," he told writer Michael Bane. "I guess it kind of bothered me that nobody else thought so. I was into a lot of negative thinking back then. I did a lot of bad things, got into fights with people. My head was just pointed in the wrong way."

With no income, no respect, and no options, he felt it was time again for a change of scenery. Leaving a pile of bills behind, he dropped off Martha, Lana and Susie, and baby brother, Billy, in Waco with Martha's mother, promising to send for them once he got settled, and steered his ugly green '46 Buick east.

The first stop was Meridian, Mississippi, where Claude Gray, the man who was making him famous with "Family Bible," was a DJ on the radio. Maybe Claude could help him find work. "Willie moved out to where I was and we palled around for six weeks, going to the honky-tonks and the dives," Claude said. "But I never could get a good job for Willie at the station. We were a small radio station."

Willie decided he might as well go for all the marbles.

He aimed the Buick, four payments behind, north. "Family Bible" was a hit. Word had spread in the business that Willie was the one who wrote it, even if his name wasn't on the single. It was time to show his face to the powers that be in Nashville, Tennessee. ★

GROVER LEWIS

Grover Lewis [1934–1995] is considered to be an "uncredited founder of the New Journalism." When *Splendor in the Grass*, a collection of Lewis' writings, was published in 2005, he was remembered as a journalist like Tom Wolfe, Gay Talese, and others, who put himself into his articles, and made the act of writing the story part of the story itself. That approach is at work here, in his profile of Lightnin' Hopkins [1912–1982] that tells us nearly as much about Lewis himself as about po' Lightnin'. The approach has its rewards, as Hopkins comes alive on the page to a rare extent. He's not exactly a heroic figure here, but he's certainly human. "Looking for Lightnin'" originally appeared in the *Village Voice* in 1968.

Looking for Lightnin'

I.

TURNING OFF THE RACING CABAL OF THE Gulf Freeway a couple of minutes south of downtown Houston, I had my first glimpse of Dowling Street, main artery of the Third Ward and home base for the legendary country blues singer, Sam "Lightnin'" Hopkins.

The neighborhood, once an opulent residential enclave, was now, in the summer of 1960, a black ghetto, shabby at the elbows and knees. Towering Victorian houses, sandwiched in among bleak rows of shotgun shacks and paintflaking juke joints, still reflected some of the old, baronial splendor, but the baroque cupolas atop the weathered mansions had bleached and cracked and begun to fall and the ornate gingerbread lacing on verandas and spires was saggy with rot.

Locating the intersection where I'd been directed, I parked beneath the marquee of a theater featuring a triple-threat combination of horror thrillers and walked past a dry-goods store's sidewalk display of outsize denim overalls "If They Fit You, You Can Have 'Em," a hand-scrawled sign challenged—back to the tin-roofed café on the corner.

The first encounter set the tone for most of the others to follow. I opened the screen door, plugged with cotton tufts to ward off flies, and stepped into an electric-charged silence. Conversation died away without a murmur; bottles suddenly stopped ringing against glasses. For a long instant, the eyes of the half dozen cab drivers sitting at checker-clothed tables in the rear—any of whom, I'd been assured, could help me find Lightnin'—all turned my way. Then, with no appreciable movement, everyone was looking somewhere else.

"What you need, man?" one of the two waitresses inquired cautiously. I explained that I'd driven in from Dallas to try to locate Sam Hopkins, a guitar player—

"Ain't no gittar player here," the second waitress said quickly.

"What you want to see this man about? You a law or does he owe you money?" the other waitress asked.

I explained I wanted to hear him play.

"What's his name again?" After I told her, she shook her head with finality.

"Naw, there ain't nobody around here like that. You know any Tom Hopkins, Lottrell? Any you boys know him?"

Lottrell shrugged and moved off behind the counter. None of the men answered for a long moment. "Naw, I don't know nothin' about him," someone finally drawled. "I never heard of him, my own self," a companion chimed in.

"You come back now," Lottrell called out brightly to my back.

Outside, waiting for the light to change, I heard the café's jukebox begin to throb—a nervous, high-pitched boogie played without accompaniment on an amplified guitar. The song was as harsh and dreary in its dogged reiteration of a mocking, sardonic central riff as the urban slum where I stood.

Now and then, the guitarist injected caustic asides on his own playing: "Now ain't that good," he sneered, a note of self-parody in his voice, after a brilliantly intricate succession of volatile, ringing runs.

There could be no doubt about the performer's identity: I'd first heard him in '48 or '49, when browsing in a grimy, secondhand record shop in Dallas' "Deep Ellum" section, I'd stood stunned with recognition listening to the raw, mournful guitar and a smoky, galvanic voice chanting:

I come all the way from Texas
Just to shake glad hands with you

It was Lightnin' Hopkins, the man I'd driven three hundred miles to hear.

When the song ended, I started walking east, laughing and looking for a likely place to resume the hunt. Midway across the intersection a battered jalopy whipped around the corner in front of me. On the rear bumper, inscribed in red tape, was the motto: "SON OF ZORRO—LOOK OUT" Still laughing, I did, and he missed me a good eight inches.

II.

At night, Houston's Dowling Street, pulsing with jukebox music and flickering neon signs tersely announcing "Beer and Tavern and Dancing," radiates an electric musk—the edgy, sinister reek of something akin to violence held in too long and spoiling to explode.

But strolling east in the steamy afternoon heat as I searched for the fabled Lightnin'—passing a grocery with banana stalks outside, a fortune-telling parlor, a used furniture store, a string of dingy bars held together by a surrealistic patchwork of metal signs, the echoing galleries of ancient boarding houses, a church called the First National Tabernacle of Matthew, Mark, Luke and John, African—I was reminded of the small, islandlike business corners of the late Thirties, before the component-parts shopping centers. In an eerie sense, walking down Dowling Street was like retreating twenty-five years into the past.

Buttonholing passersby and shop clerks to ask about Hopkins I was repeatedly rebuffed. Several people refused to talk to me at all; others were studiedly vague or evasive in their answers. The reaction of a saleslady in a record store was typical.

With narrowed eyes, she listened to my questions, and at first professed to know nothing about Hopkins. When I persisted, she blinked innocently, puckered her forehead in feigned concentration and free-associated: "Hopkins, Hopkins . . . hmm, Harry, maybe? No, he was in the New Deal."

Trying to keep a straight face, I pointed out one of Lightnin's LPs on the rack behind her.

"Oh, that," she grinned amiably. "That's $3.98."

I had better luck with a chance acquaintance named Junco Red at a bar in the next block.

"Well, I be John Brown," he boomed when he heard my question. A wizened gnome with bloodshot eyes, he tipped his truck driver's cap at a rakish angle and wheezed a phlegmy chuckle as he swung around to shake hands. He had only one leg; propped beside him at the bar was a pair of yellow pine crutches. "So you're lookin' for Lightnin', is you?"

Yes, I nodded. Had he seen him?

"Has I *seen* him?" he exploded with laughter. "Why, Sam and me's like brothers. Him and me used to travel all over the country together workin' on the ray road." He pointed at the door. "That scoun'el passed this place not five minutes ago. Well, maybe it were ten, but I know it were soon."

He mentioned a café across the sheet where Hopkins traded regularly and suggested I check over there. "I'd go with you," he offered, draining his glass and winking, "but I'm afraid I'd freeze my heat."

I asked Red if he could describe Hopkins.

"What he look like?" Red thought a minute and motioned vaguely. "Be John Brown, man, I can't say. He be just a cat put his pants on one leg at a time like everybody else." Red stared down into his lap, looking at the empty trouser leg. "Just a black man," he nodded reflectively, "like everybody else."

At the café a waitress pointed through the window to a dusty row of shotgun houses on the adjoining street. "Mr. Hopkins lives in either the fourth or fifth house," she said, "I'm not sure which." When I looked surprised at her help, she smiled: "What's the matter—the people along the street giving you a hard time?"

I knocked at the fourth house and a gaunt, impassive Negress, bearing on her hip, in the immemorial posture of the country woman and her "chap," a plump, sleeping baby, answered the door and eyed me warily as I explained what I wanted.

After I finished, she studied my face a few seconds longer and then un-latched the screen door to point across the yard to the next house. "This here be my place," she explained. "Lightnin', he stays over yonder. He be gone around the corner to the barber shop, if you want to wait." She waved at a man saunter-ing toward us from Dowling. "There be Spider Kirkpatrick now—he Lightnin's drummer, and he can more than likely help you."

Thanking her, I walked to meet the small, dapper drummer. Dressed in a skull-hugging corduroy cap and tightly pegged "drapes" dating back to the bebop period of the Forties, Spider moved with the poised, head-in grace of a jockey.

"Are you the cat be been lookin' for Lightnin'?" he asked politely.

I nodded yes and asked where Lightnin' was.

"Aw, he be around here somewhere," Spider drawled, glancing back at the intersection where a battered '54 Dodge was rounding the corner. "Some of them heads at the poolroom, they told me you was huntin' him, so I figure I'd come out and meet you . . ."

I didn't notice a poolroom, I told him.

"Everybody on Dowlin' seen you, whether you been seen them or not," Spi-der snorted with a short laugh.

The Dodge had pulled into the curb now, motor idling, about a hundred yards up the street. Because of the sun glinting on the windshield, I couldn't see the driver's face.

"Yehr," Spider mused, accepting a cigarette. "I been knowin' and drummin' for Lightnin' ten years and he be well-liked, I can tell you that . . ."

"Is that him?" I asked, motioning to the car which had pulled up abreast of us.

"Yehr," Spider nodded without looking. "That the man."

Stepping off the curb, I leaned in the car window. The driver was a thin, sin-ewy, middle-aged man dressed in rumpled slacks and a heat-wilted sport shirt. Draped around his neck in the manner of an ascot, a spotlessly white barber's towel contrasted startlingly with the deep chocolate hue of his skin. Tilted over his eyes, he wore a jaunty, Sinatra-like porkpie, and mirror rimmed sunglasses further obscured the spare, angular features of his prominent-boned face.

"Are you Lightnin'?" I asked him.

Chuckling, the man pushed his hat back with a lazy gesture and squinted across the seat at me. "Lawd have mercy," he said in a warm, raw rush of whiskey fumes. "I got to cop a guilty plea to that one. Yea, I'm Lightnin' Hopkins. What's happenin', baby?"

III.

Looky yonder what I do see
Whole lots of 'em comin' after me,
But I'm gone.
—Sam "Lightnin'" Hopkins, 1960

"You ain't just signifyin', is you?" Lightnin' asked warily. "You mean you come all the way from Dallas to hear me play?"

When I nodded yes, he searched my face quizzically and then slapped his knee and rocked back and forth with laughter. "Climb in this ol' hoopy, white boy," he crowed, leaning across to flip open the passenger door. "There's a little hell-dive around the corner that sells the coldest beverage in Houston town. Less you and me go over theh and get our heads all tore up."

Which we did. The head-tearing-up process, which was enacted in a succession of piss-smelling little beer parlors, wore on for days, at the end of which I knew considerably more about sour mash whiskey than I had counted on.

But in the end, I also knew considerably more about myself, and the South (and that knowledge ultimately freed me to leave it forever), and my own forebears, who, like Hopkins in his young manhood, had been sharecroppers. Somewhere along in there, too, in those feverish, rushing days and nights of sweet, raw whiskey fumes and mournful guitar cadenzas—even as we shyly began to feel each other out over the clattering racket of the Dodge's hoarse engine—I realized with a dawning sense of wonder that the quest I'd initiated in looking for Lightnin' had begun long before.

In the years after my first exposure to Lightnin's music, the legendary singer had became a human talisman in my breviary of values, an associative touchstone around which clustered most of my precariously balanced, double-edged feelings about the Southwest. This was 1960, recall, before the Kennedys, before McLuhan and the Beatles, before the Mississippi Summer and Lee Harvey Oswald and Jack Ruby and Sirhan Sirhan and Chicago and—oh, hell. A time so remote, in retrospect, that it virtually paralyzes memory.

Texas had changed greatly since my childhood days when, striding beside my grandfather, I roamed the heart-burstingly beautiful dogwood trails of the lower Red River Valley. The transformation, roughly coeval with my own lifetime, hadn't all been for the good.

Much of the wilderness had vanished in the decade after World War II. The vast metropolitan areas spawned by the dizzying changeover from an agrarian to an industrial economy extended suburban purlieus into the countryside, swallowing up pasture, forest, limestone hills, even rivers. The homeplaces in most outlying rural districts stood empty and desolate. The part of Texas from which I'd sprung was now a dying landscape full of sere, brown cemeteries and decaying ghost towns.

The fact that urban existence differed from country ways wasn't what disturbed me. Rather, it was the haunting feeling that something basic, vital, and valuable had been lost in the transition.

Somehow, all of us in Texas, I gradually began to understand, had left behind the old fierce, personal capacity for love and anger that engenders and sustains tribes. Collectively speaking, we were all running scared and alone. Later, traveling and living in other parts of the country, I would understand that the referent "we" encompassed not merely Texans, but Americans at large.

Growing up absurd in the Fifties, as Paul Goodman had it, I found myself increasingly attracted to the few dwindling areas in Dallas that hadn't changed beyond recognition in the span of my own memory: the hustling, feverish Farmers Market; "Deep Ellum," with its bawling street singers and gaudy pawnshops; a rundown "back o' town" section with massive stone staircases soaring crazily out of the debris-strewn foundations of demolished Victorian mansions.

Invariably, I'd encountered the two most fully articulated esthetic expressions of my rolling, lonesome native country: the wild, fellaheen plaint of the hillbilly ballad and the brooding, archaic blues sung by men like Lightnin' Hopkins.

As time passed, I'd accumulated a piecemeal fund of information about Hopkins. I learned, for instance, that he was born and raised at Centerville, a small, dusty cotton community halfway between Dallas and Houston on U.S. 75.

Hopkins' records—many of them unmistakably autobiographical—spilled over with the texture of his life. From such songs as "Tim Moore's Farm," "Sad News from Korea," "Racetrack Blues," "Penitentiary Blues," "Short-Haired Woman," and a score of others, the patterned progression of his past and present emerged—from his earliest days as a sharecropper in the black loam country of Central Texas to his abrupt appearance in 1946 as a prolific recording artist ensconced in the night club and sporting-life milieu of Houston.

All the pungent flavor of his experience, I discovered, was hidden somewhere in the canon of his music: the country dances and Baptist Association suppers in Leona and Groesbeck and Buffalo Springs, where he first heard the harsh, intense poetry of singers like Blind Lemon Jefferson and Hopkins' own cousin, Texas Alexander; the cutting scrapes that followed the dances and the prison stretches that followed the cutting scrapes; the faithless, evil women he knew in both the country and the city as a hobo, a policy gambler, and finally as the cherished pet and musical idol of Houston's black underworld.

Yet it wasn't merely the cold facts of Hopkins' day-to-day life nor his anguished, esoteric music that accounted for my unflagging interest in him. Instead, it was the burgeoning realization that, lying at the heart of both his existential experience and his intense, personal creative efforts, there existed a working fund of values of profound significance for a generation such as mine, born circa Munich.

From Hopkins' music, I learned long before I met Hopkins himself something of the essence of the bleak, barbaric microcosm of his fallen and perishing world—and in the end I understood that he had come to full terms with it. Unlike many in my generation, he'd passed far beyond the lachrymose, self-pitying posture that accompanies a frightened, solipsistic preoccupation with survival.

Accepting the bedrock necessity of unceasing struggle for existence as a simple, inflexible condition of life, he had summoned up the strength, courage, and raw marrow to forge ahead and confront a vaster dilemma: the problem of fashioning something outside oneself worthy of continued life.

At his creative zenith, Hopkins had given form and life to the kind of triumphant, victorious music that, after Faulkner's last ding-dong of doom has pealed, surely will come bubbling and ringing from the lips of the first human to ascend into the light again from his tangled underground lair.

Lightnin' Hopkins—I understood at last, had accomplished in his fashion as much as any man can do. With only one good arm and a splintered toothpick for a bat, he had coolly stepped up to the plate and knocked the concrete ball aimed at his head clear out of the largest goddamn park there is.

IV.

Houston—the South's first feverish megalopolitan dream—resembles a cocky, overdressed, temporarily successful club fighter showing off for a gallery of poolroom bums and petty chiselers on the corner.

In scant minutes, you can drive from the lawless, squalling strip of malarial bayou east of the downtown district, where nine out of ten cons discharged from the prison farms at Huntsville and Richmond congregate after release, to high-on-the-hog Afton Oaks, where oilman Glenn McCarthy's town house scowls sullenly out of a sunless clot of trees like a sybaritic weedhead who thinks the world owes him a lid.

Strolling along heat-shimmering Dowling Street with Lightnin' toward a cluster of tin-and-tarpaper bars, I was in Houston's "third city"—the black ghetto of the Third Ward. Watching our approach, a gangling, stiff-haired shine boy shot out of his cubbyhole rhythmically snapping his cloth. "How you, gate? Lemme put a glaze on them skates for you."

Hopkins waved him away moodily, a distracted frown on his face. "Naw, I ain't got no gig at a club right now," he was saying. "Me and John Lomax Jr.— you're too young to recollect Ol' Man John Lomax, which he got Leadbelly out of the penitentiary in Loozyana—me and John Jr., we got a revival out at

California University, one of them little towns out there . . ." Berkeley? "Yah, that's the one." Hopkins darted a quick, troubled look at my face. "You ever go up in the air in one of them flyin' ships?"

I nodded yes. "Man, I ain't woofin' you," he sniffed emphatically, "I'm *scared* of them molly-trotters. Why, one of them flimsy little ol' outfits could crash and burn up in a minute, and then where'd you be?" After an instant, he brightened. "Aw, well, I'll worry about that tomorrow or the next day," he grinned, recklessly. "It ain't no hurry."

Leading the way into a dim, grimy lounge called Zito's Jungle Hut, Hopkins stopped, recognizing a thin, wrinkle-eroded woman in a maid's uniform sitting at one of the scarred tables. After my eyes grew accustomed to the gloom, I could see she was young and very drunk.

When Hopkins touched her shoulder, she stared at him without replying. "Get wheelin', Mottie," he ordered sharply. "Split your ass on outta here before the man comes along and sets you to pickin' peas." Still wordlessly, the girl rose and lurched toward the door. Watching till she was gone, Hopkins shrugged self-consciously. "Ol' Mottie, she all right," he explained, "but sometimes she get too much beverage to drink."

Maybe Mottie had—but we didn't—not in Zito's, at least. When Hopkins approached the bar and ordered, the waiter answered tonelessly, "We all outta beer today, man."

"What?" Hopkins asked, uncomprehending.

Looking steadily at me, the barman mumbled, "I told you, we ain't got no beer today," and turned away to begin mopping the counter.

Stunned, Hopkins spun around and, motioning curtly for me to follow, plunged back out into the sunlight. Shifting from foot to foot, he tried to dismiss the incident as a joke, but the more he talked about it, the angrier he got. The episode seemed to trigger some hair-fine edginess in him, and in the moments that followed, he grew increasingly morose, only occasionally breaking into abrupt, unprovoked fits of hypertense laughter.

"One thing that man's still got to learn," he grumbled darkly, inspecting the ridged, hairless skin on the backs of his black hands. "This here stuff don't rub off one way or another, you know what I mean?"

Our reception was more affable next door. A gaudily lighted jukebox played a slow-drag blues, and the husky, bald bartender greeted Hopkins as we entered: "How things shakin', Sam?" "Everything copacetic," Lightnin' nodded. "Hit us with two more of the same, will you do that, Curly?"

One of the selections on the jukebox was a song by John Lee Hooker. Curious to find out Hopkins' reaction to what I supposed to be one of his rivals, I asked him about Hooker's style. "Aw, he'd be all right," Hopkins smiled crookedly, stripping the label off his bottle with a thumbnail, "if he'd just woodshed a spell and learn how to play the damn gittar."

Uneasily, trying to stave off the awkward silences that began to develop, I continued to ask Hopkins questions. Gradually, he grew more spontaneous and animated—at one point, he raised his trouser leg to display the scars left on his shin by a leg iron he wore during a stretch on a Central Texas work gang—but it was clear that he wasn't over the depression and anger caused by the ugly incident at Zito's.

"Tell you what," he said finally, cutting his eyes nervously around the room and scraping a raspy palm across his stubbled cheeks, "I never did get that shave I set out for this mornin'. I think I'll roll on down to the barbershop and get cleaned up while you got this cool place to wait for me in. Okey-doke?"

I nodded, sure.

"Won't take but fifteen, twenty minutes," he estimated. "Then I'll meet you up we'll go by where I stays at and get my box, and I'll hit a lick or two for you."

The jukebox fell silent. Swiveling around to watch Hopkins' tall, stooped figure move through the shadows toward the door, I wondered if I'd see him again and thought about the long return drive to Dallas, and then stopped thinking about anything at all and simply sat, waiting, watching Mottie, slumped half-hidden at a table in the rear, lifting and lowering her pint of Tokay until it rang empty.

V.

Oh, if it wasn't for lovin',
I believe this big world would come to a end.

But I want you to remember–
This world's gonna stand forever.
—Sam "Lightnin'" Hopkins, 1960

Looking frail and worn, swaying precariously on the edge of the rump-sprung divan on his front porch after picking me up at the Dowling Street bar more than an hour past the time he'd promised, Hopkins opened the pint of bourbon, drained off a deep, hungry swallow, weighed the cap in his hand a moment, and then flung it far out across the packed-dirt yard. Twilight was settling and a faint, tangy breeze had sprung up from the direction of the Gulf, but Lightnin's face glistened with a sickly rime of sweat.

"Well, I done made it up in my mind," he announced hoarsely, picking up his guitar and striking a jagged discord that seemed to linger, brooding and tangible, in the wan light. "I'm gonna call John Lomax Jr. tareckly and tell him I ain't goin' to California nor no place else in no airplane."

He tilted the bottle again and a tic leaped in his cheek. "Ol' John's been good as gold to me, and I hate to jump salty on him, but when it comes to any outfit that goes up higher off the ground than a fast rattler, that's all she wrote for *this* mother's son."

Ducking his head and muttering under his breath, he began to tone his strings. Next door, a sullen-faced teenager with the wispy beginnings of a mustache and boot-shaped sideburns was monotonously bouncing a tennis ball off the dust-grimed wall. After a minute, Hopkins grunted irritably, and called out: "Hey, hotshot, how you expect a man to get this box talkin' American with you makin' all that racket?"

Taking his time, the boy bounced and caught the ball twice more before sauntering across the yard and leaning indolently against the banister. "You really think you're somethin' else, don't you, doctor?"

Hopkins stiffened but didn't glance up. "Naw I didn't say that," he murmured.

"Well you ain't me, doctor," the boy drawled, "'cause I think you're somethin' else, and that's a fact." He reached over and flicked one of the guitar strings and Hopkins' head snapped erect. "You know, doctor," the boy said, calculating his shot before turning away, "there just ain't nothin' sadder in the world than a old hipster."

Wincing as though he'd been struck, Hopkins watched the boy saunter away across a yard and resume bouncing and fielding the ball. Then, lurching to his feet with a mixed look of terror and unutterable weariness, fumbling with the guitar and the capless whiskey bottle, Hopkins, reeled off the porch toward his car. "Come on if you're comin', white boy," he called in a vacant, stricken voice. "I ain't got all day."

Revving up the Dodge's engine to a throbbing, feverish wail, Hopkins jammed down the accelerator before I got the door closed, and staring dead ahead, roared through the stoplight at Dowling, heading south. After he'd whipped around a series of blind corners and careened past a vast, desolate graveyard for junked automobiles, the engine began to knock, making the car pitch and buck.

"Sounds like it's throwed a rod, don't it?" Lightnin' remarked distantly, mopping moisture from his face with the barber's towel draped around his neck. "But maybe it ain't."

The pavement ended and the road abruptly dwindled to a single span of dirt tracks. The last house fell behind. In the middle of an open field, facing a motte of sycamore trees, Hopkins braked the hissing, protesting car to a halt. The engine wheezed once and died.

Wordlessly Hopkins started toward the grove trailing the guitar through the high scorched Indian grass. As I got out and started after him, a swarm of birds soared up from the trees like a pall of dark, oily smoke. Somewhere close by, the sound of running water rustled.

Hopkins sat down on a stump near the verge of the grove and cradled the guitar under his arm, and I stood a half dozen yards away. He had just begun to play when he heard the sound.

Rising involuntarily, all the muscles in his face working in frantic chorus, his fingers unconsciously sweeping the guitar strings, Hopkins recoiled in blind, panicky anguish as the jet airliner, climbing for altitude, swept straight toward us, its metal belly gleaming only a few hundred feet above the earth in the last, thin wash of light.

Then Lightnin' pulled himself fully erect, his fingers still ripping the strings, and cried out in tormented protest—not words—but a roar of mingled horror and triumph old as the earth itself.

After the plane had passed, Sam Hopkins of Centerville, Texas, remained erect and his fingers began to remember how to play mere music again, and I sat across from him in the warm, enfolding summer grass, rapt and grateful and listening very hard. ★

ROBERT EARL HARDY

Townes Van Zandt was Houston's *poete maudit*. He was certainly a poet, and he was certainly cursed, if only by himself and his near constant abuse of alcohol and drugs. The following excerpt, which describes how Van Zandt began his career playing in Montrose folk clubs, is from veteran music writer Robert Earl Hardy's first book. Over the past twenty-five years, Hardy has published articles on twentieth-century American music, obscure baseball history, and the arts in defunct newspapers, obscure journals, and unknown magazines, most recently in the acclaimed tenth annual Southern Music issue of *The Oxford American*.

From *A Deeper Blue: The Life and Music of Townes Van Zandt*: Waitin' for the Day

THE JESTER LOUNGE ON WESTHEIMER Boulevard was one of no more than a half-dozen small nightclubs or coffee-houses in Houston that featured folk music. They were small rooms with tiny stages where mostly local acts would play for tips or for five or ten dollars a night. "At the time, the Jester was very cool. It was a real folk music club," recalls John Carrick. Carrick, along with his mother, who was known as "Ma" Carrick, ran another of Houston's seminal folkclubs, the Sand Mountain Coffeehouse, and also was among the group of local regulars who played the few—"three or four," according to Carrick—folk venues in Houston. "What we didn't know then," Carrick says, "was how cool the Jester was. Here's a short list: Townes played there, and he was one of the kids, you know. I think that was the first place in Houston that Jerry Jeff Walker played. K. T. Oslin was a regular there, and Guy Clark. A lot of the blues guys played there, including Mance Lipscomb and Lightnin' Hopkins, and a lot of musicians that people had never heard of but that were just phenomenal. Townes was one of the first around doing any stuff he'd written, although at first they were just kind of goofy talking blues songs, like 'T-Bird Blues' and 'Mustang Blues' and stuff like that."

"[T]he first place I played was a club on Westheimer called the Jester Lounge," Townes later recollected.

> That was the first place I ever got paid real money for singing. This guy, who turned out to be Don Sanders, came up to me in there and said I also oughta try this place called Sand Mountain. I went over there with him and we did a short little set. Mrs. Carrick was at her desk keeping an eye on the proceedings, and the place was almost empty at the time. There was this song I used to do at the time called 'The KKK Blues,' and I sang it that night. It was a talking blues about dropping out of the second grade to join the Ku Klux Klan, and the guy said 'you got too much education.' Then I did another one called 'The Vietnamese Blues,' which had a chorus line about leaving Vietnam to the Vietnamese. Anyway, I got through singing and Mrs. Carrick said, 'Well, that was real good, but we just don't do things like that around here.' I said, 'Well, this is a fine place, but I just can't stay here then.' Next day she sent Don as an envoy again and she said she wanted us to come back. That was the beginning.

Townes recalled meeting Guy Clark around this time. "He was at the Jester before I played there, and then [he] joined the Peace Corps. I started playing there, and then he came back [and] we met. . . ." Fran [Fran Van Zandt, his first wife] also recalls Townes and Guy meeting sometime in mid- to late-1965. "Guy was just one of these ten-dollar acts like Townes was. It was kind of an immediate friendship. Guy lived not too far from Sand Mountain, in a one-room apartment. Susie, his first wife—Susan—came in to Sand Mountain. She was a little-bitty cute thing, kind of feisty. And Guy just kind of fell for her right off. They started dating and got married and had a baby. So, all of us were just kind of hanging out there."

Since the mid-1950s, the local folk scene had been centered in the Houston Folklore Society and in the powerful personality of its leader, John A. Lomax Jr., the well-known folklorist Alan Lomax's brother, the other son of the legendary patriarch John A. Lomax Sr. The senior Lomax had collected cowboy songs in the 1920s and discovered Leadbelly and made field recordings of dozens of other American roots musicians all over the South, and he remains one of the most important figures in twentieth-century American music scholarship.

As John Lomax Jr.'s son, John Lomax III, recalls, for folk singers in Houston, the Folklore Society "was the only place to go, really." The society met monthly and held events in local clubs and coffeehouses or occasionally at the Jewish Community Center. "The meetings of the Houston Folklore Society consisted of about ten minutes of business, then the rest was essentially what they now call 'pass the guitar,'" says Lomax.

"My dad was extremely democratic, and they were all very democratic, and everyone got a song or two. . . . No matter if you were wretched or professional; the whole concept was you were doing this for fun, and numerous beverages were served. They used all the members' houses. . . . My dad would sing some in that setting. He would get up and sing real folk songs *a capella*, and sometimes he'd accompany himself with an axe and a big chunk of wood. He would stroke it with these big whack sounds, [singing] 'take this hammer . . . *whack!*' With this big fuckin' log, and it would go flying everywhere, to show how it was rhythmic. And he would talk about where the songs came from and how he learned them from his dad, who learned them from whoever.

"Guy Clark came through there when he first came to town," recalls Lomax. "My dad had a show with Lightnin' Hopkins—he managed Lightnin' at the time—and Guy had just showed up in town, and he went to a meeting, and they said, 'Oh, we're having a show day after tomorrow, do you want to play?' And he did, and Lightnin' was there. Guy was a little nervous."

Lightnin' Hopkins was in fact a regular fixture on the Houston club scene throughout the sixties, and it was through the influence of Hopkins and other black musicians like Mance Lipscomb and Josh White that the young Townes Van Zandt left the more purely white, commercial folk path and set a more deep-rooted, blues-oriented course, something that some of the other young, white folk aficionados felt ill-equipped to attempt, but that Townes seemed to take to naturally.

Van Zandt had discovered Hopkins' recordings when he was in high school, then began listening more seriously in college, copying guitar licks, slowly mastering his finger-picking technique, and gradually absorbing the nuances of his style and, critically, his attitude. As he later told the story, one day at the University of Houston, he spotted an ad in the paper for Lightnin's appearance that night at the Bird Lounge. Townes recalled that he was dumbfounded, never imagining that Hopkins was still alive and could actually be seen at a local club. He saw the show and then met Lightnin', sitting at his table and chatting with him, somewhat in awe.

Rex Bell was another aspiring folk singer, and he played bass with Hopkins during this period, later going on to play a long stint with him. Bell recalls that it was actually he who introduced Townes to Lightnin'. "Mrs. Carrick introduced me to Townes," Bell remembers. "I was her perennial opening act. . . . I think I got paid six bucks or something. So she introduced me to Townes upstairs there at Sand Mountain, and she left the room. And immediately Townes threw open the window, and he had a gallon of wine on a rope, and he pulled it up, and we both took a swig of wine, and we were friends from then on. It wasn't too long afterward that I introduced him to Lightnin'."

Fran recalls that Townes was a big fan of Lightnin', and that he got to know him on a personal level to some extent.

> I remember one time it was announced in the paper that Lightnin' Hopkins had died. It was Sunday morning, not even eight o'clock, I don't think. We got the paper and Townes read it and got real upset. We got in the car and drove over. Lightnin' lived in an apartment close to the University of Houston. We knocked on the door, and old Lightnin' always had these bodyguards, these people around, so they opened the door and we went in and Townes said, 'Oh, my God, Lightnin'. They said you were dead.' And Lightnin' just says, 'I don't think so.' So we sat there and they played guitars and talked for hours. Lightnin', you know, was drinking white lightning whiskey all the time.

Soon, to save money and to be closer to what there was of a folk music scene, Townes and Fran moved into the tiny apartment above Sand Mountain, and Mrs. Carrick became their landlady. Many of the young folk singers in Houston had lived in that apartment at one time or another, according to John Carrick. "The deal was, you'd live up there, and in return, you'd clean the club and you'd get a little bit of money." Townes became "kind of the house act," at Sand Mountain, opening shows for many of the more well-known acts that passed through, Fran recalls. "That's when he and Guy Clark got real close." Clark had in fact just returned from training for the Peace Corps: "I had a brief fling at it, but I didn't actually go anywhere. I just did the training program," Clark remembers.

***

"We both started writing about the same time," Clark says. "But Townes just did it in a way that raised it to a level of art, or poetry, whatever you want to call it, rather than just rhyming 'moon, June, and spoon.'" While Bob Dylan's writing was inspiring folk musicians everywhere, Townes' inspiration was more direct. "Townes was right there," Clark stresses, "and while you couldn't be Townes or write like Townes, you could come from the same place artistically."

Darryl Harris was another musician playing the folk clubs of Houston at the time. He had attended Milby High School in Houston with Fran. "I was a guitar player," Harris recollects. "I played some kind of schlocky flamenco and classical stuff. I was playing at the Jester Lounge, and I went out to the Jester one night, and Townes was playing there. He was with Fran, so that's really how we met. . . . And when Townes and I met, we were both going to the University of Houston, so we would then run into each other occasionally on campus. We'd run into each other and then we'd sort of talk each other into not going to class."

Harris recalls, "Townes and Guy were probably the most popular guys who played there, but most of the people there were pretty good. Although when I first saw Townes out at the Jester, he was pretty awful, really; pretty drunk. The stuff he was playing made me kind of wonder. Sometimes you hear people play and you wonder how they could ever imagine it being possible to have any kind of career in music. That was really sort of my response the first time I ever heard him."

Another singer on the scene at the Jester and Sand Mountain, who was writing his own songs, was Jerry Jeff Walker. Townes was impressed and inspired by Walker's songwriting; Fran was less enthusiastic. "Jerry Jeff was over at our apartment one day," she recalls. "He was from New York, and back then there wasn't a lot of mixture of the South and the North. Jerry Jeff had such a different sense of etiquette; he really had none." She recalls one day when "he was sitting at our dining room table eating, slumped over, not talking to anybody, and he had his hat on, and Townes' mom and dad came over," she says. "Jerry Jeff didn't stand up, didn't take his hat off, didn't even look up. So Townes' dad wouldn't let his mother sit down, and he called Townes outside and said, 'This guy has insulted your mother. How could you allow that to happen?' That is the sense of honoring women that Townes was brought up with. . . . [Townes' parents] always wanted to hear Townes sing, but if Jerry Jeff was on the bill too, they wouldn't come."

Fran remembers clearly that it was also during this time that Townes wrote the first few batches of the songs that would make up his lasting body of work. "In the first apartment we lived in there were two walk-in closets," she says. "The little one off the bathroom he decorated with posters, music posters, and made into his own little studio. There was just enough room to have a chair and a little amplifier and a little tape recorder, and a little table. You had to step in sideways to be able to sit down. That is where he started writing his first songs. He loved going in there; he would shut the door and stay there for hours." They had a small antique pump organ in their apartment, and Fran would often help Townes write out his music. "I would sound it out [on the organ] and write it because I knew music, although I could only do the treble. . . . That was for the first five or six songs."

The songs came quickly. "'Waitin' Around to Die' had to be within the first two or three songs, maybe the second or third," Fran recalls. "It wasn't the first one I heard. He might have written it first, but I think he didn't sing it for a while, he kind of just held it. . . . 'Turnstiled, Junkpiled' was another early one."

Fran was overjoyed by this creative outpouring, but she was taken aback by "Waitin' Around to Die." She asked Townes where such a song had come from. "He just said he didn't know," she says. "He would often just wake up in the middle of the night and write, and sometimes he described it like it would just tumble out of his brain and down his fingers."

"My first serious song was 'Waitin' Around to Die,'" Townes said in 1977, a statement he repeated many times when performing the song. "I talked to this old man for a while," he continued, "and he kinda put out these vibrations. I was sitting at the bar of the Jester Lounge one afternoon drinking beer, thinking about him, and just wrote it down."

"Waitin' Around to Die" is indeed a serious song for a young man with Townes' early background to have written, but unlike many "serious" songs that young folk singers come up with, it bears the weight of its seriousness almost effortlessly. It takes its subject, a young man, through a life of misfortune, from a childhood marked by his father's beating of his mother and the mother's desertion, to an adolescence of deceit and abandonment at the hands of a woman, to imprisonment for robbing a man, always with the almost offhand refrain, "it's easier than just waiting around to die." Finally, after spending two years in prison, the young man is resigned to a life of destitution with his new "friend," codeine, a drug of poverty and desperation, and he ends, "together we're gonna wait around and die."

This is a bleak vision indeed, but it is handled so deftly that there is no sense of it being maudlin. The simple three-chord progression in a minor key perfectly reflects the direct simplicity of the storytelling, Van Zandt's delivery is entirely straightforward and unaffected, and the poetic sensibility shows an already well-honed maturity—the use of the place names in each verse: Tennessee, Tuscaloosa, Muskogee; the offhand vernacular: "she cleaned me out and hit it on the sly"; "we robbed a man and brother did we fly"; and the fine-tuned balance of the verses—so that all of these things add up to a stunning personal vision of something much deeper than mere folk music. "Waitin' Around to Die" is the blues: starkly personal and universal at the same time. It's the kind of song that instantly differentiated Townes Van Zandt from his contemporaries, and that often left audiences stunned, as Fran had been. ★

LISA GRAY

Lisa Gray has worked as a writer and editor for the *Houston Press*, and at the *Houston Chronicle* as columnist and member of the editorial board. Like a lot of people, she didn't expect to stay long in that city. But she did.

In this 2000 *Press* article she profiled curator and museum director Jim Harithas, and in the process said a great deal about the contemporary Houston art scene. Since this article was written, Harithas and his wife, Ann O'Connor Harithas, have also opened The Station Contemporary Art Museum in the Third Ward. Video artist Andy Mann later died of prostate cancer.

Revolution in Chrome

"IT'S A FUNNY LITTLE MUSEUM, ISN'T IT?" asks big, white-haired Jim Harithas, surveying his domain. The answer—*oh, yes*—is too obvious to wait for, so Harithas paces around the Art Car Museum, stopping occasionally to admire the works already in place, mentally rearranging them to accommodate two new shows. But oh, yes: It *is* a funny little museum. You know it as soon as you lay eyes on the building, a silvery onion-domed thing punctuated with spikes and a red plastic star, like a stoner's model of the Kremlin. A vicious-looking barbed-wire-and-chain-link fence protects the museum from a funky stretch of Heights Boulevard—and perhaps more to the point, lends the place a tough, macho air. Nearby, a sign designates a grassy field as the museum's official parking lot. Next door, there's a Citgo station-cum-convenience store; across the street is *Carmadillo*, the hulking metal-scaled creature that lurks outside sculptor Mark Bradford's studio. The Museum District, this ain't. And that suits Harithas fine.

Outside, you see the kind of works you'd expect from something called the Art Car Museum—that is, particularly splendid examples of the genre, of vehicles used as much for personal expression as for transportation. Under the tinny carport lolls a stretched-out David Best fantasy barely recognizable as a car. Shiny, bright-colored doodads cover every inch of the surface, layers of beads, buttons and cheap toys, the detritus of a thousand Happy Meals. A tubby plastic Michelin Man serves as the hood ornament. You can't help but look.

Inside, a rotating cast of such cars offers itself for your inspection. Depending on when you're there, you might see the one that looks like a starlet's red stiletto, or the one that resembles a giant bunny, or a particularly astounding lowrider. Some of the other exhibits feel like variations on the main theme—not art cars, but car art. One of Andy Mann's video installations uses a stack of TV sets to run video clips from Houston's annual art car parade. Mel Chin covers a tire in snakeskin and calls it *Road Killer*. A backlit George Hixson photo captures smooth-headed car artist Mike Scranton, his eyes hidden behind goggles, a welding torch brandished like a weapon, a car in flames behind him.

But many of the museum's exhibits, including the two shows Harithas is now installing, have nothing at all to do with cars. Jim Hatchett's "Dirt Paintings" is four abstract canvases "painted" with soil and sand and rocks; Ron Hoover's "Mr. WTO" is a series of small unnerving paintings that mostly depict shadowy businessmen. Both shows make overt political statements: Hatchett's *Butterfly Hill* is named in honor of Julia Butterfly Hill, the eco-protester who spent two years living in a redwood; Hoover's nightmarish *Mr. Maxxam, a/k/a Charles Hurwitz* depicts her nemesis. Even the two shows' opening party, on the Friday before Memorial Day, will possess a left-wing social conscience: Houston's Green Party will be stationed at the door, soliciting last-minute signatures on its petition to add Ralph Nader to Texas's presidential ballot.

To the uninitiated, the museum's juxtapositions seem weird: Why, other than for color, is a car that looks like a starlet's red stiletto pump positioned in front of a pro-union painting of oppressed farm workers? Why would Ralph "Unsafe at Any Speed" Nader garner support at a place that celebrates cars?

But to Harithas, it all coheres. In his "Art Car Manifesto," posted near the front of the museum, he argues that art cars are revolutionary by nature: When a dull, mass-produced machine is transmogrified into something weirder and wildly personal, the artist is "rescuing the automobile from corporate uniformity," striking back against the bland consumer culture that suffocates our souls.

It's a '60s kind of argument; Harithas is a '60s kind of guy. When he calls something "subversive," he means it as high praise; "revolutionary" is even better. He knows, good and well, that the red star atop his museum can be read as something other than the Lone Star of Texas.

This latest opening excites Harithas, makes him edgy. It's a chance to show off artists he thinks the world needs to see; it's a chance to make a political statement; and it's a chance to host a raucous party, the kind he's always loved. Pacing the museum, he radiates a surprising star-of-the-school-play nervousness.

Surprising, because Harithas is hardly new to all this. At 67, he has curated hundreds of shows and presided over nearly as many opening parties. Thirty years ago, he was considered one of the hottest, most avant-garde museum directors in the country.

Such moments don't last long. In 1978, after Houston's Contemporary Arts Museum very publicly let him go, Harithas's career appeared to be over. And for nearly 20 years, it seemed that way. Harithas lay low.

But he has resurfaced, now, at this funny little museum. Obviously it's a place to show art cars and other worthy works. But it's also a place free of meddlesome board members—which means that it's a place where Jim Harithas can make as much trouble as he likes.

***

In the late '60s and well into the '70s, Harithas was famous for his ability to make a museum seem like the blue-hot pulsating center of the universe, the right place at the right time. At the straitlaced Corcoran Gallery of Art, that counted as a significant accomplishment.

In '65 Harithas was the chief curator at the Corcoran, one of the oldest museums in the country, located only a block from the White House in stuffy Washington, D.C. In '68 he took over as the museum's director, and soon afterward dispatched his curators to lure "the freak community" to a museum opening; as hippie bait, he proffered a rock band and free food and drink. The freaks arrived in droves and, Harithas remembers proudly, "the dope smell was enormous." To conservative board members, he explained that times, they were a-changing, and if the Corcoran didn't get with it, it would remain the same boring institution it had been for 35 years. The Corcoran got with it. Harithas's short reign is now remembered as the beginning of the museum's lively golden period.

In 1971 he took over the Everson (pronounced "Ee-verson") Museum of Art in Syracuse, New York—a nowhere, upstate university town that he was determined to blast onto the cultural map. Under Harithas, the museum danced on the bleeding edge. Harithas even curated the first-ever major show of video art: a little piece of museum-world history.

But the story that everyone tells first, when talking about the Harithas era at the Everson, is of the John and Yoko show. Harithas had met John Lennon and Yoko Ono at the Leo Castelli Gallery, the New York art world's equivalent of Sam's Bar: Sooner or later everyone ends up there. Practically everyone alive knew Yoko as the woman who'd broken up the Beatles, and as an artist, she was important in the scruffy band of neo-Dadaists called the Fluxus movement. But for all her notoriety, practically no one had ever seen her way-out, high-concept work. Harithas asked if she'd consider the Everson.

Later, John and Yoko invited Harithas and a curator to their home near Central Park West. They were received, of course, in John and Yoko's bedroom. Yoko lay on the bed; John was sitting at its foot. The curator went into shock— John Lennon! *the* cultural hero of the '60s!—and Harithas worried he'd faint. But Lennon produced a pair of guitars and asked the curator to play a few songs with him. The curator remembered all the words. Lennon didn't.

The United States was trying to deport Lennon, an unemployed foreign national, and Harithas was delighted to make the process more difficult by offering Lennon a job as a curator. In fact, Harithas was delighted to turn over his entire museum to John and Yoko.

He'd judged the cultural moment precisely right. On Lennon's birthday, a cold, wet night in October '71, a mob was camped outside the Everson building, waiting for the show to open. A newspaper estimate put the number at 8,000, only half of whom managed to squeeze inside. Ringo Starr and Eric Clapton showed up. John and Yoko took refuge from the crowd in the museum's garden. The opening made national news. Harithas was ecstatic.

***

Most of Harithas's museum friends warned him to forget about Houston. If you go to Texas, they said, your career is over.

At the beginning of '74, he was 41 years old, a father of three, and a hot property. Not only had he positioned the out-of-the-way Everson firmly in the avant-garde, he'd made the bookkeepers happy. He'd quadrupled the museum's annual attendance, doubled its budget and wiped out its deficit.

Harithas was hailed as a kind of miracle worker, and Houston's Contemporary Arts Museum needed a miracle. Other than a distinctive new building—the stainless-steel parallelogram was only two years old—the CAM didn't have much going for it. The museum was nearly broke. Marilyn Lubetkin, head of the museum's search for a new director, told the *Houston Chronicle* that the board was not only looking for a director, but also "looking for money to sustain the exhibitions for 1974." Rumor had it that the CAM might have to let itself be absorbed by the rich, dull Museum of Fine Arts.

Harithas saw the CAM as a gigantic overripe challenge. Houston was the fourth-largest city in the United States but a hopeless cultural backwater, a place that needed to be woken up. He took the job.

Video artist Andy Mann had known Harithas since 1972, when Mann helped an artist friend install a show at the Everson. As Mann remembers it, Harithas got drunk one night and informed Mann that he didn't have to be a mechanic, that he should be making art of his own. "Anybody can say that," says Mann. But a year later, when he approached Harithas with an idea for a video installation, Harithas came through with money.

After Harithas accepted the CAM job, Mann ran into him at a bar in SoHo. Mann was sick of the New York art scene.

"I'll go to Houston," he said.

"Okay," replied Harithas. "I'll pay your bus ticket."

As Mann remembers it, he arrived in Houston on the weekend Harithas and his wife were splitting up; Harithas isn't sure of the chronology. He says now that he "went a little crazy" after his divorce, though not in a way that affected his job. Even so, his timing was perfect: The early '70s was a crazy time, and oil-boom Houston was a crazy place.

***

In some ways, Harithas fit Houston perfectly: a swaggering, flamboyant museum director for a swaggering, flamboyant city. He was undeniably a carpetbagger; his voice still retains Yankee traces of his native Maine, and he was educated in Europe. But he had the outsize gall required to tell Texans what it meant to be Texan—and furthermore, that the state didn't appreciate its own artists enough. "I feel Houston shouldn't follow New York, it should lead it," he informed the *Chronicle* after the museum announced his hiring. "The capability is there." It didn't hurt, either, that shows by little-known Texas artists were cheap to mount.

In September, Harithas opened the first show he'd curated for Houston: "12/Texas," a group exhibition whose dozen members included rising stars Luis Jiménez and James Surls. (Harithas quickly awarded each of them solo shows.) He soon followed with the now famous sculptures that John Chamberlain had concocted of crushed car parts; the pieces were owned by Stanley Marsh, the super-rich and famously eccentric antiwar protester who commissioned Ant Farm's Cadillac Ranch. Until Harithas called, Texas museum directors had avoided Marsh; he was not their kind of person.

Harithas's shows at the CAM were criticized as "uneven," but the highs were very high. Now-familiar names jump out from the list of the CAM's exhibitions: John Alexander, Dick Wray, Jesse Lott, Earl Staley and Terry Allen. In February '76, Harithas awarded a show to Julian Schnabel, the recent University of Houston graduate who would soon come to symbolize the excess of the '80s art world. At the time, Schnabel was working as a cook; he hadn't yet shown his broken-plate paintings in New York and been signed by (what else?) the Leo Castelli Gallery. Harithas was giving the young artist a break; Schnabel's work was shown in the CAM's basement.

But the CAM, under Harithas, wasn't just a container for art; it was a center of activity. Harithas surrounded himself with bright young curators like Mark Lombardi and Paul Schimmel (now the chief curator of the Los Angeles Museum of Contemporary Art). Houston's artists and art students gravitated toward the museum's openings. The parties were wild: Fistfights broke out almost as a matter of course, and the '70s art crowd felt it almost a moral duty to embrace mood-enhancing substances and sexual liberation.

Harithas was known as a ladies' man. "Jim was always very sexually potent," remembers Mann. "One thing you had to do in the art world then was take whatever love you could find." In the mid-'70s photographer Susie Paul shot Harithas and his old friend, the painter Norman Bluhm, in front of one of Bluhm's paintings. Bluhm was one of the last and sexiest of the abstract expressionists, a painter whose cushy abstract shapes conjured fleshy breasts and buttocks. In the photo, Bluhm and Harithas stand with their thumbs hooked in their belts like cowboys: the embodiments of machismo against an orgiastic background.

Fredricka Hunter ran (and still runs) Texas Gallery, which has long shown cutting-edge Texas artists. Hunter didn't count herself among Harithas's inner circle; she remembers it as a boys' club and a "scene," neither of which appealed to her. But she remembers listening fascinated to Harithas's monologues about art, traipsing after him as he talked, the same way that everyone else traipsed after him. She liked his manic enthusiasm and love of risk, both of which made him seem more like an artist than an administrator. "It certainly wasn't as corporate a time as it is now," she sighs.

But not everyone approved. Some CAM board members didn't like the museum's scruffy image. Others objected to Harithas's shameless regionalism: If the museum was any good, they asked, why was it showing *local* artists? What about New York?

***

Harithas's relationship with the CAM's board of directors was always strained, and the museum never had enough money. He blamed the board; the board blamed him.

Those problems grew worse in June 1976. Heavy rains sent water pouring into the CAM, and in 25 minutes, the lower floor—a glorified basement used for exhibitions, storage and offices—was flooded. Harithas says he and his staff went "diving for art," trying to salvage what they could. Luckily firemen cut off the museum's electricity before the staff electrocuted itself.

Some of the wet art was shipped to NASA to be vacuum-dried, and some was placed in freezers at upscale grocery stores. Much of it, though, was beyond repair. The damage, estimated at $1 million, included the CAM's membership records, 15 years of work by Washington, D.C., painter Gil Cautrescasas and some of Harithas's own collection, including works by Lennon and Ono.

The financial hit was nearly more than the struggling museum could bear, and the CAM remained closed for almost a year. When it reopened, Harithas informed reporters that with new funding, the museum would no longer need to focus on Texas artists.

He'd partially renounced his love of regionalism, but he hadn't renounced his rowdy ways. In May of '77 the CAM reopened with a retrospective of Salvatore Scarpitta, an Italian sculptor. Among his works was *Rajo Jack*, a meticulous replica of the car driven by the first black competitor in Southwest drag racing. It was a bravura exhibition of artistic technique, but more than that, the piece also made a social statement about speed and fury and racism. To Harithas, it was the best kind of art.

In a similar vein, Scarpitta's *Lynx* was a functional replica of a light desert vehicle from World War II. At the Port of Houston, authorities refused to allow it into the country. Never mind that its surface is intricately painted, they said; it's a weapon, and can be fully mobilized.

Harithas reveled in the controversy. At one point, Joan Mondale, the vice president's wife, helped the CAM lobby the port, but as Harithas tells the story, the work's release had more to do with the head of the port, a former tank commander: "You can't tell me this is a tank," the man said, and Harithas knew then that he was home free. At the CAM, Harithas aimed the tank's guns diagonally across the intersection of Bissonnet and Main—a declaration of war on the Museum of Fine Arts, and on the forces of bureaucracy and dullness everywhere.

But it was a few months later, in October, that the anarchic spirit of

Harithas's era at the CAM crystallized into the single anecdote that everyone remembers. Antoni Miralda, a Spanish artist who specialized in theatrical celebrations, designed one in which 60 Kilgore Rangerettes first danced for the CAM opening crowd, then proceeded to build a 200-foot wall out of loaves of bread dyed red, green and blue.

Someone tore half a loaf from the wall and lobbed it across the room, hitting a woman in the head. The opening turned into a gigantic food fight. Crumbs rained down into the CAM's lower floor. Outside, a fistfight escalated into a general melee. The police broke up the party.

At his house, Harithas still keeps a black-and-white video of the Rangerettes' performance that night. He pops it into the little TV on top of his refrigerator and shakes his head as the drill team executes its trademark high kicks. "That's Texas," he says. "I *went* Texas."

***

The shenanigans further strained Harithas's dicey relationship with the museum's board. Harithas argued with the board over finances and aesthetics, and complained that its members didn't understand the museum. They didn't look at the shows, he said; they wouldn't talk to him about the artistic program. In May of '78, furious that the board had discussed hiring a business manager to handle the museum's books, he wrote a hotheaded letter of resignation. After submitting it, he thought better of it and tried to retract it. The board voted to accept it anyway. Harithas was out of a job.

"CAM supporters note cheerily that the museum's image can only go up," wrote *Houston Post* arts reporter Mimi Crossley. "The recent aesthetic has expressed itself in radical chic exhibitions formulated out of the '60s rebellion against formalism, the establishment and sexual mores." That fall the museum announced a fund-raising concert by jazz pianist Bobby Short, a society favorite; the evening would be smooth, safe and free of risks.

The CAM's Harithas era was over. But Harithas wasn't over the CAM.

In the '70s and '80s Andy Mann's friendship with Harithas was a prickly one. Harithas had a habit of throwing unwanted shadow punches at Mann—a physical metaphor for their relationship. Sometimes they were close compadres:

Harithas would help Mann land a show in Fort Worth, or Mann would spend a weekend camped on Harithas's couch; when they played chess, Harithas usually won. But sometimes they'd go for long periods without speaking. Looking back, Mann can't remember why.

Mann says that after Harithas's breakup with the CAM, Harithas began to fast; it was a cleansing ritual. The gesture annoyed Mann; at first, he thought fine, let Jim starve himself. But by day 20, even Mann was worried. Harithas's chess game had gone to hell, he looked weak, and his teeth were getting loose. He'd grown so thin that even passing acquaintances worried about him.

But not until day 42 did Harithas break the fast. Mann says that he started with a shot of scotch.

***

People talk now about Harithas's "lost years." For a long time, he lay low, keeping a polite distance from the Houston art scene he'd once led. In the late '70s he married Ann O'Connor Robinson, one of the founders of Robinson Gallery, which had stood next door to the CAM. Ann was an heir to the O'Connor oil fortune; she had a gravelly voice, a raucous laugh and four kids. Jim and his three moved into her sedate house on ritzy North Boulevard. Some of Jim's artist friends, like Mann, weren't sure they were welcome there. They weren't North Boulevard people.

But slowly Jim and Ann transformed the house into something much wilder. As a wedding present, Jim gave Ann a toilet that California artist Larry Fuente had covered in bright-colored strands of beads. Alternating rings of nickels and pennies tiled the bowl, and a statue of the Virgin Mary stood enshrined atop the tank. Ann adored the toilet; it now commands a place of honor in the Harithas living room.

Ann asked Fuente if he'd give the interior of her new Lincoln a similar treatment. Fuente said he'd rather do a whole car, preferably a '50s Cadillac. Ann ponied up the money.

Ann, in fact, was in love with art cars. In '84 she curated the "Collision" show at the University of Houston's Lawndale Art & Performance Center. The show caused a minor sensation, especially Fuente's *Mad Cad*, the car that Ann had commissioned. Fuente had encrusted the '59 Cadillac with beads, buttons and toys, given it giant tail fins made of bejeweled flamingos and carousel horses, and set sparkly swans and ducks swimming along the roof.

To fund their various projects, Ann and Jim set up the Ineri Foundation, a private entity with themselves (and not a board) firmly in control. For Ann, those projects often involved art cars. Jim's projects, though, had little to do with art. Instead, he made trips to Russia, Cuba and Central America, driving to remote towns and villages and personally handing out medicines to people who might need them.

It's hard to say what those trips meant to Harithas. They were undeniably a way for him to do something good and useful, and he probably took a certain macho satisfaction in driving through, say, El Salvador, crossing checkpoints manned by teenagers with machine guns. But it may be that those trips were purgatives, like his fast: not only a way to avoid the Houston art world, the scene of his defeat, but a way to flush the bitterness from his system.

***

The same people who talk about Jim Harithas's "missing years" now talk about "the golden age" or his "resurgence," and they usually date the beginning of that period to the opening of the Art Car Museum. Jim had somehow caught Ann's enthusiasm for art cars, or maybe, on some level, he'd always harbored a little of it himself.

Art cars were as indigenous to Houston as cockroaches, and Harithas had always supported regional movements. They also appealed to his sense that art should mean something in the real world. Cars were about speed and movement and freedom, the great themes of the modern city; art cars also had an added layer of meaning, one that wasn't at all what Ford or Toyota had intended. "All art cars are subversive," Harithas proclaimed in his '97 "Art Car Manifesto."

The Art Car Museum, which opened quietly in '98, is likewise subversive; it hijacks the very notion of a museum. For starters, it's intentionally not located in the Museum District; Harithas believes art shouldn't be segregated from ordinary people's lives.

The bulbous, exuberant building—the work of artist David Best—can be read as a rebuttal to the CAM, Houston's other silvery museum. The CAM's sleek building feels cool and detached, a slice of minimalism in a noisy, extravagant city; the Art Car Museum looks hot and engaged, and even weirder than its neighbors. From the street, the way-out building raises unnerving questions: *Is that thing really a museum? Is it safe to go inside? Why does it need that barbed wire? Are they trying to keep the weirdos out, or to keep them in?* But you do not suspect, even for a second, that the place will bore you.

On closer inspection, the Art Car Museum reminds you how much other institutions cast themselves as devices for the tasteful display of wealth. For instance, when you enter the Museum of Fine Arts, Houston's impressive new Beck building, you see donors' names carved into a massive limestone wall, enshrined for the ages. The Art Car Museum is pointedly *not* called the Harithas Collection, and in fact, Ann and Jim's role as its patrons is hard to discern; there's not even a plaque to tip you off. You might see Ann's name next to her collages, or Jim's on something he has written—that is, they might present themselves as an artist or a curator, but not as benefactors. The art is enshrined; the money behind it remains invisible.

***

"Is that too high?" asks Kari Sellers, one of the museum's three young curators. She's holding a Ron Hoover painting against the wall; below it, curator Gabriel Delgado holds another.

"This is Texas," growls Harithas. "You can hang 'em on the ceiling."

Normally Harithas and his bright young curators aren't actually *in* the museum. They work from the Ineri Foundation's headquarters, which is to say, in Ann and Jim's backyard, in the maid's quarters behind the mansion on North Boulevard. And in point of fact, half their work seems to take place in the kitchen or at the backyard table. Andy Mann and Jesse Lott wander down the driveway without calling first; other artists drop by for opinions on their work, or for help moving a large piece. The place exudes a laid-back, improvisational vibe, like the quad of a college campus, and the arguments—most often between Harithas and Tex Kerschen, the fiercest of his young curators—seem downright recreational.

But this morning, a Wednesday, Harithas and his curators are hanging their next shows. Finished with the Hoover paintings, Harithas leaves the little front gallery and walks into the museum's large room, surveying it with an eye toward Saturday night's opening. He still deploys his old formula to draw a crowd: Besides the art, there'll be free food and drinks, plus Kerschen's rock band, Japanic. And here, at the museum without a board, he's free to overtly use left-wing politics as bait: Nader's Greens will show up for the petition-signing party Friday, and maybe they'll come back.

On one side of the room are Jim Hatchett's freshly hung "Dirt Paintings." On the other is one of Harithas's favorite art cars, Betsabeé Romero's *Ayate*, a 1955 Ford Crown Victoria whose windows are filled with dried roses, its body covered in what looks like floral-patterned upholstery. It's a deeply feminine expression of immigrants' crushed dreams, and Harithas has installed it in a kind of border stage set, atop a little hill of reddish soil.

"There's dirt on both sides of the museum," he exults. The symmetry pleases him; he enjoys making the works fit together.

Faith, another art car, is as ebullient as *Ayate* is meditative. David Best covered a 1984 Camaro with bezillions of cheap religious souvenirs, Buddhas mixing easily with Madonnas. To the front grill, he attached the head of a water buffalo. "This one," says Harithas, grinning, "it's all about the influence of acid."

There are two works by Harithas's old friend Jesse Lott, who has been billed as "the star of the Art Car Museum." Lott, like Hatchett and many of the museum's other artists, tends to work in "found" materials. *Black Madonna*, left from Lott's show last year, looks like an icon carved from driftwood; the new one, *Spartacus*, is a nearly human-size crucifix constructed from wire and scrounged metal. In part, Lott chose his materials from necessity: Stuff you find is cheaper than stuff you have to buy. But the discarded materials also give the works a haunting flavor; they seem more personal, more homemade, more a part of the world we live in now.

In the back room, there's *Know-Mad*, a video game designed by Mel Chin and a team of programmers from MIT. It's basically an arcade driving game, the kind with a steering wheel and gas pedal. The screen depicts a nomadic camp somewhere in the desert; the player drives from tent to tent seeking gold balls. The text on the wall explains the piece's heady artistic intentions—the juxtaposition of modern cultures with traditional ones, the effect of speed on a nontechnological society, the beauty of traditional rugs set against the beauty of driving—but the high-flown ambition doesn't frighten away neighborhood teenagers, who play the game after school.

Chin is another old friend of Harithas's. Like Lott, he grew up in the Fifth Ward; unlike Lott, he left Texas and became nationally prominent. "Mel Chin, John Alexander, Julian Schnabel," says Harithas, shaking his head. "They had the sense to leave." His meaning is clear: Houston doesn't support its own.

Octo Quad Ring, Andy Mann's latest video installation, glows in the back room. Seventeen TV screens beam versions of the same image, oriented differently, as if reflected in a kaleidoscope, and in the center is a mirrored pentagram. The images, of flowers and clouds and fire, are natural and timeless; if you position yourself just right, you see your own face reflected in the pentagram's sides, part of all that swirling beauty and terror. At the end of the cycle, the screens go dark. The effect, to use one of Harithas's favorite words, is "spiritual."

Andy Mann was recently diagnosed with terminal prostate cancer, and the news hangs heavy on Harithas's mind. Mann, he declares, has always been a terrific artist—"the first socially conscious video artist! one of the best cameras in the world! Houston is lucky to have him!" When Mann told Harithas that he had cancer, Harithas pushed him to work, pushed him to consider his audience: "You want them to think better of you than they do now, don't you?"

It must be Houston's lousy air, Harithas grumps: Everyone he knows is undergoing chemo, or dying, or dead. It's hyperbole, of course, but it contains a grain of truth. Lately he has felt surrounded by death.

Only days before, Ann's mother died. A few months ago artist Mark Lombardi, once one of Harithas's bright young curators at the CAM, committed suicide. And last year Harithas's old friend Norman Bluhm, the sensual abstract expressionist, died of a heart attack.

Harithas delivered Bluhm's eulogy at the Whitney, and he wrote a moving essay for a posthumous Bluhm tribute show. In the essay, you can hear echoes of Harithas's life: Bluhm's work fell out of fashion, but he stuck stubbornly to his vision of the world. Bluhm's work wasn't fully appreciated "by the New York art establishment." He lived a life "that tolerated no compromise." And his late phase—the mature works, the last ones he painted—was his most profound.

You figure that Harithas thinks a lot about his own late phase, that he wants "them" to think better of him than they do now. Sometimes, when he talks about the future, he's bullish. He and Ann are considering sites for a second little museum in yet another Houston neighborhood. The new one might or might not show art cars; they haven't decided. And after that, there might be even more little museums—maybe a whole string of them—scattered through Houston, like so many rebel bases. Soon, he says, his young curators won't need him anymore; they'll be ready to run the places on their own, and he'll show up only to watch them work.

Other times, Harithas is quieter. He and Ann might leave the Art Car Museum and its offspring to the city of Houston, he says, but he's not sure the city is interested.

He stares for a few seconds at Andy Mann's video screens, then snaps to attention as Bryan Taylor, the museum's shaggy front man, ambles into the main room.

Taylor explains art to visitors, and Harithas wants to make sure he gets it right. Harithas gives him a penetrating look and points toward Jim Hatchett's show: "What are you going to say about these 'Dirt Paintings'?"

"I don't know," shrugs Taylor. "I just saw them half an hour ago."

"Well, you can say this. Say, 'Texas artists have been treated like dirt for so long that now they're working with it.'"

Taylor nods, and Harithas once again starts pacing. ★

ROBB WALSH

Houston Press food critic Robb Walsh has won a James Beard Award for magazine journalism and a James Beard broadcast award. He has served as the food columnist for *Natural History* magazine, published by the American Museum of Natural History, and has written for *Gourmet, Saveur,* and *Fine Cooking.*

His books include *Legends of Texas Barbecue Cookbook: Recipes and Recollections from the Pit Bosses*; *The Tex-Mex Cookbook: A History in Recipes and Photos*; *Are You Really Going to Eat That? Reflections of a Culinary Thrill Seeker*; *Sex, Death & Oysters: A Half-Shell Lover's World Tour*; and *The Tex-Mex Grill and Backyard Barbacoa Cookbook.*

Here he tells the compelling story of Hugo Ortega, who went from being an undocumented alien living on the streets of Houston to renowned restaurateur. This article also explores the importance of undocumented workers to the restaurant industry, in Houston and across the nation.

Guess Who's Cooking Your Dinner?

My TABLEMATE DIPPED HER DOUGHNUT INTO the cup of hot chocolate and purred while she chewed. "Is this the best thing you ever ate, or what?" she said. We were splitting an order of *churros* and hot chocolate, which the waiter recommended as the best dessert on the menu at Hugo's, the popular upscale Mexican restaurant on Westheimer.

A churro is a Mexican doughnut made by extruding dough through a nozzle into a deep fryer. The nozzle gives the long stick-shaped doughnut pronounced ridges, which trap the cinnamon and sugar topping. At Hugo's the kitchen doesn't fry the churros until they're ordered, so they're served piping hot. Hugo's also cuts them in three pieces, fills the inside with the caramel syrup called *dulce de leche* and serves them on a plate with a dainty scoop of mocha ice cream.

There are hundreds of Tex-Mex cantinas, authentic Mexican restaurants, *taquerías, carnicerías, panaderías* and taco trucks in Houston. But ever since it opened in 2002, Hugo's has been the best Mexican restaurant in the city. In the 2003 "Best of Houston" issue, the *Houston Press* named Hugo's Houston's "Best Restaurant," period.

The restaurant roasts its own cocoa beans and grinds them by hand in an old-fashioned stone mill imported from Oaxaca. The fresh-ground cocoa powder is used to make its signature mole poblano, as well as the cup of hot chocolate that comes with the doughnuts.

The churros and hot chocolate at Hugo's are sensational. Churros are a common street food snack in Mexico City, which is fitting since Hugo Ortega, the owner and head chef, grew up in one of Mexico City's worst slums. Ortega entered the United States illegally, and like an enormous number of Mexican immigrants, he found work in the restaurant industry.

The restaurant industry is the nation's largest employer of immigrants, according to the National Restaurant Association, which estimates that 1.4 million restaurant workers in the United States are foreign-born immigrants. Seventy percent of them work in the lowest-paying jobs, as dishwashers, busboys, prep cooks and cleaning help.

The National Restaurant Association lobbies on behalf of restaurant owners, and predictably, it's one of the loudest proponents of immigration reform. "While the government claims stepped-up enforcement . . . will discourage future illegal immigration across our nation's borders," the NRA Web site says, "in reality, all they are doing is eliminating a sizeable portion of the workforce without providing any legal avenue to hire foreign-born workers to do jobs that Americans are no longer taking."

Meanwhile, anti-immigration groups such as U. S. Border Watch, which intimidates day laborers as they wait for employers to pick them up, remain active. "It makes me sad," Ortega says about a recent confrontation in northwest Harris County. "If immigrants are selling drugs or committing crimes, then put them in jail or send them back to Mexico. But please judge immigrants as individuals and for their contributions to society."

"You only hear one side of the immigration debate, because the people who really know what's going on can't say anything," one Houston restaurant owner told me. "If you own a restaurant and you speak out about immigration, you make your business a target."

There's a weird disconnect between perception and reality for those who work in the business. Thanks to media demagogues like Lou Dobbs, much of the American public is ready to "send 'em back to Mexico." Meanwhile, Spanish is what you're most likely to hear in a restaurant kitchen.

Author and TV star Anthony Bourdain is one of the few chefs who's been willing to speak frankly on the issue. He says the American restaurant industry would be in big trouble if all the illegal immigrants in this country were rounded up and deported. "The bald fact is that the entire restaurant industry in America would close down overnight, would never recover, if current immigration laws were enforced quickly and thoroughly across the board," Bourdain told me. "Everyone in the industry knows this. It is undeniable . . . I know very few chefs who've even heard of a U. S.-born citizen coming in the door to ask for a dishwasher, night clean-up or kitchen prep job. Until that happens, let's at least try to be honest when discussing this issue."

***

The two roasted poblanos were stuffed with shredded pork shoulder that had been slowly braised with pears, peaches and raisins, and spices. I ate some of the filling with the spiciest part of the chile, the thick flesh around the stem. There was so much going on—the sweetness of the pork, the kick of the fiery green chile and the creaminess of the thick walnut sauce, sparked with the intense tartness of pomegranate seeds that burst as I chewed—it was a baroque fugue of flavors.

"I learned the secret of the walnut sauce from a lady in Puebla," Hugo says. The secret is to buy walnuts in September when they're still white inside and then soak them in milk until the bitter skins slip off easily.

155

Hugo's serves chiles *en nogada* through the fall or as long they can get fresh pomegranates. In the summer, the menu switches over to dishes made with squash blossoms. The restaurant also serves such exotica as *huitlacoche* (corn fungus) and sautéed *chapulines* (grasshoppers) when they're available.

The chiles en nogada at Hugo's are the best I have ever eaten—even better than the supposedly definitive version I once sampled at Osteria San Domingo in Mexico City.

The dish is associated with Mexican patriotism. The green chiles, white walnut sauce and red dots of pomegranate garnish are traditionally arranged in the order of the colors of the Mexican flag. Chiles en nogada were created by the nuns of the Santa Monica convent of Puebla in 1821 to commemorate the arrival of Agustín de Iturbide, architect of Mexican independence. Iturbide's celebrity was short-lived; he was crowned emperor in 1822, deposed in 1823 and executed in 1824. So maybe the fiery chiles en nogada should also be considered symbolic of the cruel fate that befalls so many Mexicans.

It's hard to picture the soft-spoken, slender and genteel-in-his-chef's-whites Ortega climbing over a barbed-wire fence with the Border Patrol in pursuit. Like so many others, he crossed the border for little more than the promise of washing dishes and busing tables.

"My teen years were pretty awful," he says, remembering his struggle to take care of seven brothers and sisters and his decision to cross the border. "My dad was beating my mom and me. He hardly ever came home. When I was 15, I quit school and started working for Procter & Gamble in Mexico City loading boxes of soap into cartons on an assembly line. My family was going hungry. I was buying rice and beans, but that was it. There was never enough. Then my mom had twins and got sick. I was raising the kids and working. It was a bad deal."

Ortega couldn't earn enough to live, no matter how hard he was willing to work. Hope arrived in the form of a letter from a cousin named Pedro (not his real name) who had made it to Houston.

Pedro wrote about the terrible journey. The van he was riding in blew up. He had to walk across the desert with nothing but a couple of tacos to eat. But he made it. He was living in a shotgun shack between Taft and Montrose. "He said he was making $200 a week," Hugo remembers. "That sounded like a lot of money.

"I was young. I wanted to do something with my life. And I wanted to help my mom and my family," he says. "What would you do?"

In April of 1983, at the age of 17, Ortega decided to go to the United States. "My mom was very sad and very concerned when I left. When I quit my job at Procter & Gamble, I got 200 pesos in back pay, which was less than $20. I bought a bus ticket to Juárez with the money."

Ortega arrived in Juárez along with an older cousin, who was 23, and three other friends. A coyote met them as soon as they got off the bus and asked if they were going across. "You have to give him a phone number of somebody in the U. S. If you don't have a phone number, they won't cross you. My cousin and I gave him Pedro's number in Houston. Pedro had to agree to pay $500 for each for us. He really stepped up to the plate."

For five days, Hugo and his group stayed in a junkyard in Juárez, sleeping in wrecked cars and eating potatoes and eggs. On the fifth day, they attempted to cross the border.

"We had to inflate a plastic boat by blowing into it. There were 35 people including little kids and fat ladies who could barely walk. We took turns going across in the boat. I was scared to death because I couldn't swim. The mosquitoes [helicopters] came with their lights, and we tried to hide in the bushes. The coyote cut a barbed wire fence, and we ran. We got to a road. It was perfectly smooth, with no potholes. I thought, 'Wow, what an amazing country.' We got caught by the Border Patrol. They tied up our hands and put us in a van, took us to the bridge and sent us back across the border. We crossed again three more times, but we kept getting caught.

"The fifth time, we all split up, and the young guys who could run fast went by themselves. We crossed two fences and got to the railroad tracks where we were supposed to wait. Someone opened the door of a railroad car and then they locked us and two coyotes in there. The coyotes told us if we coughed or made a noise, they would kill us. I believed them.

"They had a special seal so that the customs people wouldn't open the rail car. We were in there for three hours before the train moved. After awhile, we could barely breathe. We took turns putting our faces up to a crack in the floor to get air.

"When we got close to San Antonio, the coyotes had to hack through the railcar's wooden wall with a pickax so they could get the door open. One of the coyotes cut his hand open, so there was blood everywhere. We had to jump out while the train was still moving. Finally we got to a house in San Antonio. People were talking, and it was half English and half Spanish. That was the first time I ever heard English.

"They had taken the seats out of a green Impala and put blocks on the shocks. They crammed 13 people into that car. I was one of five guys in the trunk. We drove to Houston and stayed in a house until Pedro came to get us. We were so dirty and skinny, he didn't recognize us.

"I hated Houston at first. It seemed like a ghost town after Mexico City. There was nothing going on in the streets, no music, no soccer, nothing," Ortega remembers.

He took a job cleaning offices. When his cousins decided to try their luck in California, he stayed in Houston so he could keep his job. But the company he was working for relocated, and Hugo found himself unemployed and homeless. "I was broke and sleeping outside on Dunlavy Street behind where the Fiesta is now. I was really depressed."

Ortega's culinary career began by chance. Some fellow immigrants he met playing soccer offered to take him to Backstreet Café off Shepherd where they worked so he could apply for a job. Owner Tracy Vaught was impressed with Hugo's attitude and industriousness from the first day. At Backstreet, Hugo slowly worked his way up from busboy to prep cook to line cook.

Ortega says the restaurant didn't know he was illegal. "I gave them a Social Security number," he says.

Soon after they arrive, illegal immigrants buy fake IDs and Social Security cards at flea markets or on the street. As a result, of course, they're paying income tax and Social Security—and never see income tax refunds or Social Security benefits.

But Ortega says this didn't bother him. "I didn't care," he says. "I was just happy to be able to work."

***

The dark brown sauce that cloaked the chicken leg quarter was dotted with sesame seeds. The version of mole poblano served at Hugo's was velvet on the tongue. The incredibly smooth texture married the rich taste of dried chiles, fresh-ground cocoa powder, toasted sesame seeds, aromatic almonds and other nutty flavors. But there was a deeper wave of flavor in this version of mole po-blano, a wonderfully complex fruitiness and a shining high note of tartness that I'd never encountered before.

"Very few restaurants in Puebla serve mole poblano," Hugo Ortega says. "Because everybody's grandmother makes it better."

Ortega's mole has unusual fruit flavors. "That's the raisins and the plan-tains you're tasting," Hugo says. I have made a lot of moles from recipes in Mexican cookbooks, but I have never seen a mole poblano recipe that called for plantains.

American foodies make the mistake of thinking that reading Diana Ken-nedy or Rick Bayless's cookbooks is all it takes to master Mexican cuisine. Cookbooks only skim the surface. Native chefs like Ortega are a reminder of how deep Mexico's culinary traditions really go.

The Ortega family has mole in their blood. A relative of Hugo's makes the mole at the restaurant. "She learned from her mother, who learned from her mother and so on. [Her] mole poblano is fourth-generation. You should taste the mole that my grandmother makes back in Puebla," Hugo says with a grin.

Hugo Ortega's favorite childhood memories are of his days in Progreso in the state of Puebla. His family moved back to their ancestral village when his father became too sick to work. This period came before his father began abus-ing his family. Hugo was nine years old when he arrived in Progreso. He was sent to the mountains with a herd of goats to tend.

"I was scared to death at first," he remembers. But he learned how to herd goats and was happy in the country. In Puebla, he learned about Mexican cook-ing traditions from his grandmother. Some days he would help his aunt, who was the village baker. Other times he would assist his uncle, who lived in the mountains and made cheese.

But Ortega's childhood in the country came to an end when his father recovered and moved the family back to the slums of Mexico City.

Hugo's maternal grandmother remained in Progreso. There, she's the member of an informal club, a group of around a dozen women who travel around the countryside cooking dishes like mole poblano for weddings and other celebrations.

Hugo recently returned to Progreso to attend a family wedding. He was shocked by what he saw. "There's only women and children left in the village. All the men and boys are in the United States. It's like that all over Mexico. Things are different. The younger generation isn't picking up the old traditions. Where are the women who will go from village to village cooking mole for weddings after my grandmother and her friends are gone? I am afraid that Mexico's culinary culture is going to disappear."

***

On my most recent visit to Hugo's, I sampled one of the nightly specials, a mesquite-grilled black Angus tenderloin. The steak was medium-rare and nicely charred around the edges. It sat in a luscious puddle of *guajillo* sauce. The rich dried-chile flavor was rounded off with butter and garlic. On the side, two mole tamales and some grilled asparagus spears sat on a bed of sautéed spinach leaves.

To go with my steak, the waiter recommended a glass of 2005 Tikal "Patriota" wine, a Malbec-Bonarda blend from Argentina. It was a big, bold red that stood up brilliantly to the dried chile sauce.

My dining companion tried another entrée from the list of specials, a thick salmon steak cooked rare in the middle and balanced on a bed of mashed Peruvian purple potatoes. The fish was garnished with mussels, and a disk of corn pudding was served on the side.

This isn't traditional regional Mexican cuisine, and it isn't supposed to be. This is modern American cuisine with a Latino spin, and it speaks well of

Hugo Ortega's culinary training. "The dinner specials are different, more innovative," he says. "I learned French techniques in cooking school, and I apply them to Mexican cooking."

Hugo Ortega was issued a Temporary Resident (green) card in April of 1988 under the "Reagan Amnesty." With the help of Tracy Vaught, he enrolled in the culinary arts program at Houston Community College. He graduated in 1992 and worked as chef and executive chef at Backstreet Café and Prego before opening Hugo's in 2002. He has made two guest chef appearances at the James Beard House in New York City.

And there are a lot more Hugo Ortegas on the way, thanks to philanthropists like Kit Goldsbury, heir to the Pace Picante Sauce fortune. Last year, Goldsbury contributed $35 million to a small San Antonio cooking school called the Center for Foods of the Americas. His goal was to create a top-rank culinary academy specifically for young Latinos.

The nation's foremost culinary school, the Culinary Institute of America, became a partner in the project. The San Antonio cooking school is now known as the Culinary Institute of America's Center for Foods of the Americas. It will offer extensive financial aid to struggling Hispanic students and, for the most talented, a chance to transfer to the CIA's prestigious main campus in Hyde Park, New York.

Hugo Ortega and Tracy Vaught were married in 1994, and in February 1997 they had their first child, Sophia Elizabeth. Ortega became a naturalized American citizen in 1996. As a citizen, Hugo was entitled to bring members of his family to the United States. "I think I am more patriotic than most Americans," he says. "I love this country like my mother. When I hear the national anthem of the United States, it sometimes makes me cry."

His mother and father live in South Houston, and all of his siblings have joined Hugo here as well. Alma works for Mary Kay selling cosmetics. (One day she hopes to own a pink Cadillac.) Ruben is a pastry chef at Backstreet Café and Hugo's. Sandra works as an administrative assistant during the day and at a local restaurant at night. Rene, a graduate of Reagan High School, works as a mechanic for Admiral Linen Company. Twins Gloriela and Veronica now sell real estate in the Heights. And Jose Luis, who worked in the kitchen with Hugo, recently moved from Houston to Belize to become the chef at The Victoria House.

Hugo's nephew Antonio will graduate from South Houston High School in May of 2008. Tony has received scholarship offers from Harvard, Yale and Rice, among others. It's a difficult decision. But because he doesn't want to be too far away from his family, he's leaning toward Rice.

Hugo is working on a cookbook that will combine old family recipes from Mexico and innovative dishes he created in Texas. ★

PART II

VISITORS

HOUSTON HAS ATTRACTED ITS SHARE OF literary visitors, and they came for wildly varying reasons. In the very early days of the city, James Audubon arrived to make drawings of the local birds, but he also left behind a pithy account of the "city" itself (not excerpted here), in which he took note of the squalor that President Houston lived in. Frederick Law Olmsted came the following decade as part of his journalistic investigation into the slave economy of the South. Here we read his report on Houston.

Humorist Alexander Sweet arrived on a purely literary mission in the late nineteenth century. He was laughing his way across Texas, and his time here yielded some mirth.

The noteworthy twentieth-century writers included here came to Houston on a variety of missions. H. L. Mencken came to write about the 1928 Democratic National Convention. Simone de Beauvoir made Houston a stop on her de Tocqueville-meets-Kerouac tour of the U. S. made shortly after World War II. Norman Mailer was in the area to write about the Apollo 11 mission. Jan Morris and Stanley Crouch both arrived in the early 1980s: Morris on a *Texas Monthly* assignment to profile the city, and Crouch here at the behest of the *Village Voice* to write about blues and capitalism.

One of these pieces was not written by the traveler in question. But the *Civics for Houston* magazine account of a long-ago visit by Maurice Ravel was too charming to ignore.

FREDERICK LAW OLMSTED

Frederick Law Olmsted [1822–1903] is most famous, of course, as the nation's great designer of parks. But before he imagined Central Park, Prospect Park, or any others, he was a working reporter and an abolitionist. *The New York Times* sent Olmsted on a tour of the South to report on the slave economy. His reports were later compiled into books, including one that deals directly with Texas. This book may well be our best record of life in Texas in the 1850s. Olmsted later founded *The Nation* magazine.

From *A Journey Through Texas*: Along the Eastern Coast

HOUSTON

HOUSTON, AT THE HEAD OF THE NAVIGATION of Buffalo Bayou, has had for many years the advantage of being the point of transshipment of a great part of the merchandise that enters or leaves the State. It shows many agreeable signs of the wealth accumulated, in homelike, retired residences, its large and good hotel, its well-supplied shops, and its shaded streets. The principal thoroughfare, opening from the steamboat landing, is the busiest we saw in Texas. Near the bayou are extensive cottonsheds, and huge exposed piles of bales. The bayou itself is hardly larger than an ordinary canal, and steamboats would be unable to turn, were it not for a deep creek opposite the levee, up which they can push their stems. There are several neat churches, a theatre (within the walls of a steam saw-mill), and a most remarkable number of showy bar-rooms and gambling saloons. A poster announced that the "cock-pit is open every night, and on Saturday night five fights will come off for a stake of $100."

A curious feature of the town is the appearance of small cisterns of tar, in which log-handled dippers are floating, at the edge of the sidewalk, at the front of each store. This is for the use of the swarming wagoners.

Houston (pronounced Hewston) has the reputation of being an unhealthy residence. The country around it is low and flat, and generally covered by pines. It is settled by small farmers, many of whom are Germans, owning a few cattle, and drawing a meagre subsistence from the thin soil. A large number of unfortunate emigrants, who arrive with exhausted purses, remain in the town at labor, or purchase a little patch or cabin in the vicinity. The greater part of the small tradesmen and mechanics of the town are German.

In the bayou bottoms near by, we noticed many magnolias, now in full glory of bloom, perfuming delicately the whole atmosphere. We sketched one which stood one hundred and ten feet high, in perfect symmetry of development, superbly dark and lustrous in foliage, and studded from top to lowest branch with hundreds of great delicious white flowers.

A Captured Runaway

Sitting, one morning on our stay, upon the gallery of the hotel, we witnessed a revolting scene. A tall, jet black negro came up, leading by a rope a downcast mulatto, whose hands were lashed by a cord to his waist, and whose face was horribly cut, and dripping with blood. The wounded man crouched and leaned for support against one of the columns of the gallery.

"What's the matter with that boy?" asked a smoking lounger.

"I run a fork into his face," answered the negro.

"What are his hands tied for?"

"He's a runaway, sir."

"Did you catch him?"

"Yes, sir. He was hiding in the hay-loft, and when I went up to throw some hay to the horses, I pushed the fork down into the mow and it struck something hard. I didn't know what it was, and I pushed hard, and gave it a turn, and then he hollered, and I took it out."

"What do you bring him here, for?"

"Come for the key to the jail, sir, to lock him up."

"What!" said another, "one darkey catch another darkey? Don't believe that story."

"Oh, yes, Mass'r, I tell for true. He was down in our hay-loft, and so you see when I stab him, I *have to* catch him."

"Why, he's hurt bad, isn't he?"

"Yes, he says I pushed through the bones."

"Whose nigger is he?"

"He says he belongs to Mass'r Frost, sir, on the Brazos."

The key was soon brought, and the negro led the mulatto away to jail. He seemed sick and faint, and walked away limping and crouching, as if he had received other injuries than those on his face. The bystanders remarked that the negro had not probably told the whole story.

We afterwards happened to see a gentleman on horseback, and smoking, leading by a long rope through the deep mud, out into the country, the poor mulatto, still limping and crouching, his hands manacled, and his arms pinioned.

There is a prominent slave-mart in town, which held a large lot of likely-looking negroes, waiting purchasers. In the windows of shops, and on the doors and columns of the hotel, were many written advertisements headed, "A likely negro girl for sale." "Two negroes for sale." "Twenty negro boys for sale," etc.

***

To The Trinity

Leaving Houston, we followed a well-marked road, as far as a bayou, beyond which we entered a settlement of half-a-dozen houses, that, to our surprise, proved to be the town of Harrisburg, a rival (at some distance) of Houston. It is the starting point of the only railroad yet completed in Texas, extending to Richmond on the Brazos, and has a depth of water in the bayou sufficient for a larger class of boat from Galveston. Houston, however, having ten or fifteen years, and odd millions of dollars, the start, will not be easily overridden. Taking a road here, by direction, which, after two miles, only ran "up a tree," we were obliged to return for more precise information.

At noon, we were ferried over a small bayou by a shining black bundle of rags, and instructed by her as follows:

"Yer see dem two tall pine in de timber ober dar cross de parara, yandar. Yer go right straight da, and da yer'll see de trail somewhar. Dat ar go to Lynchburg. Lor! I'se nebber been da—don'no wedder's ary house or no—don'no wedder's ary deep byoo or no—reckon yer can go, been so dry."

Two miles across the grass we found the pines and a trail, which continually broke into cattle-paths, but, by following the general course, we duly reached San Jacinto, a city somewhat smaller than Harrisburg, laid out upon the edge of the old battle-field.

Upon the opposite shore of the river lies the "town of Lynchburg," which has been recommended, by a commission, for a national naval dépôt. It consists, at present, of one house and out-buildings. Within this house is the city post-office, where, when we mailed a letter, we received, for the first time in six months, a *cent* in change. A Texan, who was standing by, demanded to see it, saying that he had never known before that there existed such a coin; he had supposed it as imaginary as the mill. The South has no copper currency, the fraction of a dime being considered too minute for attention. There is a certain vague and agreeable largeness in this, but the contrast of her working and lounging class with the penny-papered and penny-lettered corresponding class in the copper-circulating States is not so pleasing. ★

ALEXANDER SWEET

Alexander Sweet [1841–1901] was probably the first Texas humorist of any prominence. His columns, called "Siftings," which ran in *The San Antonio Express*, *The San Antonio Herald*, and, most notably, *The Galveston Daily News*, reached a national and even international audience. His weekly humor magazine, *Texas Siftings*, was in so much national demand that he moved it from Austin to New York in 1884. His work was widely read in England, and remained in print there even after his death. His success was doubtless due to his work's surprisingly high literary quality. He wrote about rough-and-ready Texas with wit and sophistication. The following excerpt is from his 1883 travelogue, *On a Mexican Mustang, Through Texas*.

From *On a Mexican Mustang, Through Texas*: "Giving Galveston Hell"

THERE ARE MANY "OLDEST" INHABITANTS IN Houston. They generally open out on a stranger by stating, that, when they came here in '40, there was only one two-story house in the place. After you have listened to the talk of one of these pioneer veterans for some time, you begin to feel that the creation of the world, the arrangement of the solar system, and all subsequent events, including the discovery of America, were provisions of an all-wise Providence, arranged with a direct view to the advancement of the commercial interests of Houston. One of the old inhabitants told me all about the New-Orleans railroad, which, he said, was expected to leave Galveston high and dry on the quicksands of adversity, while Houston would keep on flourishing like a green bay horse in a Blue-grass pasture. I said that I did not see how a road direct to New Orleans could help Houston much.

"Well, no," he said, "that's so: it won't help us much, except to the extent that it will give Galveston hell."

There seems to be an innate animosity towards Galveston; and almost every conversation on the resources and prospects ends with some remark that reminds one of the *delenda est* of the old Roman senator. It does not do to express your opinion about any particular Houston institution, unless the opinion is prepared expressly for the Houston market. For instance: I was in a drug-store, getting some medicine, and had a very interesting meteorological conversation with the proprietor while he was folding up a little powder that he took out of a bottle labelled "Pluribus Unum, Nox Vomica, Vox Populi," or words to that effect. As he was about to hand me the powder, I inadvertently remarked, —

"Your city seems to be pretty well laid out."

All in the world I meant to say was, that the streets were broad and straight; but, before I could explain myself, all present jumped to their feet. My special friend the druggist glared at me, and then bawled out, —

"Houston is well laid out, is she? you leprous outcast from Galveston! I tell you, you vile Galveston emissary, that Houston is a lively enough corpse to lay out that little fishing-town at the other end of the bayou. You come here swelling around, and trying to break up our trade, do you? So Houston is well laid out, is she? We will see who is laid out next!" and he began blowing a police-whistle.

The cashier ran upstairs for his shot-gun, while a junior member of the firm bawled out to the porter, —

"John, turn the bulldog loose: it's time to feed him."

These episodes tended to make my stay in that portion of the city monotonous. Besides, I was afraid, if they kept on, I might become exasperated: so I said, "Don't let me detain you from your business," and adjourned *sine die*.

It was the same everywhere we went. After the doctor had returned to the hotel to get his shoes scraped, he made some remark to the hotel clerk about the dust on the street being in a rather juicy condition.

"Yes," said the clerk, with great complaisance: "we never suffer from drouth here, sir; and we never have to dig sand out of our ears, as they have to do in Galveston. Down there they had to dig an artesian well twenty-five hundred deep, and use it as a sort of anchor to keep their old sand-bar of an island from moving off."

I had heard about Houston being a seaport, but I thought it was a joke. I knew, however, there was a bar; for one of the very first gentlemen I was introduced to took me to see it. It was very much like the bars at other seaport towns I had seen. There were two inches of water on the Houston bar, in a tumbler; and I supposed the rest of the seaport was to match. The next man that said seaport to me, I took him off to one side, told him that I always liked to get the latest marine intelligence, hence I wanted to know seriously if there was any seaport in town. He said he was willing to make an affidavit that there was a seaport in town. Then I told him I wanted him to take me out for a drive on the beach, where I could disport in the ocean's wild roar, and see the white-winged messengers of commerce laden with cloves from where the spicy breezes blow soft o'er Ceylon's Isle, and other condiments from far distant Cathay. The Houston man looked me square in the eye, and said, —

"It seems to me you have a damned sight of curiosity for a stranger. Do you want to see it right away?"

"Right off," I replied.

"Well, le'me see," he mused: "I have an engagement with a man, and it's nine o'clock already. If I don't hurry up I'll miss the street-car." And off he went.

Still I was dissatisfied. I yearned to see that seaport, even if I had to employ a detective to hunt it up. I knew it was in Houston concealed somewhere, but I was afraid it would be removed to a place of safety before I could see it. The next gentleman I was introduced to also had something to say about that seaport. I asked, —

"Do you let strangers see it every day, or only on Sundays, or how? Does it keep open all the season? Money is no object, if I can only get to see it. I don't suppose it will take me very long."

Said he, "Come with me, and I'll show you the shipping."

He took me down behind the Hutchins House; and, in a slough at least forty feet wide and three feet deep, I saw the fleet. One of the merchantmen had two masts, and carried at least three wagon-loads of sand. It did not seem to have much first-class accommodation for passengers who might want to cross the Atlantic in any thing like style. The other vessel had only one mast, and did not have as many tons' displacement as the larger craft.

"How did they get here?" I asked. "By the ship-channel?"

"By tug."

"They must have a pretty heavy tug of it getting up here. I do not see any iron-clads or ships-of-war. Can you not show me the tug of war between here and Galveston?"

"Oh, yes! you may joke; but this is a seaport, all the same, according to an Act of the Legislature."

I had heard that Legislature made laws, but I never knew it made seaports.

"Why," said my Houston friend, "we cannot help being seaports. The other day there was a porpoise killed right near the city."

"On purpose?" I asked; for I was hungry for news.

"How can we help being a seaport? Did you ever hear of a porpoise being killed in a town that was not a seaport?"

I took a last look at the fleet, —one of which a man, in the mean time, had pulled out on the land to dry, —sighed, and went back to the hotel.

***

All seaport towns suffer from those marine monsters known as mosquitoes. In inland towns you have to raise them in a cistern, or worry along without them. Both coast towns, Galveston and Houston, have fine natural facilities for raising mosquitoes. I have tried both brands of mosquitoes, or rather both of them have tried me; and I cannot tell which is the best to avoid associating with. . . . In Houston they showed me affidavits stating that in Galveston the mosquitoes were so large as to be included in the cow ordinance, while in Galveston I was told that the Houston mosquitoes wore forty-five inch undershirts. There is probably a happy medium between the two. I do not know how happy the medium is; but if he is not under a mosquito-bar, there is a limit to his bliss. The truth is, that the coast-town mosquito rarely exceeds in size the ordinary Texas mocking-bird. ★

CIVICS FOR HOUSTON

Civics for Houston was one of Houston's first magazines. It was started by Will Hogg [1875–1930], an early (and often frustrated) proponent of city planning for Houston. *Civics for Houston* was the publication of the Forum of Civics, an organization Hogg founded to promote planning. In 1923 *Civics for Houston* published a letter from a black Houston minister that "contained the most comprehensive view of the city's black population many whites had ever seen," in the words of a *Houston Review* article. The magazine also published unsigned art and music reviews, and features such as this one on Maurice Ravel's 1928 visit to the city.

Lifting Music's Curtain

MAURICE RAVEL, DISTINGUISHED FRENCH composer, was presented at the Scottish Rite Cathedral the evenings of April 6 and 7 by Rice Institute Lectureship in Music.

He was assisted on this occasion by Barbara Lull, violinist and Esther Dale, soprano, in giving a program of his own compositions.

These were evenings arranged for the student of music and the intelligently enquiring, though we venture to say that the casual concert-goer had frequent glimpses into that realm of strange beauty wherein Ravel dwells. We were deeply conscious that before us was a modern master, an unassuming little man offering us the results of a life's work—the greatest living representative of a school of music which has exerted such a powerful influence, not only on French art but on European and English, with a distant and distinct echo in our own incoherent efforts.

We have heard Ravel in Carpenter, Griffith, in Gershwin, to name a few—we have heard him in jazz. But on this night we heard jazz in Ravel!

Surely there is hope for American music! And it is significant of the value of this material when such a sophisticated artist frankly acknowledges his debt as he did in the violin sonata.

***

Ravel's music was novel to most of his audience. Little of his work has been heard in Houston. He is a bold, yet aristocratic, innovator, scornful of the obvious, austere and sometimes obscure, but with a reverence for classical tradition which gives a delicious and peculiar charm to his music. A better acquaintance with such music brings rich reward in enjoyment, but one needs to hear it more than once. We shall look forward to the publication of his lecture in which he characteristically declines, by the way, to dwell upon his own art, but clearly professes his faith in an aesthetic of abstract music.

***

[Glimpses of a drive to Galveston with Maurice Ravel]

Senor Eyquem [a Rice Spanish teacher who served as Ravel's interpreter] had arrived to take Monsieur Ravel to Galveston, but the weather was disagreeable and his car was open.

Our car was closed.

Monsieur Ravel wanted to see Galveston.

We wanted to see Monsieur Ravel—voilà.

We went to Galveston.

***

Ravel chatting on every subject, except Ravel, laughing gaily at everything, enjoying the day of play as a boy out of school.

Ravel at the luncheon at the Galvez, listening to our strange words, watching our faces for the meaning, telling his quaint stories, Senor Eyquem translating for us.

***

When told the story of Frederick the Great and the chicory he shook his head and laughed. He knew that one.

Then his story, told by an epicure, of the rare olive, to be carefully prepared and dipped in precious sauces.

Then, he told us, the olive was to be placed inside a very small bird, just large enough to hold it. This in turn was to be placed inside of a quail that had been carefully dressed and prepared. The quail was then placed inside a chicken and the chicken in a duck, until finally all was placed in a large turkey. They were then put in an oven with a slow fire and cooked carefully for a matter of many hours.

When this rare dish reached its height of perfection it was removed from the oven, each bird removed from its casing and lastly the olive.

"Then" we were told, "you throw away everything but the olive, which you eat." ★

H. L. Mencken

Satirist, critic, and newspaperman (the list of the literary hats that he wore could go on) H. L. Mencken [1880–1956] was skeptical about democracy. He famously termed the American middle class the "booboisie," and warned, "On some great and glorious day the plain folks of the land will reach their heart's desire at last, and the White House will be adorned by a downright moron." In 1931, the Arkansas legislature passed a motion to pray for Mencken's soul after he described the state as the "apex of moronia."

Nevertheless, he was the country's most important political commentator, and in 1928, when he came to Houston to cover the Democratic National Convention (which nominated the ill-fated Al Smith), he was at the height of his sardonic powers.

A brilliant and influential prose stylist, Mencken wrote for the *Baltimore Sun* from 1906–1948, when he retired from writing. In 1908 he became the influential literary critic of *The Smart Set*, and in 1924 started the famed cultural journal *The American Mercury*. Some thirty-plus books have been published under his name.

From *Thirty-five Years of Newspaper Work: A Memoir*: Knavish Dishonesty

WHEN WE GOT TO HOUSTON THE NEXT morning, June 23, we found a band playing in the station, and learned that it was there to welcome [the New York Democrat] James W. Gerard, who had come in on our train, not to attend the convention, but to harangue a gathering of West Texas Babbits. A large committee of welcome was present, and the plan was that the open automobile bearing Gerard should head a parade following the band. But when Patterson, Hyde and I jumped into a taxicab the driver barged in directly behind the band, and so we proceeded to the Rice Hotel, with Gerard looking daggers at us for stealing his spot. I had spoken to him in the station, but saw no more of him after the parade was over. He had by now shrunk to nothing, politically speaking, and none of the assembled politicos paid any attention to him. Our quarters on the eleventh floor of the sixteen-story Rice Hotel were comfortable enough, but we had run out of alcoholic refreshment, and looked forward to a dry week. Relief arrived quickly from two directions. First the Hogg brothers, sons of a former Governor of Texas, sent word that they had opened a house of mirth in another hotel, and invited us to use it. Secondly, Amon Carter arrived from Fort Worth the next day with an immense stock of liquors, and these he laid out for his friends in rooms near ours, with the sheriff of Fort Worth, elegantly bebadged and heavily armed, in charge. The Hogg brothers had converted a ballroom into an old-time saloon, with a wooden bar and sawdust on the floor. It served beer only. Hyde and I set out to investigate it at once, and came back with the melancholy report that everything was lovely save the beer, which had been made in Texas and was quite undrinkable.

***

I had to endure a number of other unpleasantnesses at Houston, and left it at last with a considerable distaste for it, and in fact for all Texas. Texans were simply not my kind of people, and even when they were trying to be nice to me I found myself unpleasantly conscious of that difference. Amon G. Carter's hospitality at Fort Worth, though it was earnest and lavish, was more of a nuisance than a joy, and at Houston his attentions were worse. He came into my room two or three times a day, usually accompanied by his friend and retainer, the sheriff of Fort Worth, and the two of them wasted a great deal of my time. I had plenty to do to cover the convention for the *Evening Sun*, but in addition I was hard beset by *American Mercury* business, for several large packages of manuscript were waiting for me when I arrived at the Rice Hotel. One day the Fort Worth sheriff dropped in on me alone, with a copy of the *American Mercury* for July, 1928, under his arm. He had just read an article in it by Jim Tully, entitled "Shanty Irish," and wanted to discuss it. He had no objection, it appeared, to the article itself, but he considered the title an insult to the great race of Irishmen. Inasmuch as he was drunk, it was impossible to argue with him; moreover, I was too busy. I finally got rid of him by telling him that Tully, an Irishmen himself, looked upon "Shanty Irish" as an epithet of honor. He went away muttering, and tried to resume the debate every time I met him thereafter. He was a gigantic fellow, always drunk, and carried in a holster a huge pistol studded with rubies—a present from his admirers among the Fort Worth bootleggers.

Carter himself dropped in on me every few hours, and often brought strangers to be introduced. They were always tight, as was Carter himself. One afternoon, as I was sitting in my undershirt trying to knock out a dispatch for the *Evening Sun*, he appeared alone in very ebullient spirits, and refused to be got rid of. Finally, I had to turn my back on him, and resume my work. Suddenly he pulled a pistol and fired three shots out of the window. The aim of his volley, as I learned, was simply to entertain me pleasantly in the Texas fashion, but what ensued was an uproar that kept me busy for two hours. The cartridges, it quickly appeared, had been loaded with ball, and the three bullets hit a hotel across the street, close to the window of a room in which the Ku Kluxers were holding a caucus, with one of the town judges of Houston presiding. The Ku Kluxers, headed by the judge, rushed out howling that Al Smith had turned loose the Pope's sharpshooters on them, and in five minutes the Hotel Rice was swarming with Texas Rangers. As I found out afterward, some of them had to hoof all the way upstairs to the top floor, for the elevators, as usual, were jammed. Working downward they then began a systematic search of the whole building, to the tune of a great deal of shouting and running about. When a party of them knocked at my door Carter slipped his pistol under the mattress of my bed, and made off through the room adjoining, leaving me to engage them alone. I pretended, when they barged in and explained their business, to be greatly surprised, and protested that I was a hard-working newspaper correspondent, as they could see by my costume, and carried no arms, and knew nothing about any shooting. I had pretty well convinced them when one of them, smarter than the rest, espied the three bullet-holes through the fly-screen of the window. They then announced that I was under arrest, and would have to go to the lockup at once. While I was still arguing with them, the town judge, who had been following them, came in, and on his heels came Carter.

Carter had become miraculously sober, or so, at least, he seemed, and he proceeded at once to tackle both the judge and the cops. If I were cast into jail, he said, the whole country would ring with the scandal, and Texas would be made ridiculous. I was known as a peaceable and virtuous character by millions of people, and the charge that I had tried to shoot up Houston would make the whole world laugh. But what of the bullet-holes? demanded the cops. It was easy, replied Carter, to explain them. Eminent though I was, I was still subject to the calls of nature. Obviously, some miscreant had sneaked into my room while I was in the bath relieving my bladder and then fired at the Ku Kluxers and run off. It was, as everyone knew, a way that such enemies of the Southern *Kultur* had. And how came it that I had not heard the shots? Because the toilet made a noise, the bands playing outside in the street made more, and the convention hubbub in the hotel made still more. The town judge admitted that there was something in this defense, but insisted that my room was no place to try me: I should be taken before the proper authorities, and heard according to law. Meanwhile, the rangers searched my baggage, my writing table, my typewriter case, my bureau drawers, and even the clothes hanging in the closet, but by great good fortune they overlooked the bed, though the pistol under the mattress made a visible lump. I was in fear that they would find the last bottle of our stock of booze in the closet, but it did not appear, and I learned later that Patterson had taken it away that morning. While they searched Carter wrestled with the town judge, and finally, to my considerable astonishment, His Honor ordered the rangers to go no further. He was convinced, he said, that I knew nothing of the shooting. It must have been done by prowling Catholics from the North. He advised the rangers to round up all such persons then in town, and to give them brisk work-outs. I should add that His Honor, like nearly all the other Houstonians I met, was in liquor. But the cops were sober, and went away reluctantly and in bad humor. The instant they were out of sight I got Carter's pistol from under the mattress, handed it to him, and desired him to clear out at once.

Later in the day he fired it again—this time through a glass elevator door.

As I have said, the hotel elevators were all jammed, and often a passenger waiting for one would have to wait while half a dozen went past him. This irritated Carter, and his protest took the form of firing through the door after the fifth or sixth elevator had flitted by. This time he was seized by bystanders, but the city cops, not connecting him with his first offense, let him go on the ground that no one had been hurt, and that firing a pistol was a natural sign of discontent in Texas. Later on the fact that he had fired the three shots from my window were known, but by that time he was back in Fort Worth and safe under the protection of his sheriff. All sorts of legends grew out of the two episodes. It was widely reported and believed that Carter and I had got into a quarrel, and that either I had fired at him or he had fired at me. It was also reported that he had fired through the elevator door in an elevator full of people, and wounded several of them. I suspect that he propagated these stories himself. He was a vain fellow, and eager to be respected as an exponent of Texan truculence. Indeed, he always spoke of himself, not as a simple Texan but as a West Texan, which connoted a familiarity with firearms and a willingness to use them. After we got back to Baltimore Patterson wrote to the manger of the Rice Hotel asking him to send on the fly-screen with the three bullet-holes in it. This was done, and a segment of it showing the holes was framed. For some years thereafter it hung in Patterson's office. ★

SIMONE DE BEAUVOIR

Not long after World War II, French writer and philosopher Simone de Beauvoir [1908–1986] set out on a Greyhound bus tour of the United States. She began in Chicago, where her sometime lover Nelson Algren introduced her to the city's dark side, which apparently wasn't hard to find. From there she traversed much of the country, occasionally stopping to lecture at a university, as she did at Rice.

This excerpt shows that de Beauvoir took a deep interest in the racial tensions of the day, and that she was not a big fan of professional wrestling, or of Houston, for that matter.

From *America Day by Day*

FOR THE TOURIST, HOUSTON IS AS GLOOMY as Buffalo. At the heart of this urban sprawl we find the same street that we walk along in every town and village where the Greyhound stops; we know its lights and displays by heart. Fortunately, a movie theater advertises "thrillings." We go in. We see Victor Francen in the role of a brilliant pianist who is paralyzed in one hand and who dies pathetically at the beginning of the film [*The Beast with Five Fingers*]. His adoptive son, Peter Lorre, who devotes himself to mysterious scholarly works, is threatened with expulsion from the mansion's library by a band of self-centered heirs. Death is unleashed; a mysterious hand strangles brothers, nephews, and cousins and threatens a pretty niece. It is Francen's hand, which Peter Lorre has cut off and put in a box, but we see it leaving its box by itself to go off and play concertos on the piano. In the end it attacks Peter Lorre himself, just as he's about to murder the gentle heroine. He throws the hand into the fire; it writhes about in the flames, escapes, and slowly reaches for the throat of the unfortunate man. Despite the stupidity of the plot, that enormous spidery hand lifting the lid of a dish or creeping along a table is as disturbing as the opening scenes of *Un Chien Andalou* [by Luis Buñuel and Salvador Dalí].

***

M. [Marcel Morand], who has been a professor in America for twenty years, takes me to Rice University. The buildings stand amid lush lawns flowering with camellias and azaleas. We have lunch at the faculty club. These clubs are reserved for men, which gives the meal a touch of austerity; but in the universities, as elsewhere, men's clubs passionately refuse to open their doors to women. Women demand too much attention and consideration; men prefer to be bored—at least there are no constraints. After the meal M. takes me for a drive. On the outskirts of town we cross large parks that are extensions of the unspoiled woods. The trees, entangled with vines and veiled with Spanish moss, have a tropical lushness. Idling in their shade are those lazy, languid rivers called bayous. On the edge of the forests are the luxurious houses of the oil barons; they're built in the old plantation style, in wood with porches and verandas, but they're fresh and shining. In front, tall, placid black men mow the sunny lawns. Azaleas, camellias, golden grass, well-trained servants—all is peace, order, and beauty. In this limpid world, only the Spanish moss recalls the mysterious disturbances of growth and of all prosperity.

M. is a mischievous old man, a rare sort who judges America without either hostility or complacence. Among other things, he's amused by the mixture of strictness and hypocritical license that one encounters here, as in the rest of the country. For example, it's forbidden to bring alcohol to Rice University. If you want to enter the campus carrying a bottle under your arm, you won't be allowed to pass, but if you're just careful enough to put it in a bag, no one would dream of searching you. In fact, students and professors are hard drinkers, and there are some faculty members who are never seen except in a state of inebriation. Free love is frowned on, but the marriages are highly elastic. A certain professor intrigued his colleagues by coming back one autumn with a young wife who was totally different from the fiancée he'd taken to Mexico at the beginning of summer vacation. He'd had time to be married, divorced, and remarried. He admitted to having precipitated matters in the hopes that his first wife's face would be forgotten and that the second one would be welcomed unquestioningly as the only Mrs. Z. His first marriage had been merely a trial marriage: he'd ended it after a week.

M. tells me many other anecdotes, proving that French universities don't have a monopoly on jealousies and rivalries. Then he talks a little about the race question. Tension is greater than ever, with the blacks indignant at being given no reward for the services they rendered during the war, and the whites dreading that they might claim certain privileges and treating them even more arrogantly than in the past. The blacks look for any opportunity to avenge these insults. If a white person hires a black cook or an extra servant for a dinner party, the blacks will make formal promises, then fail to show up at the last minute—and it just so happens that no one can be found to replace them, that all the cooks and extra servants are busy that evening. Since leaving the army, blacks have demonstrated a sense of racial solidarity and a will to revolt. M. also tells me that last year, while visiting a nearby black university, he was welcomed with special warmth as a Frenchman. But when the moment came for lunch, they led him to a little room where they'd set a table just for him. "You cannot eat with us," the black professors said apologetically. "We would run into terrible trouble if it were known that we allowed a white man to sit at our table."

In most towns the elegant restaurants, like the nightclubs, are situated in the suburbs. We have dinner far from the center of town, in a place typical of Houston—a large, startlingly white wooden inn. The South is the only region in America where food is not just consumed but cooked according to time-honored traditions. We have an excellent regional meal. I'm told that it's a shame that I can't see a cockfight in Texas. They're illegal, but that only makes them more attractive. On the Mexican border a rough group of cowboys gathers in more or less secret spots to bet passionately on the winner. They have to be careful to keep a straight face and never lift a finger, because the bookmakers interpret the slightest blink as a wager and always turn that to one's disadvantage.

In the absence of cockfights, a professor takes me to a wrestling match after my lecture; this may not be especially Texan, but at least it's typically American. We arrive toward the end of the match in a huge sports arena filled with a delirious crowd. The women shout, "Kill him! Kill him!" in raucous voices. In the ring the wrestlers confront each other with looks of bestial hatred, studiously imitating the stance and snarl of King Kong. It's instantly clear that this is a performance and not a real fight. One of the wrestlers throws the referee over the ropes; another hurls his adversary onto the floor of the hall. At the end of one match the loser suddenly pretends to be furious, grinding his teeth and throwing himself on the winner, who abruptly flees, terrified. They chase each other through the stands, reunite, and fight while the spectators shout hysterically. They must know it's just a show, but they refuse to believe it. Besides, they're getting their money's worth: hard knocks are exchanged, and blood flows. We leave after half an hour. L. takes me for a drink on one of Houston's main streets. Here no one drinks whiskey; instead they drink beer in large jugs. The walls are covered from floor to ceiling with huge photographs of prize bulls and cows. In one corner stands a pioneer's covered wagon with its green canvas, and giant bulls' horns hang almost everywhere. It seems that most of the cafes are decorated in this style. This evening I'll go to sleep with no regrets. I don't think that any of Houston's seductions remain hidden from me. ★

NORMAN MAILER

One of Norman Mailer's [1923–2007] thirty-plus books brought him to Houston. Rather, the launch of Apollo 11, brought Mailer to NASA. Arguably at the height of his cultural significance—he'd just completed an unsuccessful but entertaining campaign for mayor of New York, and was looking for a suitably big project. The moon launch, with its celebration of technology, WASP culture, and denial of the human body, brought together many of his obsessions.

When the astronauts left the moon for their return trip home, Mailer decided to decompress by attending a dinner party at the de Menils. He already knew them fairly well; John de Menil had appeared in Mailer's film, *Maidstone*. Evidently agitated by the moon mission, here Mailer broods over a Magritte and takes part in some cringe-worthy race banter with another guest, an African American intellectual who was apparently something of a rival. As always, you get the complete package with Mailer, the good, the bad, and the embarrassing.

From *Of a Fire on the Moon*: A Dream of the Future's Face

EARLY ON THE AFTERNOON OF JULY 21, THE Lunar Module fired its ascent motor, lifted off Tranquility Base, and in a few hours docked with Columbia. Shortly after, the astronauts passed back into the Command Module and Eagle was jettisoned. It would drift off on a trajectory to the sun. A little before midnight, out of communication for the last time with Mission Control, traveling for the final orbit around the back of the moon, Apollo 11 ignited the Service Module engine and accelerated its speed from 3,600 miles to 5,900 miles per hour. Its momentum was now great enough to lift it out of the moon's pull of gravity and back into the attractions of the earth—the spacecraft was therefore on its way home. Since the trip would take sixty hours, a quiet two and a half days were in store and Aquarius decided to get out of Nassau Bay and visit some friends.

His host and hostess were wealthy Europeans with activities which kept them very much of the time in Texas. Since they were art collectors of distinction, invariably served a good meal, and had always been kind to him, the invitation was welcome. To go from the arid tablelands of NASA Highway 1 to these forested grounds now damp after the rain of a summer evening was like encountering a taste of French ice in the flats of the desert. Even the trees about the house were very high, taller than the tallest elms he had seen in New England—"Wild pigs used to forage in this part of Houston," said his host, as if in explanation, and on the lawn, now twice-green in the luminous golden green of a murky twilight, smaller tropical trees with rubbery trunks twisted about a large sculpture by Jean Tinguely which waved metal scarecrow arms when a switch was thrown and blew spinning faucets of water through wild stuttering sweeps, a piece of sculpture reminiscent of the flying machines of La Belle Epoque, a hybrid of dragon and hornet which offered a shade of the time when technology had been belts and clanking gears, and culture was a fruit to be picked from a favored tree.

The mansion was modern, it had been one of the first modern homes in Houston and was designed by one of the more ascetic modern architects. With the best will, how could Aquarius like it? But the severity of the design was concealed by the variety of the furniture, the intensity of the art, the presence of the sculpture, and the happy design in fact of a portion of the house: the living room shared a wall with a glassed-in atrium of exotics in bloom. So the surgical intent of the architect was partially overcome by the wealth of the art and by the tropical pressure of the garden whose plants and interior tree, illumined with spotlights, possessed something of that same silence which comes over audience and cast when there is a moment of theater and everything ceases, everything depends on—one cannot say—it is just that no one thinks to cough.

There had been another such moment when he entered the house. In the foyer was a painting by Magritte, a startling image of a room with an immense rock situated in the center of the floor. The instant of time suggested by the canvas was comparable to the mood of a landscape in the instant just before something awful is about to happen, or just after, one could not tell. The silences of the canvas spoke of Apollo 11 still circling the moon: the painting could have been photographed for the front page—it hung from the wall like a severed head. As Aquarius met the other guests, gave greetings, took a drink, his thoughts were not free of the painting. He did not know when it had been done—he assumed it was finished many years ago—he was certain without even thinking about it that there had been no intention by the artist to talk of the moon or projects in space, no, Aquarius would assume the painter had awakened with a vision of the canvas and that vision had he delineated. Something in the acrid breath of the city he inhabited, some avidity emitted by a passing machine, some tar in the residue of a nightmare, some ash from the memory of a cremation had gone into the painting of that gray stone—it was as if Magritte had listened to the ending of one world with its comfortable chairs in the parlor, and heard the intrusion of a new world, silent as the windowless stone which grew in the room, and knowing not quite what he had painted, had painted his warning nonetheless. Now the world of the future was a dead rock, and the rock was in the room.

There was also a Negro in his host's living room, a man perhaps thirty-five, a big and handsome Black man with an Afro haircut of short length, the moderation of the cut there to hint that he still lived in a White man's clearing, even if it was on the very edge of the clearing. He was not undistinguished, this Negro, he was a professor at an Ivy League college; Aquarius had met him one night the previous year after visiting the campus. The Negro had been much admired in the college. He had an impressive voice and the deliberate manner of a leader. How could the admiration of faculty wives be restrained? But this Black professor was also a focus of definition for Black students in the college—they took some of the measure of their militancy from his advice. It was a responsible position. The students were in the college on one of those specific programs which had begun in many a university that year—students from slum backgrounds, students without full qualification were being accepted on the reasonable if much embattled assumption that boys from slums were easily bright enough to be salvaged for academic life if special pains were taken. Aquarius had met enough of such students to think the program was modest.

The education of the streets gave substantial polish in Black ghettos—some of the boys had knowledge at seventeen Aquarius would not be certain of acquiring by seventy. They had the toughness of fiber of the twenty-times tested. This night on the campus, having a simple discussion back and forth, needling back and forth, even to even—so Aquarius had thought—a Black student suddenly said to him, "You're an old man. Your hair is gray. An old man like you wants to keep talking like that, you may have to go outside with me." The student gave an evil smile. "You're too old to keep up with me. I'll whomp your ass."

It had been a glum moment for Aquarius. It was late at night, he was tired, he had been drinking with students for hours. As usual he was overweight. The boy was smaller than him, but not at all overweight, fast. Over the years Aquarius had lost more standards than he cared to remember. But he still held on to the medieval stricture that one should never back out of a direct invitation to fight. So he said with no happiness, "Well, there are so many waiting on line, it might as well be you," and he stood up.

The Black boy had been playing with him. The Black boy grinned. He assured Aquarius there was no need to go outside. They could talk now. And did. But what actors were the Blacks! What a sense of honor! What a sense of the gulch! Seeing the Black professor in this living room in Houston brought back the memory of the student who had decided to run a simulation through the character of Aquarius' nerve. It was in the handshake of both men as they looked at each other now, Aquarius still feeling the rash of the encounter, the other still amused at the memory. God knows how the student had imitated his rise from the chair. There had been a sly curl in the Black man's voice whenever they came across each other at a New York party.

Tonight, however, was different. He almost did not recognize the professor. The large eyes were bloodshot, and his slow deliberate speech had become twice-heavy, almost sluggish. Aquarius realized the man had been drinking. It was not a matter of a few shots before this evening, no, there was a sense of somebody pickling himself through three days of booze, four days of booze, five, not even drunk, just the heavy taking of the heaviest medicine, a direct search for thickening, as if he were looking to coagulate some floor between the pit of his feelings at boil and the grave courtesies of his heavy Black manner.

By now it showed. He was normally so elegant a man that it was impossible to conceive of how he would make a crude move—now, you could know. Something raucous and jeering was still withheld, but the sourness of his stomach had gotten into the sourness of his face. His collar was a hint wilted.

He had a woman with him, a sweet and wispy blond, half plain, still half attractive, for she emitted a distant echo of Marilyn Monroe long gone. But she was not his equal, not in size, presence, qualifications—by the cruel European measure of this richly endowed room, she was simply not an adequate woman for a man of his ambitions. At least that was the measure Aquarius took. It was hard not to recognize that whatever had brought them together, very little was now sustaining the project. The Black man was obviously tired of her, and she was still obviously in love with him. Since they were here enforcedly together, that was enough to keep a man drinking for more than a day. Besides—if he was a comfortable house guest of these fine Europeans, he might nonetheless wish to leave the grounds. Being seen with her on Houston streets would not calm his nerves.

But there were other reasons for drinking as well. America had put two White men on the moon, and lifted them off. A triumph of White men was being celebrated in the streets of this city. It was even worse than that. For the developed abilities of these White men, their production, their flight skills, their engineering feats, were the most successful part of that White superstructure which had been strangling the possibilities of his own Black people for years. The professor was an academic with no mean knowledge of colonial struggles of colored peoples. He was also a militant. If the degree of his militancy was not precisely defined, still its presence was not denied. His skin was dark. If he were to say, "Black is beautiful" with a cultivated smile, nonetheless he was still saying it. Aquarius had never been invited to enter this Black man's vision, but it was no great mystery the Black believed his people were possessed of a potential genius which was greater than Whites. Kept in incubation for two millennia, they would be all the more powerful when they prevailed. It was nothing less than a great civilization they were prepared to create. Aquarius could not picture the details of that civilization in the Black professor's mind, but they had talked enough to know they agreed that this potential greatness of the Black people was not to be found in technology. Whites might need the radio to become tribal but Blacks would have another communion. From the depth of one consciousness they could be ready to speak to the depth of another; by telepathy might they send their word. That was the logic implicit in CPT. If CPT was one of the jokes by which Blacks admitted Whites to the threshold of their view, it was a relief to learn that CPT stood for Colored People's Time. When a Black friend said he would arrive at 8 P.M. and came after midnight, there was still logic in his move. He was traveling on CPT. The vibrations he received at 8 P.M. were not sufficiently interesting to make him travel toward you—all that was hurt were the host's undue expectations. The real logic of CPT was that when there was trouble or happiness the brothers would come on the wave.

Well, White technology was not built on telepathy, it was built on electromagnetic circuits of transmission and reception, it was built on factory workers pressing their button or monitoring their function according to firm and bound stations of the clock. The time of a rocket mission was Ground Elapsed Time, GET. Every sequence of the flight was tied into the pure numbers of the timeline. So the flight to the moon was a victory for GET, and the first heats of the triumph suggested that the fundamental notion of Black superiority might be incorrect: in this hour, it would no longer be as easy for a militant Black to say that Whitey had built a palace on numbers, and numbers killed a man, and numbers would kill Whitey's civilization before all was through. Yesterday, Whitey with his numbers had taken a first step to the stars, taken it ahead of Black men. How that had to burn in the ducts of this Black man's stomach, in the vats of his liver. Aquarius thought again of the lunar air technologists. Like the moon, they traveled without a personal atmosphere. No wonder the Blacks had distaste for numbers, and found trouble studying. It was not because they came—as liberals would necessarily have it—from wrecked homes and slum conditions, from drug-pushing streets, no, that kind of violence and disruption could be the pain of a people so rich in awareness they could not bear the deadening jolts of civilization on each of their senses. Blacks had distaste for numbers not because they were stupid or deprived, but because numbers were abstracted from the senses, numbers made you ignore the taste of the apple for the amount in the box, and so the use of numbers shrunk the protective envelope of human atmosphere, eroded that extrasensory aura which gave awareness, grace, the ability to move one's body and excel at sports and dance and war, or be able to travel on an inner space of sound. Blacks were not the only ones who hated numbers—how many attractive women could not bear to add a column or calculate a cost? Numbers were a pestilence to beauty.

Of course this particular Black man, this professor, was in torture, for he lived half in the world of numbers, and half in the wrappings of the aura. So did Aquarius. It was just that Aquarius was White and the other Black—so Aquarius could not conceal altogether his pleasure in the feat. A little part of him, indefatigably White, felt as mean as a Wasp. There was something to be said after all for arriving on time. CPT was excellent for the nervous system if you were the one to amble in at midnight, but Aquarius had played the host too often.

"You know," said the professor, "there are no Black astronauts."

"Of course not."

"Any Jewish astronauts?"

"I doubt it."

The Black man grunted. They would not need to mention Mexicans or Puerto Ricans. Say, there might not even be any Italians.

"Did you want them," asked Aquarius, "to send a Protestant, a Catholic, and a Jew to the moon?"

"Look," said the Black professor, "do they have any awareness of how the money they spent could have been used?"

"They have a very good argument: they say if you stopped space tomorrow, only a token of the funds would go to poverty."

"I'd like to be in a position to argue about that," said the Black. He sipped at his drink. It trickled into his system like the inching of glucose from a bottle down a rubber tube. "Damn," he said, "are they still on the moon?"

"They took off already," said Aquarius.

"No trouble?"

"None."

If the Blacks yet built a civilization, magic would be at its heart. For they lived with the wonders of magic as the Whites lived with technology. How many Blacks had made a move or inhibited it because the emanations of the full moon might affect their cause. Now Whitey had walked on the moon, put his feet on it. The moon had presumably not spoken. Or had it, and Richard Nixon received the favor and Teddy Kennedy the curse? Was there no magic to combat technology? Then the strength of Black culture was stricken. There would not be a future Black culture, merely an adjunct to the White. What lava in the raw membranes of the belly. The Black professor had cause to drink. The moon shot had smashed more than one oncoming superiority of the Black.

***

That night Aquarius had trouble falling asleep, as if the unrest of the Black professor at the passage of men's steps on the moon had now passed over to him. Nothing in the future might ever be the same—that was cause for unrest—nor could the future even be seen until one could answer the obsessive question: was our venture into space noble or insane, was it part of a search for the good, or the agent of diabolisms yet unglimpsed? It was as if we had begun to turn the pocket of the universe inside out.

He had had at the end a curious discussion with the Black professor. "It's all in the remission of sin," the Black man had said. "Technology begins when men are ready to believe that the sins of the fathers are not visited on the sons. Remission of sin—that's what it's all about," he said in his Black slow voice.

Yes, if the sons were not punished, then the father might dare, as no primitive father had ever dared, to smash through a taboo. If the father was in error, or if he failed, the sons would be spared. Only the father would suffer. So men were thereby more ready to dare the gods. So that love on the cross which had requested that sons not pay for the sins of the fathers had opened a hairline split which would finally crack the walls of taboo. And the windowless walls of technology came through the gap. Back to Sören the Dane. You could not know if you were a monster or a saint of the deep.

In the Nineteenth Century, they had ignored Kierkegaard. A middle-class White man, living on the rise of Nineteenth Century technology was able to feel his society as an eminence from which he could make expeditions, if he wished, into the depths. He would know all the while that his security was still up on the surface, a ship—if you will—to which he was attached by a line. In the Twentieth Century, the White man had suddenly learned what the Black man might have told him—that there was no ship unless it was a slave ship. There was no security. Everybody was underwater, and even the good sons of the middle class could panic in those depths, for if there was no surface, there was no guide. Anyone could lose his soul. That recognition offered a sensation best described as bottomless. So the Twentieth Century was a century that looked to explain the psychology of the dream, and instead entered the topography of the dream. The real had become more fantastic than the imagined. And might yet possess more of the nightmare. ★

JAN MORRIS

The Welsh historian, author, travel writer, and, most famously, portrayer of cities, Jan Morris [b.1926] was brought by *Texas Monthly* in the early 1980s to write about Texas places. Her tart evocation of Houston is still a powerful read today. In the introduction to her *Among the Cities* anthology she writes that it is one of her most frequently anthologized pieces.

From Boomtown! Houston U.S.A.

WHAT ELSE? SURELY, YOU ARE SAYING, THE famous Galleria? Well, yes, but not its architecture especially, nor the predictably obscene profusion of its merchandise, but something I saw happening on the ice-rink there, as I sat drinking my coffee on the terrace above. Suddenly the strains of "Yellow Rose of Texas" were gigantically blasted into the glass roof of the arcade; and looking down below me I saw a group of Houston ladies preparing to practice an ice-chorus routine. They struck me, to be frank, as a mature class of chorine, but they swung wonderfully robustly into the gliding steps of their performance—*swing right, one two, swing left, one two, cross over, cross back, into circle one two three*—while all the while the "Yellow Rose" went thump thump from Neiman-Marcus to Lord and Taylor. It was evidently an early stage of their preparations, and just occasionally somebody fell over; but with what dauntless diligence they kept at it, how resolutely they repeated themselves, how indefatigably their leader shrilled her instructions, how untiringly the record player returned, ever and again, to the opening drumbeats of their anthem!

They were your archetypical *doers*: and the true astonishment of Houston, the allure that draws the migrants and fuels the imagination of the nations, is not what it is, still less what it looks like, but what it does.

193

***

To grasp what it chiefly does, on my third day I went and sat upon a grassy bank beside the Houston Ship Channel, with my back to the old battleship *Texas*, the last of the world's dreadnoughts, now berthed for ever in its dock at San Jacinto Park, and my front to the waterway itself. It is not at all a straight-forward waterway, like the Suez Canal, say, since it is really the same old Buffalo Bayou in disguise, and it winds its way sinuously up from the sea by way of Black Duck Bay and Goat Island, and spills frequently into the side-basins and creeks, and is gouged away at the edges into mooring berths. But up and down it night and day the sea-traffic of Houston inexorably proceeds, and I sat in the sunshine there and watched it pass: tankers from Arabia, peculiar Japanese container ships, long strings of blackened barges, queer truncated tugs, ferries, speedboats, sometimes heavy old freighters—ships from sixty nations in 1980, ships from the whole world heading up the old bayou for Houston, Tex.

And the minute they pass the battleship there, with a formal hoot of their sirens sometimes, they enter a stupendous kind of ceremonial avenue, Houston's truest Mall or Champs Elysées: for all up the banks upon either side, jagged and interminable stand the oil, chemical and steel plants that have brought Houston into its future—plants with the magical raw names of capitalism, Rohm and Hass, Paktank, Diamond Shamrock, Bethlehem, plants with towers of steel and ominous chimneys, with twisted assemblies of pipes or conduits, with domes, and tanks, and contrapuntal retorts—hissed about here and there by plumes of steam, hung over by vapours, one after the other far away into the haze of the city centre, as far as the eye can see towards the distant blurred shape of the skyscrapers.

The Ship Channel takes its vessels almost into the heart of the city, well within the freeway loop. On the western side of town, the suburban side, you would hardly know this staggering complex existed: but it seemed to me down there beside the water as though some irresistible magnetism was impelling those ships willy-nilly upstream into town. Houston is now the first inter-national port of the Western Hemisphere, the place where American's ocean lifeline, as the editorialists like to say, comes ashore at last: that spectacle before me, those ships, that channel, those eerie tanks and towers, really is one of the most significant sights of modern travel.

The power that created Houston also redeems this otherwise banal metropolis. Power must stand in the middle of any Houston essay, for it is power in its most elemental form, the power of physical energy that has turned this once provincial seaport into a prime force among the Powers. Houston's publicists like to speak of it as the Giant City, but the truth is far greater than the image, a reversal I think of the Texas norm, and from the indomitable skating ladies of the Galleria to the metallic splendor of the Ship Channel, it was the mighty resolve of the place that most moved me about Houston. ★

STANLEY CROUCH

Stanley Crouch [b. 1945] was already master of long-form critical essay when he wrote this piece for the *Village Voice* in 1981. In the essay he brings to bear his deep knowledge of, and feeling for the blues, along with his appreciation of Southern culture and a personal connection to Houston, to produce a review that remains compelling almost thirty years after the performance.

Crouch also wrote a novel that was partly set in Houston, *Don't the Moon Look Lonesome*. He is now a columnist for the *New York Daily News*.

From Blues in the Capital of Capitalism

THOUGH WE MISSED THE FIRST CONCERT, which took place a few days before I arrived, my mother, my sister, and I attended all of the others, the first of which we heard at Emancipation Park in the Fourth Ward. The performances—all professionally paced and supervised— were presented by SUM Concerts, a nonprofit organization that was founded in 1969 by Lanny Steele, a white man, Vivian Ayers, a black woman, and Bob Morgan, another white man. Ayers and Morgan have since left SUM, which is now directed artistically by Steele, a professional musician and assistant professor of music at Texas Southern University. SUM raises money to present everything from Stockhausen and Sun Ra to Arnett Cobb and Lightnin' Hopkins. They have been giving a free Juneteenth Blues Festival in conjunction with the city of Houston and private sponsors since 1977.

With each successive year, their festival has become a larger event, culminating in the presentation of an award from the mayor's office to a major blues artist on the final night. According to Steele, it is harder to raise money for the blues festival than for their fall jazz festival because the former music is regarded as black and the latter isn't. Given that Steele had to lobby heavily to get saxophonist Billy Harper into the famous North Texas State Jazz Band as its first black player, this comes as no surprise. There was a great controversy the first year of the festival because it was feared that Miller Outdoor Theater would be destroyed by "thousands of undesirables" due to an incident involving the notorious professional redneck Jerry Jeff Walker. When Walker appeared there in a rock concert in 1977, he exhorted the white audience to drink up its Lone Star Beer and then throw the bottles at somebody. A riot broke out, the SWAT squad was sent in, a girl was raped in the dressing room, and two police cars were overturned.

There was no violence at any of the SUM concerts, but the gang was all there. The culture of poverty and the desperate, mumbling imbecility bred by near illiteracy would be juxtaposed against the jovial or sober dignity of those Negroes, both young and old, who carried themselves as if they knew they'd won a hard uphill battle on greasy ground. Whether the women I'd loved or the bitches I'd hated, the men I'd admired or the fools I'd despised, all were so committed to freedom that every one, regardless of personal warmth, was given to that distance individuality makes inevitable. These were the kinds of people who had produced the nameless cowboys and the famous black crooks of the Old West; these were the descendants of the 9th and 10th Cavalry, those Buffalo Soldiers black legend claims not only whipped many an Indian but chased Geronimo down into Mexico and brought him back, only to have white officers push them out of the photograph. From this mix had come Henry Flipper, the first Negro to graduate from West Point and the first to be recognized as a professional engineer; Bill Pickett, the "dusky demon" who invented bulldogging; and Rube Foster, purportedly the first great black pitcher, definitely the first black manager of a professional team—the Texas Yellow Jackets—and also one of the founders of the Negro National League in 1920. Scott Joplin too was a Texan. But maybe in this context one should think most of Blind Lemon Jefferson, the down-home Homer and Aesop of the blues, whose "Prison Cell Blues" (Milestone Records) provides a straight line to the big thinking, do-it-yourselfing, convention-be-damned genius of Ornette Coleman.

***

The violence, bitchiness, and stubbornness of which Texans are capable coexists with courtliness especially evident in the rearing of children. Unlike the mannerless brats one becomes accustomed to in Northern middle-class, liberal, or bohemian households, the black children of Houston radiated a sense of individuality and community, for they were from a world where absolute lack of discipline or respect for adults didn't equal "freedom" or "creativity." It is that thorough awareness of individual style and communal responsibility that accounts for so many major jazz innovators being either literal Southerners or from the second-floor South of enclaves like black Philadelphia. It is the closeness to the slave experience and segregation that creates a willful individuality one is hard put to find in places like Manhattan, where fad and fashion are too often all.

Though Arkansas's Larry Davis played with an authoritative gutbucket lustre and Lightnin' Hopkins was well-received, the most impressive performance of the first few nights was that of James Cotton. Sandwiched between talented young Sherman Robertson and master of the erotic mantra John Lee Hooker, Cotton's group, with its control of tempos, nuance, and intensity and its amiable showboating, proved that there is a future for the blues in the hands of young black players. During Cotton's set, the sun went down and the night, full of people who had become three-dimensional shadows, was touched up by the rhythm of green phosphorescent loops spun to the four-on-the-floor beat of the drummer Ken Johnson. Something of an innovator in the idiom, Johnson knows all of the black rhythms and mixes jazz, latin, disco, skipping triplets, and surprising accents into the beat. The upshot is that the audience is captured by the tension and the release, the familiar and the exotic. Young lead guitarist Michael Coleman, tenor saxophonist Doug Fagan, rhythm guitarist John Watkins, and bassist Herman Applewhite were also quite fine. Cotton was definitely the leader, however, and a version of "Going Down Slow" was as moving as I've ever heard. During an encore, Cotton's harp quoted a Basie riff, Nat Adderley's "Work Song," and "When the Saints Go Marching In." While Cotton was reaching for a deeper groove, I overheard two black boys of about 13 saying to each other as they swayed to beat, "He's getting down now! He's getting down, man." I could never imagine that from Harlem boys. Finally, Cotton reached what he was looking for, that mood of a house party high on the wing of the night. At that point, spontaneous dancing had a domino effect and the audience reached that ritualistic level wherein all those hair styles, caps, cowboy hats, shapes, outfits, and colors connect in a deceptively imperishable moment of transcendence. The audience was ecstatic.

***

On the evening of Juneteenth, I attended a party for SUM Concerts at the mansion formerly owned by the late Jesse Jones, who was a pivotal figure in developing the alliance between business and government in Texas. Jones was from Tennessee and is a mythic figure in the West. He conceived the idea of the ship channel which runs 40 miles inland and makes Houston a port city, now the third largest in the country. He started the Texas Commerce Bank, owned real estate, founded the Federal Loan Administration, and became Secretary of Commerce under Roosevelt's New Deal. Jones dispensed 50 billion dollars in federal funds and with a small group of associates ran the city of Houston from a room in the Lamar Hotel that led to the term "the 8F Club" (also known as *the* card game in town). An important member of that club was George Brown, who received government contracts through his associations with Jones. Brown built NASA's Manned Spacecraft Center, the Mohole Project (to penetrate the earth's mantle), and the American facilities in Da Nang, which he sold for a rumored 37 million dollars.

Wandering through the late power broker's mansion that evening were blues singers and players, some of Houston's recent successes and arrivals, plus a bit of old Houston money. In that huge backyard, under those trees, while the Fifth Ward's Big Mama Thornton sat in a sullen stupor, James Cotton strolled about, amiable, chuckling, and talking about how much he'd liked playing for the black audiences in Houston and New Orleans. The members of his band were all authentic hambone Negroes. They bemoaned the fact that more younger black musicians weren't interested in blues but felt that this was slowly changing. The liquor flowed and the food was good.

A black corporate executive said something to me at the party that illuminated much of what I'd seen. "Whether people like it or not, the center of the drive for independent energy sources is in Texas, and the way Texas goes is the way the country is going to go as far as energy is concerned. There's no future in crude oil, but there's plenty of coal, shale oil, and in the Southwest in general all kinds of important minerals like uranium. That's where the Mexicans and the Indians come in. This could turn out to be another Oklahoma for Indians because a lot of those valuable minerals are on their reservations. The business people know it, the Indians know it, and so do the Mexicans. In fact, they're just beginning to talk about 'Mestizo Power,' you know. A coalition based on them being mixed up in each other's family lines. Now what the black people are going to have to do is stop being stupid and talking about dumb Mexicans and start trying to deal with these people politically, socially, and economically. If they don't, they won't need a blues festival cause they'll be singing the blues every goddam day."

The last shows were on Saturday, one in the afternoon, one at night. They started quite beautifully with Milton Larkin and His All Stars, featuring Arnett Cobb and Jimmy Ford. Larkin's set wasn't folk blues, it was hard jazz blues, including ballads and a disco tune he wrote for his great-great-grandchildren. From his metal crutches Arnett Cobb filled up the stage with his grand sound, and Jimmy Ford, veteran of Tadd Dameron's band, proved once more how much better Southern white players sound in jazz bands than their Northern counterparts. He was a perfect foil for the Texas tenor of Cobb, whipping out eloquent lines in Charlie Parker's language. Albert Collins played wonderfully at both concerts, with a weight to his guitar sound that made each note sound twice as thick as normal. The set began with rhythm and blues but moved into hard shuffle when Collins came on, so much so that an unidentified drunken Negro came on the stage and did a leg-wiggling dance as authentic as it was unexpected (and unwanted by the performers). Big Mama Thornton, butched up in cowboy hat and cowboy outfit, her clothes padded to give what she must think is an image close to her nickname, arrived at the festival in a dark blue Lincoln Continental which had "Big Mama" written on the right side of the windshield in gold sequins. Her entourage consisted of her sister and two militant, muscular Houston homosexuals with cowboy hats, sleeveless dark blue shirts, jeans, boots, and handlebar mustaches. Her set wasn't as interesting as her entrance, but she was in stronger voice than when I had heard her last.

By the time Eddie Cleanhead Vinson came on, people had been barbecuing for hours in the trees a few hundred yards from the bandstand, beer had been given away, and the crowd had sunk into the dark bliss of a hot summer evening. Vinson was suave and professional, teasing, and sophisticated in a way few of the previous performers had been. Here was a man who breathed the blues and its bebop extensions with such command his distracted appearance on the stage made his virtuosity even more apparent. Far more than Jimmy Ford, he showed how much range there is to the blues idiom and how many notes are now associated with the sensibility only because of the innovations of men like Charlie Parker.

Between Vinson's set and Clifton Chenier, one of the performers handed the other a beer, then lifted his own to toast.

"Cheers."

"What we got to cheer about? The white folks got all the money."

"Well, long as you living, you got a chance."

"I guess you right about that."

"How's that old knucklehead?'

"He's all right, but he ain't big enough to be a star and he ain't good enough to do nothing but play the blues for the white folks. You know how they are: they like anything."

"Who you telling."

"But if you good enough, I mean all around good enough, you can play the blues all the goddam way from California to Calcutta."

"Well, you goddam right about that, too."

Clifton Chenier and his Red Hot Louisiana Band came on to excited applause. Chenier introduced his group by saying, "This here is what you call the real zydeco. I took the zydeco all the way from Opalusa, Louisiana, to Israel, Europe, and Africa." Playing his fancy new accordion and leading his group through a fiery set, Chenier's music rocked everyone within hearing distance. The ensemble, which includes electric guitar and bass, alto saxophone, trumpet, washboard, percussionist (bongos, scrapers, etc.), and trap drums, was the most exciting at the festival. The alto sound in the group achieves a color close to that of the harmonica and, in tandem with the accordion, provides extraordinary timbres. Synthesis is the essence of Chenier's achievement, for the music is protected from the sentimental by the heavy, rattling, scraping, thumping percussion that sets one foot in Africa and the other in the gutbucket. There are mock melodramatic ballads nearly country-and-western in feeling, Lester Young motifs, Louis Jordan alto spirals, sensual, pugnacious riffs, and barrelhouse boogie back home as the house farthest down in the swamp.

As Chenier went into "It's All Right," the entire audience had been transformed. No longer bothered by the heat or the mosquitos, the listeners became a huge polyrhythmic pulsation. The Mexicans did Hispanic steps, the whites clog-danced, and the Negroes, their identities deepened by so many miscegenations, were an encyclopedia of facial and body types, chanting voices and rhythms. As I looked at them I thought how prepared these descendants of mountain men, cowboys, frontier women, and daredevils seemed to be to move through the tragedy so basic to the black American story. For just as the Chicago bluesmen met the challenge of electronics and Clifton Chenier has transformed a polka pumper into a blues shouter, black Americans must conquer the frontier of the Information Society. As John Biggers, artist and teacher at Texas Southern University, says, "These black schools are falling apart. Desegregation has sent us all the bad white teachers and the dwindling budgets and the poor administrators. The white people found out the Civil Rights Movement came off these campuses and decided to destroy them. But now is the time for us to branch out and take over the big white institutions—not with bullshit, but with quality. A lot will be hurt and a lot will be left behind, but that's the way our history is. But the old people who came before us, the runaways and the rebels, that's the way they wanted it to be. They expected us to travel on. They just didn't want us to stumble into oblivion."

Texans, are, to use Octavia Paz's phrase, labyrinths of solitude, with cultural and ethnic pedigrees appropriate to human mazes. The Spaniards conquered the Indians of Mexico with Chinese gunpowder on horses and Moorish saddles, brought the architecture of the Alhambra to the country under a cover letter of vernacular Catholicism, introduced the big cattle-raising vision of the *rancho grande*, then created the mulatto race we know as Mexicans. They also brought African slaves whose ethnicity became part of an Afro-Indian race observed near the Rio Grande by the 1570s. Then came the white Americans and northern Europeans—hardy, self-righteous, and xenophobic Protestants. Like John Wayne's Ethan in *The Searchers*, they absorbed the severity, the flair, the fraternity, the pride, and the solitude of the region until, for all their connections to England, Scotland, Ireland, Wales, and Germany, they became akin—in spirit and often in blood—to their Indian and Mexican adversaries. So that in the end they were like the fellow in the Talmud who was spooked by an animal at night, only to realize it was a man as he came closer—and, finally, that the stranger was his brother. ★

PART III

THE CITY ITSELF

I ONCE ASKED A HOUSTON POET WHY THERE weren't more poems written about the city. But the question could be addressed to almost any genre. (Though after putting this anthology together I must admit that the question makes me feel greedy.) His off-handed reply still brings me up short: "That's the beauty of Houston. You don't have to write about it."

I'm not really sure that any writer *really* wants to live in a place that makes so vague an impression, even if that vagueness would free you to ponder the eternal verities rather than the intersection of Westheimer and Montrose. But, as essayist Phillip Lopate declares in "Houston Hide and Seek," the city really is "a strangely non-imposing environment."

This hasn't always been true. The blandness of the physical city is largely the result of Houston's unique brand of development after World War II, and its lack of historic preservation for buildings, both of which have left the city with a surprising (especially if you're from the urban northeast) number of gaps in its urban fabric. Buildings get knocked down; entire neighborhoods get leapfrogged by developers.

But in its early days, the city was all too imposing, as historian Stephen L. Hardin recounts in the hair-raising and darkly humorous excerpt from his *Texian Macabre*.

Over a century later, the city's lack of zoning, and its absolute exaltation of the automobile, attracted seekers, such as *The New York Times* architecture critic Ada Louise Huxtable (included here), who famously, if not as flatteringly as it sounds at first blush, called Houston "*the* city of the second half of the twentieth century." In his book *Edge City*, Joel Garreau took a more focused look at the city—he concentrated on the Galleria area—and found a new type of city structure, one that leads to "pretty society," rather than a "pretty city," in the words of an Indian restaurateur. Meanwhile, poet and former University of Houston professor Mark Doty issued a sort of Valentine to Houston on the occasion of his permanent departure. He sees Houston's urban shortcomings, but finds that the place grew on him anyway, which is a position the many Houstonians take who find themselves liking Houston more than they had expected to when they arrived to work at the Medical Center or an energy trading firm. Rice professor Terrence Doody considers the effects of the Houston cityscape on its citizens' senses of place and privacy.

Donald Barthleme is the only native Houstonian included in this section. Far too much the ironist to ever wax lyrical, instead he analyzes the cultural shortcomings of Houston in the early 1960s. And Tony Diaz, novelist and founder of *Nuestra Palabra*, criticizes the city's cultural elite for being so oblivious to the *vatos* who wait on them as they prepare for a night at the opera house.

Stephen L. Hardin

Historian Stephen L. Hardin is both an unusually vivid writer and a dogged, clever researcher, as he demonstrates here in this painfully detailed description of life in Houston during its brief, and apparently squalid, run as the new nation's capital.

Houston readers will likely have a dual reaction to *Texian Macabre*. They'll wonder how anyone could stand to live in the Houston of the 1840s, and then they'll be struck by how similar it sounds to the Houston of today.

From *Texian Macabre*: "The Most Miserable Place in the World"

THE CITY SUFFERED ALL THE ILLS OF DESULtory development. By 1838 the Allen brothers' dream had become a nightmare. Houston resembled not so much a city as a perverse burlesque of one. Even the most zealous booster had to admit that much of the year it was a contaminated cesspit. In the summer, swarms of flies carried the bacteria that caused dysentery. Winter brought typhus, influenza, cholera, and tuberculosis. Almost yearly yellow fever epidemics swept through the city claiming vast numbers of victims. A ghastly assortment of detritus littered the muddy streets. One official was dead on target when he referred to "this detested, self-poluted, isolated mudhole of a city." Mrs. William Fairfax Gray averred that she "never saw anything like the mud here. It is a tenaceous black clay," she continued, "which can not be got off of any thing without washing—and is about a foot or so deep." Francis R. Lubbock recalled Houston as a "very muddy place, almost the entire town tract being black, stiff land, and with poor drainage, so that, with the immense wagon trade, the roads and streets, although wide and handsome, were almost impassable in wet weather." So too, were the "roads from Houston to the country in almost any direction." Likewise, Samuel Maverick of San

Antonio mocked the "seat of Government" as a "wretched mudhole." Dr. John Washington Lockhart recalled the avenues were "very muddy, and it was not an unusual thing then and long afterward to see ox wagons bogged down on the principal streets." Frequent rains liquefied the black dirt and horse droppings. Wagon wheels further whipped the mixture into a putrid slime. With good reason, "the Father of Texas Medicine" Ashbel Smith requested a New Orleans friend to procure for him a "pair of India Rubber overshoes." And never ending, like a symphony of squalor, the maddening buzzing of the flies. As night draped its cloak over Houston, citizens endured another one of nature's recitals: "the howling of wolves." Many shared Nacogdoches Representative Kelsey H. Douglass's opinion that Houston was, "the most misera[b]le place in the world."

It was no mystery why Houston was so muddy. Much of the land the Allen brothers selected for the town site was swampland. One of their nephews, O. F. Allen, later depicted the difficulties involved in reclaiming the area. "One could hardly picture the jungle and swampy sweet gum woods that a good portion of the city is built upon." Allen claimed the "southwestern portion of the city was a green scum lake, studded with giant sweet gum trees, and water from one to two and a half feet deep." Reflecting the racial sensitivities of his day, Allen recalled the backbreaking and deadly work required to drain those wetlands. "The labor of clearing the great space was done by negro slaves and Mexicans, as no white man could have worked and endured the insect bites and malaria, snake bites, impure water, and other hardships." The slaves could not either, for as Allen reproached, "many of the blacks died before their work was done."

The rancid streets functioned more as obstacle courses. Because of the Borden brothers' prescience, streets measured eighty feet wide and ran ramrod straight. The exception was Water Street. It was one hundred feet wide and mirrored the meanderings of Buffalo Bayou. Even so, "streets and squares," one resident reported, "were still covered with trees and stumps that obstructed the way, especially at nighttime." If that were not enough, stray horses, dogs, cats, rats, and even hogs ran feral through the streets.

Dead animals posed an even greater hazard than live ones. The carcasses lay where they fell and festered alongside the refuse that littered Houston boulevards. "[It] was said that enough oxen had been killed on the roads from Houston to the high rolling country to build the first twenty-five miles of the Houston and Texas Central railroad," recalled Dr. Lockhart. He was not certain if such claims were factual, but he did know that he had personally seen "the roads lined with carcasses." Add horse droppings and raw sewage, and the stench was nauseating. The place smelled less like a town than a charnel house.

More than animal carcasses sullied the avenues. Dr. Moore recalled that "instances have been known when three or four dead bodies have been picked up of a morning in the street, and that sickness and death visited almost every family." He noted that these fatalities were "more owing to the exposed situation of the inhabitants than the unhealthiness of the climate."

Moore took the board of health to task for their negligence. He upbraided the members for the offal that "has been suffered to lay unremoved in our vicinity, so near as to impregnate the atmosphere with its putridity." He further excoriated officials for allowing the "washings of the kitchens and back yards of the whole city . . . to be thrown into the streets and gutters, there to rot and emit a stench disgusting and poisonous in the extreme." Shamefaced, Congressman Douglass admitted to his wife, "we live like hogs."

Naturally, citizens sought to avoid the fetid quagmires that passed for roads, but that produced another quandary. The city council subsequently approved an ordinance that forbade local jehus from riding horses or driving carriages and wagons on the sidewalks.

Then there was the vermin. Traveler C. C. Cox decamped in the loft of a Houston home. His bed consisted of a few blankets thrown upon the hard plank flooring, which the Ohio native allowed would have been adequate but for "other company": "The fleas were as thick as the sands of the sea. Our clothes were actually bloody, and our bodies freckled after a night of warfare with the Vermine."

Nor could Houstonians elude the maddening attention of flies and mosquitoes. An American tourist reported the ravages of the "blister fly" that he "found along the waters of the lower country, where they lie in wait for horses and cattle in such numbers that, when they light, they literally cover their victim and drive it to distraction." He swore that he had seen flies terrorize a horse until it was "covered with gore and champ his bit in the agony of torment." It was, of course, not only mounts that suffered. "Musquetoes and other insects," the author of a popular emigrant's guide asserted, "annoy the over-heated emigrants by day and night." An English traveler noted the "myriads of mosquitoes, which are so venomous and troublesome as to render existence hardly endurable." On a business trip, Francis Lubbock became lost and had to spend the night in the Brazos bottom. "The darkness," he recounted, "was made hideous by the yelping of wolves, the cries of the Mexican panther, and the never ending hum of mosquitos." He survived his night in the woods, but upon returning to his boarding house discovered his face "so disfigured by mosquito bites that my wife scarcely recognized me."

If Houstonians suffered a dazzling assortment of vermin, rats were the worst. As soon as Houstonians snuffed their candles, the skitter of rats lulled them into slumber. Gustav Dresel, a young German immigrant, described the scourge of these loathsome creatures:

> Thousands of these troublesome guests made sport by night, and nothing could be brought to safety from them. All the provisions were soon begnawed by them, and the best rat dog became tired of destroying them because their number never decreased. Human corpses had to be watched the whole night because otherwise these fiends ate their way into them. The finger of a little child who lay alone in the cradle of a few hours was half eaten away. This I saw myself. . . . Rats often dashed across me by the half-dozens at night. In the beginning this proves annoying; of course, later one gets accustomed to it.

One might accuse Dresel of exaggeration were his observations not corroborated by others. "I cannot convey an idea of the multitude of Rats in Houston at that time," C. C. Cox recollected. "They were almost as large as prairie dogs and when night came on, the streets and Houses were litterly alive with these animals. Such running and squealling throughout the night, to say nothing of the fear of losing a toe or your nose, if you chanced to fall asleep, created such an apprehension that together with the attention that had to be given our other Companions made sleep well nigh impossible."

The oppressive heat and humidity were also well nigh impossible to endure. From the beginning, the city achieved a reputation for its astronomically high temperatures. The summer of 1980 registered temperatures that *exceeded* one hundred degrees for fourteen consecutive days. Modern Texans can hardly imagine how debilitating such heat would have been before the advent of air conditioning. Numerous citizens of the Texas Republic cursed the hellish Houston summer. One reporter proclaimed the atmosphere "dry, hot, and oppressive." Citizens thought it paradoxical that streets were quagmires when it rained and "dusty and disagreeable" when it did not. Edward Stiff claimed that the climate was "decidedly unfriendly to health; quite as much so as New Orleans. . . . The morning sun beams down with scorching and sickly heat; and

From mountain dell or stream,
Not a fleeting zephyr springs;
Fearful lest the noontide beam
Scorch its soft, its silken wings.

President Houston learned that the privileges of his office did not include relief from the summers in his namesake city. On an especially blistering day, he beseeched: "God keep me clear of the heat of the natural as well as the political season." Physician John H. Bauer remembered one summer so hot that "we worked in Genl. Houston's house in Houston until nearly morning—stripped of all clothing except our shirts."

So crushing was the heat and humidity that the entire city seemed to sink into a slough of lethargy. Ashbel Smith bemoaned, "the heat is so severe during the middle of the day, that most of us lie in the shade and pant—morning and evening." The editor of the *Morning Star*, left a vivid record of the misery:

Oh for a good cold norther! One of your real old-fashioned ones, early though it be for them. We are tired of gazing upon burning, brassy skies; upon hot looking clouds, and parched earth. We are weary of throwing open all the doors and windows, and placing ourselves in the draught, in hopes to catch one breath of cool air to cool our fevered brow. We are weary of staying home in the day time, lest we should be scorched with intense heat; and of being obliged to remain within our mosquitoe-bar at night, lest we be devoured by the mosquitoes. We are weary of feeling the perspiration coursing down our cheeks as we sit at our desk puzzling our brains, or rummaging over the mails, in order to present something interesting to our readers. We are weary of this lassitude, and languor; this constant relaxation of mind and body, which incapacitates us alike for mental and physical labor. We want something to brace us up. And what is better for that purpose than a good cold norther?

The sweat-soaked editor should have been careful what he wished for. Winters proved as frigid as summers were charring. Again, Houston's location was a factor. Buffalo Bayou provided the city's northern boundary; to south and west, "stretching far in the distance," recounted one resident, "is an extensive prairie with here and there a grove of timber." (Indeed, one of these groves would be the site of the gallows that feature so prominently in this unfolding morality play.) "The country westward of Houston for some thirty miles or more, is a level prairie," observed A. B. Lawrence, "with scarcely a sufficient inclination to carry off the water of the rains that fall upon it." All this wide, open space allowed icy winds to sweep through unimpeded, cutting scythe-like through dwellings and clothing. The buffeting winds made the city cold; the marshy bayou rendered it damp.

Hearty Houstonians might have endured the cold and abided the dampness, but the combination proved lethal for great numbers of them. Dr. John Washington Lockhart recalled that two consecutive winters were especially vicious. "In 1837 and 1838 there was a sleet," he recounted, "that broke all the large limbs off the old trees; and after melting, left the appearance as if a great cyclone had devastated the forest." The *Telegraph* noted that on February 16, 1837, the city experienced "Remarkably cold weather," with the mercury plummeting to "within ten degrees of zero." Dresel explained that residents were ill equipped for such conditions. "When fall came with its northers and there were only three stoves in the whole of Houston, we used to light fires in front of the saloon in the evening, stand around them and enjoy—not excepting the President—hot drinks with merry speeches." Lubbock concurred: "Stoves at that time were very seldom if ever seen." Even the president's cabin had no fireplace, "nothing but a small clay furnace in the room for him to get over and warm his fingers, Indian fashion." Writing his wife, Congressman Douglass grumbled, "The room that I occupy has no fire and I all most frose Last night." He cut his letter short: "I am quite cold so farewell." John Hunter Herndon bewailed the city's "cold disagreeable weather," which was, he believed, "worse than Kentucky." On 4 February 1838, his diary entry was laconic in its melancholy: "Several persons freeze to death."

Describing the winter of 1838, Mary Austin Holley lamented: "The excessive bad weather for a month & a half past has defeated all objects, & interfered with all business. The few who could get about have had their labor for their pains," she concluded. "It has been truly unfortunate having such a winter—a thing unheard of before—so different from what the early season promise[d]. There has been no getting about for storms—Every body had to stop just where they were overtaken by them & use the best shelter they could." If winter proved a hardship, on occasion it at least provided spectacular landscapes. On February 16, Mrs. Holley noted, "Water froze solid in my room during the night. The prairie was like a sea of glass, glittering in the sunshine. It continued shining & freezing all day. As cold as Boston Commons."

Most of Houston's dwellings—makeshift, ramshackle, and foul—did little to protect their inhabitants from the ravages of the weather. While barely fit for human habitation, vermin felt perfectly at home. Rats in their thousands, having feasted on the putrescent offal in the streets, then disputed possession of the shanties. On January 23, 1838, John Hunter Herndon received his first view of the city. "Arrived at Houston at 3 O'clock P.M.," he recorded in his diary. "Formed bad opinion of the place which time will correct or confirm. The buildings are all indifferent, some small, unfinished frames, the rest of boards and shantys." Dr. Smith admitted, "few of our houses have chimnies. And, indeed, we have as yet in this country but few of the comforts of civilized life." The small clapboard house belonging to Francis R. Lubbock and his French Creole wife, Adele, was typical of those throughout the city. It was constructed of "three-foot pine boards and covered with three-foot pine boards, and contained all told one room about twelve feet square and a smaller shed room. There was one door leading into the main room and one door from that room into the shed room, both of three-foot boards, with all the hinges made of wood. There was no window in the house," Lubbock recalled. "When air and light were wanted, a board was knocked off." San Jacinto veteran Mosley Baker and his wife also lived in a two-room clapboard house. In the larger room a carpet covered the dirt floor, which he explained, "gave an air of comfort contrasting strongly with the surroundings."

With memories of the Runaway Scrape still fresh in their minds, Houstonians were hesitant to invest in permanent dwellings when they might have to abandon them at a moment's notice. "Apprehensions of another invasion not having yet wholly subsided," Smith reported, "the improvements are for the most part of a temporary and unsubstantial nature." ★

DONALD BARTHELME

Donald Barthelme [1931–1989] remains Houston's most celebrated writer. (This short summary can't begin to do him justice, and I urge interested readers to pick up Tracy Daugherty's biography, *Hiding Man: a Biography of Donald Barthelme*.) He grew up in a brilliant family, led by prominent Modernist architect Donald Barthelme Sr., and was a man of divided loyalties. He chafed at the restrictions of provincial life, as the following *Texas Observer* essay shows. (It was written in 1960 before he'd begun publishing fiction.) But he also remained loyal to Houston, and in the early 1980s returned from New York to teach in the University of Houston Creative Writing Program. As a writer, he was among America's most celebrated post-modernists and a mainstay at the *New Yorker* for three decades.

From the *Texas Observer*, an untitled essay

IT IS FREQUENTLY PAINFUL FOR A TEXAN TO decide that he is not, after all, a cowboy. The role is glamorous, sanctioned by the community, and not difficult to play. Adults can manage it far more easily than they could, say, Spaceman. But there are some serious disadvantages.

The trouble with being a cowboy, even a counterfeit cowboy, is that although exquisitely sage in matters of horses and cattle, the cowboy tends to be somewhat limited outside these areas. This has more to do with the ritual demands of the role than with his innate gifts. Certain important areas of thought and feeling are closed to him; like a cloche hat or an interest in the United Nations, they are simply unbecoming.

A number of talented improvisers have attempted to enlarge the role, giving us, for instance, the scholar-cowboy: "All I eat is beans cooked over a mesquite fire but I also speak Chaucer." The role is legitimized by the cachet of scholarship, and we are made more comfortable in it. It is not necessary that we too speak Chaucer; it is enough that we are told that Chaucer and mesquite fires may safely co-exist.

A community of largely bogus cowboys, or cowboys who are uneasy in their roles, provides interesting examples of amateur or do-it-yourself schizophrenia. Thus we have the moneyed cowboy whose money proceeds not from cattle but from a nice little plastics plant. To complicate the picture insanely, let us say he is also, in his rough-hewn way, a patron of the arts. Note that the drama here is generated by the delicious incongruity he presents—in his role of the cultured cowboy: "I died with my boots on of boredom in the Art Museum." When we remember that he is in fact not a cowboy at all but a plastics engineer, the multiple level of the charade is revealed, the lostness of the leading character established.

These charades are sometimes played on a grand scale, with the entire community taking part. This can be seen in the recently advanced proposal, apparently seriously intended, that Houston's new Museum of Natural History be built in the shape of the state of Texas. When we begin building things in the shape of other things (hot dog stands in the image of giant wieners, tourists courts à la Indian tepees) we immediately betray a desperate inadequacy of the imagination. Not content to let the thing be what it is, we insist that it pretend to be something else—usually something we can despise. Luckily, the Houston museum will escape this fate. But the inappropriateness of this maneuver in regard to a museum, which usually despises us, is clear.

Role-playing is a complex business, and the role of cowboy is certainly both gross and obvious; all of us are involved daily in dozens of subtler impersonations. What is significant, for the moment, is our choice of models, what we select from tradition and other sources as images of what we are and what we can be.

Most of these models come today from the mass media. The rather proprietary interest displayed by the press, radio, and television in certain agreed-upon objects of admiration—Dr. Albert Schweitzer, the United Fund, General de Gaulle, urban renewal, Mr. Bang-Jensen, juvenile delinquency, Gamble

Benedict's grandmother—solicits our sympathy without really involving us. My admiration for Dr. Schweitzer is considerable but it is also almost meaningless, because I do not believe that he is real; he has approximately the same status in my world as that other celebrated physician, Dr. Lionel Barrymore, and sometimes I am not sure that they are not one and the same. In this way the mass media siphon off our powers of concern; the models they propose, as proper subjects for thought and feeling and emulation, are if not spurious at least safe, distant, and "approved."

My complaint about the ideas and attitudes received from the media—as well as from such homegrown myths as the myth that every Texan is in some sense a cowboy, or capable of being one, or should possess the cowboy virtues—is that they are second-hand, weak, and flat. In the choice of such models is to be found the meaning of provincialism.

Not long ago I heard a local jazz group among whose obvious merits was a distinct resemblance, in style and attack, to the Modern Jazz Quartet. The latter is the most accomplished, most original jazz unit in the country. I know that this is so because I read it in the *New Yorker*, and because I have heard their records. What I felt while listening to the local group, along with pleasure in their proficiency, was how much I missed having heard the Modern Jazz Quartet.

What made this clear was both the excellence of the imitation and its imperfections. For one thing, the musicians had hands and faces. For another, the drums were a little loud, the bass a little dim, the vibes a bit hasty—as is absolutely never the case when listening to music in the comfort of your own living room, where everything is always cool, meticulous, perfect. The quality of the experience was fresh and vivid: it made listening to records seem a very pale enterprise indeed.

I rehearse all this in order to place myself in a position to say that I think we know what we know of our principal sources of innovation in our culture in pretty much this pale, unsatisfactory way. This too is part of the definition of provincialism. John Crosby recently remarked that although he'd been pleasantly surprised by the number of legitimate theatres he'd encountered in travels around the country, he did wish they'd all stop doing "Bus Stop." Like the cowboy, Dr. Schweitzer, and Leopold Stokowski, "Bus Stop" is a piety—a lovely myth that enables us to avoid the arduous business of seeking out and experiencing The New.

***

In a way, this is simply a function of one of our traditional obligations to neglect artists, writers, creators of every kind—or to patronize the wrong ones. In this way a Starving Opposition is created, and the possibility of criticism of our culture provided for. Neglect is useful: consider what "La Bohème" would be if, in the second act, Rodolfo entered and declared, in a passionate aria, that he had just received a two-year grant from the Ford Foundation.

I think that on this score we may consider ourselves safe. As far as I can see, neglect is proceeding at appropriate levels. But those of you who are contrary, cross-grained and generally unruly might give some thought to Cyril Connolly's acute insight that to a writer whose work one has admired, one should send money—"anything between half-a-crown and a hundred pounds." I suggest that a dollar in the mail to Tennessee Williams, for having written that remarkable line "I have always depended on the kindness of strangers," would not be amiss. Better still, find a Tennessee Williams of your own. ★

Ada Louise Huxtable

Ada Louise Huxtable is one of the country's most noteworthy architecture critics. Born in 1921, she worked as a Curatorial Assistant for Architecture and Design at the Museum of Modern art from 1946–50, before beginning her writing career. She was a contributing editor at *Progressive Architecture* and *Art in America* until she was named the first architecture critic at the *New York Times* in 1963. She held that position until 1982, and in 1975 wrote this contemplation of Houston. In 1970 she won the Pulitzer Prize for Criticism. She currently writes architecture criticism at the *Wall Street Journal*, and in 2004 published a biography of Frank Lloyd Wright.

Deep in the Heart of Nowhere

THIS IS A CAR'S-EYE VIEW OF HOUSTON—BUT is there any other? It is a short report on a fast trip to the city that has supplanted Los Angeles in current intellectual mythology as the city of the future. You'd better believe. Houston is the place that scholars flock to for the purpose of seeing what modern civilization has wrought. Correctly perceived and publicized as a freeway city, mobile city, space city, strip city and speculator city, it is being dissected by architects and urban historians as a case study in new forms and functions. It even requires a new definition of urbanity. Houston is *the* city of the second half of the 20th century.

But what strikes the visitor accustomed to cities shaped by rivers, mountains and distinguishing topography, by local identity and historical and cultural conditioning, is that this is instant city, and it is nowhere city.

Houston is totally without the normal rationales of geography and evolutionary social growth that have traditionally created urban centers and culture. From the time that the Allen brothers came here from New York in 1836 and bought the featureless land at the junction of two bayous (they could not get the site they really wanted), this city has been an act of real estate, rather than an act of God or man. Houston has been willed on the flat, uniform prairie not by some planned ideal, but by the expediency of land investment economics, first, and later by oil and petrochemical prosperity.

This is not meant to be an unfavorable judgment. It is simply an effort to convey the extraordinary character of this city—to suggest its unique importance, interest and impact. Its affluence and eccentricities have been properly celebrated. It is known to be devoutly conservative, passionately devoted to free enterprise and non-governmental interference. It is famous, or notorious, for the fact that, alone among the country's major cities, it has no zoning—no regulations on what anyone builds, anywhere—and the debate rages over whether this makes it better or worse than other cities. (It's a draw, with pluses and minuses that have a lot to do with special local conditions.)

Now the fifth largest city in the country, Houston has had its most phenomenal expansion since the Second World War. At last count it covered over 500 square miles and had a population of 1.4 million, with 1.8 million more in surrounding Harris County. A thousand new people move in every week. This record-setting growth has leapfrogged over open country without natural boundaries, without land-use restrictions, moving on before anything is finished, for a kind of development as open-ended as the prairie. It has jumped across smaller, fully incorporated cities within the vast city limits. The municipality can legally annex 10 percent of its urban area in outlying land or communities every year, and the land grab has been continuous and relentless.

Houston is a study in paradoxes. There are pines and palm trees, skyscrapers and sprawl; Tudor townhouses stop abruptly as cows and prairie take over. It deals in incredible extremes of wealth and culture. In spite of its size, one can find no real center, no focus. "Downtown" boasts a concentration of suave towers, but they are already challenged by other, newer commercial centers of increasing magnitude that form equally important nodes on the freeway network that ties everything together. Nor are these new office and shopping complexes located to serve existing communities in the conventional sense. They are created in a vacuum, and people come by automobile, driving right into their parking garages. They rise from expressway ribbons and seas of cars.

Houston is all process and no plan. Gertrude Stein said of Oakland that there was no there, there. One might say of Houston that one never gets there. It feels as if one is always on the way, always arriving, always looking for the place where everything comes together. And yet as a city, a 20th-century city, it works remarkably well. If one excepts horrendous morning and evening traffic jams as all of Houston moves to and from home and work, it is a lesson in how a mobile society functions, the values it endorses, and what kind of world it makes.

Houston is different from the time one rises in the morning to have the dark suddenly dispelled by a crimson aureole on a horizon that seems to stretch full circle, and a sun that appears to rise below eye level. (New Yorkers are accustomed to seeing only fractured bits and pieces of sky.) From a hotel of sophisticated excellence that might be Claridge's-on-the-prairie, furnished with an owner-oilman's private collection of redundant boiserie and Sèvres, one drives past fountains of detergent blue.

Due south [*sic*] on Main Street is "downtown," a roughly 20-block cluster of commercial towers begun in the 1920s and 30s and doubled in size and numbers in the 1960s and 70s, sleek symbols of prosperity and power. They are paradigms of the corporate style. The names they bear are Tenneco, Shell Plaza, Pennzoil Place, Humble and Houston Natural Gas, and their architects have national reputations.

In another paradox, in the country of open spaces, the towers are increasingly connected by tunnels underground. Houston's environment is strikingly "internalized" because of the area's extremes of heat and humidity. It is the indoors one seeks for large parts of the year, and that fact has profoundly affected how the city builds and lives.

The enclosed shopping center is Houston's equivalent of the traditional town plaza—a clear trend across the country. The Post Oak Galleria, a $20-million product of Houston developer Gerald Hines and architects Hellmuth, Obata and Kassabaum, with Neuhaus and Taylor, is characteristically large and opulent. A 420,000-square-foot, 600-foot long, three-level, covered shopping mall, it is part of a 33-acre commercial, office and hotel complex on the West Loop Freeway, at the city's western edge.

The Galleria is the place to see and be seen: it is meeting place, promenade and social center. It also offers restaurants, baubles from Tiffany and Neiman-Marcus, a galaxy of specialty shops equivalent to Madison Avenue, and an ice-skating rink comparable to Rockefeller Center's, all under a chandelier-hung glass roof. One can look up from the ice-skating to see joggers circling the oblong glass dome. The Galleria is now slated for an expansion larger than the original.

These enterprises do not require outdoor settings; they are magnets that can be placed anywhere. In fact, one seeks orientation by the freeways and their man-made landmarks (Southwest Freeway and Sharpstown, West Loop and City Post Oak) rather than by reference to organic patterns of growth. Climate, endless open topography, speculator economics and spectator con-sumerism, and, of course, the car have determined Houston's free-wheeling, vacuum-packed life and environment.

For spectator sports, one goes to the Astrodome to the southeast, which has created its own environment—the Astrodomain [*sic*] of assiduously culti-vated amusements and motels. Popular and commercial culture are well served in Houston. There is also high, or middle culture, for which the "brutalist" forms of the Alley Theater by New York architect Ulrich Franzen, and the neutral packaging of Jones Hall for the performing arts, by the Houston firm of Caudill, Rowlett, Scott, have been created. They stand in the shadow of the downtown oil industry giants that have provided their funding.

Farther south on Main are the Fine Arts Museum, with its handsome ex-tension by Mies van der Rohe, and the Contemporary Arts Association build-ing, a sharp-edged, metal trapezoid by Gunnar Birkets. They cling together among odd vacant lots in a state of decaying or becoming, next to a psychoana-lytic center.

Because the city has no zoning, these surreal juxtapositions prevail. A ham-burger stand closes the formal vista of Philip Johnston's delicate, Miesian ar-cade at St. Thomas University. Transitional areas, such as Westheimer, not only mirror the city's untrammeled development in 10-year sections, but are freely altered as old houses are turned into new shops and restaurants, unhampered by zoning taboos. (Conventionally zoned cities simply rezone their deteriorating older residential neighborhoods to save their tax base and facilitate the same economic destiny. This process just takes a little longer.)

Houston's web of freeways is the consummate example of the 20-century phenomenon known as the commercial strip. The route of passage attracts sales, services and schlock in continuous road-oriented structures—gas stations, drive-ins and displays meant to catch the eye and fancy at 60 miles an hour. There are fixed and mobile signs, and signs larger than buildings ("buildingboards," according to students of the Pop environment). Style, extracted as symbols, becomes a kind of sign in itself, evoking images from Rapunzel to Monticello. There are miles of fluttering metallic pennants (used cars), a giant lobster [*sic*] with six shooters, cowboy hat and scarf (seafood), a turning, life-size plaster bull (Charolais Breeders Association), and a revolving neon piano. The strip is full of intuitive wit, invention and crass, but also real creativity—a breathtaking affront to normal sensibility that is never a bore.

Directly behind the freeways, one short turn takes the driver from the strip into pine and live oak-alleyed streets of comfortable and elegant residential communities (including the elite and affluent River Oaks). They have maintained their environmental purity by deed restrictions passed on from one generation to another.

Beyond these enclaves, anything goes. Residential development is a spin-the-wheel happening that hops, skips and jumps outward, each project seemingly dropped from the sky—but always on the freeway. The southwest section, which was prairie before the 1950s, is now the American Dream incarnate. There is a continuing rivalry of you-name-it styles that favor French and Anglo-Saxon labels and details. If you live in Westminster, authentic-looking London street signs on high iron fences frame views of the flat Texas plains. You know you're home when you get to Le Cour de Roi or Robin Hood Dell.

Because Houston is an urban invention, this kind of highly salable make-believe supplies instant history and architecture; it is an anchor to time and place throughout centuries of civilization—identity, intimacy, scale, complexity, style—are simply created out of whole cloth, or whole prairie, with unabashed commercial eclecticism. How else to establish a sense of place or community, to indicate differences where none exist?

Houston is a continuous series of such shocks. Its private patronage, on which the city depends for its public actions, has a cosmic range. There is the superb, *echt*-Houston eccentricity of Judge Roy Hofheinz's personal quarters in the Astrodome, done in a kind of Astrobaroque of throne chairs, gold phones and temple dogs, with a pick-a-religion, fake stone chapel (good for bullfighters or politicians who want to meditate), shooting gallery and Presidential suite, tucked into the periphery of the stadium, complete with views of the Astros and Oilers. At the other end of the esthetic scale there is the Rothko Chapel, where the blood-dark paintings of the artist's pre-suicide days have been brought together by Dominique de Menil—a place of overwhelming, icy death. One welcomes the Texas sunshine.

***

Houston is not totally without planned features. It has large and handsome parks and the landscaped corridor of the Buffalo Bayou that are the result of philanthropic forethought. There are universities and a vast medical center.

But no one seems to feel the need for the public vision that older cities have of a hierarchy of places and buildings, an organized concept of function and form. Houston has a downtown singularly without amenities. The fact that money and population are flowing there from the rest of the country is considered cause for celebration, not for concern with the city's quality. This city bets on a different and brutal kind of distinction—of power; motion and sheer energy. Its values are material fulfillment, mobility and mass entertainment. Its returns are measured on its commercial investments. These contemporary ideals have little to do with the deeper or subtler aspects of the mind or spirit, or even with the more complex, human pleasure potential of a hedonistic culture.

When we build a new city, such as Houston, it is quite natural that we build in this image, using all our hardware to serve its uses and desires. We create new values and new dimensions in time and space. The expanded, mobile city deals in distance and discontinuity; it "explodes" community. It substitutes fantasy for history. Houston is devoted to moon shots, not moon-viewing. The result is a significant, instructive and disquieting city form.

What Houston possesses to an exceptional degree is an extraordinary, un-limited vitality. One wishes that it had a larger conceptual reach, that social and cultural and human patterns were as well understood as dollar dynamism. But this kind of vitality is the distinguishing mark of a great city in any age. And Houston today is the American present and future. It is an exciting and disturbing place. ★

PHILLIP LOPATE

Phillip Lopate [b. 1943] is likely the University of Houston creative writing faculty member who took the greatest interest in Houston as a city, and, for that matter, as a problem. Here he attempts to reconcile his fondness for the city, and his recognition that, as a city, it has numerous deficiencies—some of which, such as a shortage of public spaces, have been ameliorated.

From *Against Joie de Vivre*: Houston Hide-and-Seek

DRIVING ALONG KIRBY AVENUE LATE AT night—a nondescript nowhere corridor with billboards and fast-food stands and darkness, a way to get from one place to another but without much profile in it-self—you are sucked in, as with so much of Houston, invited farther and farther along with no real opposition, nothing to bounce off of, until you notice that the place you're sucked into is your own inner self. Somewhere, always just beyond reach, is the city, all that flat, exploding, diffuse, strip shopping center galaxy, outside, but never bigger than, one's car window. The automobile is a moving monk's cell, it forces you back on your thoughts, while only marginally attending the vaguely urban streets. "Perhaps only through a kind of inattention, the most benevolent form of betrayal, is one faithful to a place" writes architect Aldo Rossi. If so, Houston invites fidelity; it is a strangely nonimposing environment.

Too much is made of the explanation that Houston lacks zoning, as though the presence of a saloon next to a private convent school could explain the weirdness of this place. All big cities have such surreal juxtapositions. No, what makes Houston so peculiarly itself is the alternation of being and nothingness. Driving around Houston, one grows conscious of that rhythm of negative and positive space, the lacunae, the gaps between teeth, the no-man's-land of vacant lots, speculatively held, which Nature has been busy reclaiming with high weeds and broken cars, rusting abandoned machine parts, mini-swamps, since, as we know, nature abhors a vacuum.

So do developers, but sometimes the economy is simply too sluggish for them to make their move, thank God. We owe to Houston's recession the continuing existence of the Fourth Ward, that amazing shantytown of shotgun wood-frame houses and churches and rib joints and poor blacks sitting on porches, a bit of Mississippi Delta that trembles just beyond the itchy paw of downtown. The Fourth Ward is historically important, the oldest black urban settlement in Texas, originally occupied by families from East Texas and Louisiana cotton farms who built modified versions of the old slave cabins, adding front porches for coolness and communal life. The city has been neglecting the area for decades, stingy with garbage pickups, sewer maintenance, nonpotable water pipes, as if hoping the district will disintegrate of its own accord or that one good fire will clear the land for redevelopment. But the Fourth Ward obstinately holds on.

Houston became officially integrated only in the mid-1960s, through a coalition of black organizers, Texas liberals (a doughty breed), clergymen, and moderate businessmen who saw the writing on the wall. The change occurred without anything like the degree of ugly incident that took place elsewhere; Houston has a justifiable reputation around the state for tolerance and progressive politics. However, there is still a good deal of de facto segregation—or racial distance, if you will—in residential and recreational activity. Much of the vitality of Houston's nightlife, for instance, is hidden below the surface, in the barrios and ethnic neighborhoods, and you need a guide to help you explore.

Take the zydeco. I was first brought to a zydeco dance hall, the Continental Lounge, by my friend Lorenzo Thomas, a black poet. It was a big square barn with red walls and couples hugging in the middle. Somehow it reminded me of Renoir's paintings of country dance halls, except all the dancers were black. Many of the couples on the raised wood-planked dance floor were middle-aged or gray-haired: some dressed sharply in three-piece suits, others wore simple farm clothes; a few were in cowboy hats. Even the teenagers looked countrified, sweet-natured, and somehow from an earlier era. They danced to the music called zydeco, that haunting harmonic blend of sweet French Cajun and piquant Negro blues. The accordion-saxophone combination supplies the main spice; the rhythm section consisted of drums, a bass guitar, and, what struck me as most timeless, a man wearing an aluminum washboard over his chest, thumping himself to play.

We took seats at a table on the side and ordered beer and hot boudin sausages. The dance floor was packed, yet not claustrophobically so; the same swaying, relaxed motion passed from body to body. It was mostly touch dancing, and the strong rhythm more or less dictated what to do, as I discovered when my date and I (the only two whites) took the floor.

Individual styles gradually began to emerge from the dancers. One gray-sideburned, thickset man in a white suit and white tie rooster-strutted around his amused partner, inventing a little drama of attraction and rejection, working himself into a lather of romantic feeling, pausing only to take out a red bandana and dot his forehead. An intense young pair breezed through a slick, economical bunny hop. Nearby, another man, drunk, was dancing by himself with a half-grin that seemed to repeat the curve of the bags under his eyes. A black policeman took the mike and wished everyone a happy new year (it was mid-January) and announced that the police force was there to help so they should cooperate with the police in the coming year; nobody listened much, though they weren't rude to him either.

Having diplomatically left us alone at first, people now began coming over and extending hospitality. The white-suited man invited us to his home and to be his guest at other zydeco events. It seemed that zydeco moved from place to place every week like a traveling fair. There were no newspaper ads; you just had to *know* by seeing the Xeroxed handbills or belonging to the proper information circuit.

Since then I've returned on occasion to that strange, beautiful zydeco milieu, sometimes at the Continental or in the parish hall of a church out by the airport. It's just one of the many near-invisible worlds that make up buried Houston, the real Houston each resident seeks out individually, for want of a discernible mass focus. You end up putting together an interior city from the handful of locations that are charged with personal meaning. The milieu to which I mainly belong—the intelligentsia or "art crowd"—is another hardy scene that nevertheless eludes the world's image of Houston, maybe because intellectuals are less easily packaged into mythology than cowboy boots.

The art crowd consists of about two hundred visual artists, gallery owners, curators, architects, historians, writers, critics, musicians, dancers, patrons, students, hangers-on, and dilettanti who bump into each other year after year at the same art openings, performances, parties, and the same ten restaurants. There is much running around in packs, a hedge against loneliness as well as intimacy; sometimes two eventually pair off and marry, or friends quarrel and avoid each other, finally growing friendly again, because there aren't that many people to talk to, the cast of characters is so limited. Every once in a while a new curator or artistic celebrity moves to town and is feted, courted, scrutinized, privately dissected. Every so often, too, one of the regulars, like a Chekov character who keeps sighing, "I must go to Moscow," actually picks himself up after years of threats to do so and moves to New York or Los Angeles or Washington, D.C. These defectors later return for visits, wistfully reporting that they have never been able to find elsewhere anything like that warm camaraderie of the Houston art crowd. On the plus side, the art scene here is exceptionally cohesive, supportive, and loyal, on the minus, this close-knit courtesy has so far stifled the development of honest, tough-minded public criticism, which means that some local artists are never challenged to go beyond producing half-baked work.

One of the hallowed places for the art crowd is Brown Auditorium, in the Museum of Fine Arts. A splendid hall—and here I have only praise for Mies's handiwork—graced by perfect acoustics and sight lines, its scale allows for both intimacy and formality. With its ambitious programs of repertory cinema, poetry readings, chamber music concerts, art history lectures, panel symposia, community meetings, and so on, Brown Auditorium functions as a truly democratic space, a sort of Town Hall for Houston's culture-hungry.

Another hallowed space is the Brazos Bookstore, which is surely one of the best literary bookstores in the country. For years it has been at the heart of the city's artistic life, an agora where one drops in expecting to meet friends, or to steal a few minutes' spicy if harried conversation with the impish, punning owner of the store, Karl Kilian, who will also tell you about the latest choreographic whiz or minimalist composer coming to town, for whose concert Karl happens to have a bunch of tickets to unload. We authors come by the Brazos to attend book-signing parties and readings, but also secretly to check where Karl has placed our own books and perhaps to bug him about it afterward.

The universities in town are of course great attractors and multipliers of culture. Rice University has an air of placid gentility; its Byzantine Revival quadrangle by Cram and Goodhue (who designed St. Bartholomew's Church in New York) is perhaps the most harmonious campus ensemble in America. The University of Houston exudes more of a nitty-gritty, messy, working-class atmosphere, as befits a state public institution. The University of St. Thomas, a small Catholic school with a strong Thomistic bent, has a trim, effectively severe campus designed by Philip Johnson in his Mondrian phase. All of these schools have played host to extraordinary cultural moments in the city's history.

The Rothko Chapel is another special place in my interior map of Houston. How many times have I trotted visitors from out of town over to that shrine and watched their differing reactions—some awed, some mildly impressed, others left cold—and with each I have tended to agree. I've sometimes allowed myself to think (blasphemously, in this town) that those paintings are not as great as one might have hoped from Rothko. They are from his late, blackened period and do have a grim grandeur. My feelings toward them are as changeable as the natural illumination that filters through the chapel's skylight from hour to hour: I've gone there in the mornings when the building is empty, save for a long-hair meditating on a cushion; I've stared at a purplish-black canvas so long I was spooked when I looked down at my green Adidas and saw ebony shadows in them; I've felt peace and panic and pleasure and indifference and itchiness in that sacramental cube, wondering where the recessed niches led; in short, the Rothko Chapel plays back to me, for better or worse, my own mind. Then there are those "ecumenical" occasions when the chapel is packed, hosting a Sufi whirling dervish troupe, a Steve Reich concert, a human rights award ceremony—or a memorial service. Each time the art crowd loses one of its own we pour into the Rothko Chapel to comfort each other. The occasion is sad, but there is some consolation in realizing that we are, in fact, a community still holding together. Precisely because Houston's art-making pool is so finite—unlike New York's or Paris's, where the inexhaustible riches of cultural life render it impossible for any one artist or writer even to meet all of his/her peers—this town values its creative people, and gives them a chance to play a larger civic role.

***

Houston is perceived by the outside world as a thoroughly modern environment, a sterile mélange of concrete and glass, so that people who have never been here are surprised when you tell them that, first, it is an exorbitantly verdant place, and second, that it retains much that is old. For myself, who am by nature more attached to the past than the present, this evidence of the old is very healing. I keep trying to root out the vestiges of old Houston, to understand what it was like before I came. My archaeological itch has taken me to the various cemeteries around town, where I stare at headstones and fantasize about the days when people routinely picnicked among the graves if the weather was nice; it has taken me though the charming old residential neighborhoods like the Montrose, the Heights, the Binz, Southampton, MacGregor Drive—which comprise for me the true heart of Houston, with their wonderfully diverse stock of vernacular bungalows, split-level ranch houses, and Bauhaus-style cottages made elegant or cozy by their owners' loving touches; it has taken me into the old tumbledown wards and the new ethnic areas in search of a polyglot, international Houston; it has taken me into the orderly, regulated suburbs like Kingwood, where clotheslines are forbidden and where the American Dream has been achieved to a degree that scares the hell out of me; and into the abandoned suburbs far beyond Loop 610, where the American Dream suddenly stopped in its tracks and ran out on its mortgage. In a vain effort to grasp firsthand the city's economy, I have ridden around the obscure area of the Ship Channel, whose construction sixty years ago catapulted Houston over Galveston into one of the major ports in North America (a fact one so often forgets, even living here); out by the oil fields where mechanical grasshoppers paw the ground; and through the enormous Medical Center, a virtual walled empire of

Disease (health care, not the oil business, is Houston's largest employer). But riding around and imagining can teach you only so much, and the history of Houston is not that easy to come by. This is not a city that wears its past on its sleeve. Quite the contrary, it is an amnesiac city, one that keeps forgetting its intriguing antecedents in a headlong rush to embrace the shock of the new (or the *schlock* of the new, like Jean-Michel Jarre's laser light show during Texas Sesquicentennial Year).

In the City of the Future, even native Houstonians fall into the habit of waiting expectantly for the Age of Culture to commence with the next new arts facility's construction (a necessary fund-raising strategy, I suppose), losing sight of the fact that the city has always had its share of culture, from the Ballet Russe de Monte Carlo and other major dance companies who have performed here, to Leopold Stokowski holding sway at the Houston Symphony, to locally developed writers like O. Henry, William Goyen, June Arnold, Donald Barthelme, Vassar Miller, Larry McMurtry. Streets have been named after the generals of the Texas War of Independence, but not in commemoration of the heroes of the common people, like Lydia Mendoza, the great Chicana singer who made her home in the Houston Heights, or Lightnin' Hopkins, the blues artist who lived and died here. Houston is profligate with its anticipations (the latest being a plan to snare a Disney operation for the Space Center), stingy with its memories.

Nowhere has this civic amnesia wreaked more damage than on the urban environment itself. In the last thirty years, the old, retail, walking downtown, a congenial gathering place with department stores, movie palaces, and eateries, was for the most part demolished and replaced by a colder set of freestanding corporate towers alternating with surface parking lots. One is no longer invited to dally, meander, window-shop. This single-use downtown closes up at six o'clock; at night or on weekends, it resembles nothing more than a huge deserted warehouse.

Interestingly, Houstonians are very proud of their new slab tower central business district, which they see as a triumph of architectural up-to-dateness. And indeed, several of the new buildings are architecturally interesting, and—seen from a distance—there is something inspiring about the skyline of Houston as a whole; those chimerical salmon- and jade-colored reflecting glass surfaces vying for the eye's attention with the latest Mayan-topped or Dutch Guild Hall-inspired postmodernist skyscraper. It's not surprising that Houston became the sketch pad for Philip Johnson and other postmodernist practitioners. As critic M. Christine Boyer has written: "Architecture made to be seen from the road demands an image which is immediately understandable to a public concentrating more on traffic than on a building's details or structure. This architecture must offer a spontaneous theatrical spectacle manipulating images in simple combinations and patterns that are part of our collective recall. . . ." This is sixty-miles-per-hour architecture, and the freeway offers the best vantage point from which to experience Houston as an urban place. The problems begin when one descends to street level and finds oneself surrounded by such an unnuanced, impermeably monumental stage set. Since Houston's downtown blocks are so short (250 square feet), a single contemporary office tower will usually occupy a whole block: there is rarely any sense of variegated, historically layered street wall; instead, one finds that odd condition of constructional uniformity that architect Jacqueline Robertson has called "the Hiroshima effect."

There are social as well as aesthetic drawbacks to the new downtown. Regrettably, at the same historical moment that Houston officially brought in racial integration, it converted its downtown into a monolithically white-collar (if not white) universe, while redistributing its shopping and popular entertainment functions to outlying malls, where preexisting residential patterns would reinforce de facto segregation. The only type of entertainment that the city kept downtown was high culture: a performing arts complex for opera, ballet, the symphony, and repertory theater, whose ticket prices and cultural vocabulary tend to exclude the working class and poor. The old social-mix role of downtown was further diluted by an underground tunnel system, put in with the new office buildings, which leached an entire retail economy from ground level, taking much of the area's street life with it. Whereas any stranger can happen upon interesting shops while wandering a city's streets, Houston's tunnels are a maze into which only those who work downtown venture. In these minimalist corridors, slight differentiations of material or lighting seem like giddy refinements, and the sudden entry into a radial underground "plaza" becomes a thrilling event. Ultimately, though, it is a mole's life, with torpor-inducing vista restrictions and monotonous duplications of retail offerings—soup and salad bars, travel agencies, novelty card shops—lopsidedly geared for a lunch-hour trade.

The tunnels are part of Houston's general tendency to avoid the street (i.e., the weather), a tendency that has yielded skyways between buildings and giant interiorized shopping malls like the Galleria, which have all the élan of an airport terminal. Actually, Houston's weather is not so terrible: our best-kept secret is that the city has one of the mildest and pleasantest climates of any North American metropolis—for about seven months. If the remaining five come close to being insufferably hot or wet, that average is no worse than those of London, New York, Chicago, or New Orleans, all excellent walking cities. In my view, Houston has overdone this business of climate control: in moving so much of its life indoors for "comfort" it has developed a kind of unhealthy phobia against its own natural environment. It was the city's misfortune, in a way, that its building boom coincided with the advent of new air-conditioning technologies, which sealed off buildings from the outside street.

I think I could more easily accept the self-cannibalization of the old historical business district, knowing that it came at a period (the sixties and seventies) when disastrous urban renewal policies were gutting downtowns all over the United States, were it not for the fact that Houston continues to dismantle its historical heritage, or what is left of it. In addition to the Shamrock, the distinguished Medical Arts Building, the old Lamar Hotel where the city fathers used to decide policy over poker hands, and John Staub's graciously designed Crabbe House in River Oaks have all recently fallen to the wrecking ball; the exemplary, small-scaled Allen Parkway Village public housing complex in Fourth Ward was cynically allowed to deteriorate by the Housing Authority; it is now half boarded up (though its defenders have just gotten it added to the National Register of Historic Places). The grand Rice Hotel, with its majestic portico, is on its last legs, also boarded up and vulnerable to demolition; and the Pillot Building, a handsome example of nineteenth-century cast-iron architecture, was first neglected and then, in a sloppy repair job, de-roofed, promptly causing part of the building to collapse. A "facadectomy" (the facade saved like a Hollywood set, the rest cleared for a new office building) became its only option for survival.

Whenever I am away from Houston and try to picture it, what comes to mind are the white concrete silos of the American Rice Company elevators that rise like Egyptian pyramids above the greenish waters of Buffalo Bayou. The rice elevators are a noble example of pure industrial architecture and probably my favorite Houston structure; now they, too, stand in grave danger of demolition. If they can no longer turn a sufficient profit, surely some other recycled use can be found for them—even as architectural ruins. All development proposals for Houston agree that the waterfront-park area along Buffalo Bayou will play a key part in the city's future, and when that day comes, how we'll groan and tear our hair out, if we allow that chalky prominence to disappear.

It isn't just a matter of being sentimentally attached to old buildings, but of appreciating that cities need local landmarks to be spatially comprehensible, to be readable by their citizens. Whether it's an actual monument, or a commercial, industrial, or residential structure that stands out, by virtue of singular scale, materials, or design excellence, or a durable, gracious train terminal like Los Angeles's Union Station, landmarks create a sense of place around which memory and continuity accumulate. You need the big clock where lovers rendezvous, and you need that clock to stay in the same spot for one generation after another. Houston is sadly short of landmarks. It *has* history, but it doesn't go out of its way to make it visibly apparent.

Take Allen's Landing, the very spot, tradition tells us, where the city was founded by our very own Romulus and Remus in 1836. Granted, the Allen brothers were two New York land developers out to make a bundle, but still it's thrilling to be able to point to a spot and say, Here's where it all started. I was living in Houston for years before I even found out about Allen's Landing, and when I finally did visit the unmarked site along the bayou, lured by an arts organization benefit, I was amazed at how pretty it was, how luckily close it was to downtown, and what an appalling highway bridge had been allowed to be built almost directly over it, obscuring and overwhelming what should have been the city's ancestral heart.

I am forever looking backwards, I admit it. Still, when I ask a Houstonian to do the same, it is not to freeze the city in a static conservatism, or to prevent it from acting upon fresh visions, but so that, when it reaches for those visions, it can proceed from a more confident, mature sense of self, such as only comes from making peace with one's past. In order for a place to have a soul, it has to bear visible witness to a past. Without that manifestation of history, Houston will become what its detractors already claim it to be: a brash, thin-souled, post-modernist theme park. It is as necessary to create the past as to create the future. Again, this is not simply a matter of preserving what is already in our midst, but of coaxing from an analysis of the past those promising hints that were left undeveloped, and reforming the present defects accordingly. For instance, Hermann Park was meant to be our own Golden Gate Park or Central Park, but its original Olmstedian vision was blurred as acreage got nibbled away by hospital grabs, roadways connecting downtown with the Medical Center, and surface parking lots. It is still Houston's most popular and heavily used public space; the zoo is one of the few places in town where families of all social strata parade on a Sunday, and where the energy of urban life is both concentrated and mellowed. The Juneteenth blues concerts and Shakespeare in the Park at the Miller Outdoor Theater give us a glimpse of how lively this city could be. But Hermann Park needs nurturing, landscaping attention, and a retrieval of its initial "City Beautiful" impulse before its true scenic and recreational potential can be realized.

The Astrodome was once Houston's greatest achievement—"the Eighth Wonder of the World"—until domed stadia started cropping up everywhere. Built in the middle of Houston's love affair with the space program (and perhaps deriving its iconography more from NASA than from the sporting field), the Astrodome is like a flying saucer landed on a lunar landscape. There is no sur-rounding neighborhood to absorb or detain you here; once the game has ended, you have no choice but to head for the parking lot and sit in your car until an opening presents itself in the exit lane. Compare this situation to Wrigley Field, Madison Square Garden, or the Boston Garden, where fans can spill directly into the streets and walk off their exuberance or disappointment, or crowd into bars and subway trains and carry on. There are few opportunities to linger *en masse* in Houston after an event, to savor oneself as part of an emotional crowd. It wouldn't be bad, either, if a city park were landscaped beside the Astrodome, so that people could play catch with their kids before or after a game, or have a picnic under shade trees. The glory of Houston is in its trees. Yet whenever a new facility is built, it seems to always be aproned in harsh concrete.

Houston has a general lack of neighborhood parks, plazas, promenades, fountains—attractive public space where people can congregate to watch the spectacle of humanity and celebrate festivals and local rituals. In this sense, however friendly Houstonians as individuals are, the built environment wears a more hermetic face to outsiders, because there is so little effective public space to mediate between private homes and the impersonal workplace. It almost seems as though Houstonians have lost the habit of public space. One obvious reason for this atrophy is the privileging of the car at the expense of foot traffic and mass transit. Walking and public space have always been deeply intertwined: the great plazas and town squares did not bloom in a void; they were fed by rich circulation patterns of surrounding pedestrian streets.

In Houston, the rights of the pedestrian are held in contempt. For example, outside of downtown, contractors are not even required to reconstruct a public sidewalk after tearing it up to permit new construction. Try walking in most neighborhoods of Houston, even along major thoroughfares. If you are lucky you will find a semblance of sidewalk, one narrow square of concrete, usually cracked, buckled, roiling, edged on both sides by grass plots that, after a rain, resemble flooded rice paddies; it is difficult to walk two abreast and carry on a conversation, but even single-file you cannot advance very far without being stopped by a ditch; an impassable puddle, a miasma of weeds and vines, someone's property fence, or a parked car forcing you into a roadway—down which most Houstonians choose to walk (if they walk) anyway, daring the cars. Should you swerve in the other direction, you find yourself crossing someone's lawn, with the awkward sense of trespassing. Houston's badly kept sidewalks give off a blunt message, "Don't bother, take the car," which is particularly hostile to citizens who don't have cars.

Not that all areas are so inhospitable to pedestrians. Among the most agreeable sections to walk are the parallel avenues of North and South Boulevards, with their double lanes of live oaks touching over a lovely brick promenade and forming a nave of sunlight. Even on the hottest days of August, one feels invited to stroll down the shady esplanade and peek at the old Edwardian and neoclassical mansions on either side of the street. These boulevards make one realize how breathtaking a city this could be, since its climate is ideal for supporting any number of live oak avenues. Lately, the local civic associations have pledged themselves to an ambitious tree-planting operation downtown and elsewhere, the fruits of which may take fifty years to be appreciated, but at least it is a start. Houston could certainly use a few broad landscaping or street design maneuvers, like real boulevards, to bring about a more harmonious whole. Until now, the town's wealthy benefactors have shown little interest in urban design; we are lacking not in millionaire-donated hospital pavilions or cultural edifices but in those gestures that would help bring the city itself together more as a work of art.

Such synthesizing gestures need not be pharaonically expensive; they can also be quiet, subtle. We have a good example in the blocks around the Menil Collection, which the locals call "Do-Ville" (after Dominique de Menil). First, all the cottages that the Menils owned in the area were painted gray, giving these blocks a uniform look. Then a museum was built that related with sublime contextual tact to the gray wooden houses, being itself a sort of oversized gray clapboard house. So something new is created that completely respects the neighborhood and its past—even, in this case, a partly manufactured past.

On the other hand, to cite a hellish example of lack of design, the Post Oak area around the Galleria shopping mall is noteworthy for having the greatest concentration of buildings it is possible to assemble without at the same time achieving anything like an urban texture. Today's architects are trained to build freestanding objects; quite apart from whether the result is good or bad architecture, what you get when you keep placing one freestanding object next to another is a proliferation of objects. What are needed are not so much objects as *places*. Much of Houston suffers from floating placelessness. Of course, what I am describing is not unique to Houston. It is only that Houston, having been at the forefront, is sometimes blamed for the phenomenon, as when some architectural critic warns against the "Houstonization" of his fair city. Obviously, there are larger, global forces at work that account for the increase in spatial privatization and the decrease in the art of city-making.

In Houston, we have all sorts of wonderful excuses and rationalizations for our deficiencies in good public space and urban design, which we trot out enthusiastically: the weather (though many South American cities abound in lively outdoor plazas); the lack of zoning (but zoning would not necessarily bring improved public space either); the rapid population growth (still, Chicago grew from 300,000 to nearly two million between 1871 and 1900, and pioneered in urban design); the low-density spread (then what to make of many Scandinavian cities? besides, downtown Houston is hardly low density); the prohibitive cost of public space in the present economy (was it ever cheap?); and the free-enterprise, anti-tax climate in this part of the country (perhaps this is beginning to change with the voters' approval of a mass transit system).

Houston's resistance to city planning strikes me as partly a way of putting off acceptance of its urban nature. Anti-city values saturate the state's rugged-individualist, agrarian, Chamber of Commerce religion, Texana; and Houston, as the largest city in a state that has become predominantly urban but refuses to recognize the fact, has long been caught in the contradictions of that denial. The creation of public space is after all the most self-consciously urban act that a municipality can undertake. It signifies a city's maturation, through the recognition of its responsibilities to the public to exist as a collectivity. Houston is often spoken of as an adolescent: the question is whether this immaturity is a phase (albeit a protracted one) or a permanent personality trait.

Some have argued that older cities had more of a need for good public space (as well as cafes, pubs, clubs, and community halls), because people's homes were generally less comfortable. In offering its citizens a much higher standard of domestic comfort, this argument goes, Houston represents a new type of suburbanized city where private convenience reduces the necessity, and the yearning, for public interaction. Perhaps, though I can't believe that the political vitality and conviviality of urban areas are not somehow diminished in the process. Still, most Houstonians do seem at peace with their city, find it reasonably easy to navigate, and don't seem to feel the same ache of placelessness that I, as a transplanted New Yorker, intermittently experience. For instance, I can't help noticing the oddity of two major thoroughfares crossing each other without anything more dramatic than a 7-Eleven convenience store and gas station to mark the juncture. It seems to me that major intersections should be commemorated by an intensification of city life—a department store, a big movie theater, a dance hall, a public square or park, *something*—but Houstonians do not seem to share this uneasiness. Each Friday and Saturday night I look at the cars piling into the intersection of Montrose and Westheimer streets, drawn by the magnetic attractions of these crossroads, and I think, Wouldn't it be better for these young people to have something to *do* once they get there, besides honk their horns and participate in gridlock? But no, they seem to like to sit bumper to bumper, perhaps entertaining the fantasy of picking up some cuties in the next car. Who knows?

The problem with looking at Houston from a strictly urbanistic perspective is that one inevitably falls into the trap of judging it by the cherished traditional values of urban form (real streets to walk in, real public spaces to be in). By these standards Houston must be seen as a failure, even while they ignore the degree to which it seems to work on its own terms. On the other hand, the proclamation of local champions to "Let Houston be Houston" has a smug Panglossian ring and dodges responsibility for correcting the very real deficiencies of the place. If you ask me, Houston will never become a great, "world-class" city. But it's an intriguing, evocative, comfortable, one-of-a-kind place with plenty of surprises. So it seems that once again I'm parked at the intersection between Tenderness and Chagrin, where I'll leave it alone for the present. ★

JOEL GARREAU

Joel Garreau [b. 1948] was a long-time *Washington Post* reporter. A series of articles that he wrote about the new types of urban development that are growing on the "edges" of many cities led to the book *Edge City*. Here he looks at the Galleria area as a relatively positive example of this type of development. His is one of the most optimistic views of Houston's often-maligned pattern of development.

From *Edge City*: Texas

"HOUSTON IS MUCH FUNKIER THAN PEOPLE think," says John Ashby Wilburn, editor of the *Houston Press*, the arts and entertainment weekly. "When I first came here, I just felt like I'd stepped off the edge of the world, that I'd made a horrible mistake. In New York, everything is so above the surface, you see so many things because everything is so squeezed together. It took me a year to realize that (a), there were interesting people here, and (b), I could find them. You do bump into them, but it takes longer, because they're farther apart."

Jennifer Womack can testify to that. One spring morning in the Galleria, at all three levels of the rails above the ice rink, people were stopped, gazing at this arresting brunette in a loose orange Reese's Pieces T-shirt and black Spandex tights. She would start at one end of the ice, dig in, and, at midpoint, she would achieve escape velocity and leap, spin, twirl, and then leap, and leap again, to spin to a stop in a bursting shower of ice flakes.

Phew, you could hear spectators exhale, explosively.

She would intently glide back to her precise starting point, eyes down, a study in concentration, and go through the same routine. Again and again. Two dark-skinned middle-aged gentlemen were among the spectators. They appeared to speak little English. They made hand gestures at the only other figure on the ice, a man who obviously was finding it all he could do simply to keep his rented skates under him. They twirled their index fingers as if mixing a drink. Go ahead, try a spin like that, they mimed. That gave everybody on the rails a good laugh.

Jennifer Womack, it turns out, once skated with the Ice Follies. Then she fell in love with a man in the "awl bidness"—the Texas oil business—and followed him to Houston. There she found herself in culture shock. She emphasizes the word "shock" with her light hazel eyes open wide. Home to her was the cool, laid-back land just north of San Francisco across the Golden Gate, in Marin County. In Houston she was utterly lost. The different pace of life. How loud people spoke. The flat coastal plain. The Gulf heat. She is still able to recall in considerable detail sitting home for months, experimenting with air-conditioner settings.

That has changed, though. She has begun to feel comfortable in Texas. "Did you know that armadillos can jump?" she asked. But she doesn't think she could have made it if she hadn't stumbled on the Galleria and its rink.

She made friends there, on the ice. She found people with whom she had much in common.

"I owe this place my sanity," she says. "I found community here."

***

Trolling around within sight of the Galleria area's office towers, seeking out civilization—hunting for mine canaries, if you will—you discover that the 1980s' oil bust had interesting side effects on Houston. There was an explosion of intriguing ethnic neighborhoods—Vietnamese, Hong Kong Chinese, Salvadoran, Honduran, Iranian, subcontinent Indian. Houston was a bargain for immigrants in the 1980s. Cheap place to buy a house, buy an office building, start a business. Now that the place has bottomed out and is turning around, you find a plethora of diverse shops. Peel off the Southwest Freeway at Hillcroft, outside Loop 610, and there's a discount warehouse sari emporium.

Didn't used to always be this way in Texas.

Some things never change, though. The *Texas Monthly* crowd is especially high on a restaurant called the Bombay Grill, so that is where the crowd ends up for dinner. Those who know absolutely nothing about Indian cuisine let those who do order lamb shahi korma, chicken tikka masala, peas pullao, and a sauce called raita.

Mickey Kapoor, the owner of the place, then asks if the table would like "bray-yad." Eager to learn as much as possible about the exotic customs of colorful lands, the stranger in the crowd goes up for the bait like a marlin.

Certainly. Great idea. Now what, exactly, is "bray-yad"?

You know. Bray-yad. The stuff on either side of the meat in a sandwich? Slices of bray-yad? Pronounced in Texas the same as in southern India?

The next evening, somewhat more seriously, Kapoor talks about the countries he has lived in, and the cultures he has encountered, and what led a nice Hindu boy like him to try to bring civilization to an Edge City in Texas.

Bringing cosmopolitan, authentic, high-end Indian cuisine to Houston has provided him with more than his share of adventures, he acknowledges. There were all the people who wanted to know what kind of Indian restaurant his was. Navajo? Comanche? Then, when he was running the place called the Taj Mahal, there were the people who wanted to talk to Mr. Mahal, the short guy with the glasses. All the waiters learned to say, Oh yeah, you mean Taj, and sent Kapoor out front.

For reasons that are inexplicable even now, the location of his first place was on the southeast side of Houston, on the way to the Edge City of Clear Lake–NASA, three miles from a saloon and dance hall called Gilley's. Remember the movie *Urban Cowboy?* Remember the mechanical bull? Remember the pickups and the shotgun racks? That was Gilley's. Real "Bubba and Skeeter country," Kapoor recalls, in his clipped Empire sing-song.

Yeah, I've really done my bit for civilizing this market, he deadpans. There was this redneck who sauntered up to Kapoor once as he was shopping for a car. Jabbing a middle finger in Kapoor's chest, he bellowed that he believed he'd located a "stupid Iranian." That indictment was a real hazard to your health in Texas at the time. No, sir, Kapoor explained, sir. "I am a stupid Indian, sir." Reincarnation or no, passing for a Persian was the last way Kapoor figured he needed to die.

But getting more serious, Kapoor notes there is a difference between a beautiful city and a beautiful society. Kapoor really hoped that this strip-shopping-center world he found himself in at the Bombay Grill was a transitory phase for Houston and for America. That it was part of an evolution toward a finer structure. "Things do happen by accident, but they do evolve to a higher form of perfection, which lends credence to the concept of God," he notes. "Because, you know, whatever we do, we are propelled forward by some natural forces beyond our comprehension and our immediate senses."

As far as he could tell, though, "we haven't changed much from the village concept except that these Edge Cities are self-contained little villages intertwined and interconnected and compacted into a larger thing called the metropolis. Eventually, in my mind, a perfect form of this would be that in a particular neighborhood everything should be so accessible that a final form will develop; even, I think, where you won't have to drive that much. You will work closer to home; you will have shopping closer to home; and it is only in cases of extreme necessity that you will do the traveling and commuting. The ecology, the air—taking all this in consideration, the sooner we go with this into areas where people work where they reside, or reside where they work, people can stay closer to home; it eventually will resolve some of the more troubling issues."

Right now, Kapoor feels, the reason his restaurant's neighborhood is interesting is that it is on a border between the fancy environs of the Galleria area and "the large and very sizable Indian community that lives within a five-mile radius. There are Indian grocery stores, Indian clothing stores, Indian appliance stores."

Indeed, you talk about cosmopolitan climes. No more than two miles from the Galleria there is something called the Fiesta Market. The simplest way to describe it is as a kind of Third World village market run by a sophisticated, knowledgeable, sympathetic, and sensitive American outfit with an organizational firepower reminiscent of Safeway.

The sign over the entrance to the Fiesta says WELCOME, then BIEN-VENUDO, and then goes on in five more languages in which not even the script, much less the alphabet, is familiar. This place is so international, so sophisticated, so diverse, that all the *important* signs are in English. Just English. The multilingual possibilities and combinations are just too hard. Nobody has enough else in common. Makes your head hurt.

Yet the prices are right, the selection stunning; and Fiesta has become a chain that is carving up market share left and right in Houston, even in Anglo neighborhoods.

Why is the Indian community out here? I ask Kapoor. Out past the Loop? Out past 610? Not in the older, denser areas? I thought Indians were accustomed to density.

"Density is something they would like to get away from," says Kapoor, who is Rajasthani. He is from that tan, desert area between Gujarat and the Punjab, up against the border with Pakistan—not much farther from either China or Afghanistan than Houston is from Dallas.

"Yeah, sure. It's like privacy. In India you don't get a thing like privacy. There's no such thing. Because you live in a house with thirty other members of the family. But here, you get your first taste of privacy. It becomes very precious all of a sudden. Oh, yes."

The previous day I had chatted with Stephen Fox, who teaches at Rice, and who had just written the *Houston Architectural Guide*. We had been talking about what was wrong with Houston, and what had to be made right. And he, quite independently, mentioned that he had students from around the world, and the first thing he asked them to do was write a paper describing the architectural history of their home places.

He said he had been struck especially by the Malaysians, who described their place in terms that to him seemed idyllic. Tightly knit. Dense. Walkable. Surrounded by community that was generations thick and centuries deep. But it was they especially, he reported, who seemed most to love Houston. They were singularly articulate about the limits of where they came from. The stifling rigidity. The paternalism. Yes, Houston is nuts. But it's so much fun. There is such individualism. You have so much freedom.

"I take that for granted," Fox noted sheepishly.

I tell all this to Kapoor, who says, "The thing is that Americans—native-born Americans—I don't know whether they understand it, but they probably undervalue the elbow room they have. That is commonly known as freedom.

"The liberty that we have over here. It's not comparable with anything anywhere in the world. You cannot compare, not even Canada. Not England, not Germany. Not even close. The enjoyable thing over here is that you can express yourself. You can just be yourself. You can be left alone if you want to be left alone. Not so in even the more advanced or self-professed civilized countries of the world. And I have lived in ten or eleven of them.

"When I say Americans don't understand it, people ask what I mean. The basic things are taken for granted over here because they are just given to you at birth, like a kid given a Cadillac on his sixteenth birthday. You know, simple things like ten people can get together and start a political party if you want to. You can deride anyone you want to. You can write a letter to the newspaper if you want to. You can just assemble on the street and start talking.

"You can start a business if you want to. You can quit a job if you want to and get another one if you want to. To an American these are everyday things. You can turn on the telly, turn on the radio, listen to any station you want to, read any newspaper you want to, adhere to any belief you want to. To Americans these are like, so what is the big deal?

"Well, the big deal is that you cannot do this in any other place in the world. In England you cannot just go and start a business. I could never have a restaurant this big. First of all the hindrance would be getting a lease. They would want references. Money in the bank. Need everything cash up front. You have to belong to a certain class of people over there.

"In New York, Houston, you can sell an idea and fructify the idea into something solid. Very, very different to do it any other place in the world.

"Civilization is not just physical attributes or the structure of buildings. It is the quality of life, the psychological impact. The evolution, I think, cannot be on the level of just the structure. It must be the people who live in the structure, too. How are we going to be thinking?

"What I think we must think now, about Edge City, is that this is screwed

246

up. If this is evolution, then I'm happy. But if it is closer to the final product, then it is very scary.

"I am not saying that everything that is haphazard has to be controlled. It's not what you do, it's a state of the mind—being urbane. An urbane person, to me, is someone who, in a fire, can stand in line and wait to get out. Know which way things are going. Not just dress up and at the critical moment go bonkers. That is not very civil.

"Houston is already there. The one thing that impressed me about Houston when I came here twelve years ago was the basic friendliness. That 'howdy' attitude they had. That they still do. Even if they think my first name is Taj. If it comes from the goodness of their hearts, that is quite acceptable to me.

"It is a sense of community. You have to create the conditions. Create the environment, for someone to evolve to that final product.

"What are you wanting, eventually? A pretty structure? Or a pretty society?" ★

TERRENCE DOODY

Terrence Doody teaches courses on the novel at Rice University and at the Women's Institute of Houston. He is the author of *Confession and Community in the Novel* and *Among Other Things: A Description of the Novel*. He is currently working on a book on the literature of the city. Doody frequently writes about Houston and city life in general, and for several years served on the editorial board of *Cite: The Architecture and Design Review of Houston*.

Immanent Domains

CELEBRATION STATION IS AN ENTERTAIN-ment complex at 6767 Southwest Freeway, on the inside feeder road between Bellaire Boulevard and Westpark. It consists of a dark arcade filled with electronic games, children at parties, and unbearable noise. There is also a go-cart track, a pool for bumper boats, and three eighteen-hole miniature golf courses laid up and down a fake "mountain" that rises to about forty feet in height. The mountain has concrete appliqués painted the color of sandstone, a waterfall and slow stream, an open-ended cave that you play through, and a number of holes that step several levels down the terraced layout. It is a very neat place and, by far, our family's favorite venue for miniature golf.

One very hot Sunday afternoon last summer, I noticed a Latino family—husband and wife, three very small children, and a grandmother, all in black—not playing miniature golf, but strolling the courses. They were, I realized, "tourists" taking in the scenic vistas and dramatic overview of US Highway 59. It was a moment of some pathos.

However, I have wondered since then if pathos was the right response. We were there for essentially the same reason they were, but we were disguised as golfers and it cost us $30. At no cost at all, they were improvising their pleasure in a city with few sidewalks, fewer parks, and elevated prospects available only from freeway overpasses. They were taking a walk, and redefining the city for themselves in the ambiguity of the commercial space that can so nicely facilitate this kind of appropriation. They started me thinking about the nature of place, about public places like entertainment facilities and malls, about our definitions of privacy in public, and, of course, about cell phones.

We usually experience places from the outside in. They are there already before we arrive and are defined in some way by their function; places usually have names, and they contain things. We put ourselves in places and behave appropriately. But we can also experience places from the inside out as we appropriate them by acts of the imagination and redefine their purpose. This appropriation can be both simple and complex. It starts in gestures like using a sewer top for home plate as we play in the street. It can be the designation of the romantic corner in a restaurant that then becomes "ours," in the way a song becomes "our song." Neutral landscapes, with private associations or evocative qualities, suffused with possibilities or memories, are available both on the way to school and in cultural moments like Wordsworth's Tintern Abbey. And think about what's going on when Christo wraps a large public building or a bridge. Gestures like these, from creating home plate to the installation of a controversial sculpture, I like to think of as establishing immanent domains. They are private acts in public, and they can play with our civic senses of "zoning."

II

Immaculate Nikes, a purposeful stride, and eyes as cloistered as a monk's all mark the seniors who walk The Galleria. She never carries a purse. He is not dressed to be seen. They are not shopping. They are exercising. And they are obvious.

If they were walking like this through the sidewalkless streets of my neighborhood in Bellaire, you would hardly notice; and there are people in other cities who walk to work down Michigan Avenue, Madison Avenue, Commonwealth Avenue, with a purposeful stride and fixed gaze, who are not shopping either. (Does anyone walk through Highland Village on their way to work? Can you walk through Highland Village in the first place?)

But public streets are always both means and ends, theaters as well as bazaars, but thoroughfares first, and the place where strangers are least legible and most interesting. The avenues of a mall, however, don't go anywhere else, aren't routes, have no other rationale, and mark strangers as shoppers. These avenues are as focused in function as an escalator. It is almost reasonable, therefore, that one mall manager argued that the mall-walkers ought to be banished during the Christmas shopping season because they take away parking places from orthodox consumers and they crowd things. Imagine! Crowds at Christmas! He lost the argument. History and custom were not on his side.

In 19th-century American cities commercial spaces, like modern malls, were developed not to exclude the foreigner and the unorthodox, but to offer another opening into the new world. Department stores were intended not simply to sell things but also to be the agent and stage of a changing order, "a form of real emancipation" from "the boredom of familial confinement or the drudgery of domestic routine."

> A millionaire [such as Marshall Field] who greeted his customers and responded to the grievances of a shopper on the crowded floor of his store elevated an obsequious act to the level of a public service.
> A poor woman's self-esteem was elevated by her ability to share a display counter with a rich woman, who in turn achieved her satisfaction from the admiration of clerks and customers.

These passages are taken from Gunther Barth's *City People* (1980), but his points are anticipated and dramatized in Emile Zola's novel about a Parisian department store, *The Ladies' Paradise* (1883), and in Theodore Dreiser's novel *Sister Carrie* (1900). Novels, among the many other things they have always done, have always explored, or even exploited, the zone between the private and public, between immanence and the common social order.

In any daily urban life, it seems, we live in that zone all the time. What the poor woman at the counter thinks about herself and her place, in every sense, is what establishes in her mind the meaning of her life. What the rich woman thinks does the same thing. The invisible zones of their consciousness, as a novel can give them to us, as we can imagine them watching people in the mall, enrich the place they're standing in a way the place can never fully contain.

The cafes-concerts in the Paris of Haussmann and the Impressionists' paintings of them did some of this kind of social work, but American cities had a much more heterogeneous populace to work with, and the class issues Barth identifies are still obvious in the differences between the Galleria and the Alameda Mall, where there is no Tiffany's, and in the reputation certain cities have for blue-collar football teams—Oakland but not San Francisco, Pittsburgh, but not Miami. But deeper than class is commerce. Money makes the world go round and helps us all identify and disguise ourselves. In places like malls we are neither private individuals nor exactly public citizens; we are free to be many other things at once, visibly and invisibly at the same time.

III

Sidewalk visionaries, talking to their unseen gods, used to be schizophrenics and the homeless. Now it's the guy who has a little cell phone plugged in on the other side of his face. Because phone technology is still so imperfect, he is speaking very loudly. He is violating your privacy as he forces you to overhear him, and we don't yet have a word for this inversion of eavesdropping—which is a truly spectacular word itself. The boundaries of public and private are contested in this relationship between a cell phoner and his unwilling audience, and I think of this relationship as a commercial space too, created not out of any deep human need to be talking to someone miles away as you stroll the city or fight the freeway traffic, but out of the communication industry's Darwinian aggression. Nature, one of my students told me, is what is possible. And we can now select to be two places at once, talking to someone who is not here but there in another domain.

One sign the Apocalypse is nigh was the woman I saw walking down the white line in the middle of University Boulevard, at about 8:20 A.M., morning traffic streaming past her on both sides, her eyes on the high horizon, her ear on her cell phone. Where, in what world, was she? "Up there in air-space," Salman Rushdie writes in *The Satanic Verses*:

> Up there in air-space, in that soft imperceptible field which had been made possible by the century and which, thereafter, had made the century possible, becoming one of its defining locations, the place of movement and of war, the planet-shrinker and power-vacuum, most insecure and transitory of zones, illusory, discontinuous, metamorphic. . . .

This air-space is also the domain of the electronic media that are now essential to the other defining location of our experience in postmodernity, the city—which in Rushdie's novel is equally Bombay and London. The world is incompatible, one of his characters says, and "the locus classic of incompatible realities" is the city, because there is nothing like the city in all its messy splendor that resists clear-cut binary orders of public and private, social and individual, functional and free, or legible and opaque.

Maybe one simple reason It's All At The Mall, or at Celebration Station, is that any place that takes our money gives us some freedom in return. Or it may also be that some places with high-intensity definitions encourage our resistance: They push against us so hard, we have to push back to make rooms for ourselves.

The poet Wallace Stevens defines the imagination as the pressure inside us that resists the pressure of the reality outside; and he is perfectly comfortable with the implication of this position that all of us are necessarily poets, that the gestures by which we establish our immanent domains in the world are acts of art. Stevens is as democratic in this belief as Walt Whitman is, but more radically anarchic because he writes without Whitman's hope in community. And because he is neither a novelist, nor an architect, nor a city planner, but a poet of exquisite abstractions, he says of himself: "Life is an affair of people not of places. But for me life is an affair of places and that is the trouble."

In Houston, the Borders bookstore I know best has books and magazines, CDs and DVDs for sale, a snack shop and coffee bar, and a massage station. Upstairs there are many soft reading chairs, and one Saturday I saw a couple, their laps piled with books and magazines that they hadn't bought, their empty latte cups at their feet, sound asleep.

Sleeping in libraries is perfectly natural. Sleeping in stores, however, is the projection of a kind of privacy hard to gauge. An immanent domain, for sure, and all they had to buy was the caffeine that didn't keep them awake. ★

TONY DIAZ

Novelist Tony Diaz is the author of *The Aztec Love God* and *The Protesters Handbook*. Originally from Chicago, he earned an MFA from the University of Houston Creative Writing Program. He is also the founder of Nuestra Palabra: Latino Writers Having Their Say, a nonprofit organization that promotes Latino literature and literacy. He hosts the NP Radio show on 90.1 FM, KPFT, and is editor of the magazine *Aztec Muse*. He is also an English professor at Houston Community College.

In this essay, originally written for the *Nuestra Palabra* website, Diaz describes a night when he found himself straddling two worlds; the relatively wealthy and inevitably white world of the downtown literary reading, and that of the *vatos* who clean up after it.

A Night at the Opera

A NIGHT AT THE OPERA: BOOKS WILL NEVER go away, just like Opera has not. But as with Opera, the audience will simply get older and whiter. I say this as I see how the publishing and academic world have made an art out of missing the Latino demographic.

This dawned on me actually, in January of 2008, before the Depression of 2009, before Hurricane Ike, and just down the street from where the Enron building once stood in downtown Houston.

My parents had come to the U.S. for this.

Their son was loose on the streets of downtown Houston, Texas, about to enjoy literature.

Of course, I was in my late-thirties, and I had assumed the American Cultural Dream just in time for it to go away.

It was a Monday night. It was January 2008, a tough beginning to a tough year. I didn't know what was awaiting us, so I was still looking for entertainment, distraction, wisdom, knowledge with a good time, an edifying experience.

Thus I used my boy's-night-out-pass, and my baby sitter chip to attend a reading.

It was 7:10 P.M. I was late for the reading.

As I pulled up to the Wortham Theatre, I passed Birroperetti's on the corner, a restaurant/bar, and I caught site of the vatos working inside, carrying trays, wiping off tables, out-numbering the number of nicely dressed customers as they, and I, subsidized the Houston culture not watching Monday night football.

I wasn't attending just any reading.

This was a reading put on by the mainstream literary nonprofit, in honor of a writer who was a literary star, in Houston's opera hall, the Bayou City's red carpet treatment.

I pulled into City Parking at Bayou Place and paid five bucks, and I walked to the Wortham via the underground tunnels.

It was hard to find. I didn't know there was more than one hall in Wortham Hall. The first worker I asked about the reading told me I could read a book anywhere I wanted. The second worker had no idea that an event was going on there that night. He thought it was a dark night. When I spoke to a third person, I insisted she take me to the event that I knew was occurring, that I had a flyer for. We found it. But we had to then go in through the balcony, as no one could enter late through the main doors. This event was definitely not made for those of us who run on Latino time.

There were a lot of older white folks in the audience below. Old white folks are a good audience. They listen. They like plays on words. They have money to spend on books. They have time to read.

The young people there were students, as evidenced by their notebooks in hand, scrawling all the phrases they would need to complete their compulsory assignments or their extra credit.

And because of the topic of the book, and because Houston has a huge middle class, there were those of us who are multicultural.

But we were at the Opera House.

As a novelist, I ask myself, if given a choice, which would I want to be, a rock star or an opera star?

I wanna be a regattón star, baby.

Books will never go away. That sentiment is true. Just like Opera never went away. It morphed, into musicals, into Broadway, into movies. Its audience got smaller, defined by wealth, education, and free time, like Monday nights, instead of working, not worried about waking up late for work, so you can roam in the caverns of the opera house. With enough education and audacity to say, not only do I belong here tonight, mutherfucker, but I'm expected, and even if I'm late, let me in.

With enough money to not have to work that night, to pay $5 for parking, to spend 2 hours at a reading, to spend the $25 for the hardcover, $39 if you buy an additional paper back, with enough experience with genteel, old art, to know that it was a good night, it was a good show. It was a good reading.

The vatos at work at the restaurant/bar on the corner, or any restaurant or bar open Monday nights, or any night of the week, will not join me in an opera hall or a reading for a long time. Perhaps some day they will, or their kids will, or their grand kids. And it is unimaginable to Houston, at the time, the things I will have to do to make that happen.

Ever competitive, I imagine how I would have organized the event.

All the events Nuestra Palabra organizes have more people, less money, more color.

It's Monday night. My friend has just won the Pulitzer Prize. Yet 50% of kids who look like me, who form 50% of the Houston Independent School District, will drop out of school.

In a few short months the publishing world will be rocked just like every industry is about to be rocked in America.

And on that night of plenty, those very same people who need my people the most are missing us, are not even coming close to attracting us.

That night, as one of just a few Mexicans in the crowd, I think, I need to re-evaluate this relationship. Maybe I need to go with younger technology, different ways to convey cultura. I think that maybe every time I say I will never give up my books, I should substitute "I will never give up my tablets of stone."

I leave, after waiting in line, shaking the star's hands, not a divo, but nonetheless, an opera star. I stroll towards the undergound tunnels, books in hand, with deep thoughts, never turning back to see the dark, looming Opera House. ★

MARK DOTY

Mark Doty's *Fire to Fire: New and Selected Poems* won the National Book Award in 2008. The John and Rebecca Moores professor in the department of English from 1998 until 2008, he now teaches at Rutgers University and lives in New York. This essay originally appeared in *Smithsonian Magazine*.

Southern Comfort

IT DOESN'T TAKE LONG IN HOUSTON TO REalize that the beauty of the place is in the sky. The swamplands and fields that became the fourth-largest city in the country are almost entirely flat, and the availability of cheap land and an exuberant appetite for sprawl have kept most of the town low-slung and horizontal. So the sky seems vast, and from any parking lot you can watch big white towers of cloud sail up from the Gulf of Mexico 50 miles to the south as if they were navigating the ship channel beneath them. The expanse of sky is so wide, there's often more than one thing going on. Rain may darken the western rim while a fierce sun illuminates cloud towers in the center and a brilliant blue fills the east. How can you forecast the weather when it's doing three things at once?

I've only just started describing the place, and already I've had to employ a whole vocabulary of scale: *largest*, *vast*, *big*, *wide*. Indeed the sky's a huge, open relief from all the busyness below, but that cluttered landscape is itself immense. Houston's a universe of visual detail. Drive down the freeway (this is a city built on the premise of the personal vehicle, a private sphere to propel you through public spaces) and you become a reader of the telegraphic messages the city pulses out all day, all night: Bail Bonds, Paternity Tests, Taqueria, Weight Loss, Wireless, Margaritas, No Credit? Bad Credit?, God's Got a Plan for You,

Gentlemen's Club, Nails, BBQ, Christian Singles. The city's welter of signs is a crazy patchwork of human desires given material form.

I've been coming to Houston for a decade now, teaching one semester each year in one of the country's best creative writing programs. I used to joke with my friends in the Northeast that every fall I descend into Texas like Persephone, only to return, come spring, into the light. But after a few years, my feelings about the place shifted. I can tell you everything that's wrong with it: no zoning, bad air quality, impossible climate. Tiny, malicious mosquitoes so tough and persistent you get bitten on Christmas Day. Poor drainage, so that the ubiquitous storms create floods of biblical proportion. It's harder to name just what it is about the place that's gotten under my skin, holds my attention here, makes me want to come back.

In spite of its international petroleum-based economy, its layered ribbons of freeways and corporate spires, Houston still feels Southern. Imagine a hybrid of New Orleans and Los Angeles, with a dash of Mexico City thrown in. True, it doesn't have the regional feel it once did, but you can still find it in my neighborhood, Montrose, an arts/alternative/liberal district near the center of town. Here the city's splendid tradition of patronage is on its best display, so the great old live oaks thrust their bowing branches out beside the Cy Twombly Gallery and the Rothko Chapel. The limbs dip perilously toward the ground, and the roots heave the sidewalks beneath them into little concrete alps, but since nobody walks anywhere it doesn't make much difference. In summer the trees resound with cicadas, like electronic versions of the Mormon Tabernacle Choir chorusing an insanely repetitive song. Gangs of bronzy black birds—boat-tailed grackles—prefer smaller trees in busier areas; they like grocery store parking lots and the drive-through lanes at the Taco Cabana, and they shriek and holler long into the night, as if in avian parallel to the traffic below. They're the loudest part of a plethora of urban wildlife: opossums, raccoons, the occasional snake slithering across the road, a sadly large population of stray dogs. Coyotes roam the cemetery north of Buffalo Bayou, where Howard Hughes is buried. All over town, tiny green lizards hold their heads up with notable alertness. My friend Mark's iguana, a giant version of those local denizens, escaped into a wisteria arbor and remained there for months before finally consenting to be lifted down.

Southern culture still lingers. There is, for instance, conversation with strangers. In my other life, in New York City, I'll walk into a deli and the guy behind the counter will shout, NEXT, and I shout back, COFFEE WITH MILK NO SUGAR. This brusque exchange is not rude, though visitors sometimes think otherwise; it is designed to make life easy for a large number of people, part of the unwritten civil contract that makes an enormous city work. If the server or I behaved this way in Houston, we would be seen as rude or crazy or both. Our exchange would more likely go something like this:

—How are you today?

—I'm doing well, thank you, and I sure am glad it's not as warm as it was.

—Oh, me too, I was just melting in that. Now what can I get for you?

I understand that this is simply social convention, so maybe I shouldn't find it so touching, but I do. When I first arrived, I went to a Whole Foods store in my new neighborhood to order some dinner from the deli there, and after I'd asked for some grilled chicken breasts the server said, "Would you like some green beans with that?" in a warm East Texas inflection, and I found myself tearing up then and there, almost unable to say yes. Hers was a version of the voice of my grandmother, who was from Tennessee and spent her life pleasing people with food. Would you like some green beans with that? meant I love you with all my heart, and what can I do to make you happy?

This particularly Southern social fabric, with its suggestion of a slower pace of life, no hurry in all the world, is eroding. That's not entirely a bad thing; in comes new energy, more urbane possibilities, new futures. Since Houston is about transformation, it seems by nature to be a city without much allegiance to history. If there were a motto on the town flag, I think it might read NO NOSTALGIA.

The city's a world capital of erasure. I'll often go away for a few days and return to find a familiar building gone. In fact, it's so common to drive down some street and find the built landscape changed that one loses the very habit of familiarity. I find it almost impossible, in a way that's not true of any place else I've lived, to remember what's gone. What stood on that corner last year?

What was here before they built those new condos with the coffee/wine/tapas bar on the first floor? The past starts to seem irretrievable. There's a neighborhood near downtown called Freedmen's Town, for instance, that gained its name from a 19th-century community of former slaves. The streets were lined with small, orderly houses of the kind called "shotgun," one room opening into the next, so that if the front door were open you could see—or fire a shotgun—all the way out the back. These repositories of history are almost entirely gone now. In a flash, after decades in which the exurbs seemed to be most peoples' goal, it became fashionable to live downtown. So the old neighborhood disappears, to be replaced by something more anonymous, and while I tend to think the destruction of the past is regrettable, I admit I've had my preconceptions brought up short.

A friend asked a black student if he'd visited the city's historical African-American enclaves, and the student said, "Why would we want to see that?" That's a characteristically Houstonian attitude: What's so hot about yesterday? Let's go forward, let's see who we can be *now*. A historical preservation organization has been raising concerns that a handsome Art Deco theater in the city's River Oaks neighborhood will be torn down to build a high-rise. But I've come to understand the principle at work, if not its application: Houston is about the new, about transformation and ambition, the making and remaking of the self and the environment. Of course we make mistakes, but in ten years they're gone, and there's space for the next set of possibilities.

Whatever they are—our hopes, successes and mistakes—they're put in perspective by what Shakespeare called "this brave o'erhanging firmament." When the clouds conjoin and a storm pushes up from the Gulf, look out. I've seen a tornadic tropic fury pour in, tingeing the day an evil green, and the whole city suddenly resembles some underwater kingdom. Wiser drivers pull over and wait for the storm to pass. The foolhardy plunge forward, plowing through channels of rainwater filling the intersections. Sometimes whole school buses float away. Everyone hopes for reprieve. Which won't be long in coming, so that we can forget about the sky and return to the theater of our aspirations, the daily traffic, this new city's strange promises and invitations. ★

PART IV

EVENTS

I HAVE TO ADMIT THAT IT SEEMS ODD TO HAVE only six entries under the heading "events." Houston is popularly considered short on history, but more than six things have happened here. But I used the term as something of a catchall to help round up some dramatic stories that didn't really fit elsewhere in my scheme.

Actually, the city was born in a burst of real drama; the battle of San Jacinto led directly to the founding of a city named for that strange encounter's putative hero. Not to knock the *Sword of San Jacinto*, but Stephen L. Hardin's gripping account of the battle, taken from his *Texian Iliad*, shows that the events of April 19, 1836, happened almost in spite of Houston, rather than because of him. I've also included a Mexican view on the battle's disgraceful (to the Mexicans) outcome—an excerpt from José Enrique de la Peña's *With Santa Anna in Texas*.

From blood and guts history we leap to a couple of twentieth century cultural showdowns, one which led to the formation of the Houston Symphony, as described by longtime Houston critic Hubert Roussel, and another which took place in the Chinese Consulate, where, in what became an international incident, Houston Ballet dancer Li Cunxin was detained by the Chinese authorities after he married an American dancer without their permission.

From these intense but small-scale collisions we turn to the three events from recent years that focused the world's attention. Stephen Harrigan has a moving essay on the *Columbia* shuttle disaster, and I've excerpted two books about the Enron implosion, Mimi Swartz and Sherron Watkins' *Power Failure* and Bethany McLean and Peter Elkind's *The Smartest Guys in the Room*. The *Power Failure* excerpt looks at the origins of the company, while *The Smartest Guys in the Room* excerpt tries to pin down exactly where it all went wrong.

Enron gave Houston a black eye, and called into question the city's business-friendly ethos. But before long the Katrina disaster, as chronicled by Jed Horne, gave the city an opportunity to render a remarkable and big-hearted service to a wounded neighbor.

Hopefully the next ten years won't be quite as exciting.

STEPHEN L. HARDIN

Historian Stephen L. Hardin's account of the Battle of San Jacinto is unusually vivid, even cinematic. Would that more historians, *all* historians, wrote with his gusto.

From *Texian Iliad*: "Nock There Brains Out"

IN THE TEXIAN CAMP, THE TROOPS WERE IN a near frenzy. It was noon, and Houston had already wasted half the day. Any more delay would surely bring additional Mexican reinforcements. Some speculated that Houston was simply seeking another excuse to avoid battle.

Eight disgruntled officers demanded a council of war, and Rusk, heretofore a staunch Houston supporter, took part in it. The meeting lasted from noon until two o'clock. Accounts of what occurred differ. Robert Coleman, who in 1837 wrote a vicious anti-Houston polemic, claimed that the general had ordered a withdrawal across Buffalo Bayou, but the officers told him that "he *must fight*, that a further delay would not be countenanced by either soldiers or officers." Finally, according to Coleman, Houston resentfully replied, "Fight then and be damned!"

The pro-Houston forces told a different story. They swore that Houston was fully committed to an attack on April 21. Charles Edwards Lester wrote in his patently partisan biography that upon awaking that morning the general "sprang to his feet, and exclaimed, 'the sun of Austerlitz has risen again.'" Houston was, Lester claimed, "probably the only man in that camp over whose mind flitted no anxious vision." Marquis James, in his Pulitzer Prize-winning biography, *The Raven*, expressed few doubts. According to him, the general, not his officers, called the meeting to decide whether they should attack the Mexicans or await attack in the splendid defensive position provided by the oak grove. "Houston expressed no opinion," James wrote, "and when the others had wrangled themselves into a thorough disagreement he dismissed the council."

Two distinct images of Houston emerge. One is of a timid man, who schemed to avoid combat until his troops literally forced him into action. The other is of a stalwart hero in the Kipling mold, a confident commander who kept his head while petty and presumptuous subordinates were losing theirs. Neither view is entirely true nor entirely false. Since Houston was careful not to reveal certain aspects of himself, there will always be an air of mystery surrounding the man. It is equally true that many of the scurrilous charges against him—such as the one that the vial of hartshorn that he periodically sniffed was in reality opium—were made by those who resented his political power or envied his fame.

Whatever his motivation, between three and four o'clock on the afternoon of April 21, it was Sam Houston who called the Texians to battle. The army advanced in two parallel lines, with the two six-pounders in the middle and the mounted riflemen screened behind an oak grove on the enemy's left. The Texian horse now had a new commander. Lamar, a private the day before, had so distinguished himself in Sherman's unauthorized charge that Houston had awarded to him the cavalry command. The insubordinate Sherman was back at the head of his Kentucky infantry.

A slight rise covered by high grass concealed their approach from the Mexicans. With luck, they would cover most of the five hundred yards between the Texian camp and Santa Anna's breastworks before their presence was discovered. As the rebel army began its advance, "Deaf" Smith rode down the line yelling, "Vince's Bridge is down!" The destruction of the bridge would hinder the approach of [further Mexican reinforcements] on the Texian rear, but it also cut off their primary line of retreat. It was now a case of win or die.

It was no splendid army of Napoleonic proportions that grimly stalked toward the Mexican camp. The men composing the rebel line represented every frontier variant. The backwoodsman in greasy buckskins stood elbow to elbow with the townsman in frockcoat and top hat. One [rebel] in partial U.S. army uniform advanced next to a southern beau in planter's hat, waistcoat, and cravat. The Kentucky Rifles, a unit recruited and outfitted by Sidney Sherman, donned

266

trim, military-cut uniforms. They did, however, have a few traits in common; all were mudstained and unshaven; all were tired of running from an enemy they despised; all were anxious to avenge the deaths of those who had fallen at the Alamo and Goliad.

Among them, Juan Seguín led a detachment of about nineteen *tejanos*. Their presence in the line of battle was all the more impressive because they had been excused from combat duty. Since the execution of Fannin and his men, animosity toward Mexicans—all Mexicans—had run high. Houston was fearful that in the heat of battle his vengeful rowdies might not pause to make distinctions. Before leaving Harrisburg, therefore, the general ordered Seguín's company to stay and guard the baggage. Seguín angrily reminded Houston that not all his men were with him. Some had fallen at the Alamo. Besides, all of his soldiers hailed from the Béxar area, and until Santa Anna and his army were driven out of Texas, they could not return home. Seguín steadfastly asserted that his men had more reason to hate *santanistas* than anyone in Texas and wanted in on the kill. "Spoken like a man!" Houston exclaimed. But he insisted on one precaution; the *tejanos* must place pieces of cardboard in their hatbands to distinguish them. Consequently, with the distinctive cardboard insignia in place, they advanced upon the enemy with the rest of the army.

Meanwhile, all was quiet in the Mexican camp. Santa Anna had expected the rebels to attack the night before. Failing that, he was certain that they would attack the morning of April 21. Then at nine o'clock, Cós had arrived with five hundred additional troops, not the veterans that His Excellency had requested, but recruits who were exhausted and hungry after the forced march from the Fort Bend area. Still, the arrival of Cós's reinforcements had shifted the odds in Santa Anna's favor. His force now consisted of at least 1,250 men, against Houston's band of about 910. Santa Anna reasoned that Houston had seen Cós arrive and could also detect the newly erected breastworks. He doubted that the rebels would throw themselves against barricades but ordered constant readiness. Noon passed, as did early afternoon. As the shadows of late afternoon fell across the field, Santa Anna relaxed his vigilance and ordered his troops to stand down. His own force had been awake constructing defenses and Cós's troops had spent the night marching. The weary Mexicans welcomed the opportunity to sleep. Santa Anna also needed rest. He had spent a nervous night supervising the construction of the breastworks and awaiting the arrival of Cós. But now he could enjoy his repose; if the rebels had not attacked before Cós arrived with reinforcements, they were not likely to do so now. Thinking the situation well under control, Santa Anna retired to his camp bed.

Not all of the Mexican officers were as confident as their commander. Lamenting the pitiful defensive ground his general had selected, Colonel Delgado noted:

> We had the enemy on our right, within a wood, at long musket range. Our front, although level, was exposed to the fire of the enemy, who could keep it up with impunity from his sheltered position. Retreat was easy for him on his rear and right, while our own troops had no space for maneuvering. We had in our rear a small grove, reaching to the bay shore, which extended on our right as far as New Washington. What ground had we to retreat upon in the case of a reverse? From sad experience, I answered—None!

Delgado sought out General Castrillón, the gallant officer who had attempted to save the lives of Crockett and others at the Alamo, to discuss his concerns. He found him standing just outside His Excellency's tent. "What can I do, my friend?" Castrillón asked caustically. "You know nothing avails here against the caprice, arbitrary will, and ignorance of that man!" Delgado was surprised that the normally mild-mannered Castrillón expressed his contempt in such an "impassioned voice" and well within Santa Anna's hearing.

The unseen insurgents marching toward the Mexican camp were about to justify Delgado's concerns. Houston described the advance:

> Our cavalry was first dispatched to the front of the enemy's left for the purpose of attracting their notice, whilst an extensive island of timber afforded us an opportunity of concealing our forces and deploying from that point agreeably to the previous design of the troops. Every evolution was performed with alacrity, the whole [army] advancing rapidly in line and through an open prairie without any protection whatsoever for

our men. The artillery advanced and took station within two hundred yards of the enemy's breastworks, and commenced an effective fire of grape and canister.

The battle opened around 4:30, and with the firing of the Twin Sisters, events unfolded quickly. Lamar led his horsemen in a charge on the Mexican left flank. About the same time, a four-piece band broke into a titillating ballad, "Will You Come to the Bower?" Houston, out in front astride a huge stallion named Saracen, called for the infantrymen to hold their fire. He finally halted the line, dressed ranks, and shouted orders to fire; the entire line erupted in smoke and flame. After the first volley, Houston attempted to halt the line for reloading, but Rusk rode onto the field shouting, "If we stop, we are cut to pieces! Don't stop—go ahead—give them Hell!" The Texian line disintegrated. Men surged forward in open skirmish order; losing control of his army, Houston could only follow. Rusk was correct. At that juncture, momentum meant everything. Not bothering to reload, the rebels swept over the barricades swinging clubbed rifles, wielding flintlock pistols and Bowie knives. While few Mexican soldiers knew the language, they knew only too well the deadly message of the vengeful battlecry: "Remember the Alamo! Remember Goliad!"

The surprise was complete. Some Mexican officers attempted to rally their men. "The utmost confusion prevailed," Delgado recalled. "General Castrillón shouted on one side; on another Colonel Almonte was giving orders; some cried out to commence firing; others, to lie down to avoid grape shot. Among the latter was His Excellency . . . I saw our men flying in small groups, terrified, and sheltering themselves behind large trees. I endeavored to force some of them to fight, but all efforts were in vain—the evil was beyond remedy: they were a bewildered and panic-stricken herd."

Actually, commanders on both sides lost control of their troops. Houston had envisioned a more formal battle in which ranks would advance, fire, reload, and continue. Had the Texians proceeded in such a manner, however, the Mexicans may well have had time to form behind their barricades and return effective musket fire. As Houston's line dissolved into clusters of shock troops, the Mexicans had no main body against which they could direct their volley fire. Yet in open skirmish order, the rebel riflemen *could* rely on individual aimed fire, which proved extremely effective.

Texians flooded over the barricades; most of the defenders fell back. There was one, however, who won the lasting admiration of his adversaries. General Castrillón directed the gun crew manning the Golden Standard. Rifle fire soon killed most of the Mexican artillerymen, and those who had been cut down were "running like turkeys, whipped and discomfited." His men called out for the general to come with them, but he stubbornly refused to budge. "I have been in forty battles and never showed my back," Castrillón answered. "I am too old to do it now." With these words he manfully turned to face the onslaught.

Viewing this remarkable demonstration of courage, Rusk sought to preserve the gallant officer's life. He rode along the line, shouting, "Don't shoot him! Don't shoot him!" The secretary of war even knocked up the rifles of nearby soldiers who were aiming at Castrillón. But as the young Walter P. Lane looked on, others rushed past Rusk, drew down on the "old Castillian gentleman," and "riddled him with balls."

The actual battle lasted no more than eighteen minutes, but the slaughter continued much longer. Determined to avenge the loss of those killed at the Alamo and Goliad, the bloodthirsty rebels committed atrocities at least as beastly as those the Mexicans had committed. Sergeant Moses Bryan came across a Mexican drummer boy with both legs broken. The frightened child had grabbed a Texian soldier around the legs, all the while screaming *"Ave Maria purissima! Por Dios, salva mi vida!"* (Hail Mary, most pure! For God's sake, save my life!) Bryan begged the man to spare the youth, but the pitiless brute, in a threatening gesture, placed a hand on his belt pistol. Bryan backed away and watched in horror as the man "blew out the boy's brains."

If the Mexicans expected mercy from Seguín's men, they were soon disabused of that belief. Shouting *"Recuerden el Alamo,"* the *tejanos* pitched into the midst of the fight, transforming the odd bits of cardboard in their hatbands into honor badges for their unit. As the slaughter ensued, a Mexican officer recognized Antonio Menchaca as an acquaintance from Béxar and pleaded with him as a "brother Mexican" to intercede for his life. Menchaca fixed him with a cold gaze and replied, "No, damn you, I'm no Mexican—I'm an American." Then turning to his Anglo comrades, he curtly instructed: "Shoot him!" They summarily ended the pleading. For better or worse, Seguín and his *tejanos* had cast their lot with the Republic of Texas; the bitterness of San Jacinto demonstrated that for most there could be no turning back.

In their haste to escape the bloodthirsty Texians, many Mexicans threw down their arms and plunged headlong into Peggy Lake. For the riflemen on the bank, it was quite literally like shooting fish in a barrel. Colonel Delgado caught a glimpse of Colonel Almonte swimming with his left arm while holding his right above the water, still grasping his sword. The waters of Peggy Lake turned red: "It was there that the greatest carnage took place," Delgado reported. Dr. Labadie found a helpless Mexican officer who had become bogged to his knees and could not move. "Oh, I know him," one of Seguin's *rancheros* remarked, "he is Colonel Batres of San Antonio de Béxar." The doctor had just extended his hand to help Batres when he observed the approach of several menacing Texians. "Don't shoot! Don't shoot!" Labadie cried, "I have taken him prisoner." Despite the surgeon's pleas, a man fired at point-blank range. The ball shattered Batres's forehead. The doctor recoiled in horror as the helpless Mexican's brains splattered his hand and clothing. This villainous deed was not, however, the worst offense Labadie beheld, for he lamented that afterward he "witnessed acts of cruelty which I forbear to recount." The imagination reels when it considers just what those acts might have been. But it is known that several of the Mexican corpses on the battlefield had been scalped.

General Houston, with a smashed ankle and mounted on his third horse of the day, rode among his soldiers trying to halt their wanton killing. Seeing the uselessness of his efforts, he admonished: "Gentlemen, I applaud your bravery, but damn your manners." The vindictive Texians were displaying bad manners indeed. Private Robert Hancock Hunter recounted the instructions of one captain upon hearing Houston's orders to take prisoners. "Boys," he told them, "you know how to take prisoners, take them with the butt of yor guns, club guns & remember the Alamo, remember Labaher, & club gun right & left, and nock there brains out!"

***

Careless, or perhaps chauvinistic, writers have alleged that Texians defeated the Mexican army at San Jacinto; that they most assuredly did not do. The contingent that was decimated along the banks of Buffalo Bayou was but a small portion of the total Mexican army in Texas. Forces under Filisola and Urrea were still a threat, and around nightfall Houston revealed his justifiable fear of an attack. His shattered ankle was causing him much pain, and he finally dismounted. While the general was waiting for Dr. Labadie to treat his wound, Rusk and other were rounding up prisoners. Amasa Turner described his commander's behavior as he saw the herd of prisoners of war approaching the Texian camp. "Houston threw up his hands and exclaimed: "'All is lost! All is lost! My God, all is lost!'" Turner was firmly convinced that "when the general first saw Rusk and the Mexicans on the prairie he thought it was Filisola's column coming from the Brazos."

On April 22 Santa Anna justified those anxieties when he came before Houston as a captive. "You have whipped me, I am your prisoner," His Excellency admitted, "but Filisola is not whipped. He will not surrender as a prisoner of war. You must whip him first. But," Santa Anna quickly suggested, "if I give him orders to leave the limits of Texas, he will do it." Most of the rebels were eager to hang the Mexican general from the nearest limb. Houston realized, however, that alive, Santa Anna was a powerful diplomatic card; dead, he would be of no more use than the other bloated corpses that littered Peggy Lake. Houston well knew that a victory over Filisola or Urrea would be harder to achieve even if his men were in a condition to fight. It was time to run a bluff.

Obeying Houston's demands, Santa Anna dispatched orders for Filisola, his immediate subordinate, to retire to Béxar and await further instructions. Urrea, de la Peña, and others harshly criticized the Italian-born Filisola for submitting to orders issued under duress. Filisola always maintained that, orders or no orders, he had no recourse but to retreat. The heavy rains continued to render movement difficult; supplies were running out; and many *soldados* were stricken with dysentery. Santa Anna had taken the army so far from its logistical bases that supply lines had broken down. According to Filisola, it was not the Texians who defeated the once proud Mexican army but the "inclemency of the season in a country totally unpopulated and barren, made still more unattractive by the rigor of the climate and the character of the land." Consequently, Filisola withdrew the Mexican army, not to Béxar, but across the Río Grande.

Several factors had produced rebel victory at San Jacinto. Before April 21, 1836, most observers thought the revolt crushed. Speaking for many of his ilk, Yankee newspaperman Horace Greeley concluded that the twin disasters of the Alamo and Goliad "must naturally, if not necessarily, involve the extinction of every rational hope for Texas." Many were astonished, therefore, when the same Mexican soldiers who performed so resolutely at the Alamo on March 6 were utterly routed on April 21. Many Texian veterans condemned them as cowardly, a label that the facts hardly warranted. The troops that Santa Anna brought to Buffalo Bayou were hungry, demoralized, and far from provisions. They appeared, furthermore, to have lost all confidence in their commander. Texian insurgents, of course, were not brimming with love for Sam Houston, but they did have enormous faith in themselves. Much of that faith was justified, for once committed to battle at San Jacinto, the ferocious volunteers were unstoppable. When Santa Anna, contemptuous of the rebel army, made the fatal blunder of separating his detachment for the fruitless drive on Harrisburg, the rebel army stood ready to exploit his mistake. The fact remains, however, that the mistake was his. Houston had been able to surprise the Mexicans only because Santa Anna neglected his camp security. His Excellency had, furthermore, confidently moved his army off the prairies where his superior cavalry enjoyed an advantage and had ventured into wooded marshlands where the Texian riflemen could employ the terrain to advantage. San Jacinto was not so much a battle that Houston won, but rather than one Santa Anna squandered.

Six months earlier, William H. Wharton had been unhappy in his position as the insurgent army's judge advocate. In a rancorous letter of resignation to General Stephen F. Austin, he denounced the "failure to enforce general orders" and asserted, "I am compelled to believe that no good will be achieved by this army except by the merest accident under heaven." In more ways than one, the Battle of San Jacinto had been that accident. ★

José Enrique de la Peña

José Enrique de la Peña's *With Santa Anna in Texas: A Personal Narrative of the Revolution* excited a tremendous controversy when it was published by Texas A&M Press in 1975. De la Peña [1807–1840] was a member of the Mexican army during the Texas Revolution, and it was he who reported that Davy Crockett had been captured and executed, rather than gone down swinging Old Betsy as Fess Parker had it. Some historians responded to the very late appearance of this manuscript with extreme skepticism, but today it is generally seen as authentic, if not completely accurate. But no such document ever is.

There's far more to this book than a rather stale controversy, however. No one ever mentions that it's a sensitive and beautifully written book, and that de la Peña might have found a career as a literary man. A foe of Santa Anna, de la Peña died under suspicious circumstances in Mexico City.

From *With Santa Anna in Texas*

"BEWARE," SAID TURENNE, "OF UNDERESTImating your adversary, for surely this is one of the greatest risks in war"; but General Santa Anna greatly deprecated an enemy whom heretofore he had vanquished in every encounter when he had dared to show his face. He was over-confident, and he communicated this feeling to those under him, giving the enemy an advantage that he could not have had otherwise.

A slave appeared before Houston at three o'clock the afternoon of the 21st, informing him that General Santa Anna was sleeping and that his camp had delivered itself over to a feeling of confidence and great abandon. Houston hurried to take advantage of the beautiful opportunity that presented itself to him, to be freed of a critical and anxious situation, mobilizing his force immediately with the greatest caution, then giving the sign for the attack. This circumstance explains why he decided to battle an enemy who had just received reinforcements of four hundred men when the previous day he had not accepted combat offered to him with inferior numbers. For men who had been placed in the cruel dilemma of either vanquishing or dying, who knew by past experience that no quarter would be given, it was not difficult to overcome an enemy that slept and was unprepared to resist. So, to advance, to surprise our advance post, to introduce confusion and disorder, and to spread terror and death in our camp was the work of a few moments. The cry *Remember the Alamo!* that the enemy shouted as he dealt his blows served to increase his fury during that terrible moment, to make the conflict more bitter for our men, and to avenge twice over their comrades who had fallen at the place of that name. The thirst for vengeance that dominated them when they recalled the scenes at the Alamo and Goliad, so fresh in their memory, was so strong that they became intoxicated with the carnage and could not be controlled in their devastating fury by those of their leaders and companions who, though justly indignant at the inhumanity with which our own leader had conducted himself with their men, did not wish to stain their victory with the same excesses that had blotted our own.

Nothing speaks more convincingly for the instantaneous surprise registered in our camp and the fact that it was carried out with a horrible carnage of men who showed no resistance than Houston's dispatch, in which he reveals he had only 2 dead and 23 wounded.

***

Houston has purposely withheld from his dispatch the circumstance to which he owed his victory, in order not to diminish the renown it has bestowed on him, for certainly without such a complete surprise, the more reprehensible because it was at midday, he never could have obtained it. General Santa Anna had under his command forces superior in both number and discipline; he had excellent officers, and though there were some recruits in his ranks, these were the lesser numbers; of choice companies he had ten, and among the fusiliers of the other contingents there were veteran soldiers, soldiers who on more than one occasion had decked their foreheads with the laurels of victory. Houston, on the contrary, had forces inferior in number which, though composed of men of courage, were not subject to the discipline that makes the soldier; they did not follow any specific tactics nor had they mastered the fundamentals of war. It can be said of them that they were all recruits, courageous men, who tried only to save or to sell their lives dearly, for which reason the defeat at San Jacinto appears the more humiliating, for in defeat disgrace is quite possible, just as one can be vanquished without necessarily losing honor; but on the 21st of April everything was lost, men, arms, and reputation.... ★

HUBERT ROUSSEL

Hubert Roussel was a feared and admired music and drama critic at both the *Houston Press* daily and the *Houston Post* from 1933 to 1966. As an editor at the *Post* he was also feared by his young writers, such as Donald Barthelme. Tracy Daugherty's biography of Barthelme refers to Roussel-the-editor as a "no-nonsense perfectionist."

Before his tenures at the dailies, Roussel served on the staff of a New York magazine, and later as associate editor of the weekly *Houston Gargoyle* (see Antonya Nelson's piece "Eminent Domain" for a fuller description of that publication), where he first demonstrated his sharp wit and supple style for Houston readers. Both those qualities are on full display in this excerpt from his history of the Houston Symphony.

From *The Houston Symphony Orchestra, 1913–1971*

THE WAR LEFT HOUSTON A MORE COMPLEX, restless city. In material ways it had benefited from the great industrial effort brought on by the conflict; socially it had acquired a variety of new characteristics, due to heavy gains in population that had not as yet been fully assimilated. The public temper was impatient, erratic, and fickle. Such indeed was the atmosphere over the nation as a whole. And as the second decade of the century gave way to the one later to be known as the Roaring Twenties, the meaning of this reaction to the war's frenzy was not to be guessed. It was a strange lingering fever. The resumption of old habits had not occurred as most people had expected; the past seemed very much past. It was a time of new pressures, dissatisfactions, and doubts.

The Houston orchestra had been disbanded without disbanding its supporting organization. Officially, there was still a society. This continuance was chiefly the work of Miss [Ima] Hogg, who had become president of the association in 1917 and had seen to it that occasional meetings were held. She had hoped to reestablish the orchestra as soon as conditions were normal, but now, though the crisis was over, she found little to encourage her idea. The immediate postwar air did not invite art projects whose goals were necessarily distant. A year after the conflict Miss Hogg suffered the illness that caused her to remain long in a hospital [Editor's note: probably from depression], and when it ended she was not at once able to resume her accustomed activities.

In 1921 she was succeeded as president of the association by Mrs. H. M. Garwood, and there were other official rearrangements. But this led to no immediate action. The association adopted a waiting policy, and it easily turned into a habit. The mad Twenties were very bemusing. Time passed, and there was no move to reassemble the orchestra. But after a while, in order to hold some public position, the society began to present occasional programs of chamber music, with members of the original orchestra, and to act as joint sponsor of certain visiting musical attractions. For the latter purpose it made an arrangement with Mrs. Edna W. Saunders, who had recently come into prominence as a booker of cultural entertainment for Houston; this connection resulted in appearances of the St. Louis, Minneapolis, and other symphony organizations of note. Altogether, however, thirteen years were to pass, from the time of the orchestra's disappearance, before Houston's own symphony movement would be fully revived. When this did happen, the time was entirely unlikely and the circumstances not lacking a note of the comic.

In the summer of 1929 the nation was at the peak of a wild economic boom, and this giddy prosperity, which had been mounting for more than a decade, manifested itself in an orgy of freak fads and extravagant projects. No other time could have made flagpole-sitting an interest. Among the period's more grandiose ventures that found ready financing was Chicago's Century of Progress Exposition, the plant for which was then under construction. The aims of the exposition included a representative showing in the nation's regional culture, and thus it occasioned a certain venture in Houston.

The Houston musical colony had for many years been enlivened by a personality of rare color, temerity, and impulse, Mrs. John Wesley Graham, whose impatient rushes to conquer the heights of Olympus left many a legend. She was a teacher of voice, choir director of the First Methodist Church, and organizer extraordinary of sundry ventures intended, as she individually reckoned, to hasten the coming of the city's full cultural glory. The announcement of Chicago's plan to survey regional theater art was to this excellent lady a direct and imperative challenge. "Ma" Graham—for so she was fondly known to her considerable flock—reacted in a typical manner. It became her conviction that Houston should be represented in Chicago by an opera company of full mettle and weight, in the form of a spectacular production of Verdi's *Aida*, elephants included, which she would personally undertake to finance, organize, and direct.

Nobody in Houston said nay to the ideas of "Ma" Graham; the prudent had learned to take cover and give her full freedom of movement. Though the exposition would not open for more than a year, she felt there was no time to be lost; the opera company would need seasoning at home. She accordingly started with a propaganda barrage of her own brand; Mrs. Graham was a pioneer in the saturation technique of publicity. Her campaign had proceeded for some weeks and was just getting the city well blanketed, when the Wall Street market collapsed on October 28. The inflationary bubble had burst. Within a very few weeks, drastic retrenchments of every kind had become the order of American life.

It might have been supposed that such a scheme as the Houston opera enterprise would rank high among locally dispensable items. But that was to reckon without "Ma" Graham. She was not the sort of woman to be turned in her purpose by a mere national calamity. Houston did not at once feel the depression too keenly and was never to suffer its worst blight. Mrs. Graham simply redoubled her efforts. In the summer of 1930, with certain backing secured in her own ways, she left for Europe to scout some of its operatic ideas and available talent. Her trip was to have dramatic results, for things happened that way with Mrs. Graham.

She first visited Italy, and while in Milan met an opera coach and conductor whose talents impressed her. This was Uriel Nespoli. He was still youngish, well regarded, and apparently on his way up. Mrs. Graham thought so well of his qualities that she made him an offer to become the conductor of her enterprise. Though he probably never understood her completely, Nespoli gladly accepted. He had never been in America and the offer had a flattering sound. Mrs. Graham then left to continue her travels in England, France, and Germany. She was not to be home until September; Nespoli was to meet her in Houston at that time.

But there was a hitch in the plan. Complications developed, and as a result Mrs. Graham arrived in the city in high dudgeon. She had sent back news of the conductor's appointment, and now there was no conductor to meet her. She explained things in a statement given the press. It appeared that when Nespoli, acting on her instructions, had attempted to leave for his new post, he had been told by the Italian authorities in Milan that the quota of immigration to the United States was exhausted for the year, and summarily ordered to forget his plan. Mrs. Graham was indignant and furious. In view of the reason for Nespoli's hiring, she considered this interference an outrage. She suspected a plot against American art, and held Mussolini responsible. The conductor was no less than a prisoner in Italy, she protested, and she would demand state action if necessary.

As a preliminary, however, in order to strengthen her position, to make clear the rare qualities of this musical artist, and to show the absurdity of the law, she would place Nespoli under a new, ten-year contract of spectacular gravity and conditional specifications. She proceeded to do so with all speed. (Her counsel, and the author of this remarkable document, was a handsome and indulgent young Houston attorney, Maurice Hirsch.) She sent a copy of the contract to the American consul in Milan, with a letter demanding redress. When he chose to ignore it, the situation became fully operatic. Mrs. Graham moved on Congress, where she was not altogether without friends. Washington smoked for three days and capitulated. The case wound up in the office of the secretary of state, where it was conveniently found that a small error had been made and that after all one more entry was possible under the immigration quota. As a result the conductor set sail on the first available craft—a cattle boat. It will never be known what he expected to find.

But all this had consumed time, and the season was moving along. It was mid-January before Nespoli finally arrived—tagged and delivered to Mrs. Graham much in the way of a piece of baggage, for he was utterly innocent of English. Nespoli was a stocky, nervous, eruptive little man of forty-seven, myopic and beginning to bald, who peered at the world through round, thick-lensed glasses with the aspect of an unusually emotional salmon. A Neapolitan by birth, he was in fact a simple Italian provincial. He had been a pupil of the celebrated Leopoldo Mugnone, Verdi's favorite conductor. Mugnone could not have had a more diligent or worshipful protégé; to Nespoli, he was a god. But whatever his training in Italy, it had little prepared Uriel Nespoli for the circumstances in which he found himself now. Houston overwhelmed him completely; he could never get used to its ways. It was an alien world of incredible habits, and, although he had been taken into the household of Mrs. Graham, he was bitterly homesick and when not at work wandered about in a daze. He knew much about music and loved it passionately; he was emotional to the point of embarrassment. To watch him rehearsing the opera chorus in Houston was to watch a man suffering acute pain in his effort to communicate. It was pitiful because he lacked the advantage of a ready verbal exchange with his singers. All the same, his direction was clear, and nobody could doubt his sincerity. It was like that of a child. For a time he drudged faithfully at training the volunteer choral performers. But his expression grew increasingly melancholy.

Musical politics are in any case apt to be confusing, and a visitor less alien than Nespoli could have found himself sorely befuddled by the picture in Houston that winter. For "Miz Graham," as he called her, was not alone in running the show, and the whole of it was a curious mixture. While businesses flickered and failed over town in the depression's gathering gloom, other musical ventures had sprung up. They now began coming to light.

Before leaving for Europe Mrs. Graham had announced her intention to form a full orchestra for the opera company. She had pointed out that the orchestra's usefulness need not end there; it could also be presented in concerts. Her statement had undoubtedly been noted with interest by members of the quiescent symphony board, though they probably thought the idea would remain strictly an idea in the head of this lady. But once Mrs. Graham had gone as far as to provide herself with a European conductor, the matter began looking a little different. Now there was not much time for the symphony faction to think it over, for with Nespoli's coming the other developments thrust forward.

The most surprising was another orchestra that suddenly sprung out of nowhere—complete with conductor, repertory, sponsoring body, and a plan to do immediate business. There was an odd story behind it. This venture had begun in the winter of 1929 when a group of the city's musicians, mostly professional but including talented amateurs, anxious to make serious music and weary of waiting for the chance, had decided to act for themselves. The result was an informal association or club consisting of some fifty performers, who paid membership dues of five dollars to be used for the rental of scores. As a conductor they had selected Victor Alessandro, then director of band and orchestra music in the Houston public schools. As a meeting place they had borrowed the basement of the First Christian Church, and for more than a year they had gathered on two evenings a week to rehearse. Having by then worked up a considerable repertory, they became interested in giving public performances.

For that purpose they needed a sponsor, and they found one in N. D. Naman, a quiet cotton and real estate broker, who had long been a lover of music. Invited to one of the orchestra's meetings, he liked what he heard and agreed to furnish a modest underwriting (about $350 a concert) for a series of public appearances. He thereupon, with four associates, chartered the organization as a non-profit enterprise; the name was the Houston Philharmonic Orchestra, which suddenly made itself known by advertising a course of concerts to be given on Sunday afternoons in the auditorium of Scottish Rite Cathedral. The first was scheduled for March 15, 1931, Mr. Alessandro to conduct.

The public was a little surprised by the news; it was not a time to expect such ventures. But hardly had it finished digesting this morsel when it got a companion *bonne bouche*. Still another orchestra and still another series of concerts was announced. This time it was the Ellison Van Hoose Little Symphony.

***

Meanwhile in its own corner the *Aida* chorus was lustily hymning the Pharaoh. But Mrs. Graham had picked up a competitor. Mary Carson, a Houston soprano with red hair and a European reputation in opera, had returned home to pursue aims as an impresario and was stormily rehearsing a production of *Carmen*—also with civic opera intent. Otherwise Houston was quiet as spring settled in 1931.

The humor of this situation was not lost upon those who could follow the game. At this juncture the *Houston Gargoyle*, a sprightly news magazine that recorded the follies of the day, appeared with an article entitled "Unfinished Symphonies," whose subheading inquired: "Organized Your Orchestra Yet?" It was certainly the seasonal fad. The town's musical factions were clearly divided, and the gossip was lively and apt to be slightly malicious. At smart gatherings the guests winked at each other when the subject was mentioned, thereby implying the obvious question: where was the Houston Symphony Association in all this cultural fury?

***

The Association was now sharply aroused. It was given the spur, and the spur hurt. The new movements ignored its existence. Finding itself treated in that rather unceremonious way, the association was in no humor to bow meekly and surrender the franchise.

***

At the same time, the presence of Nespoli in town was embarrassing from the standpoint of the association. Because of the flamboyance of his sponsor, Mrs. Graham, the circumstances of his arrival, and his own idiosyncrasies, he had caused a considerable curiosity. His mannerisms were good "copy" and the press had been having its inevitable holiday with the doings of a strange visiting maestro. It was discovered that for some curious reason he could only shave one side of his face. His favorite amusement in Houston was streetcar riding. Because of his podium furies he was nicknamed "Little Caesar," after the fulminous hero of an Edward G. Robinson movie, and when this was picked up by the Italian press and came back over the Atlantic as *Piccolo Cesare*, the local historians were delighted. In one way and another, he had created more interest than the Philharmonic announcement. It was also apparent that he was training a chorus quite ably and that Mrs. Graham's opera endeavor, if it was to be further developed, would soon have need of its own orchestra. To much of the public, Nespoli had become the symbol of new musical stirrings in town.

One result of all this was that Ima Hogg made a trip to New York. She went as a representative of the Symphony Association to interview conductors who might be suitable to head a revival of the Houston venture. Before she had got far with that effort, however, there was another local development. Nespoli let it be known that he was very discouraged with prospects for the operatic endeavor. His lament was heard where he meant it to be. In late February, the Italian conductor was quietly consulted by a friend of the Symphony Association as to how he would look upon a chance to organize and direct an orchestra for this sponsoring body, an activity which, it was pointedly mentioned, could very well be carried on without affecting his duties to the opera company. Nespoli by now had his Italian advisers in town (Mrs. Marie Vescova, in particuar) and through one of these submitted his contract with Mrs. Graham to a legal authority for examination. When told that it seemed to leave room for the orchestral job, he accepted at once with enthusiasm. But he was bidden to say nothing about this to anyone for the moment.

***

By mid-April Nespoli was rehearsing for the association an orchestra whose personnel he had selected. They were a mixture of professional and amateur players, including some who had participated in both the Philharmonic and Little Symphony ventures. As might have been supposed, Josephine Boudreaux was installed as the concertmistress. The first rehearsals took place in a cotton warehouse of the new Merchants' and Manufacturers' Building, a great desolate room that, with its low ceiling and baled cotton stacked high against three of its walls, could not have been better designed by a genius from hell to resist and defeat musical sound. The use of it was free, however, and economy was the governing idea. To a man of Nespoli's temper and sensitive hearing, this cavern was a torture chamber fit only for Dante's description. He bore it as he did the other bewilderments of a mad and impossible land, but his nightly distress, as he stood on a deal table before his players and wept, was such as to make that of Canio in the first act of *Pagliacci* seem a relatively undemonstrative form of chagrin. Eventually those sessions were moved from the cotton loft to the salesroom of a dairy concern.

On the whole the results were rather better than anyone might have expected. Nespoli's choice of players spoke well for his judgment and probity; he had made the most of his chances. Also, his preparation of the orchestra again showed him to be a tireless and indeed fanatical worker, which at least meant there was no wastage of time. And this challenge was good for his spirit. His new patrons were understanding and sympathetic with his musical aims, and if the working conditions were somewhat odd, he had the comforting knowledge that this experiment, if it came off well, could offer more solid and lasting benefits than those promised by the rather nebulous opera scheme. The incentive was there to put forth his best, and this he attempted to do by presenting the new band with an order of work that was a flattering estimate of its ready resources—not to mention, perhaps, his own.

Selling tickets for the concerts was no problem at any rate. The real attraction was not the program, but the town's musical war, obviously made hotter by the Symphony Association's return to the field. Everyone wanted to be present to see what happened. When the night for the first concert finally arrived, the Palace Theater was full and the air somewhat more than expectant. That gathering of May 7, 1931, was discreetly referred to by the press as a "representative audience," which meant that all factions in this struggle were represented in force. There was a tension in the auditorium, hardly diminished when ceremonies began with certain formal remarks from the stage, all carefully emphasizing the fact that the Symphony Association had founded and fostered the orchestra movement in Houston and was here resuming an effort that had only been stopped by a world war. The inference was that it was now time to revive this excellent civic aim—but of course in the orthodox way.

The lights then failed for a moment. When they came up brightly again the spectators beheld, in all proper detail, a stage crowded by an orchestra of seventy-four, and out of the wings strode Nespoli, red, damp, and heroic, to address himself to the gods present and past. Drama had been duly observed. The program itself likewise aimed for the limit in that respect; it was nothing if not dramatic, and was drawn from the canon of the art. It opened with Wagner, the

Prelude and Liebestod from *Tristan und Isolde* (for some reason given under their French titles), and included that master's Good Friday Spell music from *Parsifal*. Between these came the Beethoven Fifth Symphony.

***

Doubtless this program was intended to discourage the competitive ventures by indicating the limits of their reach. But it likewise showed the limits of its own. The program asked too much of an orchestra put together as this company had been; the band was clearly ill fitted to deal with the problems, tonal and stylistic, of such a list—even under a leader who bore the name of an archangel and was more than ordinarily willing to wrestle with the other celestials on any terms.

But the effort was not a total disaster. Nespoli's passion, though that of a furnace, did not sweep him away; his work showed enough sign of respectable judgment and method; and the orchestra, catching this intensity well, often met his demands with some grace.

***

The evening had invited attention to certain incidental delights, one of which was that the shoes of the little Italian conductor squeaked loudly. They always did, inside the theater or out. His other mannerisms, worthy of Salvini in *Hamlet* (he had a way of clapping his hand to his forehead, at a moment of stress, in a manner rendered more widely familiar by the movie performances of Ben Turpin), had likewise amused those who had come looking for sport. All the same, he had probably brought off the most impressive orchestral performance yet heard from the city's own talents. When this popular verdict was underwritten by all published reports of the concert, the quibblers were left with very little to chew on. The association had made a definite point. ★

Douglas Pegues Harvey

This article by San Antonio architect Douglas Pegues Harvey was not published in *Texas Architect* until 1990, but it explains the way that the Astrodome made its very first spectators feel that that they were stepping inside a building—and into infinity. While Harvey calls the Dome "the archetypical social form across the land," circa 1990, he also points to the reason why that form was not, in fact, eternal. Once the spectator turned his attention from the building to the game itself, he felt that he was watching it on television, and eventually that got old.

Harvey also articulates the connection between the Dome's and NASA's senses of "space," and points to the way that Houston became the world center in the quest for infinite space. Given the challenges facing NASA today, and the sad status of the Dome, we have to admit that that quest did not last for an infinite period of time.

From Il Duomo

ONE OF THE RECURRING THEMES IN AMERICAN cultural history is the quest for Zion: breaking out into infinite space to create (or regain) the ideal landscape and community—to get back to the Garden. When NASA began giving that quest its ultimate form, a conceptual boundary was created that demanded a new understanding of architectural "space." The significance of the Astrodome ... lies in [its] re-presentation of this quest as an introspective one, by establishing the possibility of an infinite interior space.

The Astrodome engages the sense of the infinite paradoxically. A single-space building, no matter how huge, appears larger inside than outside. Once inside, we lose the scalar cues the landscape and sky normally provide and have only the structure itself as a frame of reference. But our personal and evolutionary experiences with the natural world have conditioned us to interpret the background as all-encompassing. Therefore we read the distant walls as the natural background, and perceptually "overscale" any uncommonly large interior; the larger the room, the more pronounced the effect.

The Astrodome simply raises this effect to a higher order of magnitude. It encloses so much volume that the roof's visual weight is inadequate to delimit the scale, and the space becomes perceptually unbounded. Viewed through our prejudice in favor of overscaling, it reads as bigger than immeasurably big— infinite. The roof is no more than a gossamer web of steel clouds drifting above the field, completing a vision of the cosmos. Because an infinite space cannot be "inside" anything, in the Astrodome, you are not, therefore, "inside."

A parallel physiological effect then reinforces this message. When we gaze into the distance, the alignment and focus of our eyes gives us a certain neuromuscular feedback that we associate with the wide-open spaces. In neuromuscular terms, a sufficiently distant roof is the same as the sky.

The meaning derived from these phenomena are profoundly different from those evoked by the sense of being inside. Freed of ultimate closure, the Astrodome becomes a microcosm, as though it were a colony in space or on society's conceptual frontier (which, in a sense, it was), with a wholeness independent of the outside world. It is even a *dome*—a form loaded with historical references to the sacred and the infinite. Its location at the edge of the limitless prairie, in a nearly infinite parking lot, heightens the air of surreality, while its name appropriates the aura of outer space on behalf of inner space.

Subjecting the building's functions to such an articulate vastness gives them a *jamais vu* quality. By its association with the cosmic vision, any mass spectator event instantly becomes a grander, more intense, more focused spectacle; its emotional equations are transformed. The first indoor baseball game became, figuratively, the first game of all time.

However, intensifying the ritual to such a degree also transforms it into entertainment. Beginning with the first baseball game, the sense and even the pretense of continuity and reciprocity between the participants and the spectators (such as that postulated by the Texas A&M "twelfth man" tradition) were forever abandoned. The first spectators in the Astrodome became the live audience of the world's largest television studio, furnished with *theater seats*, not bleachers, and with a scoreboard that lit up like a game in a video arcade. Finally the Caesars in the skyboxes had a suitably spectacular barbarity to entertain them.

Success, it is said, has a thousand fathers. It may already be too late to establish with certainty who really originated the idea for a covered, air-conditioned baseball stadium. It is clear that various business leaders in Houston during the 1950s were campaigning to bring major league baseball to town. There were studies for a "War Memorial Stadium" that eventually became the Astrodome in order to cement the deal with the National League.

Public sentiment credits Judge Roy Hofheinz, the Dome's guiding genius and co-owner of its master lease. One story has it that he got the idea for a roofed sports stadium as a tourist in Italy, on learning that the Colosseum (home to blood sports and human sacrifices) had had a retractable sunshade. Prior to getting involved in baseball, certainly, the Judge was in a race (won by Frank Sharp at Sharpstown) to develop Houston's first air-conditioned shopping mall, and he was thoroughly familiar with the design and construction of long-span, air-conditioned assembly spaces. Moreover, the idea was already in the air. Tycoon Glenn McCarthy may have proposed a covered stadium during the 1940s. Walter O'Malley considered building a covered stadium for the Dodgers while they were still in Brooklyn, and Harris County officials met with him in Los Angeles in the late '50s.

But in mythological terms the Colosseum connection is true, regardless of its factuality. It evokes the laying-on of hands, conveying the splendor of ancient Rome from its Pantheon to the new cathedral of America's sports religion. In an article in *Architectural Design* in 1970, Peter Papademetriou equated the Astrodome to St. Peter's as a gigantic urban-edge project that established a defining physical and social form.

In the beginning, the glory of Rome gave a desirable gloss to the Astrodome's image. But today comparisons to either St. Peter's or the Colosseum are redundant. The *Dome*, not Rome, is the archetypical social form across the land. With the coming of the Dome, spectacle at last reached the intensity necessary to bridge the mythic distance from baseball, diffuse and subtle, to football, especially professional football, a gladiatorial contest worthy of the first Colosseum. ★

DAVID KAPLAN

David Kaplan is a business reporter for the *Houston Chronicle*. He occasionally writes essays for the paper. He was previously a freelance writer for *Houston City* magazine and *Cite* and a feature writer and columnist for the *Houston Post*. He is the author of *Roundup: A Texas Kid's Companion* and co-editor of Th*e Best of Bum: The Quotable Bum Phillips*, both published by Texas Monthly Press. Like many Houstonians, he has conflicted feelings about the long empty Dome. In this short piece, published in *Cite* magazine in 1986, Kaplan captures both the thrill Houston felt at the Astrodome's 1965 opening, and how quickly the excitement faded.

Let It Rain

FOR AN EXHIBITION BASEBALL GAME, LIMousines pull up, carrying men in tuxedoes, women in mink. They've come, not for peanuts and foul balls, but to enter the future.

Spaceship-like, it beckons. They walk the ramp, step inside. Vast, a clear span twice that of any previous structure. A crowned city, filled with great color and humanity. Skybox butlers wearing white gloves surround the highest realm.

A visiting sportswriter observes that when man first steps on the moon, five, ten, or twenty years from then, he'll feel a similar awe. A visiting pitcher asks, "Is it all right to chew tobacco?"

As LBJ peers through his binoculars, Mickey Mantle hits a home run, and the $2 million electronic scoreboard, compared in the program to the aurora borealis, erupts with shooting stars, ricocheting bullets, and a snorting steer. That was opening night, 9 April 1965.

Twenty-one years later, we approach the Dome in Toyotas, hoping for a foul ball. The Dome itself, we pay little mind. Now it means the past, and a place where we've witnessed too many Oiler games.

Beyond the local though, the Dome still holds its own. Among famous Texas buildings, it's second only to the Alamo, built in 1757. Open a Rand McNally city map; the Astrodome is the only building illustrated. Internationally, it's Houston's best known structure.

"Listen to the truckers talking into their CBs," muses Houston Sports Association Chairman John McMullen. "Houston's handle is the Dome City."

The Dome in fact makes a good city symbol. It epitomizes Houston: spacious, adaptable, air-conditioned, audacious, and out in the middle of nowhere.

Yet we've turned our backs on this intriguing monument. It's time we give the Dome its due.

The Dome was conceived in 1960, to lure major league baseball to Houston. Glenn H. McCarthy toyed with a roofed stadium scheme 15 years earlier, but Herbert Allen, who helped conceive the handsome and innovative Rice Stadium, may have originated the dome idea for this project. Popular opinion credits Judge Roy Hofheinz. Hofheinz, a businessman, politician, and circus lover, was certainly its promoter.

The design was touted as daringly innovative and a "geometric nightmare," but according to S. I. Morris, whose firm, Wilson, Morris, Crain and Anderson was one of the architects on the project, "Nothing about it was new. It just hadn't been done that big. We all had an awareness it could be done. The biggest question was whether we could air-condition a thing that big."

Legend holds that the Astrodome was architecturally inspired by the Roman Colosseum. The Dome did have a model, but it wasn't the Colosseum. It was the Channel 13 Studios, at 3310 Bissonnet, designed by Hermon Lloyd and W. B. Morgan, who were associated with Morris in the design of the Dome.

During construction, fans had to settle for Colt Stadium, where parking lot attendants in orange ten-gallon hats directed the entering fan to "Wyatt Earp" and other cowboy theme parking areas. Inside, a "triggerette" led fans to their seats. Clouds of insecticide floated above. Hofheinz kept watch on the rising Dome from a Shamrock Hotel balcony.

For the playing of baseball, the Astrodome offered problems: grass wouldn't grow and the players couldn't see fly balls. Solving the glare problem was easy. They blocked the sky with paint.

To solve the problem of dying grass, Hofheinz brought in Monsanto Corporation, which led to the birth of Astroturf. The judge called up the president of the National League and told him that the newly invented polyester carpeting was about the same as grass. The president didn't quibble.

For Hofheinz, the Dome was more than the "Eighth Wonder of the World." It was home. He lived behind the scoreboard. His five-story apartment came with a presidential suite, built for LBJ, containing Louis XIV and XV furnishings, a medieval chapel, a miniature bathroom, trick elevator, trick bar, a shooting gallery, barber shop, and one-lane bowling alley.

For Hofheinz, the Dome became an obsession, his kingdom, his shell. There were stretches of time when he saw little of the undomed world. But in 1976, he lost control of Houston Sports Association. He left a good-bye message on the scoreboard and moved out.

The grand Dome myths, which Hofheinz helped invent, slowly unraveled with time. Time worked on the Dome as it would a '65 Cadillac.

The appearance of other domes considerably dimmed the Astrodome's luster. Who can forget that embarrassing moment in the early 1970s, the unveiling of the Superdome, which was bigger, newer, more expensive, and had more skyboxes?

The reality principle brought a more critical assessment of the Dome. Anti-Dome romantics began singing their folksongs of Fenway Park and Wrigley Field, with their ancient timber, their sky and breezes.

They have a point. As a sports stadium, it's not even the best in town. It wasn't built for baseball physically, in the sense that Rice Stadium was created to house football. The Dome does offer comfort, but it's too distracting. As Joe Jares of *Sports Illustrated* tried to tell us early on, the Dome actually creates a new indoor sport, "a combination of baseball, pinball, and *1984*."

The Dome merits recognition, not as a sports or architectural wonder, but for its symbols and its place in time. It's the Arc de Triomphe of Texas, a classic piece of pop-culture.

And pop-culture is as notable as any other, a point made by Peter C. Papademetriou in "The Pope and The Judge," a treatise comparing the Dome with Vatican City, which appeared in the July 1970 issue of *Architectural Design*.

Vatican City may indeed be a reasonable paradigm for Astrodomain. Both were begun near, but on a fringe, of their cities, at the site of the original cult centre (old St. Peter's/old Colt 45 Stadium). Both have as their symbols the main building (St. Peter's Basilica/Astrodome) and a public space of great scale (Piazza S. Pietro/Astrodome parking lot), which is adjacent to a collection of outbuildings (Vatican Palaces/Astroworld hotels). In both cases there exists a large collection of gardens (Pontifical Gardens/Astroworld) at a more intimate scale, and finally both the Pope and the Judge reside within each complex.

I take the tour. They still offer three a day. The indoor vastness still amazes first-timers. The tour begins with a lecture. We're given the dimensions of the Marlboro, Budweiser, Coke, and First City Bank signs. We're taunted with a list of skybox accoutrements. We're shown a multi-screen slide slow entitled "The Astrodome Experience," which is like a trip back into the sixties. For the most part, this is the original Dome pitch (In the beginning, gladiators fought in the Colosseum of Rome). Some slides are badly faded.

What a tour they could give. Stories the Dome could tell. So much it has seen: circuses, tractor pulls, a Cajun wedding, a secret convention of women, bull fights, Billy Graham and the Rolling Stones. The Guru Maharaji came, to usher in a thousand years of peace, and, as a rumored bonus, levitate the Dome. His more radical fringe believed that a flying saucer would come down to lift the guru, his disciples, and the Dome to Uranus.

Sadly, no one keeps records of the Dome. Its strange and fascinating young history could make a wonderful archives, but says Paul Darst, scoreboard operator and 15-year veteran, "Every time somebody new comes in, more files get cleaned out." One more way in which the Dome is like its city.

Darst recalls his first encounter with the Astrodome, the thrilling moment when he and his Boy Scout troop, dressed as astronauts, marched out onto the field of the brand new Dome.

It's 21 now, this Eighth Wonder, this giant Channel 13. On this spring morning, the Dome's roof glistens. Across the street, at a trailer camp, a man is cleaning his goat.

As the world's economy looks to the East, as they dazzle us in Hong Kong, let's not forget our shining Dome, and April of '65, when the world looked at Houston and held its breath.

We showed them that nothing could stand in our way. Let the Texas sun blaze. Let the sky fill with mosquitoes. Let it rain. ★

LI CUNXIN

Li Cunxin was one of the first two cultural exchange students allowed to go to America to study under Mao's regime. Starting in 1979, he danced with the Houston Ballet for sixteen years, becoming a principal in 1982. He also guest performed around the world with some of the best ballet companies and won two silver and one bronze medal at three international ballet competitions. He is now a senior manager at one of the biggest stockbroking firms in Australia.

In Houston, Li began began a relationship with an aspiring American dancer, Elizabeth Mackey. In 1981, they rushed their marriage so that Li could remain in the United States without having to defect. But when Li and Elizabeth went to the Chinese Consulate on Montrose Boulevard, they were detained by the authorities, and Li's Houston friends and supporters had to spring into action.

From *Mao's Last Dancer*: Defection

WE WERE TAKEN TO A MEETING ROOM WHERE Ben [Stevenson, founding director of the Houston Ballet], Clare Duncan and Jack, the Houston Ballet's company lawyer, were already waiting. Consul Zhang was there, and his wife who was the translator, and several other consulate officials. The only one missing was the consul general himself.

I was surprised to see my friend Zhang there too. He looked tense and upset, and when our eyes briefly met he quickly turned away.

It was about six in the evening by now. Ben, Clare and Jack were all dressed in their evening wear ready for another farewell party at Louisa's house that night.

I looked around the room. I had been in this meeting room before when I'd had to report to the consulate on weekends. It was a big square room with black-and-white Chinese landscapes and calligraphy on the walls. There were some sofas and chairs in the middle of the room and some extra chairs added for extra people. I still had Lori's "Don't let the turkeys get you down" badge on my jacket.

The atmosphere was tense. The Chinese host gestured for Elizabeth and me to sit. The consulate officials seemed relaxed and friendly, but Ben was clearly furious. He wouldn't even look at me.

We were offered tea and soft drinks, and there was a lot of small talk about China and the improving relationship between the two countries. Charles [Foster, his immigration lawyer] and I were perplexed: nobody was talking about why we were there at all! The officials seemed very content for everyone just to have a good time. I was perspiring and shivering. I was very scared. I could not stand the suspense much longer.

Then one of the officials asked Charles and Jack to speak with him, alone, in a room down the hall. I wanted Charles to stay but he gave me a reassuring look, and he told me later he'd thought it made sense anyway since he was effectively my attorney and Jack was the attorney acting on behalf of the Houston Ballet. They would engage in some serious talk about my situation and spare the rest of us from all the legal unpleasantries.

But it didn't seem like that to those of us left in the room. It seemed as though the consulate officials were deliberately keeping the conversation going, trying to distract us, while they gradually eliminated my friends from the room.

People disappeared one by one, and each time a friend left I squeezed Elizabeth's hand tighter and tighter. It wasn't long before only Clare, Zhang, Elizabeth, myself and two officials were left in the room.

Eventually Consul Zhang asked everyone, except me, to go to another room. He wanted a private conversation.

Elizabeth refused.

We begged Clare and Zhang to stay with us, but the two officials simply shoved Clare and Zhang out the door.

Then four security guards stormed in, heading straight for Elizabeth and me.

We screamed.

Clare and Zhang looked back and screamed too.

The building echoed. It took only a few seconds for the four Chinese guards to separate me from Elizabeth. I tried to kick them away but I was completely helpless against those highly trained guards. They quickly grabbed my arms and legs, carried me to the top floor and locked me into a small room, only big enough for two single beds and a small chest of drawers.

I was struggling to breathe. I was scared. Truly scared.

In the meantime, downstairs, Charles Foster realized what was happening. He demanded to see his client.

From then on, Charles said later, the atmosphere changed completely. In a very loud and strident voice the consulate official ordered Charles to sit. He was on Chinese territory, and he was expected to follow orders. The two employees who were serving drinks dropped their trays and assumed a defensive stance. They blocked the door. Charles charged forward but was pushed and shoved as he tried to get through. He could hear my voice yelling from above, "Help, they are taking me! Help, they are taking me!" By the time Charles and Jack got back to the main room everyone was there, except me.

From my room on the top floor I could hear the guards talking outside the door. "Could have killed that bastard!" said one of them. I was terrified. I remembered the executions I had witnessed as a child during the Cultural Revolution, and I saw my own death flash in front of my eyes. I felt desperately alone. Nobody could save me that night. It was just a matter of time before they stuck a gun to my head or forced me back to China where I would suffer an unbearably slow, humiliating death in the cruelest prison in the land.

I tried to think about my niang and her sweet laughter. I tried to think about my dia and his humble stories. I tried to think about Elizabeth, the smell of her perfume. I remembered the Bandit and our blood brothers' poem, but I couldn't hold on to any one comforting thread.

I looked out the tiny window and down at a pool on ground floor. It was too far to jump. Escape was impossible. Death here, at least, would be simpler and quicker than the suffering and humiliation of a Chinese prison.

The door opened. Consul Zhang came into the room. He sat in front of me on the other bed and attempted a smile, but he seemed very sad. He looked straight into my eyes, like a chess player trying to figure out a strategy. I wanted to turn away but I thought this would suggest to him that I was wavering, so I forced back a smile.

We sat there just looking at each other. I was perspiring profusely. I couldn't stand this silence. If I sat there any longer, my heart would simply explode. I had to do something! What to say to Consul Zhang? What *was* there to say? I knew the outcome would be the same: I was scum, a defector, the most hated traitor of all.

Consul Zhang finally broke the silence. "Cunxin, what have you done?" he said calmly.

There seemed so many different ways to answer, but I knew none of my answers would satisfy him. "Nothing," I replied.

"Do you understand what you have done?" he asked, this time with more urgency.

"Yes, I love Elizabeth and I married her. Is this against the law?" I replied.

"Yes! What you have done is against your government's wishes and it's illegal in China! You're a Chinese citizen! *Your* government doesn't recognize your marriage. And you're too young to know what love is."

"Consul Zhang, my lawyer, Mr. Foster, told me that China *does* recognize international marriage law. I'm married here in America, and American law should be observed. As to my love for Elizabeth, it's a personal matter. I won't discuss it with you."

He was incensed. "Do you think a foreigner could really love a Chinese? The foreigners will use you, abuse you, and dump you like a piece of trash!"

"How do you know what it is like to be loved by a foreigner?" I snapped back.

For a second he wasn't sure what to say. "Have you seen any marriages between Chinese and Americans?"

I couldn't think of any.

"It's not too late to change your mind. You can just tell Elizabeth that you have made a mistake and you want to walk away from it." It was as though he was encouraging me to do something immensely heroic.

"No," I said, "I don't want to divorce Elizabeth. I want to spend the rest of my life with her."

"We are not talking of divorce. As far as we are concerned, you were never married. We don't and won't recognize your marriage as legitimate. *You* don't decide what you're going to do with your life, the Communist Party does! You're a Chinese citizen. You follow Chinese laws, not American laws."

By now I was angry. "If you think Mr. Foster has informed me wrongly, let's ask him now," I said.

Consul Zhang looked perplexed. "Mr. Foster and your friends have left. They are disgusted with what you have done! You are alone. They are no friends of yours. *We're* your friends. Everything will be forgiven if you go back to China as planned. You will be loved and respected by all your people!"

I didn't believe for a moment what Consul Zhang said about my friends. But I did think they must have been thrown out of the consulate and that the Chinese government would promise me anything to get me back to China.

There was a knock on the door, and Consul Zhang left for a brief discussion with another man. I could hear whispers, but I couldn't make out what they were saying. Then Consul Zhang came back. He was trying hard to control his anger. "I want you to think about what we have just discussed, and I'll come back soon."

I felt a sense of relief when he closed the door. I needed to regroup, to gather my courage. I felt exhausted, but I knew this was only the beginning of a long and nerve-racking night.

A few minutes later the door opened again. This time one of the vice consuls general entered. He was an older, slightly taller man, and he spoke with a heavy southern-Chinese accent. He was very friendly and offered me something to drink. I politely refused. So he began to try to convince me to go back to China, listing all the benefits there would be for my family. "Think of your parents and all your brothers back home! How proud of you they must have been! You don't want to let them down. You don't want to create any problem for them, do you?"

This was my greatest fear. If anything terrible happened to my family because of what I had done, I would never forgive myself. But there was no reason to involve my family! The Chinese government was responsible for my education, not my parents.

"I left my family when I was eleven. I have nothing to do with them, and they have nothing to do with me," I tried. I couldn't implicate my family in all of this. My family had no idea what I'd done.

"You're the property of China," the vice consul general continued. "We have given you everything. We have the power to do anything that we want with you. We don't want to lose our star dancer! You simply *have* to listen to what we say. It is for your own good. The party knows what's good for you. Have faith in the party. Have you forgotten what the party has done for you? Have you forgotten what you have sworn in front of the Communist Youth Party flag?"

I remembered the years and years of lies about the West. I thought of Minister Wang who had refused to see me about my return to America. I thought of my lack of freedom in China, the desperate poverty that they had made sound so rich and glorious. "I don't want to talk about the party," I said.

"You don't expect the party will listen to you! *Do* you? The party listens to no one! Everyone listens to the party! Who helped you to get married? Is it Ben?" he asked suddenly.

"No. I made my own decision."

"Tell me the truth!" He raised his voice. "We already have the facts. Don't underestimate your government! Is it Ben? Someone in the American government? Someone in the Taiwanese government?"

Under different circumstances I would have burst into laughter. What he was suggesting was completely ludicrous. "No one has helped me. Would I have come to the consulate if I had a political agenda to hide or if the Americans or the Taiwanese had helped me? Would they have advised me to come tonight?" I asked.

"It's not for you to ask me questions! I'm asking *you!* Who helped you?"

"Nobody helped me. Didn't you hear me? I won't answer any more of your questions," I replied angrily.

The conversation with the vice consul general went on for another half an hour, but I spoke little. Then another consulate official replaced him for another half an hour of interrogation and persuasion. It was like musical chairs.

Every half an hour another official would take over the interrogation. Each left without any progress. In a strange way, after the initial fear and despair, I felt calmer as time went on. What do I have to fear if I am about to lose my life? I thought.

A couple of times during the interrogations I touched the scar on my arm, the one I received as a baby, the one that caused so much anxiety for my parents and that had now become a symbol of my niang's love. When I touched it I could feel her love. It gave me comfort. It gave me courage. It reminded me of where I came from and where I wanted to be.

I didn't regret what I had done. In a strange way I felt at peace with myself. Elizabeth was my first love. Our marriage was not a marriage of convenience. I knew I could have stayed in America by qualifying on my own artistic merits. Charles had told me this at our very first meeting. But still I felt a strong sense of sorrow for my parents. I hadn't even sent them a single dollar yet.

I felt the tears pushing upward through my throat. My poor dear niang. She had suffered enough hardship already. I thought of her wrinkled face and the sorrow she would feel if she never saw me again. Oh, how much I loved her! She was the most innocent and loving niang on this earth. She had given me everything, yet I had nothing to give her in return. Would my niang ever recover from her despair at losing one of her beloved sons? This would surely kill her.

I thought too of my teachers who had invested so much of their time and effort in me, hoping that I would one day put Chinese ballet on the world map. Their hopes would be dashed. I would never see them again. But I was determined not to allow consulate officials to see my tears or to sense my weakness.

***

Downstairs, in the main room, everyone was shaken. The consulate officials changed their approach and went back to their pleasantries again, offering everyone drinks and engaging in idle conversation. Charles told me later that he'd sat there, bewildered, but at last he could stand it no longer. "Wait a minute, my client was just dragged out of here and I don't know about the rest of you but I am not leaving until you have released him! You are in violation of U.S. law!"

"I don't understand, Mr. Foster," Consul Zhang spoke up with genuine surprise. "You just told us that you strongly supported good U.S.–Sino relations."

"Yes, I did and I do," Charles replied.

"Well, what is good for China and for the United States is for Li to return to China. If he does not, U.S.–Sino relations will be harmed. So will the Houston Ballet and their planned tour to the People's Republic of China."

Charles responded. "While we all may agree with you about what's good for U.S.–China relations, there's one problem with what you say. In the U.S., Li gets to make that decision."

They then proceeded to have lengthy, almost philosophical conversations about individual rights versus group rights. Charles later said he'd almost enjoyed it, except for the fact that he was concerned about my safety. He was working on the assumption that they would hold me through the night and then take me to the airport and fly me out of America the following morning.

But Ben and my friends would not leave the consulate without me. They refused to leave. So the consulate officials turned the lights out. The free tea, soft drinks and crackers were withdrawn. Only the use of the bathrooms was allowed.

About twenty minutes later the officials came back into the room. Kind and polite persuasion changed to cold, threatening words.

Ben and my friends continued to resist.

By now, rumors about my detention at the consulate had started to spread to Louisa's party. By 10:30 p.m. they suspected something terrible had happened. Two people in particular wanted to find out the truth: Anne Holmes and Carl Cunningham were dance critics for the *Houston Chronicle* and the *Houston Post*. They'd planned to interview me that night, but as time dragged on and I was still missing they eventually enlisted the help of some Houston Ballet board members and discovered that I was being held at the consulate against my will.

Hours had passed. People were beginning to gather at the side entrance to the consulate. Charles was asked by Consul Zhang to go and deal with them. That was ironic, he thought: the small crowd included a few newspaper reporters, and the Chinese officials seemed to be putting an unusual amount of faith in him, asking him to talk with the press.

Anne and Carl, the two dance critics, were among the small crowd gathering outside. Charles could only say to them that there was a discussion going on inside and they were about to resolve the situation. He believed that if he told them the truth it would make the situation even more inflammatory.

He went back inside. "Look, there are members of the press out there, and they are not going to go away," he told the Chinese officials. "They are going to make this into a big story." But to Charles's surprise the Chinese officials kept on insisting that, as a lawyer, he should know how to control the press. Charles laughed. This was America, he explained several times. In America even lawyers could not control the press.

***

At one o'clock in the morning, after many hours of interrogation, I was collapsing with hunger and exhaustion. My head was throbbing. I couldn't think anymore. I hadn't had anything to eat since breakfast the previous morning. I asked one of the consular officials for something to eat. I didn't care if they put something terrible in my food like sleeping pills or poison. I just needed food.

They found me some leftover fried rice and a Tsingtao beer, a bittersweet offering—it reminded me of my parents back home. At least I would taste something from my hometown before I left this world, I thought.

After my fried rice and beer they wanted to resume the interrogation. I told them that my brain couldn't take any more. Please, just leave me alone, and if they wanted to kill me they should do it now. I had made up my mind. I wasn't going back to China.

To my surprise they agreed to stop their interrogation, and they assigned one of the guards to sleep in the room and keep an eye on me. I thought I'd just feign sleep, so I pretended to snore. But the guard simply told me to stop it, and we both twisted and turned all night.

About the same time, Charles had his final discussion with Anne and Carl outside the consulate. They wanted to know all the details. They knew this was a front-page story. Charles asked them to withhold writing anything until the matter was resolved. They said they appreciated that, but they had a greater duty to the public and they had deadlines to meet. Charles went back inside and asked to use the telephone. First he rang Federal Judge Woodrow Seals, a feisty old guy who had been appointed by President John F. Kennedy.

"Charles, this better be good," he said. It was about two in the morning by now.

Charles briefly explained the emergency, and Judge Seals told him that he would meet him at the federal courthouse at 6 a.m. along with the chief justice of the Southern District of Texas, John Singleton. Charles then called his legal assistant to help draw up the documents.

Then, unknown to the consulate officials, Charles made another crucial call. He rang the U.S. State Department. He asked to speak to the duty officer for China. He said this was a critical matter. The U.S. government should act. Charles related the story of Simas Kudirka, a Lithuanian seaman who had been on board a Soviet trawler that was suspected of spying in U.S. waters in the early 1970s. Kudirka had jumped from the deck of the Soviet vessel onto the deck of a U.S. Coast Guard vessel. Soviet sailors forcibly removed him, and a long investigation followed. Everyone in the Coast Guard chain of command who had allowed Kudirka's removal faced the possibility of court-martial.

Kudirka eventually ended up in America. Charles had hosted him in Houston. He knew the U.S. State Department had internal regulations about the forcible repatriation of foreign nationals, particularly when it came to communist countries. He knew he'd said enough.

The Chinese officials at this point became suspicious and told Charles that he could no longer use their phones. In any event, he knew he had to leave the consulate to help draft the legal documents. There were only a few hours left until morning, and he wanted to speed things along.

After Charles left the consulate, the Chinese officials had had enough. They demanded all the Westerners follow Charles and leave the consulate at once. But everyone was determined. They refused to leave until they saw me safe and sound. This irritated the Chinese hosts even more. They cut the phone off and turned off the lights once more.

When Charles left the consulate the morning papers were already out on the streets. Charles was shocked to see the headlines. "Chinese Consulate Holding Eight Americans Hostage." He returned to his office, then went to the federal courthouse with the finished legal documents, ready for signature.

Federal Judge Woodrow Seals and Chief Justice John Singleton were there as arranged. "Charles," said Singleton bluntly, "I hope you know what you are doing."

"Well," Charles replied, "there's not much time, so we just have to try our best."

***

Once the documents were signed, Charles rang Chase Untermeyer, executive assistant to the then Vice President George Bush. Charles cited the Kudirka story again and said this was a critical matter. "Chase," he said, "Vice President Bush's wife, Barbara, is a trustee of the Houston Ballet. The vice president should know the Chinese consulate is holding a Houston Ballet dancer, Li Cunxin, against his will." Charles knew the vice president would take appropriate action.

Chase in turn immediately contacted Vice President Bush, who had Chase call James Lilly, who was then the Asia Specialist on the National Security Council and was later to become the U.S. ambassador to China.

Charles then returned to the consulate with a federal marshal to serve both orders, one ordering the consul general to produce me and the other enjoining the consul general from removing me from the country. The handful of people waiting outside had grown, and they were mostly press. One man, looking very much like Clark Kent with pad and pencil in hand, walked up to Charles and whispered in his ear. He was FBI. "The consulate is surrounded," he said. "We have the floor plans. There is no way they can take Li out."

Charles knocked on the door of the consulate, with the U.S. marshal, trying to serve the court orders. "Go away," said an official, "there is no one here."

For the rest of the day Charles went to and from the consulate, but he was not allowed back in. He received many phone calls both from the federal court and from Washington. FBI numbers outside the consulate began to grow.

Charles then received another call. It was from James Lilly in the White House. President Reagan was inquiring about the status of the case. Then the State Department called and asked Charles to go back to the consulate and tell them to reconnect their phones. The Chinese embassy was trying to contact them to give them instructions.

Charles returned to the consulate around 4 p.m., and by 5 o'clock he was again in a room by himself talking to Consul Zhang. Consul Zhang was almost in tears. He asked Charles again, did he *have* to release me? "Yes. The problem won't go away. If you don't release Li, it will only get worse."

The crowd outside now numbered around two hundred. All the major networks were there, television cameras in the back of flatbed trucks, cameras over the heads of the crowd, and the parking lot of Walgreen's drugstore next door had been turned into a mini-TV studio. In my room at the top of the consulate, I was, of course, completely unaware of these developments.

Soon after 5 p.m. Consul Zhang returned to my room. "Cunxin, for your own good, and for the last time, I'm going to ask you: will you go back to China?"

Here is the turning point of my life, I thought. I was prepared for the worst. "No, I won't go back. Do whatever you like with me."

He looked at me long and hard. Finally he said sadly, "I'm sorry you have chosen this road. I still believe you will regret it later. I'm sad we have lost you to America. You're now a man without a country and a people. But I want to warn you, there are many reporters outside. What you say to them now or in the future will have a direct effect on you and your family back in China. You should consider seriously anything you say or do. We will be watching you."

I could hardly believe what I had heard. I was going to be *free*.

All of sudden, I felt only compassion toward Consul Zhang. I understood that he only represented the government's desires, what was best for China and the Communist Party. But, unlike me, he *had* to go back and he would probably never manage to get out again. He had been kind to me the whole time I was in Houston. "I'm sorry, Consul Zhang," I said sincerely.

He looked at me with a barely detectable hint of empathy and led me downstairs to Elizabeth and Charles. ★

MIMI SWARTZ AND SHERRON WATKINS

===

Mimi Swartz and Sherron Watkins are the co-authors of *Power Failure, The Inside Story of the Collapse of Enron*. Swartz is one of the leading explainers of Houston, and indeed Texas, to the world. A frequent contributor to the *New York Times*, she is an executive editor of *Texas Monthly*. Swartz has been a National Magazine Award finalist three times. She began her magazine writing career at *Houston City* magazine, where she worked from 1979–82.

Watkins is the former vice president of Enron Corporation who alerted then-CEO Ken Lay in August 2001 to accounting irregularities within the company, warning him that Enron "might implode in a wave of accounting scandals." Watkins joined Enron in 1993, initially working for Andrew Fastow, and resigned in November 2002. She later testified before the House and Senate committees investigating Enron's collapse, was named one of *Time* Magazine's Persons of the Year, and began a career as a lecturer on business ethics.

===

From *Power Failure*: Mythology

FROM THE BEGINNING, ENRON WAS A STORY with a mystery at its center, for Ken Lay was a mystery to many people. Just about everyone who met Lay for the first time liked him, from world leaders to the ministers from Houston's poorest neighborhoods. A very rich man as early as the mid-eighties, he was always able to convey, at least from a distance, that he was a man of simple tastes and good works. His dark eyes were unusually soulful, though they could turn as hard as onyx, and he had the oversized, enveloping hands of a farm boy, which he had been. He also possessed the politician's gift—or the habit of the minister's son, which he also was—for remembering not just your name but the name of your sister, and the ability to recollect when she had recovered from her last heart surgery. He knew when your son had graduated from high school, which classes he excelled in, and what college he wanted to go to, and that it was a good school. In short, Ken Lay made it easy to believe that he had not forgotten where he came from. This talent, when coupled with the great success of his company, meant that he was able to walk into a room of international power brokers in Washington or New York or into a Houston church social, and the effect was the same. The crowds parted for him with something like awe, and he, in return, shook every hand and knew every name, and business could proceed with a feeling of the very best intentions.

Later, when Enron began to teeter, and then rumble into chaos, people would be forced to reconsider their idea of Lay, an activity that was particularly painful in Houston. It would be easy for East Coast reporters and midwestern senators to paint him as another imperial CEO, representative of the narcissistic greed of the times, a man who lived large at the expense of his shareholders. But in Houston, Lay's fall would cause the kind of soul-searching, teeth-gnashing, and rending of garments alien to this inherently optimistic city. Lay had been one of them, and maybe better than them; he brokered countless peace agreements between warring political factions, donated untold millions to the arts and various charities, built a state-of-the art baseball field, promised a future that guaranteed the greatness Houston lusted after. Seeing all that in shambles made people wonder whether they had ever really known him at all.

In fact, Ken Lay belonged to Houston as much as Houston belonged to him. Enron's rise and fall had much to do with the pressures of Wall Street and the malleability of Washington, but no one could understand Ken Lay or the company he built without understanding Houston.

***

People who visit Houston for the first time are often surprised by how green it is. They come expecting the classic Texas of cactus and tumbleweeds, and find instead a messy collision of tropics, coastal plain, and piney woods—a thick, overgrown semi-swamp, riven by bayous, that in summer exudes a humidity that is, literally, breathtaking. It was and still is an environment that speaks to a particular kind of person: Houston has never been conventionally pretty; but, hot, shady, and overgrown, it's always been alluring to those who saw, or more likely sensed, opportunity in its overwhelming, almost overweening, fecundity.

Geography was destiny. In most of Texas—western, central, southern, the Panhandle—the mythological load fell on the cowboy. That land was suitable for ranching—that's about all it was suitable for—the spaces immense, attracting the independent, expansive, and irascible. But Houston was different. It took a certain kind of person to study the swampy, wooded topography, and the distance from other thriving urban centers like New Orleans, and see opportunity. That's what happened in 1836, when two brothers from New York, Augustus and John Allen, placed an ad in papers around the United States for the sale of lots in what they called "The Town of Houston."

As Houston historian Marguerite Johnston wrote—admiringly—in *Houston, the Unknown City, 1836–1946*, "No twentieth century marketing expert could have promoted a city more shrewdly." The Allens' ad promised that there was "no place in Texas more healthy." Houston was "handsome and beautifully elevated." It "had an abundance of excellent spring water" and a "sea breeze in all its freshness." Situated near the sea and just northeast of Mexico, not far from New Orleans, this new city, they promised, would "warrant the employment of at least ONE MILLION DOLLARS [caps theirs] of capital, and when the rich lands of the country shall be settled, a trade will flow to it, making it, beyond all doubt, the great internal commercial emporium of Texas."

There is an old gambling expression that has always been popular in Texas, the phrase "betting on the come." It pretty well describes what the Allen brothers were up to. They discovered a natural turning basin upstream on Buffalo Bayou, an as-yet-unnavigable waterway that flowed into Galveston Bay. From that, the brothers envisioned a major inland port. "Envisioned" is, of course, the operative word: In reality, their hilly, breezy utopia was flat and maddeningly hot, and the bayou was so choked with flora that the brothers had to hire a steamer to prove its navigability. (It barely made the trip.) Their Town of Houston consisted of twelve ragged squatters and one log cabin. But none of that mattered: Four months after publication of the ad, by November 1836, Houston had a population of 1,500 hopeful, ambitious souls.

This creation story marks the moment when the local distinction between optimism and hucksterism would forevermore depend on the outcome of a given proposition. From then on, Houstonians would tell themselves that here anything was possible, and that they could make "anything" happen—preferably without interference from anyone else. As the city grew, this passion evolved into a generalized love of "progress." Houstonians have always told themselves, and still tell themselves, that vision and determination are the only things that matter here; pedigree, formal education, and history do not.

That notion became an article of faith after 1901, when oil was discovered in east Texas at a place called Spindletop. The well gushed 800,000 barrels of oil into the air for nine days—more oil than any single field had ever produced in history—and flooded the surrounding countryside with gooey black muck. It would subsequently produce 142,000,000 barrels of oil, as well as Houston's fervor for the energy business and all its attendant metaphors.

Almost overnight, the young city became the capital of the oil business. (Beaumont, closer to the oil play, was too mean and scrubby to fit the bill.) Houston had the rail lines and a nice gloss of culture—it had the ambition and the kinds of places where you could show off your money—and it was all too happy to abandon a constricting cloak of southern gentility to make the new oil-rich feel at home. No one cared when the town was overrun with specula- tors, because Houston was growing, and it was growing very, very rich. By 1906, following another massive find in nearby Sour Lake, the city could boast thirty oil companies, seven banks, and twenty-five newspapers, and the installation of the wildcatter as the central figure of myth.

The wildcatter was a different sort of heroic figure from the cowboy, though both characters liked to see themselves as solitary and shrewd, more comfortable outside than inside. But the wildcatter was bolder: He took bigger risks, seemed a lot more comfortable around women (in general, he liked them), and had the courage—or so he said—to fail. He was flexible: In contrast to the South's land-bound gentry, he leased his acreage and moved on if things didn't work out. When they did, he made a lot more money than his archetypal cowboy cousin, and was therefore a lot more fun. The classic example is Jett Rink, the wildcatter of Edna Ferber's *Giant*, whose character was based on a real wildcat- ter, Glenn McCarthy. (It was McCarthy who built the Shamrock Hotel for $21 million in 1949, and entertained guests by throwing a weighted $100 bill across the enormous swimming pool, which was, of course, the world's largest.)

This was the kind of Texan just about everyone could like: rich, funny, a bit of a rogue, and, outsiders could tell themselves, kind of a hick. Eventually, as Houston became known for its hospitable business climate, wildcatter worship turned into entrepreneur worship. Houston became a haven for developers who were just a little more inventive than the norm—guys who hired world-class architects for their skyscrapers, mansions, and malls; guys who put an ice-skating rink in the middle of an upscale shopping-center (in a city that rarely sees a thirty-two-degree day), even guys who built a ski slope at the intersection of two freeways. Like Las Vegas, everyone was welcome to come to Houston and try their luck.

Houston's entrepreneurial role model was a man named John Henry Kirby. Born five years before the Civil War, he was Houston's first tycoon, the so-called Father of Industrial Texas, and the state's first multimillionaire, and as such, the man who instantly changed Texas's opinion of itself and its possibilities. Kirby had the speculator's passion for risk, the oilman's optimism, and a grandiosity that was all his own. He had the requisite childhood of great American financiers: Poor and self-educated, he left home first to become a lawyer and then to create a corporate empire. According to the *Houston Chronicle*, "Those who knew him were well aware of a burning ambition on his part to organize a timberland company of monumental size—one which would provide a vehicle for consolidation of his own holdings together with those land properties which he already controlled and managed for others." Soon enough, Kirby owned more timberland than anyone else in the world. Soon after that, he created an oil/lumber conglomerate worth $40 million. He hobnobbed with President Woodrow Wilson too.

Anyone familiar with the lives of many prominent Houstonians can probably predict what happened next: By 1904, Kirby fell out with his Boston partners and was missing loan payments. His backers sued, and then his situation got worse. ("How about my allowance this month?" his daughter, Bessie Mae, cabled in 1909. "Can't send it. Haven't got it" was Kirby's answer.) Even so, Kirby had the money to build a $300,000 shingled, gabled, and onion-domed mansion that covered an entire city block, and accessorized the place with faux rustic gardens, a sprawling greenhouse, and an indoor pool with a ballroom upstairs. When asked, he blamed his problems on Wall Street, launching another great local tradition.

Of course, Kirby died nearly bankrupt at age eighty. He remained loyal to Houston to the end. "I don't think there is any limit to Houston's future growth," Kirby told a reporter on his seventy-ninth birthday.

Houston, however, soon forgot John Henry Kirby, as it would forget all but the most glorious shapers of its past. It became a city without memory, hell-bent on the future, which was always going to be bigger and better than what had gone before. Allen's Landing, the site of Houston's founding, would become a barely locatable marker in a forgotten corner of downtown. The Astrodome, which for decades called itself the Eighth Wonder of the World, was abandoned. Freeways flourished in a constant state of rebuilding and repair; there would be no historic districts to speak of. Houston's passion was always for the new.

Most locals now know only the boulevard that carries Kirby's name—fittingly, it's the major thoroughfare through River Oaks, the city's wealthiest neighborhood. But several of Kirby's businesses remain, as well. The most famous is the Kirby Oil Company, which endured a series of sales and mergers to emerge more famous at the beginning of the twenty-first century than it was at the start of the twentieth. By then, of course, it had a new name.

It was called Enron. ★

BETHANY MCLEAN AND PETER ELKIND

Now a contributing editor at *Vanity Fair*, McLean made her reputation with her reporting on Enron at *Fortune*, where, famously, she was the first journalist to question Enron's inflated stock value. She and Peter Elkind co-authored *The Smartest Guys in the Room*, which later became the basis for an Oscar-nominated documentary. Elkind is an editor at large at *Fortune* magazine where he specializes in investigative stories. A former *Texas Monthly* writer, Elkind is also the author of the true-crime book *The Death Shift*.

From *The Smartest Guys in the Room*: The Hotel Kenneth-Lay-a

> *Reported earnings follow the rules and principles of accounting. The results do not always create measures consistent with underlying economics. However, corporate management's performance is generally measured by accounting income, not underlying economics. Therefore, risk management strategies are directed at accounting, rather than economic, performance.* —Enron in-house risk-management manual

WHEN, EXACTLY, DID ENRON CROSS THE line? Even now, after all the congressional hearings, all the investigative journalism, all the reports, lawsuits, and indictments, that's an impossible question to answer. There have been accounting frauds over the years where companies created receivables out of whole cloth or shipped bricks at the end of a quarter instead of products. In such cases, someone at a company has to consciously consider the fact that he or she is about to commit a crime—and then commit it.

But for the most part, the Enron scandal wasn't like that. The Enron scandal grew out of a steady accumulation of habits and values and actions that began years before and finally spiraled out of control. When Enron expanded the use of mark-to-market accounting to all sorts of transactions—was that when it first crossed the line? How about when it set up its first off-balance-sheet partnerships, Cactus and JEDI, with such reputable investors as General Electric and CalPERS? Or when it categorized certain unusual gains as recurring? Or when it created EPP, that "independent" company to which Enron sold stakes in its international assets and posted the resulting gains to its bottom line?

In each case, you could argue that the effect of the move was to disguise, to one degree or another, Enron's underlying economics. But you could also argue that they were perfectly legal, even above board. Didn't all the big trading companies on Wall Street use mark-to-market accounting? Weren't lots of companies moving debt off the balance sheet? Didn't many companies lump onetime gains into recurring earnings? The answer, of course, was yes. Throughout the bull market of the 1990s, moves like these were so commonplace they were taken for granted, becoming part of the air Wall Street breathed.

Besides, the big Wall Street investment banks, not to mention the nation's giant accounting firms, had a huge vested interest in the kinds of moves Enron was making to create accounting income. Even before the dawning of the 1990s bull market, a new ethos was gradually taking hold in corporate America, according to which anything that wasn't blatantly illegal was therefore okay—no matter how deceptive the practice might be. Creative accountants found clever ways around accounting rules and were rewarded for doing so. Investment bankers invented complex financial structures that they then sold to eager companies, all searching for ways to make their numbers look better. By the end of the decade, things that had once seemed shockingly deceptive, such as securities that looked like equity on the balance sheet but for tax purposes could be treated as debt, now seemed perfectly fine. Securitizations exploded, with everything from lotto winnings to proceeds from tobacco lawsuits being turned into securities that could be sold to the investing public.

In the wake of Enron's collapse, the mood changed virtually overnight, and creative became a very bad word, synonymous with deceptive. But it's important to remember that it wasn't always that way. That statement in Enron's risk-management manual perfectly captured the sentiment of the times. In fact, the material in the manual, developed with the help of a consulting firm, was used throughout the energy-trading industry.

Of course it wasn't *only* the times that caused Enron to get ever more creative. It was also necessity. A company like General Electric might employ a little financial ingenuity to hit its earnings target on the nose quarter after quarter (as, indeed, it did), but even without such strategies, GE had a hugely profitable business. That wasn't true of Enron. Especially in the latter part of the 1990s, Enron didn't have anywhere near enough cash coming in the door. Eventually, the whole thing took on a life of its own, with an insane logic that no one at the company dared contemplate: to a staggering degree, Enron's "profits" and "cash flow" were the result of the company's own complex dealings with itself. At which point, of course, there could hardly be any doubt: Enron had most certainly crossed the line.

But if it's impossible to mark the moment Enron crossed the line, it's not hard at all to know who led the way. That was Andrew Fastow, the company's chief financial officer. He was 28 years old when he first joined Enron in late 1990, hired as one of Skilling's early finance guys at ECT. Skilling wanted him precisely because he knew how to set up complicated financial structures, specifically securitizations. Fastow became Enron's Wizard of Oz, creating a giant illusion of steady and increasing prosperity. Fastow and his team were the financial masterminds, helping Enron bridge the gap between the reality of its business and the picture Skilling and Lay wanted to present to the world. He and his group created off-balance-sheet vehicles, complex financing structures, and deals so bewildering that few people can understand them even now. Fastow's fiefdom, called Global Finance, was, as Churchill said about the Soviet Union, a riddle wrapped in a mystery inside an enigma that was Enron's string of successively higher earnings. "Andy was a master at walking in, always at the end of the quarter or the end of the year," says Amanda Martin. "The fat was in the fire and about to ignite. He'd say, 'give me the ball,' and he'd come through every time. That's why Jeff and Ken loved him." Like everyone at Enron, Fastow was handsomely rewarded for this work. But for him it wasn't enough. So over time Fastow found other ways to pay himself. Some of these ways his superiors knew about. Others they didn't know about—but should have.

***

Desperate to prove that he belonged among Enron's heavy hitters, Fastow began lobbying Skilling to give him a division to run. And because he had become one of Skilling's favorites, Fastow got his wish. By 1996, Skilling had put Fastow in charge of a new division he'd recently set up. It was supposed to be Enron's first foray into the retail-energy business, an effort to sell electricity and gas directly to the consumer. But nobody had figured out how, precisely, Enron was going to do that; Fastow was told to come up with the business plan for the new unit.

Try as he might, he simply couldn't do it. Fastow's business plans were so poor that Skilling kept sending him back to the drawing board. "He had lots of big ideas and went in lots of different directions," recalls a former colleague. "He would talk a big game." But he never came up with anything that had a real shot at being a business. Within nine months, after many shouting matches with Skilling, Fastow was back in finance. Fastow saw his failure as a major humiliation, potentially fatal for his career at Enron. There was no glossing over the fact that he failed miserably. Some of the traders started calling him Andy Fast-Out.

But within a matter of months, Skilling sent a clear signal to the rest of the organization that Fastow was not going to be punished for his failure. On January 13, 1997, just weeks after replacing Kinder as Enron's president, Skilling named Fastow a senior vice president, in charge of treasury, risk management, pricing capital, and funding for all of Enron's business. Fastow was also named to Enron's management committee. He was now part of the inner circle. (Shortly after Fastow was promoted, his wife Lea [Weingarten], who had risen to assistant treasurer, left Enron after giving birth to their first son.)

To many who knew him well, Fastow seemed an incredibly insecure man. There were many people at Enron who kissed up to Skilling, but few did it as overtly as Fastow. "Gratuitous annual self promotion" reads an entry on Skilling's calendar next to a meeting with Fastow. Fastow named his first son Jeffrey; after the birth, as Fastow was passing out cigars in the office, he had to fend off jibes accusing him of being a "suck-ass" for naming his son after his boss. According to one former managing director, Fastow replied, "Hey, who's done more for me other than my mom and dad?"

Fastow frequently complained about money: how he wasn't making as much as he should. After getting his promotion to senior vice president, Fastow hired a personal image consultant to help him dress like a corporate executive; later, he started wearing double-breasted designer suits, buttoned up, making him a dandyish figure in the halls of Enron, where people tended toward 1990s-style casual cool (khakis and open-collar shirts). Before he bought a new Porsche, he polled women in the office to see whether he should buy a blue car or a black one.

Fastow also seemed to have a split personality; he was Enron's version of Dr. Jekyll and Mr. Hyde. "He was so mean in business but so personally delightful," says one banker who knew him well. In a company full of strident Republicans, he was not. Years before it became a public issue. Fastow turned down a coveted invitation to attend the Masters golf tournament because women weren't allowed in the club. He was a devoted and doting father. He was also a health nut who was known for taking long runs. And he took care of employees—certain employees, that is—whom he needed on his side. "You always knew Andy was out for himself, but as long as you made him look good, he always looked after you," says a former colleague.

But Fastow was also greedy and out for himself—a "take-no-prisoners political animal," according to a former colleague—who had no qualms about taking credit for things others had done. And he had a vicious temper. "You could tell when he was about to twist off," says one banker. "That mouth would go in a certain way, and then he'd stretch his neck. You knew he was going to explode, and it would be terrifying." To the bankers and Wall Streeters he dealt with regularly, Fastow's volatile fist-pounding manner came to exemplify Enron's culture. And over the years, it only got worse. "As time went on, Andy changed," says an early senior executive. "People started to become afraid of him and afraid to speak out. It almost created a fear factor between Andy and people who did not agree with him."

In late 1997, Skilling decided to search outside the company for a CFO. He met with a handful of candidates and took a particular shine to Denise McGlone, the former CFO of Sallie Mae, who in 1997 was named one of *Euromoney's* top 50 women in finance for her work in risk management and derivatives. He went to New York to talk to McGlone and was impressed enough that he had her fly to Houston to make the rounds at Enron. Fastow, recalls a former colleague, "freaked out." She continues: "I was sitting in my office. He'd been acting really weird. Skilling walked by with this woman, introducing all of us. Andy really almost had a meltdown over it. He was in his office, staring at his desk, not reading anything, not doing anything."

Rick Causey, Enron's chief accounting officer, was almost as upset as Fastow. For both men, their worry was the same: a new CFO would inevitably get between them and Skilling. They each went to Shilling and told him that either one of them would work for the other but neither would work for McGlone. They got their way. Lay told Enron's board that he felt the best candidate was an internal one: rising star Andy Fastow. In March 1998, Fastow, just 36 years old, was named CFO of Enron. Once again, Enron had installed the wrong man in the wrong job for the wrong reason.

"Andy didn't have the knowledge base required to be the CFO of a major company," says one of his former bosses at Continental. He had a narrow set of skills—creating financial structures—and lacked the experience and judicious temperament the job required, the willingness to say no to deals and the attention to basics necessary to insure that the company's balance sheet remained strong. "Andy didn't have a risk-control bone in his body," says Sherron Watkins.

He lacked something else: the knowledge that being a CFO demanded. Fastow knew so little about accounting that one person who knows him wasn't even sure he could dissect a balance sheet. "It amazes me that you'd take a corporate finance asset-backed guy and make him CFO," says his former boss. "That's not what a CFO's job really is." Of course, the man had never worked at Enron. ★

STEPHEN HARRIGAN

Stephen Harrigan was a long-time staff writer at *Texas Monthly*; since leaving there he's published four novels and three books of non-fiction. In back-to-back novels, he took on what you might call the opposing poles of the Texas experience: *Gates of the Alamo* recounted the defining battle of Texas history, while *Challenger Park* followed astronauts up into space, and then back down to earth. This essay, first published in *Texas Monthly*, recounts his highly personal reaction to the terrible day when a group of astronauts weren't able to make that return journey. Here he movingly imagines, and describes, the human suffering at NASA the day the *Columbia* broke apart. Harrigan is on the faculty of the University of Texas James A. Michener Center for Writers.

Heaven and Earth

A BLOCK OR SO AWAY FROM THE MAIN entrance of the Johnson Space Center, in Clear Lake City, is a McDonald's whose exterior is crowned with a hovering fiberglass astronaut. The astronaut is thirteen feet high. His left arm is outstretched, and in his open hand he is holding an order of fries.

When the space shuttle *Columbia* broke apart on reentry on February 1, I was in the middle of writing a novel about astronauts and the people who train them, and this fast-food monument on NASA Road 1 had become for me a strangely important imaginative locus. The book, as I was beginning to understand it, was less about spaceflight than about the consequences of ambition, about the tension between the compulsion to voyage beyond the atmosphere and the normal human obligations owed to those who count on you to stay at home.

I had set a scene in this McDonald's. One of my main characters, an astronaut who has not yet been assigned to her first mission, takes her six-year-old son there for a Happy Meal after he has suffered an asthma attack at school. As she watches her vulnerable child crawl through the restaurant's playscape, chronic fears seep into her mind, and she finds herself helplessly thinking about another astronaut, Christa McAuliffe, whose death in the 1986 *Challenger* explosion left her children motherless. When I was writing the scene, *Challenger* was real enough in memory but no longer, at least for most of us, painfully raw; it seemed harmless enough to appropriate the tragedy as literary ballast for my character. But the immediacy of the *Columbia* disaster momentarily blew the walls off my fictional world and called into question the worth and seemliness of creating imaginary people in the shadow of so much flesh-and-blood suffering.

In coming to know those imaginary people, though, I had come to know a little about their real-life counterparts and the world they inhabit, a world that is at once distinguished by an exalted purpose without parallel in human history and grounded in homely workaday particulars. For me, it was the McDonald's on NASA Road 1 that somehow best exemplified the gravitational pull of normal life in a company town whose business is sending people beyond the reach of gravity itself.

Clear Lake City, the world headquarters of manned spaceflight, is at first glance the world headquarters of nothing much. Along with a number of other communities—Friendswood, League City, Webster—with which it has indistinguishably merged, it marks the southeastern extremity of metropolitan Houston. You might find a "Watch for Alligators" sign or two poking up from the sluggish bayous that meander around the margins of Galveston Bay, but except for such tokens of primeval mystery, Clear Lake is a straightforward exurban landscape of strip malls and theme restaurants and Lasik surgery clinics. As for the Johnson Space Center itself, it seems proud not to be noticed. It's a vast, sprawling hive with no apparent buzz. The only nod to its own wondrous history is a dutiful presentation, just inside the main gate, of the massive Saturn V rocket that once sent men to the moon. Otherwise, the JSC has the rambling acreage and the architecturally blank buildings of a hospital complex or a cheerless junior college.

Overall, Clear Lake City is an unassuming community into which astronauts are unobtrusively woven. They live on streets with names like Amber Knoll and Ardent Oak. They gather at well-known hangouts like the Outpost Tavern or Frenchie's or Pe-Te's but are just as likely to be in the cafeteria line at Luby's or in the checkout aisle at Kroger. The woman cheering her kid from the sidelines of a soccer game might have come home two days ago from a mission that took her 250 miles above earth. On her bracelet she might be wearing a space shuttle charm from James Avery that her husband gave her before she went into quarantine. The polo shirts with the mission logo worn by her and her crew came from Lands' End. In her children's elementary school, hers is one of dozens of photographs in a hallway display titled "Astronaut Moms and Dads," an extensive gallery of smiling men and women in orange pressure suits.

One of the sturdiest clichés about the shuttle program is that it represents a modern-day version of the passing of the frontier—that the more multifunctional, multicultural, and unprepossessing astronauts become, the further they are from some primal ideal laid down by that generation of squinty-eyed test pilots who rode the first rockets into space. But to anyone who has glanced at the biographical sketches of the *Columbia* crew—among whom were a submarine medical officer, a former circus acrobat, and an Israeli fighter pilot who fought in the Yom Kippur War and took part in a brazen attack on an Iraqi nuclear reactor—this observation is tediously irrelevant. Astronauts are still members of an aristocracy of achievement, they still have a dazzling inner focus, and because they willingly confront dangers like being launched into space on top of a liquid hydrogen bomb containing 1.6 million pounds of explosive fuel, they are likely to have developed the enticing professional remoteness that we associate with stardom.

But spaceflight has changed in ways that have inevitably leached some of the glamour away. The shuttle is a vehicle less for exploratory voyaging than for near-shore exploitation of space. Its primary job these days is the servicing and maintenance of the International Space Station. Compared with the *Niña*, the *Pinta*, and the *Santa María*, the shuttle is more like a crew boat ferrying personnel and supplies to an offshore drilling platform. When those supplies are unloaded in the weightlessness of space, astronauts, like grocery stockers, keep track of the inventory with bar code readers. In orbit, they receive a per diem of just $2.

On the ground the reality is just as poignantly stark. In the weeks before the launch of the 1997 shuttle flight that would deliver him to the crumbling old Mir space station for four and a half months, astronaut Michael Foale recalled puttering around his house, replacing rotten doorjambs. For what, considering the alarming condition of Mir, could very well have been the last vacation of his life, he took his family not to some distant exotic getaway but to humble Corpus Christi. One astronaut told me that what struck him most upon returning home from two weeks in space was that his grass needed mowing. U. S. senator Bill Nelson, then a Florida congressman, flew as a payload specialist on *Columbia* on the last shuttle flight before *Challenger* exploded on takeoff in 1986. The same day he landed in California, he flew back to Clear Lake City and tried to check into the Hilton across the street from the JSC. He was still wearing his flight suit, and NASA had made a reservation in his name. But the reception manager wouldn't let him check in because he had left his wallet, with his credit cards, at the Kennedy Space Center, in Florida.

"Ma'am," he pleaded, "I just came back from space. I don't have any credit cards with me."

The woman, according to Nelson, was unmoved.

Such trivialities would be unremarkable in any other profession, but everyday details tend to stand out in odd relief when set against the dimensions and dangers of an astronaut's life.

"What's the reason I'm doing it this time?" an astronaut told me she asked herself as she waited, strapped into the mid-deck of the shuttle, for liftoff. It was her second mission, she had a young child, and she knew all too well the odds of a major malfunction at launch.

Launches are terrifying; it's not hard to get an astronaut to admit it. In the weeks beforehand, they make sure their wills are in order. They might write letters to their kids or make tapes for them because, as astronaut Andy Allen puts it bluntly in a recent book, "Daddy might blow up . . ."

For weeks before the launch, the pad at the Kennedy Space Center is swarming with hundreds of technicians, but when the day comes and the astronauts are finally driven out to the shuttle, there is a sudden eerie stillness that makes them feel alone and vulnerable. The great challenge of the interminable wait for liftoff is not to pee. Astronauts are equipped with diapers but are eager not to use them. Some make a point of jogging the evening before the launch or sitting in a whirlpool to force as much moisture as possible out of their bodies. During the official launch breakfast before the astronauts depart for the pad, no one even thinks about drinking coffee.

At ignition, the three main engines and two solid rocket boosters produce almost six and a half million pounds of thrust. The noise and shaking that the astronauts experience inside the orbiter as it clears the pad and storms into space is of an intensity that is still shocking after months of training. It takes eight and a half minutes to get into space. After the external tank and the solid rocket boosters drop away, the ride changes from a teeth-rattling struggle to a silken glide. The moment that every astronaut prays to live to reach is MECO—main engine cutoff. The minutes from liftoff to MECO have always been regarded as the most dangerous part of a mission, though after the destruction of *Columbia* on reentry, every shuttle flight will now be bracketed with visceral hazard.

Weightlessness is entrancing and disorienting. Every task takes longer to do; there is a dreamy lethargy of movement. For some reason no one has quite explained, weightlessness makes food taste bland, and astronauts find them-selves craving spicy condiments. A significant percentage of astronauts are overcome with space sickness and have to float around for two or three days with barf bags at the ready, though like every other weightless endeavor, throw-ing up is tricky and time-consuming. In space, the lack of gravity extends the spine and temporarily makes people a few inches taller, though it also gives them backaches. Natural posture changes from upright to a kind of fetal curl. Fluids shift to the center of the body and to the head, making legs skinnier and chests bigger, and faces puffy. Since being weightless feels a little like floating in water, there is a natural inclination to propel oneself using the breaststroke, but this action has no effect whatsoever. If an astronaut begins to weep, which happens from time to time, the tears do not fall. They just form and hover at the corners of the eyes. When it is time for bed, astronauts strap themselves into baglike sleep restraints, and when they are unconscious, their arms drift upward, as if they are slowly grasping at something in their dreams. Sometimes, as their arms move that way, they talk in their sleep.

Their waking hours are heavily loaded with docking procedures, experiments, satellite deployments, and various maintenance and construction errands involving the space station, but sometimes they steal precious time from their sleep schedules and drift up to the orbiter windows to look down on the earth. Astronauts speak of the sight of the earth from space with an enthusiasm that borders on rhapsody. Listening on their Walkmans to John Denver or Judy Collins or some other artist of folkie majesty, they watch the advancing light of the sun creep up over the rim of the nighttime planet and shatter into glorious bands of color. They see streaming plumes of smoke and ash from volcanoes, the white throbs of lightning in oceanic clouds, sometimes even the greenish pulsations of the northern lights. But at times this godlike perspective can grow sinister and isolating. "I could see the whole world, but I felt I had no connection to it," one astronaut told me. William R. Pogue, a Skylab astronaut, wrote that when he embarked on a space walk, he was so unnerved by the presence of deep, pure space that he was reminded of a Bible passage about the "horror of great darkness."

Space is such a distant and dreamlike destination that it is a little hard to imagine that when it is time for the astronauts to come home from orbit, it takes them less time than it might to drive in rush-hour traffic from one end of Houston to the other: an hour and a half, more or less, from the time the shuttle begins its deorbit burn until it lands on the Florida marshlands. The fact that *Columbia* was so close to home when it was destroyed is only one of many bitter ironies. Because I had gotten to know a few members of the training teams that prepare astronauts for their missions, when I first heard about the disaster, my thoughts turned in their direction. For a year or more before every mission, these teams work with the astronauts on an almost day-to-day basis, sitting behind consoles as they run the crews through increasingly more complex and confounding training exercises in the shuttle simulators. The bond that develops from so many months of relentless work and shared enterprise has a familial intensity. An instructor tells Henry S. F. Cooper, Jr., in his book *Before Lift-Off* that when the launch date finally arrives, the training team feels as if they are flying in the crew's bodies.

There is a venerable tradition at the Johnson Space Center that usually takes place a day or so before the crew returns to earth. The team that trained them for the mission is in charge of decorating the hallway of the building where the astronauts' offices are located. This decorating of the hall is serious business. It is, as Lisa Reed, a former training team lead, told me without a trace of self-consciousness, a "labor of love." Both sides of the hallway are garlanded with streamers and balloons. There are also cartoons, jokey top-ten lists, photographs that were taken during training or that were downlinked from the mission itself, all suitably captioned with some quip or exasperated comment or malapropism mischievously recorded during training in the instructors' logbooks.

If the hall was decorated in the usual fashion for the return of STS-107, the official designation of *Columbia's* last flight, one of the items that would have been put up, and then soberly taken down when the homecoming did not take place, was a huge color printout of the mission patch. Patches are also serious business. During one of my trips to the JSC, I asked to visit the Graphics and Publications office. Located across the street from the astronauts' gym, Graphics and Publications is housed in a drab one-story, brick and metal building that looks like the office of an oil-field equipment company. Inside, though, it is more like a hip design studio, with graphic artists peering at their Macintosh screens amid a talismanic clutter of toys and action figures.

When a crew is assigned to a mission, one of the first things they do is get together, rough out a sketch, and appoint a "patch coordinator" to present their ideas to the designers. Technically, the coordinator is supposed to be the only crew member authorized to discuss the matter, but since the Graphics and Publications building is so close to the gym, and since early in their training the astronauts have more time on their hands, they tend to drop by and badger the designers with advice.

They want the patch to represent them. It is the enduring physical legacy of each flight. It's not unheard of for astronauts to go through fifty revisions of the image before sending it to the Center Director for final approval. Sometimes they have an unrealistic grasp of the limitations of the medium. They present the designers with what are essentially engineering diagrams, depicting the shuttle or the space station with a level of detail that could never be achieved with an image made of thread. They are limited to only eight colors, but veteran astronauts who have flown before are sometimes obsessed with trying to pin down in the patch the exact shade of darkest blue they saw out of the window of the orbiter or visually charting the haunting gradations of color from sunlight to black space. They often want some subtle symbolic reference to their children or some nod to the nicknames—the Sardines, the Maggots, the Hairballs—of the classes in which they matriculated with fellow astronaut candidates.

The fate of *Columbia* was in some ways more like a shipwreck in the sky than anything we have encountered before in our sketchy catalog of space horrors. Unlike *Challenger*, *Columbia* did not blow up before it escaped the atmosphere, with its broken parts falling discreetly into the sea. Returning from space, it broke apart on the treacherous atmosphere like an oceangoing vessel splintering on a reef. The flotsam rained down upon East Texas and Louisiana, and one of the things that washed down from the sky was a mission patch from STS-107.

When I saw this patch in a newspaper photograph, it was scorched but whole, lying in the grass. Its shape was the shape of the shuttle itself, probably not a configuration the designers would have recommended, since the sharp edges of the wings and the tail would tend to fray over time. In the middle of the patch was the astronaut symbol, three soaring rays of light passing through a crown and topped off with a star. A cluster of stars on the left wing represented the constellation Columba. In the constellation were seven stars, one for each crew member, and along the margins of the wing their names were worked into the fabric: Husband, Brown, Clark, Chawla, Anderson, Ramon, McCool.

Of all the debris, this patch was among the humblest, one of many patches just like it that the crew had taken up into space to give out later as tokens to friends or family. It would certainly be useless in helping to determine the cause of *Columbia's* destruction, but I could not look at this patch without feeling that stitched deep into the fabric was some sort of discernible clue to understanding the men and women who had dreamed of flying to the heavens, and who had died trying to come home to earth. ★

JED HORNE

Born and educated in Massachusetts, Jed Horne began his career with the Boston *Phoenix*, then worked in New York as a writer and editor with Time Inc. publications. He moved to New Orleans in the late 1980s where he went to work for the *Times-Picayune*, first as city editor, then as metro editor. His work on Hurricane Katrina was included in the paper's submissions that won two Pulitzer Prizes. He later developed his Katrina reporting into the book *Breach of Faith*, from which this excerpt is taken. He is also the author of *Desire Street: A True Story of Death and Deliverance*, which was nominated for an Edgar Award for best non-fiction crime book. He and his wife live in the French Quarter.

From *Breach of Faith*: A Rockets Jersey and a Picture of Jesus

BY THURSDAY NIGHT, BUSES FROM NEW Orleans were wrapped around Reliance Center [*sic*], the complex that includes the Astrodome—scores of buses, forty or fifty at a time, disgorging shell-shocked New Orleanians, many of them in clothing they had worn for five days. Adding to the bustle and mayhem was an influx of gawkers and do-gooders and just plain folks. Texans had seen news reports of the influx and had yielded to the irrepressible impulse to visit a spot where history and TV seemed to converge. A lot of them brought along drinks and food—Texas chili, soda pop, chips—and were dishing it up to the refugees out of coolers in the backs of their pickups.

One among the thousands of evacuees peering into this thicket of late-night activity from the window of an idling coach was an eighteen-year-old named Alvin Crockett. After eight hours aboard a tour bus with no toilet, Crockett was ready to bail out, drawn as much by the allure of this big new city as repelled by the stench—there was no other word for it—of his clothing and that of fellow passengers. "I hadn't taken a shower in four days, and neither had most of them." As far as family went, Crockett—a friendly, open-faced young man with a careful coif of pipe-cleaner-thin dreadlocks—had reached Houston alone. His father was dead (drug overdose) and his mother had been in and out of the hospital dealing with her own demons, he said. His two brothers and three sisters were all older and on their own—as Crockett had been, after dropping out of O. Perry Walker High, Mayor Nagin's alma mater, in his junior year. "Things overcame me," Crockett said of his decision to quit school. He had grown up in the Fischer public housing project. As a dropout he lived for a time on the street, sleeping in cars, smoking pot—nothing too heavy. As Katrina bore down, he moved in with an uncle who, on Tuesday, was airlifted out of the city because of a heart condition. Crockett found a blue Rubbermaid storage bin in the apartment, just big enough to hold his earthly effects, and drifted down the block to a friend's place, a young woman with a couple of kids.

Two days later, after waiting three hours in the rain on an Interstate 10 on-ramp, they were loaded onto an evacuation bus headed for . . . who knew where? Who cared? Soaking wet, Crockett settled back into the warmth of the seat and was swept by a sense of relief that he doubted he would ever forget. Out of gratitude and just to while away the time, he pulled out a sketch pad and drew a picture of Jesus. But eight hours later, enough was enough. He had to get out of there. No matter that the driver was saying that anyone who stepped off the bus would not be permitted back aboard and might not be admitted to the Astrodome. What the hell. From the clamor in the street, Crocket had picked up that they weren't admitting any more people to the Astrodome anyway. The buses were reaching the front gates only to be waved on to some other shelter. Crockett pulled down the blue plastic storage bin and walked to the front of the bus. The driver reminded him that this was it, *sayonara*, and opened the door for him. Alvin Crockett stepped out onto the streets of Houston, homeless once again.

He wandered around a while, savoring the hubbub, trying to convince himself he had options. Stephan, one of his brothers, was in Las Vegas. Maybe Stephan would take him in. But Las Vegas was a long way off and Crockett was hungry, tired, starting to lose heart. He set down his storage bin and was using it as a seat when one of the reporters working the scene for the local

ABC-TV affiliate came up to him. Would he mind doing a little interview, just a few words to say who he was and what it was like to find himself in Houston after all he had been through. Crockett said okay, and all of a sudden he was bathed in light brighter than day, and the camera was rolling. He talked about this and that and held up the Jesus sketch he had done on the bus. The lights were still on, but the TV guy had wound down the interview and was looking for the next one, when a white man walked over to Crockett and said, "Are you Alvin?" Alvin said yes, whereupon this total stranger gave him a hug and said: "You're coming with me."

Clayton McKinnis, a thirty-five-year-old financial services rep of MetLife, had not set out in search of Alvin Crockett. He and his wife, Cindy, had been watching Channel 13 in their apartment directly across the street from the Reliance Center when the news came on, and the top story had been the buses and the tumult right there in the street below—the traffic jam Cindy had bucked on her way home from work as a Chico's branch manager. Frankly, McKinnis had been kind of nervous about having all these people from New Orleans in the street below and his wife not home from work. More than nervous, he was, as he recalled the moment, angry and fearful: "Angry because my wife was being delayed from coming home after working a ten-hour shift at her store, and fearful because, for all I knew, the reports of shootings, rape, looting, et cetera, that were being posted on all the airwaves were true, and those were the type of people who were being bused to Houston, directly across the street from our apartment."

But when she got home and they could settle back and watch the news, he began to relax. And when the Channel 13 crew stuck their camera in the face of an elderly woman and the grandson she was looking after, and the woman said they had nowhere to go, "It broke our hearts," Clayton would recall. The same impulse to do something—anything—the same impulse that had prompted good ol' boys with pickup trucks and tubs of chili to materialize along curbsides near the bus drop-off, sent Clayton out into the streets to look for that grandmother and the little boy and offer them a place to stay for the night—"to find us some company," as he put it.

There was more to this than sociability. Cindy and Clayton McKinnis were churchgoers: Second Baptist. Moreover, as members of a "care team" in service to the needy, they were adherents to a ministry that believed, as Clayton put it, "that everything we have been given belongs to God, and we are simply stewards of his blessings." With stewardship came a responsibility to see that blessings were used in a manner that brought glory to God. It was a matter, as Second Baptist's pastor, Ed Young, was accustomed to say, of "putting hands and feet to our faith."

"There's someone who can't be much of a threat," McKinnis would remember thinking to himself as Cindy drew his attention to the elderly woman and the seven-year-old boy. She fell to readying the extra bedroom, pulling out an air mattress, while McKinnis put his shoes back on. But in the time it took him to round up a friend in the building and reach the streets, the grandmother and her charge were spoken for. McKinnis had been within six feet of her when relatives emerged from the crowd and ABC viewers were treated to a tearful family reunion on camera. McKinnis and his friend milled around anyway, "watching history unfold before our eyes." When he called his wife by cell phone to tell her what had happened and that he'd be back in a few minutes, she mentioned this cute kid they were interviewing on TV. "He's holding a picture of Jesus that he drew, he's wearing a Houston Rockets jersey, and he's got dreads . . . See if you can find him, Clayton."

It wasn't hard. McKinnis strode over to where the TV lights were still glowing, and there was the kid in the Rockets jersey. Under normal circumstances, Alvin Crockett might have thought twice about taking shelter with complete strangers in a city he had never seen before. And in a million years, Clayton and Cindy McKinnis might never have taken in a streetwise New Orleans teenager with dreadlocks and a funky stink to him. But these were not normal circumstances. The plan was to feed the boy, give him a hot shower, let him get some sleep, and send him on his way. But in the morning, as the McKinnises got ready for work, Crockett asked if they knew how he could go about volunteering at the Astrodome. That touched them, and the boy's stay was extended another day. Three months later, enrolled again in high school—Lee High School— and an active member of Second Baptist Church, he was still living with them, though tensions, some predictable, some less so, had begun to mount.

***

"Houston" became shorthand for the East Texas part of the New Orleans diaspora, but in fact Houston—even before the Astrodome was emptied out, after some three weeks as a shelter—got lots of help from across the region. Smaller Texas towns and cities also stepped up or, somewhat more reluctantly, found that New Orleanians had holed up in their motels and shelters and needed to be tended to. One such burg was Webster, about twenty miles south of the Astrodome. Webster had a population of two hundred at the turn of the twentieth century, and as late as 1958, when it was incorporated, had a grand total of five businesses. And then, overnight, the space age arrived and Webster's prospects were suddenly sky-high.

In 1961, the sprawling gantries and hangars of NASA's space center began to poke up above the coastal plain, and in due course, the unrelievedly flat Harris County landscape, especially along Webster's main drag, NASA Road 1, was chockablock with the mundane exuberance of highway commercialism: the waffle houses, the Chinese buffet restaurants, the check-cashing and remittance services, fingernail parlors, Motels 6 and Super 8, ad infinitum, as far as the eye could see. And nestled in among the fast-food joints and winking neon and backlit plastic signage were Webster's collection of vast and anonymous apartment complexes: Clear Lake Springs, Baystone, Harbor Tree, and so on, home to some eight hundred service-sector families whose real homes were elsewhere—Mexico, as often as not, or El Salvador, or, in Katrina's aftermath, New Orleans.

Webster was a natural for the New Orleanians, given the Red Cross shelters that sprang up there within a week or two of Katrina's landfall. But there were other draws, among them its itinerant and fluid population, the low-rent apartments that housed them, and a school system that, in addition to educating the children of the prosperous professional families drawn to the aeronautical industries, had developed a subspecialty in educating the children of the families who had fetched up in Webster to trim their lawns and hedges and vacuum their pools and detail their cars.

For the younger kids in Clear Lake Springs, a typical low-rent complex of 262 units on NASA Road, the walk to school passed through a gap in the fence at the rear of the development, then went down a short blacktop path to 300 Pennsylvania Avenue, site of McWhirter Elementary. Among other attractions, McWhirter was one of a few schools in the district that offered a bilingual program, mostly for Spanish-speaking kids, in kindergarten and first grade. McWhirter had gained added resources by becoming a laboratory school for teachers training at the University of Houston's Clear Lake campus, a maneuver that shrank the number of students per teacher from twenty-two to fifteen. And there were other benefits for at-risk kids, New Orleanians among them, except that saying "at risk" was a no-no at McWhirter. Instead they were called children "of promise"—a shade of difference, perhaps, but a clue that the Clear Creek Independent School System, to give the jurisdiction's full handle, was three hundred fifty miles from New Orleans in more ways than one.

McWhirter took its mission seriously and executed aggressively. Rather than waiting around to see who turned up for a school year that had already begun, Cindy Stamps, the coordinator of federal programs for the Clear Creek district and, as luck would have it, a former principal of McWhirter, had someone check in daily with the shelters to make sure every child of school age was on greased skids leading directly to a schoolhouse door. And when the kids and their rattled parents showed up, McWhirter didn't wrap them in red tape and junk them at curbside. No birth certificate? No problema—all that was required of parents was a photo ID. Stamps also agreed not to get hung up on missing immunization records. And with Lori Broughton, her successor as McWhirter's principal, Stamps set up a parents room with coffee, newspapers, and sofas to serve as a one-stop shop for tackling the newcomers' needs—a source of delight and astonishment after exposure to the sclerotic and hostile New Orleans public school bureaucracy. Stamps also arranged for a mobile health van to visit the district each week, and got it based at McWhirter. "I take care of my own by taking care of everyone else," she said with a sly wink.

In the first weeks after the storm, about a thousand New Orleans kids flooded Clear Creek district schools, a number that fell by half over three months. By December about 10 percent of McWhirter's six-hundred-eighty student enrollment were still Katrina evacuees, an influx that had required adding four classrooms. The shock for parents was how accommodating a school system could be. The shock for McWhirter was how far behind so many of the new pupils were. Fern Hanslik had never seen anything like it in all her years teaching second grade. Take little Maurice, for example, one of the kids from New Orleans. He didn't lack ability. Hanslik knew that from testing him. But as he entered second grade, essentially he was operating at the pre-K level. "When you showed him a puppy, he didn't know the concept of a baby dog. He did not know his alphabet. Most kids his age can sit about ten minutes," Hanslik had found. "He couldn't sit at all. It was like he had no concept of classroom behavior."

Even with the testing, Hanslik might have wondered if undiagnosed developmental problems would reveal themselves in Maurice's case. But no. Maurice was strong in math. Reading was the real problem. "He told me when he arrived that he couldn't read. I said okay, but if you leave here and you can't read, that's my fault, and I won't let it happen," Hanslik said. To that end, she began downloading books for Maurice and making a gift of them, each one signed: "To Maurice from Mrs. Hanslik." She also asked his parent to sit down with Maurice and read with him. Half an hour of it every night, no matter how tired his mother might be from hassling with her four kids or her job as a waitress at Ryan's, or his father from his work cleaning houses. "Do they do it? Yes they do," Hanslik said.

There were other marked departures for the New Orleans kids. Toilet paper in the restrooms, for one thing, and toilets that actually worked. School was no longer a daylong struggle to hold it in, for fear of visiting restrooms that were not only filthy but, at many New Orleans schools, hangouts for loiterers, toughs, and juvenile drug dealers. The corridors at McWhirter were actually quiet and orderly, not free-for-alls cruised by incorrigibles while teachers locked themselves in classrooms with more docile students, as was true in New Orleans, starting in middle school if not sooner. By Christmastime, Maurice was catching up with classmates in other subject areas besides math. At a rudimentary level, he was even reading. "When a kid learns to read, their eyes change from flat to sparkly. It's a miracle," said Hanslik, who noticed that a lot of New Orleans kids wouldn't make eye contact with her when they first arrived. "It was like they did not see themselves as equals."

It did not surprise her to discover that Maurice's parents were themselves barely literate. Among many of the New Orleanians, illiteracy and the low incomes it all but guaranteed were a legacy passed on from generation to generation. McWhirter's first taste of it had been encounters with parents who could not fill out the simple forms to register their children, a problem that was addressed by assigning extra staff to assist them. Katina Henderson, an African American social worker at McWhirter, was so appalled for her people that she broke down crying at the thought of illiterate parents and the failing children she had to help with their forms. "I just don't understand how this happened," she said, dabbing at her eyes. But actually she had a theory: In New Orleans, she discovered, kids weren't pushed to keep up with their age group, they were simply held back—"retained" in the jargon of the day—and parents settled for that, even seemed to take comfort in it. Henderson found that many of the parents were afraid of the school system, because of their own lack of education. "New Orleans cradled that," Henderson said.

The astonishing thing to Hanslik as well as Henderson was that little Maurice, the seven-year-old with the pre-K classroom skills, had been considered a good student back in the New Orleans public school system. McWhirter was prepared to bend over backward to educate the New Orleans kids, but it wasn't about to cradle them. When Nadora Dregory's five-year-old stopped turning up for school, McWhirter found out why. The little girl had fallen and broken a wrist. With the bone set, McWhirter could see no reason to prolong her absence. Her mother was reluctant, at first. Henderson kept after her, and soon enough the girl was back in class. A month or two later, Dregory would cite the school's persistence as a reason why she was so glad she had enrolled her daughter there.

"They say that if a student has just one decent teacher, you carry that with you," Hanslik mused over coffee in the faculty lounge one afternoon in early December. "One teacher can do it. I can't think of a nicer way to put it, but the teachers here, we wonder, 'What went on down there? What were they doing with those kids? What were you doing with your time?' It's an awful thing to say, but it's almost as if Katrina was a blessing."

***

Alvin Crockett had left Houston and the apartment he shared with Clayton and Cindy McKinnis ... but not to return to his Algiers stomping grounds. For all the good intentions and Christian fervor on both sides, it was probably inevitable that the McKinnises' apartment would prove to be only a way station in Crockett's life. When the seams began to split on the air mattress they rolled out for him, the young couple had called Cindy's father, a furniture maker in Fort Worth, and arranged for the purchase of a bed. And Alvin had been doing well, topping off his interrupted secondary education at a Houston high school and warming to the idea of going on to a local college. He had resisted wardrobe upgrades suggested by his hosts, but the worst tension developed around the Internet. Clayton McKinnis set up an e-mail account for Alvin so he could keep in contact with his friends and family, and just to make sure that's all it was used for, McKinnis imposed very tight security on the system. "The next thing I know, our desktop computer won't even boot up because of some virus he downloaded," McKinnis said. The corker was the time McKinnis arrived at work, plugged his laptop into the docking station, and found pictures of naked men and women in amorous entanglements. That some of the men were black and the women white did nothing to soothe the soul of a man who had been worried the minute the buses started arriving from New Orleans that the ruffians he had seen on TV might pose a threat to Cindy. "I thank God I was there before anyone else could walk by and see it for themselves," McKinnis said of the laptop porn.

"He's black, my wife is white, and there is absolutely no possibility of me letting my wife's safety be compromised," he added. "We had committed to him that he was welcome to stay with us until he finished high school and went off to college, but if my wife has to walk into her own home fearful for her safety, and I have to live with the fear of my wife being violated by someone we had taken not only into our home but to our families' homes—then I will go back on my word and I won't be ashamed of it, no doubt."

Alvin was deeply dismayed by his fall from grace, appalled that his young man enthusiasm for sexy pictures could be mistaken for ingratitude towards his benefactors—or worse. He and the McKinnises patched things up, but it was definitely time to move on. Katrina had been like that, a stirring of the social pot that had made for some unexpected encounters and brief alliances. Now those who had been caught up in the maelstrom were settling back into former lives with more familiar companions. In early January, Alvin hopped a flight for Las Vegas to see what his brother was up to. ★

PART V

POETRY

HOUSTON POETRY HAS BEEN WIDELY, AND
perhaps even wildly, varied. The first area poet of note was Cedar Creek's John
Sjolander, whose early twentieth century poems seem to be from an even earlier
time, but which manage to rise above above doggerel through his skill and occasional dark vision. Vassar Miller is the greatest of native poets; she's perhaps
the finest poet Texas has produced, and it's a pity that she isn't more widely
remembered.

Most of the other poets in this section came here from elsewhere, mainly
the northeast. The Panama-born, New York City-bred Lorenzo Thomas
was something of a citizen poet, and his "Liquid City" is perhaps the nearest thing Houston has to an epic. Edward Hirsch, Robert Phillips, Martha
Serpas, and Tony Hoagland all came here to teach at the University of Houston (in Serpas' case, also to study), and the few poems they've written about
the city or its people have little in common. Daniel Rifenburgh came here to
study with these same writers and then stayed to write and also to drive an
18-wheeler. Long time resident Larry Thomas was the poet laureate of Texas
in 2008.

In general, the bright lights that the University of Houston has attracted
(including also Adam Zagaweski, Stanley Plumly, and creative writing program founder Cynthia MacDonald, none of whom are included here), like their
peers elsewhere, tend to write about universal issues of art and culture, and

don't take much notice of the city. In the case of poetry, this is perhaps to be expected.

Poets have lamented that Houston is not a very poetry-friendly city because of its lack of landmarks, and because walking, so conducive to the poet's job, is an exotic activity here.

John Sjolander

John Sjolander [1851–1939] was born in Sweden. He came to Galveston Bay in 1871, and did a number of jobs, including farming. But poetry was his true vocation. He published widely in magazines and newspapers and had a national following. *Salt of the Earth and Sea* was his only major book. Lorenzo Thomas championed Sjolander's work and helped keep his memory alive.

Cedar Bayou

On Cedar Bayou's flowery banks
    Where summer always stays,
And where the reeds in solid ranks
    Move when the Southwind plays,
And all the birds with glad hearts sing
    To them that they love best,
Oh, there we do our sweethearting,
    And there our lives are blest.

On Cedar Bayou's gentle slopes
    Where days wear sunny smiles,
And where the prairie, sown with hopes,
    Shines golden-green for miles;
And where the fleecy Gulf-cloud roams
    A dreamship far above,
Oh, there we build the happiest homes,
    And work, and pray, and love.

Dear Cedar Bayou, loveliest
    Of all the lands we know,
Where earth gives us the most and best
    For cares that we bestow;
And where no earthly joy we miss
    From love's abundant store.
Oh, there we live our lives in bliss—
    And heaven is just next door. ★

Eileen and I

Eileen and I (ah, we had just been wed)
    Sat hand in hand beside the summer sea.
Eileen's Leon had two long years been dead,
    And Marjory was more than dead to me.
But we, Eileen and I, had just been wed,
And had no thought of dead or more than dead.

Had we not planned that day a pleasant way
    Wherein our feet should tread—a way of bliss?
Each waiting what the other's lips would say,
    To whisper, "yes," and seal it with a kiss?
Yes, we had planned that day a pleasant way,
Where death, and more than death, should never stray.

We sat, Eileen and I, beside the sea,
    'Yond which the horned moon was slipping down,
It seemed the waters shivered—or did we?
    But well I know the wide sea wore a frown.
And there we clung, beside the frowning sea,
I to Eileen, and she more close to me.

And so, close-clasped, we sat, Eileen and I,
    And watched the evening star sink low the while;
Until, at last, we saw it fade and die
    Beyond a little silvery cloudland isle.
And we were lovers there, Eileen and I,
But oh! so timorous, and knew not why.

Beside the stars to watch us there was none,
    And they were peeping in the rippled sea;
And so by stealth (as in a dream 'twas done)
    I kissed Eileen and thought her Marjory.
And she sweet-blushing, dreaming, sighed, "Leon"—
Beside the stars to watch us there was none. ★

VASSAR MILLER

Vassar Miller [1924–1998] published ten volumes of poetry during her forty years of writing. All this was accomplished despite her suffering from cerebral palsy. She was named Poet Laureate of Texas in 1982 and 1988 and was nominated for the Pulitzer Prize in 1961. She also edited *Despite This Flesh*, an anthology of poems and stories about people with disabilities.

She is best perhaps best known for her overtly Christian poems. The two I have selected here deal are among the few that deal directly with Houston.

Whitewash of Houston

I

Who would have thought of her as mother small
town raunchy with cowhands coming and country
girls and boys not knowing Dr. Freud but
Moses very well as big-nosed Bach pumped both
organ and wife scattering music even
more than her cattle safely graze those meadows
of midnight and darknesses presences surrounding
her with cloud by day and night also going
before her where she only stumbles in
imagination fearing that they are
only dry holes reverberating with
some ancient terror tutored by none
but teachers' voices like a piece of chalk
scratched white across the face of midnight breaking?
Who would have thought of her as mother sleek

big-butted like black cars that bulging slickly
swim over pavement and pothole splattered with
delicate bone and gut of squirrel none
except poor folk afoot or else on bike
would ever notice much less mourn on grounds
as female as the moon her sons tromped on
galumping ghosts crumpling that most dainty
fingernail of poetry into a
fist fondling their rod that flaunts their flag
dribbling oil and slime and muck that ooze
from under her armpits as she stuffs into her mouth
with garbage drooled onto her front until
she drops dead in her tracks to bed hot for
that prick and prong of sleep's sweet long and hard?
Who would have thought of her as mother gunning
down eerie corridors of her dark self
dented and bent the shape of truth no meaning
can measure and that has no end but life
to cradle whether for its good or ill
nobody knows however life may teem
with fact outwearing pint-sized brains made all
she ought to stand straight behind her shame
before the world that tossed her to the dogs
as innocent as she once seemed with knowing
what shadow loops its coil about her legs
quickened with light and slowed to dusk on seeing
her terror driving all her children dumb
down the long chute of death and safely home?

II

Who would have thought of her as a mother mad
at morning and mad with mourning and merry

as the scissor grinder's whistle blown far dodging
February currents and her memories
bouncing it up and down like a fey bell on
her cars as keen as gray chill cuts and leaner
than Lent has stripped away the clover blossoms
long ago vanished with the honey bees
that horny fingers of the rain uncoiled
March and April meandering across
the vacant lot of Easter and back home?
Who would have thought of her as mother fed
and fudged till fattened on her lentil vigils
as open as her covert cesspools ripe
with the rich grain of avarice and April's
froth of green and dogwood's lace hung over
the land and greening all her lawns until
she lies down with her apron smelling of summer?
Who would have thought of her as mother light
could lift into corn cribs to lie until
curious as a calf she grows and swells
with moonstruck offspring pushing all awry
who have not known the hollow of her womb
more hollow than the opening leading to it
to gobble down her shacks and spires till time
has hulled them all like winter's dried pecans
dropped to her earth leaning and lurching fawnwise
mulched with the sunshine long since loamed with darkness? ★

Pilgrim Perplexed

Here in the desert of the day
or the marshes of monotony
or the flatlands of finitude
(the designation is indifferent,
because the geography is undistinguished)—
who would believe if I told him
how the air falls, a foot on my heart,
how the telephone coils, a black silent shadow,
how the light and dark form the stripes
on the back on an invisible tiger,
crouching beneath the bed
and behind the tables and chairs?
Nor would anyone guess how you are my angel
here in this terrain, in this atmosphere
drunk on its very sobriety—
you, hair awry for a halo,
a cloud of dust doing for wings,
a stammering breath for a message
which you speak by a gesture
as all love speaks anyway, talking with its hands.
I myself can scarcely conceive
here where prayer is no more
than a set mouth and clenched teeth,
and every presence fleshed in an absence,
how your eyes hold reflected that vision
which is unbearable, being
the only one mortals can bear. ★

Lorenzo Thomas

The Panama-born, New York-raised Lorenzo Thomas [1944–2005] was per-haps the closest thing to a public poet that Houston has known. He arrived in Houston in 1973 to teach at Texas Southern University, and immediately im-mersed himself in the city's cultural life, particularly the musical life of its bar-rios and wards. Indeed, in one essay he says that he moved from New York to Houston for the music. He published three collections of poetry and two books of criticism, and is still sorely missed.

His posthumously published collection of essays, *Don't Deny My Name: Words and Music and the Black Intellectual Tradition*, won the American Book Award in 2008.

Liquid City

I
This morning wakes
Sun all around my head
A small confused attempt with memory
All urge to pry
Out
Dusty leaves and shelves a song
On Nottoc mart tram cotton no
Song
Not grand relic remains in Houston
Of a derelict glory
La Carafe, sure
Glatzmaier's lunch Old

Market Square blazing in sun
A dream of builders

Hush
As Juke Boy sang
It's going to be a long long lonesome ride back home
It's going to be a long, long
Lonesome ride back home
As Juke Boy sang, something seemed wrong
Ain't nobody even missed me
All the time since I been gone

No song

A little sun,
White as a cotton bloom,
Rounded a boll or blossom
To blue dawn
Ripens to gold, and all blues
Green to noon
By fires by night, by clouds at day
No song

No song

Bring us, O givers
From towers stilted in this ancient bayou
Merchants and manufacturers
Bring us
Of survey transits, of plumbs
The tools &c intense volcanic sight
Sublime of mud commodity &c
Mud.

Up from the waters, a lush green
From the bayou from the landing
The urban the lush geology lapidiary layers peel
First banks   then markets   horizontal
Shops   hotels   then Banks
In constant replicate year by year

With dreams of songs just waking
Piano player tinkle plunk tinkle Louisiana sound
Come 5th Ward, Texas
Silver Moon Cafe busy streets downtown
It's raining in the barren parks
The city first a dream of New Yorkers
By Abe & Pappy's
A city marching proud away
Shining from its countenance
Shining

No song

II
> *And yet I cannot find my own face.*
> James Wright

No song
Sounds like eavesdropping at a cocktail party
Chit chat from strangers
About someone you'd rather not know

Facades of shining surface, blinding glass
More than a pile of stone and steel
Walls of mirrors stilted underneath
Rising above the green twine of the bayous

All brokedown W. Dallas porch
A freedman named Jules Verne invents
A century complete with all we have
A place of material dreams

Look like upper class people
Don't care how the lower class people live
Too poor to have a song to sing
When you gave all that you could give

III
No song
To expand his unconsciousness
As he sees each one
Like you look at them this way
So much like another
Can't quite come to mind
And they stretch, pout so charmingly then
Along graceful lines.

                  Graceful lines
Glimmering among each others' shadows
Socially.

                She watches, coolly
As ornate old-fashioned lines
Flex through distortions
It comes between Splendora and splendor,
News from east Texas Dallas Alice
From Manhattan from Midland
From home
Soft eyes then and sudden
Hard mouths

Chit chat from strangers
Or neighbors,

Yes, they stretch out so charmingly then

IV
Glass is a shifting liquid
            stunned by flame
        and passersby;
            a shame
Nobody understands
Shy glass. Embarrassed buildings
Houston's pride
The city first a dream of New Yorkers
In a pickup near the icehouse
A cajun named Jules Verne invents
A century complete with all we have
The 1950s realized at last
Views from Cody's fashion-cluttered roof
Only the most recent bent
That Graettinger & Kenton and Associates
So fervently outlined
Of Transco beacon light and boomtown press
Now and then, stinging as a Blues guitar
Muted and wan as April's palest rose.
City of glass

Glass is a shifting liquid
In disguise, bearing its panic with more grace
Than any man could ever understand
More delicate than any nervous sparrow
Stronger than any girl's soft, yielding hand:
Here, for who wants to see it

(Though nobody asked for a sign)
Triumph of Dubuffet's "Phantom" seen
Through hurricane of Duchamp's chance
Stressed in the glass of Milam's pyramids

City of glass, a place of material dreams
Bestowed in plain sight and transparently denied.
A town where high school children on the bus
Discourse on architecture. Would-be boyfriends
Mew, "I like that new one there. You like it too?"

Old songs from radio, ancient courting poetry and fancy talk
Magnetized here by stone striking the eye
While set designers for the TV Evening News
Frantically paste new photos on the anchorman's backdrop,
More harried than the station managers who wait for ratings

"When you show houses, you always find a way
To drive the client there along an esplanade,"
So my friend tells me. CENTURY 21 is here, unfolding.
The 1950s realized at last
An awesome isometry of reflection

Facades of shining surface, blinding glass
Where the desperate mother, the unemployed man,
The brutal or blundering thief in the night
The crazies of Main Street who wander by night,
Homeless and dazed, are vanished from the frieze

Of commerce. If they were present, would be but rendered small
Glass shadows. Vampires and victims are not reflected at all.

No song

_____

352

V

Those in these houses only are allowed.

This is but a gift, well-meant. This isn't gossip
Of invention, not malice.
Brightest intention, really
Something to expand
And why not what's unconscious
Since we don't know where light starts anywhere,
Just its most recent bent

There is no brilliance of subtropic sun
Today. Unseasonal. So cold, so calm.
This Gulf the radio reports so roilsome.
No gleam reflected from a murky thread
Of tainted bayou,
No brilliant humor jostling on the street
No hope, no dream coming to "save the day"
Unless you want one.

    Builded in mud, proverbial shifting sand
        Sand fired stands still
    Long enough to qualify as glass
Banded with steel and concrete, it can touch the sky,
        A miracle.

In all this glass, when every face is seen,
These mirrors will hold conversations with the sun

We,
Chortling from babyhood to grandest dotage, sing.
Each egotistic we
We sing to each awakening "Good morning"

We shout through disappointments in loud restaurants
Sleeping, we sing to ourselves

And still
Can neither speak nor sing
What space we share or crop into coherent beauty
Here
But shards of reflection, but glimmers of shadows
No schedule but chance of annoyance,
Distracting refraction
A petulance designed of light rebounding—languid, liquid.
There is a gulf between us and ourselves
A missed perception

We need a song that all of us can sing
A true reflecting. A moody, bright, expansive song.
In all this glass, when every face is seen,
These mirrors will hold conversations with the sun ★

EDWARD HIRSCH

Edward Hirsch's *The Living Fire: New and Selected Poems* appeared in 2010. He taught in the Creative Writing Program at the University of Houston for seventeen years. He is now president of the John Simon Guggenheim Memorial Foundation.

This poem is dedicated to Donald Barthelme, who was his friend and colleague and at UH for years. They were in Rome together not long before Barthelme died.

Apostrophe

(In Memory of Donald Barthelme, 1931–1989)

Perpetual worrier, patron of the misfit
and misguided, the oddball, the long shot,
irreverent black sheep in every family,
middle-aged man who languishes on the couch
with his head in his hands and often
spends the evening drinking by himself,
a dualist fated to deal in hybrids and cross-
breedings, riddles without answers, slumgullions,
impure waters, inappropriate longings, philosopher
of acedia, of spiritual torpor, nightsweats
and free-floating anxieties, sentencings,
sullenness in the face of existence, wry veteran
of the unresolved and the self-divided,
the besotted, the much married, defender
of the unhealthy and the uncommitted,

collagist of that mysterious overcrowded muck
we called a city, master of the solo riff
and the non sequitur, the call and response,
voice-overs and backtrackings, sublime bewilderments
and inexplicabilities, the comedy of post-
historical desires and thwarted passions,
first of the non-joiners, most unlikely,
tactful, and generous of fathers, you
who embarrassed the credulous and irritated
the unimaginative, who entertained the void
and recycled the dross, who deflated
the pretentious and deepened perplexities,
subject to odd stabbing rages of happiness,
weird bouts of pleasure, connoisseur of mornings,
of sunlight swinging into an open doorway,
small boys bumping into small girls, purposefully,
most self-conscious and ecstatic of ironists
who sang uncertainties like the Song of Songs
and dwelled in doubt like a habitation,
my wary, unreachable, inconsolable friend,
I wish I believed in another world than this
so I could think of seeing you again
raising your wineglass to the Holy Ghost,
your "main man," and praising the mysteries,
Love and Work, looking down at the weather
which, as you said, is going to be fair
and warmer, warmer and fair, most fair. ★

ROBERT PHILLIPS

Poet and scholar Robert Phillips has authored or edited some thirty volumes of poetry, fiction, criticism, and *belles lettres*, and he publishes in numerous journals. A professor of English, he was director of the University of Houston's Creative Writing Program from 1991 to 1996. His many honors include a 1996 Enron Teaching Excellence Award, a Pushcart Prize, an American Academy and Institute of Arts and Letters Award in Literature, a National Public Radio Syndicated Fiction Project Award, and Texas Institute of Letters membership. In 1998 he was named a John and Rebecca Moore Scholar at the University of Houston. He was recently named professor emeritus at the University of Houston.

From the unpublished series West Alabama Ice House

Fester

Every afternoon he sits in back
of the Ice House, gossiping with
old cronies. No beer—he gave up
drinking six years ago, when
his wife of forty-five years died.
(She'd begged him to abstain for decades.)

Every afternoon he sits in front,
harmlessly flirting with pretty
young girls, which is why cronies
call him Fester the Child Molester.

Every night he watches the TV
With his wife's photo beside him.

He's tempted to drink,
but doesn't, out of respect. ★

Gene

They call him Gene because all
he talks about is his years
as drummer in Gene Krupa's band.
"We did all the States, toured Europe,
spotlighted Atlantic City and Vegas.
Man, it was the life! And Gene
treated me real good. Gave me solos,
even gave me my own silk tuxedo."

What happened? they ask, looking at
this aged hippy with an earring,
missing teeth. He shakes his head.
Dennis gave him the Box Boy job.
What the Box Boy does is, busts down
all the cardboard cars the beer
comes in. You'd be surprised how many
there are at a place like this.

Then one day Dennis caught Gene
selling drugs right on the premises,
fired him, told him never to come back.
Every day Gene sits on the curb
across the street, wearing a bandana,
smoking, drinking convenience store beer.
He waves at Ice House customers as they park.
He sorrowfully surveys his lost kingdom. ★

RICH LEVY

Rich Levy is a poet and, since 1995, executive director of Inprint, a nonprofit literary arts organization based in Houston, Texas. He earned his MFA at the Iowa Writers Workshop, and his poems have appeared in *Boulevard*, *Gulf Coast*, *High Plains Literary Review*, *Pool*, *The Texas Observer*, *The Texas Review*, and elsewhere. His first poetry collection, *Why Me?*, was published in 2009 by Mutabilis Press. A jazz obsessive, he has three teenage children, two dogs, and one sleepy cat.

Main Street, Dusk

At this hour even those who don't
have any place to go drive as if
they do. The wind sifts a grit fine
as talc, cigarette stubs mash
to milkweed, and fire ants flare

and lug crumbs twice their size. Above us
the sealed office blocks, buzzing street-
lamps and sky—white, indistinct,
thick as wool to breathe through,
fleshy with the heft of

the tropics and thinned by an oily
mist—loom like the ponderous
seat of a fat man settling
down on a bench. Six of us
wait for buses: a Latino

in mirrored glasses that reflect
us, his Astros cap tipped low; a lame
Black nurse, one special shoe
with sole inches thick, and
her twiggy, globe-headed grand-

son holding her hand (they whisper);
a short *muchacha*, her tight black
dress stiff, shiny, and short,
headphones buzzing, who smokes, hums,
and sways on black spike heels;

a man in wire-rims with a red
frond of hair curled forward on his pate,
his pin-striped suit creased, loafers spotted,
bent in his *Post*. One by one
they board buses, 6:50,

7:05, 7:10, and
the somnambulism of
the Gulf Coast summer night softens
my glower. Still I hold my bags
as if they will float off, as if

I am waiting for snow. If
I could have, I'd have led them in
song, told jokes—annoying one-liners
about yankees, mid-life, sex (of course),
winking at the kid, ambassador

to this gathering from—where? my
soundstage of "neighborhood" that I
believe protects me, like a turtle

that clings to the living gunwale
of its shell? It's not becoming

easier, but necessary
to wait and watch as the cars slow
on Main, each filled with two, three, four men
speaking softly in Spanish, the dusk
spreading like smoke,

my bus not coming, my life
taking on the shapely wash
of a tattoo. At such moments I believe
that history loves us, renovated under
this muff of sky, mute, finicky, stuck

in time. Just then, the bus arrives. ★

MARTHA SERPAS

Martha Serpas has published two books of poems, *Côte Blanche* and *The Dirty Side of the Storm*, from which this poem is taken. Serpas is a Louisiana native who often writes of Louisiana's disappearing wetlands and coast line. She teaches at the University of Houston, and also works as a chaplain in Houston hospitals.

   This poem is dedicated to Cynthia MacDonald, founder of the University of Houston's Creative Writing Program and was written in her apartment overlooking Hermann Park.

Sunrise

The first three-floor building in lower Lafourche—
Lady of the Sea—landed like *Apollo*
11: a new Otis, paved parking, halogen
Security lights. The old blue one swam in its shadow:
Strung double-wides, wooden stairs,
An ER ramp where in the red glare
From the Rose Bowl I had my first smoke.

In New York I worked on the fifty-seventh floor.
Every morning I imagined the ride up was
The sluggish moment of dying, the snug room
Smaller, soaring, me stuck with people
I didn't know, their faces distant and smoldering.
Everyone I did know had a walk-up or a doorman.
We were never on the ground but stared intently

At blinds raised a few yards from our windows. Today
I woke up eight stories above Houston. Downtown,
A thick clump of trees in a pasture, what was once
A pasture, and what in my mind are forty arpents
Behind our house. When the levees gave,
Alligators waited it out in our high-rise backyard
All three inches above sea level.

Look how the fog paves my view. Even indoors
There's the marshy smell of land that's not really land,
Land the new light is shoring up, land in love
With these absurd buildings bobbing on
Its surface. If I jumped, the haze might net
Me the way a trawl would. The pavement would certainly
Give way, sensing how much swamp I really am. ★

TONY HOAGLAND

Tony Hoagland's third collection, *What Narcissism Means To Me*, was a finalist for the National Book Critics Circle Award. He has received grants from the Guggenheim Foundation, the National Endowment for the Arts, and The American Academy of Arts and Letters. His poems and essays about poetry have appeared widely; he currently teaches in the graduate writing program of the University of Houston and in the Warren Wilson College MFA program.

In his Houston poems he has touched on the city's elusive nature, how at first glance it appears to be a very unsatisfactory city indeed, and then you suddenly realize that it has a hold on you, that "even ugly can be beautiful," as he says below.

Education

Because It Is Houston,

the streetlights have to take the place
usually reserved for the moon in the poem

and the traffic in the background with its roar and surge
stands in for the ocean
                    tossing wrecks like driftwood on the shore.

Because it is Houston the
tight little blond talking on her cell phone

while backing her SUV at high speed through the parking lot
is a respected citizen

and the twisted, serpentine, stretched-out limbs of oaks
above certain shady boulevards

suggest how even ugly can be beautiful.

Because it is Houston
a moist wind from the south at dawn

carries a faint petrochemical bouquet
    from the landfills of our fathers
and the landfills of their fathers.

It smells good.

A morning shower
has knocked down blossoms from the honeysuckle bush
                                    into the grass,

like little ivory trumpets.

Because there is no one better qualified around,
(because it is Houston),

you are the one who gets to kneel
            and look at them in silence. ★

Larry D. Thomas

Larry D. Thomas, a Houston resident since 1967, was the 2008 Texas Poet Laureate. He has published eleven collections of poetry, many of which have won prizes and awards. In April 2009 he was inducted into the Texas Institute of Letters. The following is one of his several poems that are directly reflective of the city.

Buffalo Bayou

(Houston, Texas)

Great trees grow
along its banks,
meshing their branches

high above it,
sparing it
the bright intrusion

of sun, moon, and star.
Great blue herons
ripple its shallows,

spearing frogs and minnows.
Within its murky
depths, the big gars flourish,

unscathed by toxins
and the bloated corpses
of poisoned fish,

working their gills,
fins, and tails,
snaking their passage,

oblivious of time
and its irksome,
futile ravages. ★

DANIEL RIFENBURGH

Daniel Rifenburgh's first book *Advent* was published by Waywiser Press in 2002 and received the Natalie Ornish Award from the Texas Institute of Letters (TIL). He has also received the Robert H. Winner Award from the Poetry Society of America and a Dobie Paisano Fellowship from the University of Texas and the TIL. He works as an eighteen-wheeler truck driver in Houston.

El Vendedor

It is a brilliant day over Texas.
In an unzoned coastal city, flat,
Traversed by listless bayous,
I sell, from a pine clapboard shack
On a gravel lot, Oldsmobiles to Aztecs,

Mercuries to Mayans, Lincolns to the lithe
Bronzed *mojados*, those who crossed lately
A brown, shallow river
And escaped whatever lies, haunched,
Across a southern border.

It is a brilliant day over Texas,
Good for sales, they say,
And I am the salesman
As was my father before;
As was my father: *yo soy el vendedor.*

Out on the gravel lot the brown *mojados* kneel
On their haunches by the rowed vehicles,
Perhaps listening to their spirits. These
Are not the new Americans. No,

They're the old ones, *los ancianos*, returning,
And there they sit, unspeaking, fingering the white gravel
While the sibilant tires of the traffic
Roll down old Durham Road.

Es un día brilliante sobre Tejas
And already I speak, as I must, their lingo,
For now the men rise, breaking the rude tableaux.
They reach into dusty boot tops for bankrolls
And bring me their pictures of dead, white presidents.

Once the simple contract is signed and the money stowed
I will tell them they own both halves now,
If the car breaks in two
And they will laugh, as the poor always do. ★

PART VI

FICTION

HOUSTON MAY STILL BE WAITING FOR ITS defining novel, but a goodly amount of fiction has been set in the city, dating all the way back to William Sidney Porter's 1890 stint at the *Houston Post*. Little noteworthy fiction appeared in the first half of the twentieth century, until Rice professor George Williams published the novel *The Blind Bull* (which is also set in other locations) in 1947. Other novels began to appear in the 1960s, mostly written by Larry McMurtry, who is without doubt the city's most prominent literary defender. The scene, included here, from 1989's *Some Can Whistle*, in which Danny Deck (also the protagonist of *All My Friends Are Going to Be Strangers*) drives into Houston after a long absence, makes McMurtry's deep connection to the city clear. Houston also has a meaningful, if brief appearance in Rosellen Brown's novel *Before and After*.

The city is also the setting for several short stories. Native son Donald Barthelme's complicated feelings about his return home from New York are reflected in his absurdist but still emotional "Return." Long-time Rice professor Max Apple's affection for Houston and its athletes suffuses his acclaimed story "Bridging." Rick Bass explores the little known world of amateur hockey in "Juggernaut." Acclaimed short story writer Mary Gaitskill uses Houston as a meaningful setting in "An Old Virgin."

Barthelme biographer Tracy Daugherty has written as much fiction about the city as anyone. His story "Almost Barcelona" also draws on his relationship with his celebrated mentor. Lionel Garcia writes about Houston's Latino population in "Emergency Room," while Antonya Nelson's "Eminent Domain" evokes, with uncanny accuracy and sensitivity, the complicated relationship between Houston's elite and the artists they support.

O. Henry

William Sydney Porter [1862–1910] moved from Austin, where he edited the satirical newspaper *The Rolling Stone*, to Houston in 1895, when he was hired by the *Houston Post*. His work was very well received; however, he fled to Honduras to escape embezzlement charges from a previous job in a bank. There he coined term "banana republic." When he learned that his wife Athol was dying of tuberculosis, he returned to face charges. He was sentenced to five years in prison. Upon his release he moved to New York and reinvented himself as O. Henry.

From *Postscripts*: A Sporting Interest

IT IS A BUSY SCENE IN THE REAR OF ONE OF Houston's greatest manufacturing establishments. A number of workmen are busy raising some heavy object by means of blocks and tackles. Somehow, a rope is worn in two by friction, and a derrick falls. There is a hurried scrambling out of the way, a loud jarring crash, a cloud of dust, and a man stretched out dead beneath the heavy timbers.

The others gather round and with herculean efforts drag the beams from across his mangled form. There is a hoarse murmur of pity from rough but kindly breasts, and the question runs around the group, "Who is to tell her?"

In a neat little cottage near the railroad, within their sight as they stand, a bright-eyed, brown-haired young woman is singing at her work, not knowing that death has snatched away her husband in the twinkling of an eye.

Singing happily at her work, while the hand that she had chosen to protect and comfort her through life lies stilled and fast turning to the coldness of the grave!

These rough men shrink like children from telling her. They dread to bear the news that will change her smiles to awful sorrow and lamentation.

"You go, Mike," three or four of them say at once. " 'Tis more larnin' ye have than any av us, whatever, and ye'll be afther brakin' the news to her as aisy as ye can. Be off wid ye now, and shpake gently to Tim's poor lassie while we thry to get the corpse in shape."

Mike is a pleasant-faced man, young and stalwart, and with a last look at his unfortunate comrade he goes slowly down the street toward the cottage where the fair young wife—alas, now a widow—lives.

When he arrives, he does not hesitate. He is tender-hearted, but strong. He lifts the gate latch and walks firmly to the door. There is something in his face, before he speaks, that tells her the truth.

"What was it?" she asks, "spontaneous combustion or snakes?"

"Derrick fell," says Mike.

"Then I've lost my bet," she says. "I thought sure it would be whisky."

Life, messieurs, is full of disappointments. ★

George Williams

George Williams [1902–1999] was a professor of English at Rice University from 1923 to 1965. He was best known for his course in creative writing, where he taught Larry McMurtry, William Goyen, and David Westheimer, among many others. His book *Creative Writing for Advanced College Classes* has been used as a text at many colleges and remained in print from 1937 to 1975. His only novel, *The Blind Bull*, was published in 1952, and was later re-published as *The Flesh and the Dream*. The novel concerns the reintegration of a soldier into the booming Houston society of the post-war era.

From *The Blind Bull*: A Man May Smile

ONLY NOW, AT THIS DISTANCE IN MILES AND years, perhaps only in the last few hours, did the Major understand the course his life and his marriage had taken. Now he neither blamed nor excused; he merely understood a situation to which he had been blind. The images trooped through his head once more, disconnected yet unified.

Houston, that fabulous city, growing explosively—with skyscrapers shooting up like rockets, industrial areas rolling out from it like smoke, wide patches of ugly residential sections dropping like shattered fragments all about its perimeter, great mansions glowing within like flameflowers, and people, people hurling themselves through it.

Houston, nourished on black oil gushing from its green coastal plain; and on white cotton trundling down to Houston's port from the wide fields of Texas; and on yellow lumber from the dark pines of the Big Thicket; and on ships thronging in with their rainbow galaxy of flags.

Houston, like a wide round festering sore on the back of the coastal plain—a ringworm canker of grimy slums and fetid industrial areas inhabited by Greeks,

Syrians, Negroes, Mexicans, and Jews—a city of lavish Country Clubs, fabulous homes, and tall apartment hotels inhabited by the newly wealthy—a city of old-fashioned mansions with cupolas and steeples and gingerbread work, now crowded among filling stations, corner groceries, and skyscrapers, and converted into boarding houses or bordellos—a city of middle-class brick veneer homes, clapboard bungalows, cracker-box cottages, identical-faced rows of rent houses exactly like those in every other American city, and inhabited by people exactly like those in every other American city.

Houston, filled with graft and greed and ambition and crime and vice and poverty and Aladdin wealth and Old South aristocracy and Middle West materialism and New York capital.

Houston, a place where a man with "drive" could make money, where money elevated erstwhile roughnecks from the oilfields into the leadership of culture, where city officials were so often in the pay of millionaires and gamblers, where law had no function except to protect the rich and money had no use except to make more money, where church and school and college and family life and friendship and love moved to the rhythm of money-money-money-money-money.

In this Houston, Clem had at first moved slowly, as a stranger will, stiff, blundering, bewildered. Then, the rhythm of it beginning to sink into his nerves, and with Janice helping him keep step, he grew more confident, learning to submit himself to the pulse of the rhythm. And at last, he whirled away on that rhythm, choosing his friends, choosing his entertainment, choosing his company, choosing his work, choosing his serious thoughts, choosing his daily habits of dress and salutation and speech and opinion to fit Houston's rhythm of money-money-money-money-money.

The images trooped in slow and disconnected sequence.

Those early years of adjustment to the rhythm. The first year or two when they thought that Janice could not bear a child, and the talk of adopting one. Janice saying doubtfully, "an illegitimate child? A child of low-class people, paupers maybe? I might learn to love it."

He and Janice and their little three-year-old daughter Karen walking through the lobby of the Rice Hotel, and Karen, in new sandals, smacking her feet down noisily on the terrazzo floor. Janice leaning over and admonishing: "Don't do that, Karen! Walk like a little lady." —*Walk like a little lady! My God!*

Janice insisting that Karen be sent not to the public schools, but to a private school more expensive than they could afford at that time: "One can't be too careful about a girl's up-bringing, Clem. A girl needs to be thrown with only with the best company—much more so than a boy." —Memory of a clear voice saying to an unhappy boy on a big porch, *"A mother has to be very careful that her daughters associate with the right kind of people."*

The Early American cottage that they had first built on the outskirts of River Oaks. River Oaks, that fabulous oil millionaires' residential section of Houston with its acres of plush lawns, azalea gardens, mansions, greenhouses, garden statuary, wooded gardens, sweeping graveled drives, columns and porticoes and gables and chimney-stacks. —*"Just close enough to River Oaks to smell the privies of the millionaires," one sneering acquaintance had said at the time the cottage was building.*

The furnishings of that Early American cottage—the Windsor chairs, the antique secretary, the cricket stool, the copper plates on the mantel, the bellows and the broom beside the chimney (that burned gas), the spinning wheel manufactured in Grand Rapids, the few pieces of old glassware on the window shelves, the books on collecting antiques, the talk of Revere silver, betty lamps, and Sheraton tables, the proud array of pewter in the wall cabinet. —*Antiques and pewter and synthetic spinning wheels!*

Janice's Junior League with its projects and credit-giving and balls and teas—the afternoons at the Art Museum, the mornings at the Clinic for Underprivileged Children; the work for the Community Chest and the American Red Cross; the ticket-selling for the Symphony Society. She was a good woman, almost pathetic in her eagerness to "do her part in the community." Clem had been very proud of her in those days.

***

His career really meant more to her than anything else. As a matter of fact, his career became her career. She admired him so much that she believed he could become not only "a leader in the community" but also a leader in the state, or even in the nation. He loved her so much, and it made her so happy when he received some "public recognition in the community" that he readily went along the path she wanted him to.

And the rhythm of Houston was beginning to pulse through him. Within a few years he needed no Janice to help him synchronize his life with that rhythm. ★

LARRY MCMURTRY

Larry McMurtry came to Houston to study English at Rice Institute in the late 1950s. He also worked as a bookstore manager here and wrote freelance book reviews for the *Houston Post* and other publications. In 1961, while he was teaching at Texas Christian University, he published his first novel, *Horseman, Pass By*. He then returned to Rice where he taught English through most of the 1960s. McMurtry says that he takes as much pleasure in collecting books as in writing them. Besides his own very sizeable library, he owns three large bookstores. He owned the Booked Up Book Store in Houston for a number of years before opening his massive store in his hometown of Archer City.

McMurtry has published over forty books. Among many awards, he has won a Pulitzer Prize for his novel *Lonesome Dove*, and, with Diana Ossana, an Academy Award for Best Adapted Screenplay for *Brokeback Mountain*. McMurtry has often written that Houston is his favorite Texas city. Given his opinion of the competition, that could be faint praise. But this excerpt from *Some Can Whistle*, a sequel to *All My Friends Are Going to Be Strangers*, shows that his connection with the city is in fact very deep.

From *Some Can Whistle*

THE DRIVE TO HOUSTON DID LITTLE TO awaken the nascent travel writer that I hoped was slumbering within me. The Decatur courthouse was the last sight on the whole trip that could fairly be described as picturesque.

Once the Fort Worth courthouse had also been picturesque, but the thing that rendered it picturesque—a neon American flag with forty-eight neon stars—had been removed. Both Fort Worth and America had outgrown the flag. America had summarily added Alaska and Hawaii, and Fort Worth had added a veneer of big-cityness. Now the old courthouse, shorn of its wonderful, bright flag, was just an ugly pile of granite on the Trinity bluffs.

I had once liked Fort Worth. I never loved it as I loved Houston, but I did enjoy its hicky vigor, of which the neon flag had been a perfect symbol. Dallas would never be original enough to stick a neon flag on a public building; Dallas remained what it had long been: a mediocre big city, growing larger, but never growing interesting.

I passed through Fort Worth like an arrow and then deflected the arrow slightly eastward until it pierced I-45, the interstate connecting Houston and Dallas. Once on that interstate it was smooth but boring sailing. The black land south of Dallas receded, the horizon began to thicken with trees, but the change was undramatic; the next real sight was the huge prison at Huntsville, two hours south.

I was glad I had brought the Cadillac; it passed scores of Datsuns and Toyotas as easily as a powerboat passes canoes. Just driving it made me feel almost stable, a feeling I rarely enjoyed.

But even a brand spanking new Cadillac couldn't make me feel stable for long. Soon I was in the pine trees, which meant that Houston couldn't be far. Even if I crept along at the legal speed limit, instead of doubling it as was my habit, I was sure to be on the banks of Buffalo Bayou within an hour or two.

Then what?

Although I had traveled much in the twenty-two years since my daughter's birth, I had never been back to Houston. Many times, the city had tried to entice me back; in the years of my success, when I was the reigning genius of American television, Houston had attempted to claim me. I had been educated there—why shouldn't it claim me? I was offered banquets, honorary degrees, a Danny Deck Day, the keys to the city, etc., all of which I sadly declined.

Sadly because Houston had been, among cities, my first love. In my failed second novel, the one I had wisely drowned, the only parts that might have deserved to survive were paeans to Houston, to the city's misty beauty and sweaty power, to its funkiness and energy. I had come to it at the right time, as a young man sometimes comes to his ideal city. In Houston I began to write, formed my first young sentences. Its energies awakened mine; the ramshackle laziness of some of its forgotten neighborhoods delighted me. I walked happily in it for years, smelling its lowland smells. It was my Paris, my Rome, my Alexandria—a generous city, perfect home for a young talent.

But that time ended. Disorder and early sorrow, of a very average kind, thrust me out and propelled me westward where for many years I failed at everything. All that time I missed Houston and missed it keenly. When I would happen on an article about the city in a newspaper I would hastily turn the page; just seeing the name Houston in a newspaper made me miss the place so much that I ached.

I missed it as much as I've missed certain women—and there are women I've missed so much that I've become afraid to see them again; it becomes too big a risk, because if you miss them that much and then see them and they turn out not to like you anymore—or worse, you turn out not to like *them* anymore—then something important to you is forever lost.

Once I got famous and began to fall in love with famous women, queens of the screen and the tube, I came to understand why I preferred to skirt all mention of Houston. I soon started trying to avoid all public mention of my famous loves as well.

Perhaps in some respects all love may have common elements, but it can also have striking differences, and attempting to love famous women, women whose pictures appear regularly in newspapers and on the covers of magazines, involves dangers that don't arise in loving obscure women. The dangers don't lie within the women, of course—any suburban housewife can stab you with a paring knife just as quickly and fatally as the most high-strung movie star.

The danger develops in that brightly lit, well-patrolled area called publicity. Loving women who merit more or less continuous publicity is a specialized pursuit, rife with little dangers. The innocent and common act of going into a 7-Eleven to buy a gallon of milk acquires a new tonality if you happen to be in love with someone whose face is apt to appear regularly in *USA Today* or the *National Enquirer*. There'll she be—Jeanie, Nema, Marella—with a new or a fading husband, or a rumored new boyfriend. In all likelihood I would already know that the husband was being phased out or the boyfriend phased in, but such knowledge did little to cushion the shock. There was always a moment of unease as I fumbled for change; sometimes I marched stoutly out without buying the tabloid, only to stop and buy it at the next 7-Eleven down the road.

As much as I hated encountering my girlfriends' pictures in one of those publications, I was apparently not equipped to resist even the most absurd and fallacious mention of them, or the hastiest and most unflattering paparazzi picture. In fact, the more unflattering the picture, the worse the temptation: the sight of one of them looking wildly unkempt, hair a mess, ridiculously dressed, some lout on her arm, undid me more than the glamour shots that were always turning up on the covers of *People, Paris-Match*, or *Vanity Fair*. In the glamour shots, staged with a full complement of hair, makeup, and costume personnel, you got more or less the woman the world wanted to love; the work of the paparazzi, disgusting as it was, nonetheless gave you something more true—the woman herself, in all her bewilderment, vivacity and élan undimmed, messiness unreduced, gloriously or ingloriously female, and always, to me, deeply affecting: the woman, in short, that I *did* love.

For decades I had been a haunter of newsstands the world over, but as the years passed I gradually began to avoid them, along with drugstores, 7-Elevens, any place where I might see a picture of one of my girlfriends on a magazine cover. I didn't want to have to handle the emotional electricity such little shocks produced—and it was for more or less the same reasons that I had flipped past hundreds of mentions of Houston in the years since I left her. Houston, too, was sexy, glitzy, high-profile, her green trees and shining glass buildings a temptation to photographers of all levels of skill. Even a slick shot in an airline magazine, glimpsed high above the Pacific, sometimes made me deeply homesick for Houston, for the weedy neighborhood, the pulsing freeways and cunty smells of the Houston that I still loved.

I yearned, but I didn't go back: Danny Deck Day never happened.

Now I was definitely going back, in fact, was almost there. Huntsville and its prison were already behind me. Apprehension, which had been flitting across my nerve ends since my daughter's first call, flitted ever more rapidly. Not only would I soon have to reckon with a child I had never seen; I would also have to reckon with a city I had once loved deeply but had neglected for twenty-two years.

The women I knew always exacted an immediate price for the most minor neglect; even Gladys was not above giving me margarine rather than butter on my pancakes, though I had repeatedly forbidden her even to *buy* margarine—if she thought I was inattentive to what she called her "situation" for a few days—-her "situation" being her ever-shifting relations with Chuck, who had lately shown an increasing tendency to absent himself to places as far afield as Tucumcari.

If Gladys, my faithful cook, repaid my neglect with margarine, what would a female entity as powerful as Houston do? Would she forgive all and draw me back to her bosom? Or forgive nothing and suck me off the freeway into a bad neighborhood, where I would be shot down by a young crack dealer with an Uzi before I even got my bearings.

Twenty-two years is a long time; more than a generation, as generations are now reckoned. Even though I averted my eyes at newsstands and flipped past articles in *The Times*, I had not missed the fact that Houston had grown; huge when I left, it was now much more huge. I was scarcely past the town of Conroe when plinthlike glass buildings began to appear, at first singly, then in clusters. To the east, near the airport, a kind of minicity seemed to have risen.

I had gotten a late start; the day was ebbing and the pastels of a summer evening colored the sky above and behind the downtown skyline when I came in sight of it. A stately white battleship of a cloud was crossing the ship channel toward Galveston.

I began to relax a little; though most of the downtown had not been there when I left, the clouds, the pastel sunset, and the sky itself had a familiar and reassuring beauty.

Just as the freeway passed over Buffalo Bayou a pickup passed me on the right—a little surprising, since I was still slicing along at a comfortable eighty-five. I glanced over in time to catch a glimpse of the driver, a big, raunchy-looking girl with long hair flying. She was putting on her eye makeup while rocketing over downtown Houston at roughly ninety-five miles per hour. The hand that had been assigned to the steering wheel was also finger-tapping in rhythm with a song I couldn't hear.

The girl must have sensed my glance; she looked over and gave me a big toothy grin, eyebrow brush still poised; she honked loudly, as if to say, Let's go, then she was past. One the curve ahead I was still close enough to see her open a lipstick.

I slowed down and drifted off the freeway at the next exit, relaxed and feeling fine. I *was* fine; moreover, I was home. The spirit of Houston might have assigned that girl to pass me just when she did; where else do girls drive pickups at ninety-five while doing their eye makeup? Besides that, driving so well that you don't even have the sense that anything reckless is happening? The main thing, obviously, is getting to the party while the party's fresh.

I touched a button and my window went down, letting in the old fishy smell of Houston, moist and warm, a smell composed of many textures. I stopped at a 7-Eleven on West Dallas Street, already back in love with the place. Now all I had to do was consult a phone book, make a list of Mr. Burgers, and go meet my daughter. ★

Donald Barthelme

Donald Barthelme wrote this short fiction for the Literary Arts Panel's series of commissioned works by Houston writers. This noble experiment in civic literature did not survive the oil bust of the mid-80s, but the works that had already been written were collected in *Liquid City*, which is worth having.

In this story, Barthelme makes plain the tensions that he felt upon returning to Houston from New York in the early 1980s to teach at the University of Houston.

Return

I WENT ON THE AZALEA TRAIL, AND SHOT one, right through the heart. I took the dead azalea home and put it in my freezer, and all at once I was seized by a deep and fearful melancholy. Had I done something wrong? I had been long away from Texas, living in the wicked, sinful cities of the East—perhaps I no longer understood Texas ways, perhaps the roar and clatter of New York City had permanently damaged the delicate tissues of my flabellum. Had I misunderstood the Azalea Trail?

But I put my melancholy aside and went vigorously about the business of getting connected. I got myself connected to Southwestern Bell, and Entex, and The Light Company, and cable TV, long lines binding me once again into the community. I subscribed to two of our great city newspapers, the American one and the Canadian one, and I bought an Old Smoky barbecue pit.

I set out to sail Buffalo Bayou on a four-by-eight sheet of three-quarter-inch plywood powered by eight mighty Weed-Eaters and I saw many strange and wonderful things. I saw an egret and then another egret and a turtle and a refrigerator without a door on it and a heron and a possum and an upside-down '52 Pontiac. And I said to myself, This blessed stream contains many strange and wonderful things. It was getting dark now, and the moon had risen, and I saw a wise old owl sitting in a tree. So I throttled back my eight powerful Weed-Eaters and spoke to the owl, saying, "How's by you, boychick?"

And then I looked closely and saw that it wasn't a wise old owl at all; it was Philip Johnson, out hunting for new clients, by the light of the moon. So I congratulated him on all his great and tall new buildings, and we gazed together at the glowing tower of the city, all the great and tall new buildings glowing like the wondrous towers of Oz, we looked at them and were content.

***

But then my melancholy came upon me with doubled force, and I decided to take additional measures. So I joined the First Baptist Church of Aldine, the First Baptist Church of Alvin, the First Baptist Church of Friendswood, the First Baptist Church of Golden Acres, the First Baptist Church of Jacinto City, and the First Baptist Church of the Woodlands. Then I started in on the Methodists. Before I had finished, I was a member in good standing of some two hundred twenty congregations, and had been appointed to a number of important committees. I was on the Old Clothes Committee here, and the Potato Salad Committee there, vice-chairman of the Fellowship of Song Committee at another place, and treasurer of the Total Immersion Committee at yet another place. It felt fine, being connected.

But by this time I was a little tired of being good, you can be good just so long and then you get a little tired of it. So I decided to be bad, and went out to find some Totally Nude Live Girls. And found some, right there on South Main, acres and acres of them. Totally Nude Live Girls. And I must tell you that they were lovely, rarely had I seen Totally Nude Live Girls quite so lovely, so I sat down, and took off my shoes, and began to talk to them.

It was a slow afternoon and there must have been forty or sixty Totally Nude Live Girls in that bar, and they all began to confide in me, telling me their hopes and fears, their visions of the future, and their regrets about the parti-colored past. One Totally Nude Live Girl told me that she was from Secaucus, New Jersey, and had only been a Totally Nude Live Girl for a month, but it was better than being a mailman, which is what she had been in Secaucus, New

Jersey, because of the dogs scaring you all the time, she knew she was supposed to like dogs but she really didn't, and so on. She was very nice. I liked her.

We were drinking, me and the forty or sixty Totally Nude Live Girls, martinis and margaritas and one thing and another, buckets and buckets of them, there was loveliness in every direction, as far as the eye could see, and with a rush the melancholy came upon me once again, because nothing can make you so melancholy, sick in the heart, as forty to sixty excited, confiding, lovely, and partially drunk Totally Nude Live Girls. So with regret I put my shoes on and left them, promising to write.

That was what I was, I remembered, a writer—a strange fate but not uncongenial. I remembered that years ago, as a raw youth, I had worked for the Houston newspaper that is now the Canadian one. This was shortly after the Civil War. The newspaper building was populated with terrifying city editors whose gaze could cut brass, and ferocious copy desk men whose contempt could make a boy of twenty wish that his mother and father had never met. I loved working there. They paid us in pretzels, of course—I got about forty pretzels a week, and then, when I got back from the Spanish-American War, I got a generous raise, to fifty. Pretzels.

When I was hired they showed me my desk, an old beat-up scarred wooden desk, and they told me that it had been O. Henry's desk when O. Henry worked for the paper, as he had at one time. And I readily believed it. I could see the place where O. Henry had savagely stabbed the desk with his pen in pursuit of a slimy adjective just out of reach, and a kind of bashed-in-looking place where O. Henry had beaten his poor genius head on the desk in frustration over not being able to capture that noun leaping like a fawn just out of reach . . . So I sat down at the desk and I too began to chase those devils, the dancy nouns and come-hither adjectives, what joy.

But I had no time to dwell upon these precious memories. I had been long away from Texas and had to reacculturate, fast. So I joined the YMCA, the AAA, the American Legion, the Art League, the Fern Society, the Canary Club, the Turnverein, the AFL-CIO, the Great Books Council, the Clean Air Caucus, the Loyal Order of Moose Number 2106, Planned Parenthood, the Gay Coalition, the On Leong Merchants' Association, the Mothers of Twins

Club, and Mensa, These new associations greatly enriched my life. I was caught up in a whirl of activity, so to say, zipping over to the Fern Society to inspect a comely new frond one day and to the Canary Club to look at a bold new Meistersinger the next, protesting outrages with my brothers of the Gay Coalition in the morning and cuddling nurslings with my fellow mothers of the Twins Club in the afternoon, and thinking the long long thoughts of Mensa all the while.

***

Yet the melancholy hung about me like an unchampionship season and I realized that I needed professional help. So I went off to consult a true expert in unhappiness, the Hunchback of the Galleria. I found the Hunchback up by the running track, watching with fascination the tiny, graceful skaters inscribing ampersands on the ice far below. "Hunchback," I said to him, "what is wrong with me? Am I laboring under some kind of a curse? Can it be that the deep and fearful malaise which informs all my days is the result of my having shot that damned azalea?"

"Woe," said the Hunchback, "woe unto him who—"

"Hunchback," I said, "what is this woe-unto-him-who business? Can you give me a straight answer, or not?"

"Woe," said the Hunchback, "woe unto him who, or, take another case, woe unto *her* who—"

He could see that I was becoming a little exasperated, so he said, in the wisest possible tones, "Why are you being so hard on yourself?" and then was off, swinging on a rope through the great cathedrallike spaces of the Galleria, and I thought I heard bells ringing, but maybe I didn't. In fine, I obtained no satisfaction, any ordinary shrink could have said to me, "Why are you being so hard on yourself?" and many have, I was disappointed.

I was disappointed, so I took myself to the Opera to cheer myself up. It was a grand evening, with a lot of flash and glitter, there were Cadillacs and Rolls-Royces and pumpkins and Mercedes-Benzes pulling up to the glistening façade of the Opera. I parked my mule and rushed inside, all of us were in a high state of pleasurable tension because we were going to the Opera, going to grasp that core experience of culture which is the Opera, that irreducible minimum of irrefrangible soul stuff which the Opera is.

And as I made my way to my seat in Row GG I saw a caped and masked figure lurking in the shadows. My God! I thought, It's the Phantom of the Opera! But it was only Philip Johnson, seeking new clients in the corridors of the Opera, and I said to him, "Noble architect! Can you design for me some kind of azalea that I can plant somewhere on the surface of this wondrous city and thus redeem, in some measure, the hasty and ill-considered act of azaleacide that I would not have committed had I not lingered too long in the wicked, sinful cities of the East and gotten my values screwed up?" And the great architect whipped from his sleeve his magic Eberhard Faber 2B pencil and waved it in the air, and sketched a most beautiful stainless steel azalea nine hundred feet high. My melancholy fell away from me, and I was content. And some day, God and the Gerald D. Hines Interests willing, you'll see this nine-hundred-foot-high stainless steel azalea, taking its place with the city's other great and tall monuments in the garden of the creative imagination. ★

MAX APPLE

Max Apple taught at Rice for many years before moving on. Today he lives in Philadelphia, which he describes as a "northern suburb of Houston." He continues to write fictions that deal, however glancingly, with Houston sports figures. His most recent collection, *The Jew of Home Depot and Other Stories*, contains a story titled "Yao's Chick." The following story, published in 1984, was compared in *Newsweek* to Chekov. Richard Ford included it in his *Granta Book of the American Short Story* collection.

Bridging

IN THE ASTRODOME, NOLAN RYAN IS SHAVing the corners. He's going through the Giants in order. The radio announcer is not even mentioning that by the sixth the Giants haven't had a hit. The K's mount on the scoreboard. Tonight Nolan passes the Big Train and is now the all-time strikeout king. He's almost as old as I am and he still throws nothing but smoke. His fastball is an aspirin; batters tear their tendons lunging for his curve. Jessica and I have season tickets, but tonight she's home listening and I'm in the basement of St. Anne's Church watching Kay Randall's fingertips. Kay is holding her hands out from her chest, her fingertips on each other. Her fingers move a little as she talks and I can hear her nails click when they meet. That's how close I'm sitting.

Kay is talking about "bridging"; that's what her arched fingers represent.

"Bridging," she says, "is the way Brownies become Girl Scouts. It's a slow steady process. It's not easy, but we allow a whole year for bridging."

Eleven girls in brown shirts with red bandannas at their neck are imitating Kay as she talks. They hold their stumpy chewed fingertips out and bridge them. So do I.

I brought the paste tonight and the stick-on gold stars and the thread for sewing buttonholes.

"I feel a little awkward," Kay Randall said on the phone, "asking a man to do these errands . . . but that's my problem, not yours. Just bring the supplies and try to be at the church meeting room a few minutes before seven."

I arrive a half hour early.

"You're off your rocker," Jessica says. She begs me to drop her at the Astrodome on my way to the Girl Scout meeting. "After the game, I'll meet you at the main souvenir stand on the first level. They stay open an hour after the game. I'll be all right. There are cops and ushers every five yards."

She can't believe that I am missing this game to perform my functions as an assistant Girl Scout leader. Our Girl Scout battle has been going on for two months.

"Girl Scouts is stupid," Jessica says. "Who wants to sell cookies and sew buttons and walk around wearing stupid old badges?"

When she agreed to go to the first meeting, I was so happy I volunteered to become an assistant leader. After the meeting, Jessica went directly to the car the way she does after school, after a birthday party, after a ball game, after anything. A straight line to the car. No jabbering with girlfriends, no smiles, no dallying, just right to the car. She slides into the back seat, belts in, and braces herself for destruction. It has already happened once.

I swoop past five thousand years of stereotypes and accept my assistant leader's packet and credentials.

"I'm sure there have been other men in the movement," Kay says, "we just haven't had any in our district. It will be good for the girls."

Not for my Jessica. She won't bridge, she won't budge.

"I know why you're doing this," she says. "You think that because I don't have a mother, Kay Randall and the Girl Scouts will help me. That's crazy. And I know that Sharon is supposed to be like a mother too. Why don't you just leave me alone."

Sharon is Jessica's therapist. Jessica sees her twice a week. Sharon and I have a meeting once a month.

"We have a lot of shy girls," Kay Randall tells me. "Scouting brings them out. Believe me, it's hard to stay shy when you're nine years old and you're sharing a tent with six other girls. You have to count on each other, you have to communicate."

I imagine Jessica zipping up in her sleeping bag, mumbling good night to anyone who first says it to her, then closing her eyes and hating me for sending her out among the happy.

"She likes all sports, especially baseball," I tell my leader.

"There's room for baseball in scouting," Kay says. "Once a year the whole district goes to a game. They mention us on the big scoreboard."

"Jessica and I go to all the home games. We're real fans."

Kay smiles.

"That's why I want her in Girl Scouts. You know, I want her to go to things with her girlfriends instead of always hanging around with me at ball games."

"I understand," Kay says. "It's part of bridging."

With Sharon the term is "separation anxiety." That's the fastball, "bridging" is the curve. Amid all their magic words I feel as if Jessica and I are standing at home plate blindfolded.

While I await Kay and the members of Troop 111, District 6, I eye St. Anne in her grotto and St. Gregory and St. Thomas. Their hands are folded as if they started out bridging, ended up praying.

In October the principal sent Jessica home from school because Mrs. Simmons caught her in spelling class listening to the World Series through an earphone.

"It's against the school policy," Mrs. Simmons said. "Jessica understands school policy. We confiscate radios and send the child home."

"I'm glad," Jessica said. "It was a cheap-o radio. Now I can watch the TV with you."

They sent her home in the middle of the sixth game. I let her stay home for the seventh too.

The Brewers are her favorite American League team. She likes Rollie Fingers, and especially Robin Yount.

"Does Yount go in the hole better than Harvey Kuenn used to?"

"You bet," I tell her. "Kuenn was never a great fielder but he could hit three hundred with his eyes closed."

Kuenn is the Brewers' manager. He has an artificial leg and can barely make it up the dugout steps, but when I was Jessica's age and the Tigers were my team, Kuenn used to stand at the plate, tap the corners with his bat, spit some tobacco juice, and knock liners up the alley.

She took the Brewers' loss hard.

"If Fingers wasn't hurt they would have squashed the Cards, wouldn't they?"

I agreed.

"But I'm glad for Andujar."

We had Andujar's autograph. Once we met him at a McDonald's. He was a relief pitcher then, an erratic right-hander. In St. Louis he improved. I was happy to get his name on a napkin. Jessica shook his hand.

One night after I read her a story, she said, "Daddy, if we were rich could we go to the away games too? I mean, if you didn't have to be at work every day."

"Probably we could," I said, "but wouldn't it get boring? We'd have to stay at hotels and eat in restaurants. Even the players get sick of it."

"Are you kidding?" she said. "I'd never get sick of it."

"Jessica has fantasies of being with you forever, following baseball or whatever," Sharon says. "All she's trying to do is please you. Since she lost her mother she feels that you and she are alone in the world. She doesn't want to let anyone or anything else into that unit, the two of you. She's afraid of any more losses. And, of course, her greatest worry is about losing you."

"You know," I tell Sharon, "that's pretty much how I feel too."

"Of course it is," she says. "I'm glad to hear you say it."

Sharon is glad to hear me say almost anything. When I complain that her $100-a-week fee would buy a lot of peanut butter sandwiches, she says she is "glad to hear me expressing my anger."

"Sharon's not fooling me," Jessica says. "I know that she thinks drawing those pictures is supposed to make me feel better or something. You're just wasting your money. There's nothing wrong with me."

"It's a long, difficult, expensive process," Sharon says. "You and Jessica have lost a lot. Jessica is going to have to learn to trust the world again. It would help if you could do it too."

So I decide to trust Girl Scouts. First Girl Scouts, then the world. I make my stand at the meeting of Kay Randall's fingertips. While Nolan Ryan breaks Walter Johnson's strikeout record and pitches a two-hit shutout, I pass out paste and thread to nine-year-olds who are sticking and sewing their lives together in ways Jessica and I can't.

II

Scouting is not altogether new to me. I was a Cub Scout. I owned a blue beanie and I remember very well my den mother, Mrs. Clark. A den mother made perfect sense to me then and still does. Maybe that's why I don't feel uncomfortable being a Girl Scout assistant leader.

We had no den father. Mr. Clark was only a photograph on the living room wall, the tiny living room where we held our monthly meetings. Mr. Clark was killed in the Korean War. His son John was in the troop. John was stocky but Mrs. Clark was huge. She couldn't sit on a regular chair, only on a couch or a stool without sides. She was the cashier in the convenience store beneath their apartment. The story we heard was that Walt, the old man who owned the store, felt sorry for her and gave her the job. He was her landlord too. She sat on a swivel stool and rang up the purchases.

We met at the store and watched while she locked the door; then we followed her up the steep staircase to her three-room apartment. She carried two wet glass bottles of milk. Her body took up the entire width of the staircase. She passed the banisters the way semi trucks pass each other on a narrow highway.

We were ten years old, a time when everything is funny, especially fat people. But I don't remember anyone ever laughing about Mrs. Clark. She had great dignity and character. So did John. I didn't know what to call it then, but I knew John was someone you could always trust.

She passed out milk and cookies, then John collected the cups and washed them. They didn't even have a television set. The only decoration in the room that barely held all of us was Mr. Clark's picture on the wall. We saw him in his uniform and we knew he died in Korea defending his country. We were little boys in blue beanies drinking milk in the apartment of a hero. Through that aura I came to scouting. I wanted Kay Randall to have all of Mrs. Clark's dignity.

When she took a deep breath and then bridged, Kay Randall had noticeable armpits. Her wide shoulders slithered into a tiny rib cage. Her armpits were like bridges. She said "bridging" like a mantra, holding her hands before her for about thirty seconds at the start of each meeting.

"A promise is a promise," I told Jessica. "I signed up to be a leader, and I'm going to do it with you or without you."

"But you didn't even ask me if I liked it. You just signed up without talking it over."

"That's true; that's why I'm not going to force you to go along. It was my choice."

"What can you like about it? I hate Melissa Randall. She always has a cold."

"Her mother is a good leader."

"How do you know?"

"She's my boss. I've got to like her, don't I?" I hugged Jessica. "C'mon, honey, give it a chance. What do you have to lose?"

"If you make me go I'll do it, but if I have a choice I won't."

Every other Tuesday, Karen, the fifteen-year-old Greek girl who lives on the corner, babysits Jessica while I go to the Scout meetings. We talk about field trips and how to earn merit badges. The girls giggle when Kay pins a promptness badge on me, my first.

Jessica thinks it's hilarious. She tells me to wear it to work.

Sometimes when I watch Jessica brush her hair and tie her ponytail and make up her lunch kit I start to think that maybe I should just relax and stop the therapy and the scouting and all my not-so-subtle attempts to get her to invite friends over. I start to think that, in spite of everything, she's a good student and she's got a sense of humor. She's barely nine years old. She'll grow up like everyone else does. John Clark did it without a father; she'll do it without a mother. I start to wonder if Jessica seems to the girls in her class the way John Clark seemed to me: dignified, serious, almost an adult even while we were playing. I admired him. Maybe the girls in her class admire her. But John had that hero on the wall, his father in a uniform, dead for reasons John and all the rest of us understood.

My Jessica had to explain a neurologic disease she couldn't even pronounce. "I hate it when people ask me about Mom," she says. "I just tell them she fell off the Empire State Building."

III

Before our first field trip I go to Kay's house for a planning session. We're going to collect wildflowers in East Texas. It's a one-day trip. I arranged to rent the school bus.

I told Jessica that she could go on the trip even though she wasn't a troop member, but she refused.

We sit on colonial furniture in Kay's den. She brings in coffee and we go over the supply list. Another troop is joining ours so there will be twenty-two girls, three women, and me, a busload among the bluebonnets.

"We have to be sure the girls understand that the bluebonnets they pick are on private land and that we have permission to pick them. Otherwise they might pick them along the roadside, which is against the law."

I imagine all twenty-two of them behind bars for picking bluebonnets and Jessica laughing while I scramble for bail money.

I keep noticing Kay's hands. I notice them as she pours coffee, as she checks off the items on the list, as she gestures. I keep expecting her to bridge. She has large, solid, confident hands. When she finishes bridging I sometimes feel like clapping the way people do after the national anthem.

"I admire you," she tells me. "I admire you for going ahead with Scouts even though your daughter rejects it. She'll get a lot out of it indirectly from you."

Kay Randall is thirty-three, divorced, and has a Bluebird too. Her older daughter is one of the stubby-fingered girls, Melissa. Jessica is right; Melissa always has a cold.

Kay teaches fifth grade and has been divorced for three years. I am the first assistant she's ever had.

"My husband, Bill, never helped with Scouts," Kay says. "He was pretty much turned off to everything except his business and drinking. When we separated I can't honestly say I missed him; he'd never been there. I don't think the girls miss him either. He only sees them about once a month. He has girlfriends, and his business is doing very well. I guess he has what he wants."

"And you?"

She uses one of those wonderful hands to move the hair away from her eyes, a gesture that makes her seem very young.

"I guess I do too. I've got the girls and my job. I'm lonesome, though. It's not exactly what I wanted."

We both think about what might have been as we sit beside her glass coffeepot with our lists of sachet supplies. If she was Barbra Streisand and I Robert Redford and the music started playing in the background to give us a clue and there was a long close-up of our lips, we might just fade into middle age together. But Melissa called for Mom because her mosquito bite was bleeding where she scratched it. And I had an angry daughter waiting for me. And all Kay and I had in common was Girl Scouts. We were both smart enough to know it. When Kay looked at me before going to put alcohol on the mosquito bite, our mutual sadness dripped from us like the last drops of coffee through the grinds.

"You really missed something tonight," Jessica tells me. "The Astros did a double steal. I've never seen one before. In the fourth they sent Thon and Moreno together, and Moreno stole home."

She knows batting averages and won-lost percentages too, just like the older boys, only they go out to play. Jessica stays in and waits for me.

During the field trip, while the girls pick flowers to dry and then manufacture into sachets, I think about Jessica at home, probably beside the radio. Juana, our once-a-week cleaning lady, agreed to work on Saturday so she could stay with Jessica while I took the all-day field trip.

It was no small event. In the eight months since Vicki died I had not gone away for an entire day.

I made waffles in the waffle iron for her before I left, but she hardly ate.

"If you want anything, just ask Juana."

"Juana doesn't speak English."

"She understands, that's enough."

"Maybe for you it's enough."

"Honey, I told you, you can come; there's plenty of room on the bus. It's not too late for you to change your mind."

"It's not too late for you either. There's going to be plenty of other leaders there. You don't have to go. You're just doing this to be mean to me."

I'm ready for this. I spent an hour with Sharon steeling myself. "Before she can leave you," Sharon said, "you'll have to show her that you can leave. Nothing's going to happen to her. And don't let her be sick that day either."

Jessica is too smart to pull the "I don't feel good" routine. Instead she becomes more silent, more unhappy looking than usual. She stays in her pajamas while I wash the dishes and get ready to leave.

I didn't notice the sadness as it was coming upon Jessica. It must have happened gradually in the years of Vicki's decline, the years in which I paid so little attention to my daughter. There were times when Jessica seemed to recognize the truth more than I did.

As my Scouts picked their wildflowers, I remembered the last outing I had planned for us. It was going to be a Fourth of July picnic with some friends in Austin. I stopped at the bank and got $200 in cash for the long weekend. But when I came home Vicki was too sick to move and the air conditioner had broken. I called our friends to cancel the picnic; then I took Jessica to the mall with me to buy a fan. I bought the biggest one they had, a 58-inch oscillating model that sounded like a hurricane. It could cool 10,000 square feet, but it wasn't enough.

Vicki was home sitting blankly in front of the TV set. The fan could move eight tons of air an hour, but I wanted it to save my wife. I wanted a fan that would blow the whole earth out of its orbit.

I had $50 left. I gave it to Jessica and told her to buy anything she wanted.

"Whenever you're sad, Daddy, you want to buy me things." She put the money back in my pocket. "It won't help." She was seven years old, holding my hand tightly in the appliance department at J. C. Penney's.

I watched Melissa sniffle even more among the wildflowers, and I pointed out the names of various flowers to Carol and JoAnne and Sue and Linda and Rebecca, who were by now used to me and treated me pretty much as they treated Kay. I noticed that the Girl Scout flower book had very accurate photographs that made it easy to identify the bluebonnets and buttercups and poppies. There were also several varieties of wild grasses.

We were only 70 miles from home on some land a wealthy rancher long ago donated to the Girl Scouts. The girls bending among the flowers seemed to have been quickly transformed by the colorful meadow. The gigglers and monotonous singers on the bus were now, like the bees, sucking strength from the beauty around them. Kay was in the midst of them and so, I realized, was I, not watching and keeping score and admiring from the distance but a participant, a player.

JoAnne and Carol sneaked up from behind me and dropped some dandelions down my back. I chased them; then I helped the other leaders pour the Kool-Aid and distribute the Baggies and the name tags for each girl's flowers.

My daughter is home listening to a ball game, I thought, and I'm out here having fun with nine-year-olds. It's upside down.

When I came home with dandelion fragments still on my back, Juana had cleaned the house and I could smell the taco sauce in the kitchen. Jessica was in her room. I suspected that she had spent the day listless and tearful, although I had asked her to invite a friend over.

"I had a lot of fun, honey, but I missed you."

She hugged me and cried against my shoulder. I felt like holding her the way I used to when she was an infant, the way I rocked her to sleep. But she was a big girl now and needed not sleep but wakefulness.

"I heard on the news that the Rockets signed Ralph Sampson," she sobbed, "and you hardly ever take me to any pro basketball games."

"But if they have a new center things will be different. With Sampson we'll be contenders. Sure I'll take you."

"Promise?"

"Promise." I promise to take you everywhere, my lovely child, and then to leave you. I'm learning to be a leader. ★

TRACY DAUGHERTY

Tracy Daugherty is the author of four novels (*Axeman's Jazz* is set in Houston), three collections of short stories, one book of essays, and, most recently, a celebrated literary biography of his teacher and mentor, Donald Barthelme. The mighty gravitational pull of Barthelme is on display in this story, in which a son deals with the chatty and pugnacious ghost of his recently dead father, who appears largely inspired by Daugherty's memories of the late writer. But this story is far more than homage; its central conceit, the narrator's imaginative construction of a city that is much more Barcelona than Houston, is both charming and moving.

Daugherty has taught at Oregon State University since 1987. He's earned the title of Distinguished Professor and has served as director of the MFA program in creative writing.

Almost Barcelona

AT ABOUT THE TIME HIS FATHER'S CANCER burst uncontrollably open in colon, brain and throat, his own health began to fail. Nothing life-threatening: restlessness—a sort of itching in the skin—lack of appetite, shifting bowels. "Sick with worry," said Sarah. "Too much stress—Robbie, it's hardly coincidence."

All winter she'd waited for Robert's worries to break. In late January he'd brought his father home to Texas from the rent-controlled apartment in Manhattan. He'd arranged for round-the-clock care at the med center, and he'd temporarily suspended his own projects. His work wasn't moving much anyway—one small showing in a local gallery where, predictably, he was promoted as the son of the famous Abstract Expressionist, Frederick Becker.

Sarah, bless her, had been a tender anchor. She insisted that Robert was painting masterfully despite the slow market for his work; she patiently accepted the burden of Frederick's sickness into her life. He'd been ebbing for two years, but the final dying—the last fatal push—occurred over a six-week period.

In his dad's last days, Robert recalled how his first-grade school reports arrived in the mail every six weeks—a timeframe, filled with swift judgment, that always terrified him. "Well now, Robbie, did you finally catch fire this term?" he remembered his hard father saying.

For six weeks as Frederick shrank and Robert sat by (like a cook, he sometimes thought, watching a heavy stock boil down on a stove) Sarah paid the bills, cleaned the house—as efficiently as a Grand Prix mechanic she kept the details of Robert's life running smoothly while he said his slow goodbye.

One afternoon in the hospital, Frederick pulled Robert's face to his own. He was pale as a dime on the starchy pillow. The room smelled of mercurochrome. "I'm sorry you had to bear all this alone," Frederick whispered. The cancer had acted on his voice like a steel blade on an apple. Robert said, "Shhh"—but his father was right. His mother had died in '82; what few relatives he knew about were as vague to him as the figures Frederick sometimes buried beneath the thick red and black surfaces of his canvases.

(His father used to laugh at the "young guns"—the postwar critics—who asked in the pages of *ARTnews*, "Do these ghostly human shapes mean that Becker is abandoning pure abstraction?" In '72—several blown-apart art movements later—Frederick did a *60 Minutes* interview in which he quipped, "Throughout my career I abandoned anything that even *smacked* of purity." This statement was taken by a new generation of critics as his credo. As perhaps it was.)

Despite his acclaim, the Becker family had always acted embarrassed by one another. Years ago they'd scattered to various poor jobs, various hills and valleys around the country. Frederick's oldest sister, Fay, was the only relative Robert remembered with any certainty. He recalled her saying one afternoon (to whom was she speaking? where did the conversation take place?), "Modern art. It's all about sex, that's what it is. His paintings may not *look* like anything, but I know what the bastard's thinking."

For some reason, Robert's dad was the blackest sheep in a dark-wool family. Too "bohemian" perhaps, too much the "libertine"—words Robert imagined Fay using. Now that he had followed Frederick's cadmium blue trail into the House of Art, Robert was a bad lamb too.

Sarah volunteered to contact the funeral director and a lawyer. In the days immediately after Frederick's death Robert simply stopped. He felt, when he was conscious of feeling at all, that he'd stepped into a late Rothko and was wrapped in a dry black mist that reeked of turpentine and linseed oil.

***

Most of the last thirty years Frederick had lived in the West Village but Houston always had a strong, almost erotic, grip on the old bird. Wherever he traveled—Paris, San Francisco, Barcelona—wherever he was fêted for his work, he spoke fondly of Houston's trees, the wet, leafy arms of its wraparound willows. He loved too the beautiful brown skin of friendly young Chicanas in the barrios and mesquite-scented, lime-soaked fajitas. All his life he wore Tony Lama boots—a western affectation he never lost in the East.

Initially, then, Robert decided to bury Frederick in Texas next to his first wife, Robert's mother, under a sweeping live oak tree on a hill overlooking the Gulf of Mexico. At night a lighthouse beam cut through thick orange oil-refinery steam gathering in boxlike clouds over the Gulf; foghorns called in brief, sad bursts out at sea.

Less than twenty-four hours before the memorial service, however, Robert changed his mind. He reheard in memory, "When I'm gone, set me to the torch and blow away my goddamn ashes, will you?"

"Are you sure?" he asked his father.

"Absolutely."

This turned out to be the first of several dialogues Robert continued to have with him.

Frederick went on (words Robert *didn't* remember, though they had his father's stamp): "Collage. Random collision. I've devoted my whole life to them and I don't see why death should stop me. So go ahead and toss my leftovers into the stratosphere. Maybe a pinch of my old ass'll land in a lilac bush, a sniff in a pig's snout, an ounce or two in an empty bucket. Who knows—I may drift through a bus window somewhere and settle on the lap of a lusty woman off to make a killing in the market, eh? Viva collage!"

***

Sometimes at night now Robert and Sarah made slow, simple love together. More often they'd talk. Sarah told him she'd be patient until his grief let go, but he knew she was edgy and tired of the distance he'd shown since Frederick's death—giant *nothings* (both the distance and the death) that seemed to be growing.

***

This is how it started each night: he'd slide into bed, kiss Sarah's forehead and cheeks, then stare for several minutes at a screened window opening onto his yard and the little tin shed he'd converted into a studio out back. He imagined the blank or half-finished canvases in the cradles of their easels, the oily rags, the spattered palettes he'd left on his studio table.

Incomplete sketches: Sarah, his mother.

Then he'd recall, from fifteen or sixteen years ago, visits to his father's studio in New York. The place was crammed with line drawings after Paul Klee ("One bone alone achieves nothing," Klee wrote). There weren't any studies of people, no familiar faces—just deep gray strokes and sheets of cascading color on the stark white walls. Red, green, purple, and black swayed from the ceiling on unseen hooks and wires. Robert remembered seeing, against a wire-mesh window, the famous series of cadmium blue sponge-mop streaks entitled *Elegy*.

Each night now he stared, with burning eyes, at the memories of blue in his head. Lake, sea, iris blue. Eventually, the jumpy hues merged and became a sky unfolding like a blanket against his bedroom walls. He dropped his eyes toward the floor and found himself in a city of his own creation.

It was an American (though ornately Old European-styled) city with sidewalk cafés. Black wrought-iron tables, aromatic coffees and teas, raisin-filled cakes on silver trays. Cars (Fords, mostly, from the 1920s to the present) cruised noiselessly down brick streets. The two men, Robert and his father, sipped white wine and praised the movements and lines of the handsome women strolling briskly together—sometimes arm-in-arm—up the walk.

In recent days Robert had made a minor correction: the women now were naked—a natural phenomenon in my splendid city, Robert decided. This new touch greatly improved the tone and feel of the talks with his father.

Usually, before ordering a second carafe of wine, Frederick commented on the architecture, which differed only slightly from one evening to the next. "Robbie, I really must congratulate you," he said tonight. "This city is your best yet. It's Barcelona, isn't it?"

"Almost. I've borrowed liberally from Gaudí."

"Yes, I noticed the corkscrew roofs, the waxlike folds in the granite. The lighting's a bit harsh—too much Texas in your sunset."

"We can adjust that."

"Marvelous. Much better. Of course, I recognize certain design elements from our previous evenings together: the crosswalks that fade in the center of the street, the diamond-shaped intersections. The statue in the fountain is new. Venus, is it? But what's she made of?"

"Chocolate," Robert said.

"Chocolate? Charming. Why doesn't she melt in the spray?"

"I don't want her to," Robert said. "This *is* my city."

"Fair enough. But why chocolate?"

"I like chocolate."

Frederick nodded. "Always did. Remember your little weight problem as a kid? But I should caution you, Robbie, aesthetic choices can't be made on personal whim. I get the impression you're not *thinking through* your projects with enough discipline these days."

"You've always thought that."

"Well—"

"Ever since I returned to representation."

Frederick sniffed. "Sentimental portraits of your mother and your wife."

—which the Old Man, the Master, the Famous Iconoclast who'd helped free American painting from Subject, always held against him. Frederick couldn't abide the fact that his boy didn't demonstrate the passion or the flair for the kinds of daring, monochrome abstractions he'd pioneered in the fifties. Robert was firmly attached to the human form.

"We don't disagree, do we, that art should lance the boil of the set-in-stone?" Frederick said.

Robert laughed. "Lance the boil" had always been one of Frederick's favorite expressions. To him, Conventionality, whatever guises it took—including straightforward figurative painting—was a hideous black blemish.

"Dad, we've trampled this grass to death," Robert said. "Abstraction was a cliché by the time I started painting."

"But there were other avenues you could've explored. Junk-sculpture. Stuffed goats, car bumpers, that sort of thing. The sixties were a fertile lab of ideas. *And* a hell of a lot of fun. You didn't have to become Norman Rockwell."

Robert let that pass. "I'll grant you, abstraction's stock seems to be rising again," he said. "At the Whitney this year—"

"Balls. Dime-store imitations of Pollock and myself. The galleries are filled with stale piss instead of the wine of life." Frederick snapped his fingers. "Waiter! A carafe of your finest piss, please!"

***

Robert realized that in some cut-rate Freudian fashion he was using these talks to rehash unresolved arguments he'd had with his father over the years. He also recognized that dialogues, stripped to the bone, are power plays, often ugly: the dominant conversational partner sets the subject, tone and pace; the responder adds incidentals, details, counterweight, and heft. These recent discussions with Frederick were agitated both by habit and circumstance. *Habit* dictated that his father dominate. *Circumstance* required Robert to perform Take as well as Give.

"Ruth" and "Art" remained the two most bitter topics between them. "Ruth was too young when she married me," Frederick said in life, and again in these vivid after-death get-togethers. "Your mother had stars in her eyes. I knew we wouldn't last—I was married to my own heroic gestures, as they say—but I didn't want to crush the poor girl."

And on Robert's recent efforts: "You do what you do with great skill, Robbie, but it's merely decorative wallpaper. It doesn't advance the cause of art."

Robert was tired of hearing this. "Screw art's cause," he said. "I paint what I paint because I like my mother's face. I enjoy my wife's honest smile."

And there it was, the *real* trouble between them: Frederick's celebrated inconstancy and Robert's faithfulness to women.

"Vulnerability," Frederick said. "A synonym for 'marriage.' Lance the boil, I say."

Now as always, personal topics gave way to theory as the two men spoke. The people they knew together—Robert's wife and mother—became merely figures, then examples (what to do, what not to do in your lifelong fencing with women), then nothing even remotely identifiable—color streaks in the conversation.

***

Tonight Robert's city was almost Barcelona but it smelled of Cajun delights. Blackened redfish, filet gumbo. Female nudes mailed letters, trotted after cabs, popped open purple umbrellas. Frederick drained his glass and beamed. The ladies in their frank poses pleased him.

Moved by his father's happiness, Robert dropped his guard. "Maybe you're right about my work," he said. "It's probably not as good as it could be. But I've been distracted lately."

"By what?" Frederick ordered more wine. He picked up his knife.

Robert scraped at a mauve acrylic dab on his thumb. "The truth is, I'm having a hell of a time accepting the fact that you're gone."

"Suffer," Frederick said, and spryly sliced his fish.

***

On the streets of Houston, Paris, Budapest, and the *real* Barcelona, women, sadly, weren't naked. They wore scarves against the wind, tinted glasses against swirling dust and glare. They wore soft sneakers on the subways, saving their cruelly shaped high heels in plastic bags until they reached the office.

They were harried and tired and angry, hungry, hurtling into or out of love.

This was a world—of concrete, steel, and actuality—that Frederick didn't feel at home in.

"I'm a Romantic," he'd once told Robert. "Romantics never stop believing in possibilities. That's what makes us so appealing, but also, I confess, unfaithful and often irresponsible. We're always running after the next new thing."

A rare moment of candor. Robert must've been twenty-four or five at the time—this was ten years ago in New York, in a hotel bar on Lexington. The subject, then as most often, was why Frederick left Ruth. "My heart," he said. "It's always yearning."

Robert remembered other actual conversations he'd had with his dad, brief moments when the walls were down, the screens of violent color washed clean.

One evening, six or seven years ago, they'd walked to the Village Vanguard to hear Woody Shaw blow golden jazz. Old Max Gordon, the club owner, always hovering at the back of the room; Shaw; now Frederick—all dead, Robert realized with a start. The sights and sounds of a whole era, vanished.

That night Frederick had clucked with pleasure whenever the drummer tickled the hi-hat. He got drunker than usual. After the band's last set he stumbled on the cement steps rising to the street and roughed-up his shins. "Damn booze," he said. "It's made me clumsy and fat." Later in his studio he admitted, "I stare at my canvases now and think, 'This next series'll drive a stake through my reputation.'"

"You've said that about everything you've ever done," Robert reminded him.

"No, this is different. Age, maybe. Or too much whiskey. I worry they'll see what a fake I am."

"Dad—"

"But then I think, Fuck it, I'm going to see it through. I'm going to by God *make it work*."

And he always did.

Another time, in Houston. They were sitting in a Tex-Mex place on Navigation Boulevard, near the shrimp-stinking Ship Channel. Margaritas, palm-leaf green; piñatas, red-and-yellow paper cutouts on the walls. The day before, the Cultural Arts Council of Houston had commissioned a skyline portrait from the city's famous son. Frederick was nervous about it—normally he didn't work on commission, but this was for a celebration of Texas images, and Frederick was touched to be included. He had a large and sincere civic conscience. Near the end of the meal he leaned over his enchiladas verdes and whispered to Robert, "The thing is, you know, I can't paint the skyline."

"Why not?"

"I don't know *how* to paint figuratively—not really." He looked around the restaurant. "I paint the only way I know. Don't tell anyone."

Eventually he produced a large, abstract canvas of brown and orange and gray. *Houston Colors*, he called it. The Arts Council was thrilled.

And then, eight months ago: "I'm frightened of dying," he said.

He'd gone off Camels and Scotch, been through detox. Chemotherapy had left him gaunt and weak. His face seemed to re-emerge after years of sternness, puffiness, lack of sleep. He had high cheekbones, an angular chin, and wide, friendly blue eyes. It was at last a face that Robert wanted to paint.

"Do I look like a cancer victim?" Frederick wanted to know one day. "How apparent is it?" He and Robert were strolling the corridors of the medical center together.

"You look okay, Dad. You needed to lose some weight," Robert said.

"Hell of a way to do it, eh? People are different when you're sick," Frederick said. "You're an embodiment of frailty so they feel they can confess all their weaknesses to you. Total strangers. In the last three months I've heard more about heart murmurs and limp pricks and lost ambitions than I care to mention. How do I look? Really?"

Robert reached to steady him.

"Don't treat me like an invalid!" Frederick wheezed.

Later in the car, on the way to Robert's house, Frederick tried to make light of his illness. Snow fell in cotton-ball bursts from the sky. The streets were icing over. Robert's windshield wipers barely moved; he couldn't see the curves ahead. Frederick suggested they park the car and take a cab. "We don't want to be badly killed," he said.

***

Robert didn't hear his father's final words, but a doctor later repeated for him Frederick's last coherent sentence. He'd been given a series of disorienting drugs for his pain. The doctors kept asking him, "Do you know where you are? Mr. Becker?"

Softly, and as gently ironic as ever, Frederick answered, "I'm in the lobby of Heaven." Then he'd closed his eyes against the color of the light.

***

"Nice buttocks, don't you think?" Frederick is pointing across the central square of Almost-Barcelona. "That woman over there by the lamppost, trying to hail a taxi."

"Very nice, yes."

"*She* could be a model."

"What do you mean?"

"I mean if you insist on painting—" His lips curled. "People."

"Can we not discuss my career?" Robert says.

"Not going well, is it?"

"Not at the moment, no."

"Perhaps if you took more risks."

"Precisely what the marketplace won't tolerate."

"Balls to the marketplace." Frederick raises his voice. "I'm talking about—"

"I know. The cause of art. The cause of art doesn't feed me."

"Spiritually or otherwise?'"

"You know what I mean."

Frederick wipes his lips with a gold serviette. "So you've taken on graphic design?"

"Temporarily. It helps pay the bills."

"I left you a tidy sum."

Robert laughs. "All tied up in the courts right now. Your dealer, your former dealer, the dealer before that—they each want a piece."

"I see. And you blame me?"

Robert pours more wine.

"Oh hell," Frederick says. "You're not going to be so tiresome as to be angry at me for dying on you?"

No, Robert thinks. I'm furious at the fact of your birth.

Frederick winces.

"I'm sorry," Robert says. "I didn't mean that."

"The truth will out."

"I *am* a bit pissed—"

"Only a bit?"

Robert swivels his shoulders. The tension there cracks. "When Mother died I could've used a little help. She had medical bills up to here—"

"Your mother didn't want my help."

"Oh?"

"She knew where I was. She could've called me."

"She'd never do that. Dignity was all she had at the end."

Frederick shrugs.

"When *you* died, Fay and the others wouldn't have anything to do with the arrangements—"

"Fay's a ninny and a prig." Frederick coughs magnificently, as he was unable to do in his final days. "She stopped speaking to me when I ran out on your mother."

"Lance the boil?"

"What?"

"My engagement to Sarah," Robert says. "That's what you told me when you heard about it, remember? 'A wife is an impediment to a painter. She'll want more money than you can provide her, she'll eat into your work-time.'"

"Was I wrong?"

Robert glares at his father.

"All right, all right," Frederick says. "The wording may have been excessively harsh, but the advice is sound, I think."

At the wedding Frederick shook Robert's hand and said, "Here's wishing you a happy and fruitful first marriage."

***

Sarah stirs in bed next to Robert. He kisses her shoulder while fixing his stare on a pair of nude women window-shopping at a bakery.

"And these young lovelies?" Frederick waves at the women. "*I'm* not making them up."

"They're here for your benefit."

"Oh, I see. You get no pleasure from them whatso-damn-ever. Does Sarah know what you're daydreaming?"

"Shhh! You'll wake her."

Now all the men in the city, except Robert and his father, are naked. Waiters, bird-sellers, traffic cops. Why not, Robert thinks.

"I agree," Frederick says. "Egalitarianism."

"Dad, I love you dearly but you're a damn scrounge. You're a rotten pork chop."

"No argument from me." Frederick raises his glass.

"I've always wanted to say that to your pointy little beard."

"These recent paintings of yours, Robbie—they're like little plucked chickens from some aborted Grander Design, am I right?"

Sarah snuffles in her sleep.

Robert says, "Okay, enough of this *Bad-boy Becker* bullshit. It may play in the art press but not with me. What we *really* need to cover here—once and for all and let the dead horse rot—is Mother—"

"How I left her with no options."

"Right. And me—"

"How I never encouraged you on your own path. Does that just about do it?"

"No, goddammit! You were afraid my work would be an embarrassment to yours!"

Sarah's eyes snap open in the dark. She moves a bare knee up Robert's leg. "What's the matter, sweetie? Can't you sleep?"

"Just thinking," Robert says.

"What about?"

Frederick rolls his eyes and sips his wine. Mourning doves spin around the bedroom, the busy brick streets.

"Nothing. Go back to sleep. It's all right."

She's already dozing again. Robert smooths her hair. She smells of jasmine—her perfume—soap, heat. This lovely, patient woman, he thinks. This beautiful, beautiful boil.

Frederick sprouts unease. Open displays of emotion—messy, messy, he'd say.

A bus picks up half-a-dozen naked women. In Robert's backyard studio, a splashed-red canvas waits for morning light. He thinks of things to do with his painting, things to cook tomorrow for Sarah; he's eager for the day to begin.

He realizes he's been staring at his father with restless, quaking fists. Frederick watches him slowly unroll his hands. Then the Maestro relaxes, sighs, gazes appreciatively at his son's splendid city. Still too much Houston in the light, but what the hell. The earth-tones, the serrated windows, the statue in the fountain . . .

"Chocolate?"

"Chocolate."

"Charming." ★

ROSELLEN BROWN

Rosellen Brown is the author of ten books, including two which are at least partly set in Houston. This excerpt is from the 1992 *Before and After*, which was inspired by a Houston incident. A father went to prison rather than testify against his son in a murder trial. Brown moved the bulk of the novel to New England, but has the family come to Houston at the end of the novel, after the son has been acquitted. The beleaguered family experiences Houston as a "City of Refuge."

Half a Heart makes more extensive use of Houston as a setting. Brown taught at the University of Houston from 1982–96. She now teaches at the Art Institute of Chicago, and in Assisi, Italy.

From *Before and After*: Ben

The punishment is exile.

Did you know that the Bible talks about Cities of Refuge, where you can go if you have killed someone accidentally? They are for the blameless, who are endangered nonetheless. They are the only places that are officially off-limits for the seekers of revenge. Safe cities.

The damage you may do yourself is not forbidden.

There are some beautiful buildings here, but my buildings have always been mountains. Still, there's green. It's a fecund place, nastily moist sometimes but otherwise benign and surprisingly sweet. No snow, my grief. Cold, hard freezes even, but nothing beautiful to take the place of what disappears in winter.

The power of positive thinking: This is not an escape. It's a continuation.

Everything I've hated about cities shields us here—so I was right about them. There are 1,924,763 people within the city limits and only four of them know about my son and Martha Taverner. Everyone we've met seems to have left some kind of life behind, even the natives: a husband, a wife, a profession, a city of origin. So in our case it's a little more dire, our history, but no one knows us well enough yet to care that much. Or they have trouble imagining, even if they believe it. The kids have an expression—"location situation"—that means, as far as I can tell, "You had to be there."

What continues the connection with Jacob's guilt?

Almost nothing. Legally nothing. He was set free by the state to go in peace. He can vote. He can carry arms. If he's crazy, in another fifteen years, he can run for President.

Does that seem unfair?

Not really.

Do you feel guilty?

Yes. Really.

***

There is a whole new sky here, I'm not sure it's the same one I've looked at all my life. Gaudy at sunset, flamboyant as hell, lit red, often, at night by— refinery fires? Particles of deadly chemicals hanging snagged in the moisture? Sometimes the air smells of coffee, vaguely burnt, and sometimes of a greasy indeterminate. Often, suddenly, of flowers, as if a powdered woman has walked by out of view.

The magnolia trees are self-possessed, cool, glossy: domineering beauties. Everything about them is slick and huge—their leaves, their seed cones like hand grenades, with red seeds lined up so carefully inside. Their soft flowers more like skin than skin. I wish I could make one, but they're already made.

Women walk down the street near my house, Mexican women followed by many small children, with one long braid down their backs. Sometimes one will carry her laundry on her head. I think about Hyland, how the keeper of the Hometown Laundromat and Quality Dry Cleaners would goggle at the sight.

Always the sense of sleaze just held back at the edges—money and malls, class and power at the center, NUDE GIRLS NUDE off at the margins. There's a lot of that, but there's a lot of not-that, too. In Hyland you need permission from the zoning board to put up a sign for lettuce and fresh eggs.

Mostly it's like every other place, though—mail delivery, traffic helicopters, gas stations, cemeteries, bus stops, streetlights, green-long yellow-red. It all flows on. No matter what you've done, or not done, it flows on. Maybe if you've lived here all your life this is your small town. One cemetery is full of people with streets named after them.

Carolyn's hospital has a staff two-thirds the population of Hyland. She parks half a mile away.

I work in hard metals with welding tools now, goggles, a mask, a concrete floor to quash the sparks—my pieces have an edge, I think, a not-nice quality: not so friendly—in a warehouse that used to be full of cotton batting, Ex-Lax, and garden tools. Or so I've been told.

What it comes down to is, the worse our history the more we had to stay together—only *we* knew all the parts, good and bad, even if we added them up differently. People were surprised, I think: Don't families fly apart after "tragedies?" Indeed they do. Or might. But who can ever tell? ★

RICK BASS

Despite the fact (or perhaps because of the fact) that he grew up in Houston's suburbs, Rick Bass is a deeply committed environmentalist and wilderness advocate. He worked for several years as a gas and oil geologist until he began publishing the first of his twenty-plus books, which include memoir, environmental and wildlife advocacy, novels, and story collections. The following story is from his first collection, *The Watch*.

The Watch won the PEN/Nelson Algren Award in 1988. Bass' 2002 collection, *The Hermit's Story*, was a *Los Angeles Times* Best Book of the Year. He was a finalist for The Story Prize in 2007 for his short story collection *The Lives of Rocks*, which includes stories set in Houston. He was also a finalist for the 2008 National Book Critics Circle Award for his memoir *Why I Came West*.

Since 1987, he and his family have lived in the Yaak Valley, near the Idaho-Montana-Canada border. Bass works to protect the area from roads and logging.

Juggernaut

WHEN I WAS SEVENTEEN, KIRBY AND I HAD a teacher who was crazy. This happened in the last year before Houston got big and unlivable.

Big Ed, we called him: Eddie Odom. Mr. Odom. He taught geometry as an after-thought; his stories were what he got excited about. Class began at nine o'clock. By nine-twenty, he would be winded, tired of sines and cosines, and he would turn to the clock in a way that almost aroused sympathy—so tired!—and he would try to last his lecture out for another five or ten minutes, before going into his stories. The thrill that Kirby and I felt when he lurched into these stories following a half-hearted geometrical lecture—there would be no warning whatsoever, we would suddenly be listening to something as fantastically wild and free as geometry was boring, and we wouldn't have done anything to earn it, we'd find ourselves just pulled into it, in the middle of it, and enjoying.

He had lived in Walla Walla, Washington, for a while, he told us, the first day we were in his class, and while there he had had a pet lion, and had to move back to Houston after the lion stabbed a child in the chest with its tail.

Houston, he told us, was the only town in the country that was zoned and ordinanced properly, so that a man could do what he wanted, as he wanted. He paused for about five minutes after he said this, and looked at us, one by one, going down the rows in alphabetical order, to make sure we had understood him.

Simmons, Simonini; Kirby and I watched him sweep down the aisles, student by student. There was a tic in his eyebrow that flared alarmingly when he passed over Laura DeCastagnola, who was tiny, olive-skinned, exuberant and good-calved. Possibly he was trying to be a hero for her. All the rest of us were.

Big Ed was graying, in his late forties, possibly even fifty, slope-shouldered, of medium height—literally taller than half of us, and shorter than the rest—and he moved with an awkward power: as if perhaps once he had had this very great strength that had somehow been taken away: an injury inside, to some set of nerves, which still retained the strength, but did not allow him to use it. Like a loaded pistol, or a car parked on the hill without an emergency brake—that was the impression he gave Kirby and me.

The child in Washington had been a punk, he told us, ten years old, and foul-mouthed, but had lived anyway.

"All female lions have a claw hidden in their tail," said Big Ed—and then stopped and locked the whole class with a look as if the last thing he would ever have expected was snickers and laughs. "No, it's true."

Kirby and I listened raptly; it was only the rest of the class which was disgusted by his callousness. Kirby and I were willing to give him that doubt. It was then and is so today still our major fault. Nothing will get you into trouble so deep or as sad as faith.

While the rest of the class hesitated, froze, and drew back from Big Ed—not understanding, but reacting, an instinct they felt—Kirby and I ignored it, this avoidance instinct, shy of it, that growing-up spring, and plunged after, and into his stories. We didn't look left or right. No one could be that crazy. Besides, we were frightened of growing up.

The point of the story had to be that female lions had claws in their tails. The other was all a smokescreen. No one *truly* believed a ten-year old boy deserved to be stabbed by a lion.

He encouraged us to go down to the zoo and somehow manage to slip a hand in through the bars of the lion cage, behind them, and find out.

"It's hidden, deep under all that fringe. It's as sharp as a nail, and like a stinger, only curved: just another claw. My guess is it's left over, from a time we don't know about, when lions used to swing from the trees, like monkeys."

Feet would shift and books would be closed or moved around, when the talk edged towards the ludicrous, as it often did.

The more adult-bound of the class would even sigh, and look out the window—it was harsh spring, and green, the lawn mowers clugging thick and choking every few yards with rich wet dark grass, and its smell of fermentation—and we all had cars, that spring, as it was Houston, and Texas, and there weren't any of us who weren't handsome, or beautiful, or going places, or popular, or sure of it all. Except Kirby and me. And Big Ed would stop, slowly but also too, somehow, bolt-like—that nerve again, perhaps—his eyebrows were arched and furry, and went all the way across—and he would squint his eyes at Cam Janse, shock white bleach haired, and lanky, sun-glasses, or at Tucker White, whose lips were big and curved, like a girl's, and who *had* all the girls—who would be pretending with these adult sighs and glances out the window that they would both be glad when the discussion got back to the more interesting topic of geometry—and so then Big Ed would assign about two or three hundred problems, over things we'd not even learned yet.

When the bell would ring, the boys sitting behind and next to Laura De-Castagnola were slower getting out of their desks than the rest of the class, and they walked oddly, holding their books at a ridiculous angle, close in and below their waists, as if aching from an unseen cramp. She had a jawline that you wanted to trace with your fingers. There was never a flatter, smoother region of face than that below her intelligent cheekbones. She made A's, and she was nice, and quiet, but she laughed like a monkey.

She would explode with her laughs, giggling and choking on them. She wore her cheerleader's dress on Friday. The blouse white without sleeves, the skirt gold. There were white socks. She wasn't sweet on anybody. She was everybody's sister. When she went to the football games and cheered, she was unique, standing under that vamp of mercury haze gold twinkling light—a huge vacuum cleaner could have sucked it and all of its charged magic away, leaving us only under a night sky out in the Texas prairie—unique in that she was always conscious of the score, and cared that we won, more so than about the party afterwards.

"Go, KEN!" she would scream. Ken Sims, breaking free, getting to the sideline and racing down it in his gallop, running all wrong, feet getting tangled up, no forward body lean, a white farmboy from Arkansas, the leading scorer in the city that year. Calves like bird's legs. If Laura *had* had a boyfriend, it would have been Ken.

We'd see Big Ed, too, up in the stands, with his scarecrow wife, who looked to be ten or fifteen years older than he, and was seven feet tall, with one of those small bug-like dark rubies in the center of her forehead, though she was not Pakistani, but pale, looked as pale and American as Wichita, or Fort Dodge. Big Ed would be watching Laura as if no one else was down there, and while the rest of the stadium would be jumping up and down, moving, orchestrating to Laura's leaps—her back to us, when Ken was running—Big Ed would be standing there, as motionless as a totem.

I would nudge Kirby and point, secretly, up to Big Ed—his eyes would be riveted on her, his mouth slightly open, as if he was about to say something—and we would stop watching the game for a second, and be troubled by it. We didn't see how he could be thinking it: lusting after a student, and such a nice one.

And down on the field, Ken, or Mark, or Amos, would score. Our band would play that brassy little elephant song. And Laura would leap, and kick, and throw her arms up and out. We were on our way to an undefeated season, that senior year. Who would want to lose any games in their last year? So we didn't. And we thought we were ready for that step, going out into the real world, and beyond.

***

It was such a time of richness that there was more than one hockey team, even—the struggling Aeros weren't enough. They played in the Spectrum, and were nothing more than an oddity, like so much else in the town at that time, and destined for a short life. The only reason at all people went to see them was because Gordie Howe, the Canadian legend, was making a comeback at the age of 48, and was both playing for and managing the team, and his two sons were playing for the Aeros with him, and he was scoring goals, and winning games.

But the other team was one that no one knew about, a seedier, underground version of the Aeros, and they played far out on the west end of town, on the warped and ratty ice rink in Houston. It was out on the highway that led into the rice fields, and tickets to the game were only fifty cents. The name of the team was the Juggernauts, and they played anybody.

We were driving then, had been for a year. We were free. Kirby had a sandy blue Mercury, one of the Detroit old iron horses from the sixties that would throw you into its back seat if you accelerated hard, and we would, on Tuesdays and Thursdays, race out into the night, away from the city's suburban lights, and we would pay with pennies, dimes and nickels—for Kirby and I had vowed never to work—and we would grip our tickets and step through the low doorway and go down the steps and into all the light, to see the Juggernauts, on the arena that served as a children's skating rink in the day.

When we would get there, the Juggernauts would still be out on the ice, down on their hands and knees, with thick marking crayons such as the ones used to label timber in the woods, and they would be marking crudely the hexagrammatics and baffling limits and boundaries of their strange game. I have been to wrestling matches, since that time, and that is what the hang of air was like, though the fans were quiet, and many wore ties, and sat up straight, waiting: hands on their knees, even the women's legs spread slightly apart, as if judging equipment at an auction, or even animals. It was the way anything is, anything that is being anticipated.

The games were sometimes violent, and always fast. We could never get the hang of the rules, and for us the best part was before the game, when the players crawled around on their knees with their marking crayons, laboring to draw the colorful, crooked lines, already suited up, and wearing the pads that would protect them.

On a good night there would be maybe thirty-five fans: girlfriends, wives, and then too, the outcasts, spectators with nothing else to do. There were people there who had probably driven from Galveston, just for the nothing event. The few cars scattered around in the huge parking lot outside nearly all had license plates with different colors. Most of the players were from Pennsylvania and New Jersey, and even beyond. It seemed odd to play the sport in the springtime, as they did.

Everyone got their Cokes for free at the games. The players didn't get any percentage of the gate, and they didn't even get to play for free, but instead had to pay the Farmers' Market a certain fee just to keep the lights on and the ice frozen; they paid for that chance to keep playing a game that perhaps they should have been slowing down in, or even stopping.

None of the Juggernauts wanted to stop! You could hear them hitting the boards, the sides of the walls, when they slammed into them. They skated so hard, and so fast! It was hypnotic, and you felt you could watch it forever.

***

Ed Odom drove a forest green Corvette to school, the old kind from the sixties—older even than Kirby's—and he didn't park in the faculty lot, but rather, on the other side of the concrete dividing posts, on the students' side, and he would arrive early enough in the mornings—steamy already, the sun rising above the apartment buildings and convenience stores, turning the haze to a warm drip that had you sweating even before you got to your locker— and he would cruise, so slowly, with the windows down, one arm hanging out, around and around the school, two times, three. Everyone saw him, and he saw everyone, and would nod vaguely, a smile that looked just past and to the side of a person, sliding away. He seemed to be like an athlete, getting ready for an event.

In class, he would grow disdainful when the guys tried to ask him about his "Vette:" what it would do, how long he had had it, how much he had paid for it. He would look at some odd spot in the room—a trash can, or the place in the corner where the walls met the ceiling—and would seem disappointed in whomever had asked the question, almost frozen with the disappointment, if not of that, then of something else—and he would seem to be unable to move: pinned down by a thing. His head would be cocked very slightly.

But one day he came to class looking like a thing from a Halloween movie: all cut up and abraded, bruises the color of melons and dark fruit, and a stupid expression on his normally wary face. His arm was in a sling. He looked as if the event had just happened, and he had come straight in off the street to find a phone. There was blood soaked through his gauze. The girls gasped. He looked straight at Laura DeCastagnola, who looked a little more shocked, and horrified, and also something else, than even the other girls—and even the guys, most of whom had no stuffing—even the guys looked away, and were queasy, could not look straight at him. Kirby and I watched the class, and it seemed only Laura was the one who could not take her eyes off him: one hand up to the side of her face, the way we all wanted to do, either in the dark or the light of day, while we whispered our promises eternal to her.

He sat down, slowly, without grimacing—focusing his mind somewhere else and far away to do so, it was easy to see—and we respected him forever, for that—and he opened the geometry book, and began to lecture.

Three days later, as the bruises began to wane, and he moved more easily, he finally told us—but our anticipation had long passed, after his initial refusal to tell us, back when it had first happened, and we had grown churlish and lost curiosity, and were merely disgusted at his childishness in holding the secret—all of us except Kirby and me, who were still hoping very much to find out. It was a thing that grew, in us, rather than fading away.

He had been driving down the highway, he said, and had opened the door to empty his litterbag—onto the highway!—and had leaned over too far, and had rolled out. His wife had been with him, and she had reached over with her long left leg and arm and drove, after he fell out.

"I bounced," he said, "like a basketball. While I was bouncing, and holding my ribs to keep them from breaking, I counted." He paused and looked intelligent, as if he had trapped us in a game of chess, but by now it was agreed upon, as if we had a pact, not to give him pleasure, and no one asked him, and he had to volunteer it.

"I bounced," he said clearly, enunciating quietly and with his teeth—it was like the words were an ice cream cone, and he was eating it slowly, on a hot day—"twenty-two times."

His wife, he said, drove to the next exit, went below the overpass, and came back and got him. Helped him back in the car.

***

We drove to the hockey games whenever we could. They didn't start until nine o'clock. Obviously all the players came home from work and ate supper first. The games lasted until eleven, twelve o'clock. There were fights among the fans sometimes, but rarely among the players, as in real hockey. I think that the fact they played among themselves, again and again, too many dulling intrasquad games, is what made this different. Though too it could just have been the spring. There weren't any wars, and there wasn't any racism, not in our lives, and we weren't hungry. There weren't any demands. Sometimes Kirby would pay for the tickets; sometimes I would.

Sometimes there would be a team not from our area, playing the Juggernauts: a northwest junior college's intramurals champions' team, or another, leaner and more haggard traveling band of ruffians, hangers-on in the sport: a prison team, sometimes, or worse. On these occasions the Juggernauts would rise from their rather smooth-skinned and sallow good-natured (though enthusiastic) boys'-school-type-of-play—happy, energetic zips of the skates, long gliding sweeps of mellowness on the ice, cradling the puck along and beaming—and on these invader nights, against the teams down from Connecticut, from Idaho, and Sioux Falls, they would turn fierce, like the same boys now squabbling over

423

a favorite girl. On these nights of the visitors, the ticket prices rose to a dollar, and attendance would swell by half.

There would even be someone there with a camera and flash, a skinny youth but with a press card, perhaps real but probably manufactured, and good equipment, and he would be crouched low, moving around and around the rink like a spy, shooting pictures. And though there was no reason for a photographer to be there—the Juggernauts were in no league, none of these teams were, there was no official record of wins and losses—certainly no newspaper coverage—despite this, the Juggernauts always played hardest and wildest when the photographer was there. It could have been one of the players' sons or even grandsons, but that did not matter.

They skated with their bellies in, those nights, bumped into their opponents without apologies and knocked them to the ice (or were knocked to the ice themselves), and charged around on the ice with short savage chopping steps of their skate blades, as if trying in their anger to mince or hash the rink into a slush. Some of them would breathe through gritted teeth and shout, making low animal sounds.

The Juggernauts had a player we all called Larry Loop. He wasn't their captain, or anything—they were a band, not a team—and Larry Loop was large and chesty, and he raced down the ice in those crunching little high-knee steps whether they were playing against ax murderers or a seminarian's school. Friend or foe, Larry Loop would *run* on his skates rather than actually using them, and could travel just as fast that way, as it was the way he had taught himself to skate, and it was a thing to watch. You could tell he was not from the north. You could tell he had not grown up with the game, but had discovered it, late in life. He was big, and the oldest man on the ice, grey-headed, tufts of it sticking out from behind his savage, painted goalie's mask—though he was not a goalie—and more often than not when he bumped into people, they went over.

It was amazing, actually, how easily the people Larry Loop crashed into went over when he hit them. They were just like something spilled. I think now that he had this great tactician's eye for analyzing, and would time his approach and hits—running at this odd, never-balanced velocity—so that he always made contact when they were pretty severely off-balance themselves: his victims nearly always seemed to be waving a leg high in the air, or grasping with both arms for useless sky, as they went over. And he would run a little farther, definitely pleased with himself, definitely smug, and then remember to turn back and look to see where the puck was, if it was still even in play.

He was called Larry Loop, we decided, because as he ran, he swung his stick, high and around, above his head, in a looping, whipping, exuberant circle, like a lariat, like a child pretending with one arm to be a helicopter. We almost expected to see him lift off. When you were close to it, you could hear the whistling sound it made.

He would gallop down the ice, waving his stick, drawing penalties for it the whole way, and I think it helped wind him up for the impact. He was what is called in hockey a "goon," an enforcer-type whose best contribution to the game is usually restricted to rattling the opposition's better players.

Except that pretty often Larry Loop would score goals, too. Again, perhaps, those strategian's eyes, theory and logic, because everything was all wrong, it shouldn't have been happening, he drew his stick back incorrectly and almost always shot improperly, off-balance. But one thing the thirty or so of us had learned from watching him was that when he was open and did shoot on goal, it was probably going to go all the way in.

When he scored, he went wild. He would throw his stick down onto the ice and race off in the opposite direction, in that funny little stamping run, and throw his masked face back, up at the low ceiling, and beat on his chest with his heavy gloved hands, and shout, "I am in LOVE! I am in LOVE!" It was funny, and it was frightening, too, to Kirby and me, like a visit to New York City for the first time, and we liked to believe that all the wildness and uncertainty and even danger in the world was contained there in that tiny skating rink, set so far out in the prairie, in the spring, heavy overhead blowers spinning, inside, to prevent the ice from melting. It was more ice than any of us had ever seen, that little arena, set so far out away from the rest of the town.

The wind coming across us, our faces, driving back into town—and it was town, then, and not yet city—it was as it had been on the way out to the game, only better, because there had been hope, going into the game, and it had not let us down. Larry Loop had been good and wild.

The rules were confusing, but we liked to watch. There wasn't any danger of, say, one of the players going down with an injury, while the rest of them crowded around him, until one of them looked up into the stands, directly at us, and motioned, or ordered, one of us to go down there and fill in: substitute. Those damn rules—not knowing what to do, and the panic such a thing would give us. It would be a horrible thing. We drove with the windows down, and felt as if we had escaped from something.

***

"When you are born," Big Ed said—and he turned and looked at the farthest side of the class and crouched, as if expecting an attack—there was maybe one small snicker, though by now, this late in the spring, most of the class was tired of his old grey-headed mock-youth—"the hospital, or wherever it is you were born, records the sound of your voice." He straightened up from his crouch and looked less wild, even calm.

"They record your first cries, the squawls you make when the doctor spanks you"—his eyes were looking at the floor, drifting everywhere but over Laura—"and they catalogue them with the FBI."

He was lecturing now, not story-telling. "Because every voice is like a set of fingerprints. They have special machines that separate and classify every broken-down aspect of your voice—and you can't disguise it, it's more unique than a set of fingerprints, it'll give you away quicker than anything, on a computer. Because those things in your voice that they pick up on tape don't ever change, over your life."

He seemed to take, for once, a pleasure in the actual content of this story, rather than in just the telling of it. Emily Carr, Laura's best friend but not a cheerleader, raised her hand and asked him—and she had a deep, husky, odd sort of voice, as if something was wrong with it, and was perhaps hoping it *would* change, with age—"What if you weren't born in a hospital? Or were born in a tiny little country hospital, where there wasn't even electricity, just a midwife?" Emily was from Oklahoma, and if possible, nicer even than Laura. Maybe because her voice was funny and off, but she went out of her way to smile at you, not afraid that you might get a crush on her, whereas Laura was shy and quick with her laughing monkey flash of white teeth, as if afraid she might lead you on into thinking something else. It was maybe like she already had someone. But it wasn't Ken! Ken was always running, running: sweating with the team. Scoring those goals.

"The FBI calls you," Big Ed said, with certainty. "If they don't have you on file, they just call you up, talk to you a while about some bogus sales offer—storm windows, insurance, Japanese Bibles—and then they hang up, and they've got you."

I dialed Kirby's number two days later, and didn't say anything when he answered.

"Hello?" he said, again. I hung up. But then the phone rang, and this time it was my turn to speak into the receiver, "Hello?" and not get an answer.

We practiced changing our voices, talked like ducks, like old men, like street toughs to each other, practicing for when the FBI called, and that moment was at hand. Tears of laughter rolled down our faces. We howled like hyenas. We could laugh at anything, and the pleasure of it was odd and sincere. Who would want to leave? If we couldn't date Laura and Emily, at least couldn't we be crazy, laughing all the time?

***

One Thursday night Kirby and I went out to the game, the Juggernauts were playing the team of an insurance firm from Boston that was in Houston for a convention—there were perhaps a hundred or more people in the stands, on either side of the teams—and we saw that number 52, wild Larry Loop, had his mask off for once, and he was talking to some people in the stands, only something was wrong, he wasn't really Larry Loop at all, it was Big Ed, Ed Odom, our geometry teacher, dressed up like Larry.

He looked like a clown, the clown that he was, standing there in the bulk of Larry's uniform, ice white and heavy rich blue: again, like a little boy, playing astronaut, playing hockey player. He was wearing Larry's big mittens and holding his stick, and hanging from his belt was the wild, frozen mask, a mute, noncommittal mouth cut into it for breathing. Big Ed was talking animatedly and, we could tell, intelligently, about the sport, to a fan—a man in a business suit with a red tie and owl glasses, the tie swinging out away from him as he leaned against the glass to get closer to Larry Loop, to hear what he had to say.

We were howling again, at the audacity of Big Ed's trick at first, but even as we were registering that thought, we were taking note of the day he had come into class so battered, of the way he was now standing on the ice, in his skates, casually, and of how comfortable he appeared, talking, even while wearing the big suit.

We weren't even tempted to go down and meet him. Like quail in tall grass, we settled down deep into the back of the crowd and watched, without standing up, him play the whole game.

And the Juggernauts lost, twelve to eleven, though Big Ed, Larry, scored several goals, and we wanted to stay for the other part we liked, at the end, where the losing team—all sweaty and sore and exhausted—had to crawl around on the ice with rags, erasing the smeared and dulled blue and red stripes and boundary lines they had just put down hours before—they had to have it clean again, by morning, no signs that they had been out there and had had glory—and the Juggernauts, or whoever lost, would be crawling on the ice, wiping up the stripes, and grown men in hockey suits would be skating around with brooms, sweeping the ice smooth again—and it was a thing we liked to watch, and often did, but the crowd was gone this night, we were almost the only two left in there, and the arena wasn't the same any more, it was as threatening as a dark, slow lightning storm moving towards us, and we had to get out of there.

And walking out across the parking lot, trying to laugh and howl at the lunacy of it but also not able to—recognizing, and being troubled by, the first signs of insincerity in this paradox—we stopped, when we realized we were passing by a parked dark green Corvette, and that Laura was standing by it, and she was holding his coat and tie in her arms, the clothes he had worn in class that day, and she had the keys in her hand, and she wasn't a girl, she wasn't even Laura, she was just some woman standing there, waiting for her man, with hopes and fears and other thoughts on her mind, a thousand other thoughts, she was just living, and it wasn't pretend.

The night was dark, without a moon, and she held our surprised looks, and in two months she would be graduating, and what she was doing would be okay then, we suddenly realized, if it was ever okay, and for the first time we saw the thing, in its immensity, and it was like corning around a bend or a trail in the woods and suddenly seeing the hugeness and emptiness of a great plowed pasture or field, when all one's life up to that point has been spent close to but never seeing a field of that size. It was so large that it was very clear to us that the whole rest of our lives would be spent in a field like that, crossing it, and the look Laura gave us was sweet and kind, but also wise, and was like an old familiar welcome.

This was back in those first days when Houston was clean and just growing, not yet beginning to die or get old. Houston was young, then, too. You cannot imagine how smooth life was for you, if you were in high school, that one spring, when oil was $42 a barrel, and everyone's father was employed by the petroleum industry, and a hero for finding oil when the Arabs wouldn't sell us any. Anything was possible. ★

MARY GAITSKILL

Mary Gaitskill is the author of the novels *Two Girls, Fat and Thin* and *Veronica*, along with the story collections *Bad Behavior: Stories* and *Because They Wanted To: Stories* and the recent *Don't Cry: Stories*, which includes this story. *Veronica* was nominated for the National Critics Circle Award, and in 2002 she was awarded a Guggenheim Fellowship for Fiction. This story first appeared in the *New Yorker* as "A Dream of Men."

Gaitskill taught in the University of Houston Creative Writing Program from 1996 to 1997.

An Old Virgin

LAURA WAS WALKING AROUND HER APARTMENT in a cotton nightgown with green and yellow flowers on it muttering, "Ugly cunt, ugly cunt." It was a bad habit that had got worse in recent months. She caught herself muttering while she was preparing her morning coffee and made herself stop. But it's true, she thought. Women are ugly. She immediately thought of her sister Anna Lee making herself a chicken-salad sandwich to have with a glass of milk. Anna Lee was not beautiful, but she wasn't ugly either. She thought of her mother, frowning slightly as she sat at her kitchen table, drawing a picture of fruit in a dish. Her mother had a small, dear bald spot on the top of her head. If anyone said "ugly cunt" to her sister or her mother, Laura would hit him. She would hit anyone who said it to her friend Danielle. Well, she didn't really mean it when she said it. At least not in the normal way.

She put her foot up on the table and drank her coffee out of a striped mug the size of a little bowl. She had to be at her job at the medical clinic in half an hour; she wasn't late, but, still, her body was racing inside. Even though she'd been at the clinic for five years, every morning her body acted as if getting out the door and into the world were an emergency. This was even more true since her father died. The death had turned her inside herself. Even when she was in public, talking to people or driving through traffic or carrying forms and charts and samples in the halls of the clinic, she dimly sensed the greater part of herself turned inside, like a bug tunneling in the earth with its tiny sensate legs. All through the earth was the dull roar of unknown life forms. She could not see it or hear it as she might see and hear with her human eyes and ears, but she could feel it with her fragile insect legs.

She finished her coffee and got out the door. Houston in the summer was terribly hot and humid; the heat made her feel grossly physical. She gave a tiny grunt to express the feeling; it was the kind of grunt her cat made when it lay down and settled in deep. She opened her car; there were cassettes and mixed trash on the floor and the passenger seat, and she thought there was a sour smell coming from somewhere. She let the air conditioner run with the door open, sitting straight up in the seat with her legs parted wide under the tented skirt of her uniform. Across the street, there was a twenty-four-hour flower market in an open shack; dimly, she could see the proprietor inside, wiping his brow with a rag. He looked like he was settled deep into something, too.

Last night, she had dreamed of two men in a vicious fight. At first, they had been playing basketball. One of them seemed the apparent winner; he was tall, handsome, and well developed, while his opponent was short and flabby. Watching the game, Laura felt sorry for the little one. Then the game became a fight. The men rolled on the ground, beating each other. The little flabby one proved unexpectedly powerful, and soon he had the tall handsome man pinned on the ground. As Laura watched, he pulled out a serrated knife and began to cut off the top of the handsome man's skull. The handsome man screamed and struggled. Laura ran to them and took the knife away from the small man. He pulled out another knife and tried to stab her. She cut him open from his neck to his crotch. He remained standing; offal fell from his opened body.

She lit a cigarette and closed the car door. Her father had been a small man. When he was younger, he'd struck boxing poses in front of the mirror, jabbing at his reflection. "I could've been a bantam-weight," he'd said. "I still have the speed."

Laura lived in a run-down neighborhood that was usually slow, but today there was heavy traffic. She talked to herself as she negotiated the lanes, speeding and slowing in a lulling rhythm. When she talked to herself, she often argued with an imaginary person. This time, she argued about the news story concerning the President's affair with a twenty-two-year-old intern. "Personally, I don't care," she said. "It shouldn't really matter what they're like sexually." Stopped at the red light, she glanced at the people waiting for a bus. They looked tenacious and stoic as a band of ragged cats, staring alertly down the street or pulled tidily into themselves, with crossed legs, holding their handbags. "It's hard to tell what really went on between the two of them anyway," she continued. "Sometimes things that look awful on the outside look different when you get up close."

Her father had started dying in a hospital in Tucson. By the time Laura had got there, her mother and her sister were fighting with the doctors about his treatment. He was too weak to eat, so they'd stuffed tubes down his nose to feed him something called Vita Plus. "His body doesn't want it." Anna Lee was talking to the nurse. "It's making him sicker." It was true. As soon as Laura looked at her father, she knew he was going to die. His body was shrunken and dried, already half abandoned; his spirit stared from his eyes as if stunned. "I know," said the nurse. "I agree with you. But we have to give it to him. It's policy."

"Hi, Daddy," said Laura.

When he answered her, his voice was like an old broken sack holding something live. He was about to lose the live thing, but right now he held it, amazed by it, as if he had never known it before. He said, "Good to see you. Didn't know if you'd come."

She stopped at a crosswalk; there was a squirrel crossing the street in short, halting runs. She stopped traffic for a minute, waiting for it. A woman sitting on a public bench smiled at her. The woman sat with her knees tensely open and her feet poised on their balls. In her pointy shoes, her feet were like little hooves. It made sense that she was on the squirrel's side.

They brought their father home to be cared for by hospice workers. By that time he was emaciated and filled with mucus that he could not discharge through his throat or nose. It ran out of his nostrils sometimes, but mostly they heard it, rattling in his lungs. He couldn't eat anything, and he didn't talk much. They put him in the guest bedroom, in a big soft bed with a dust ruffle. The sun shining in the window made his skin so transparent that the veins and spots on his face became more present than the skin. He blinked at the sun like a turtle. They took turns sitting with him. Laura stroked his arm with her fingertips, barely grazing his fragile skin. When she did that, he said, "Thank you, Laura honey." He had never called her honey before.

He was so weak he couldn't turn himself, so two hospice workers had to turn him. When they did, he got angry; his skin had gone so thin that his bones felt sharp, and it hurt him to be moved. "No, leave me alone," he'd say. "I don't care, I don't care." He would frown and even slap at the workers, and, in the fierce knit of his brow and his blank, furious eye, Laura remembered him as he had been twenty-five years ago. He had been standing in the dining room, and she had walked by him wearing flowered pants that were tight in the seat and the crotch. He'd said, "What're you doing walking around with your pudenda hanging out like that? Nobody wants to see that."

***

She arrived at the clinic early and got a good place in the parking garage. On the way up to the seventeenth floor, she shared the elevator with Dr. Edwina Ramirez, whom she liked. They had once had a conversation in the break lounge during which they both revealed that they didn't want to have children; Dr. Ramirez had looked at Laura suddenly, a deep, bright spot inside her eye. "People act like there's something wrong with you," she said. "Don't they know about overpopulation? I mean, yeah, there's biology and shit. But there's other ways to be a loving person." She had quickly bent to take her candy bar out of the machine. "You know what I mean?"

Ever since then, Laura had felt good around Dr. Ramirez. Every time she saw her, she thought, Ways to be a loving person. She thought it as they rode up in the elevator together, even though the doctor stood silently frowning and smoothing her skirt. When they got to their floor, Dr. Ramirez said "See you" and gave Laura a half smile as they strode in opposite directions.

Laura went to the lounge to get a coffee. Some other technicians and a few nurses were sitting at the table eating doughnuts from a box. Newspapers with broad, grainy pictures of the White House intern lay spread out on the table. In one of the pictures, the girl posed with members of her high school class at the prom. She stood very erect in a low-cut dress, staring with focused dreaminess at a spot just past the camera.

"She's a porker," said a tech support. "Just look at her."

"Beautiful hair, though," said a phlebotomist.

Laura lingered at the little refrigerator, trying to find the carton of whole milk. Everybody else used two-per-cent.

"It makes me sympathize with him," said a nurse. "He could have anybody he wanted, and he picks these kinds of girls. Like, they're not models, they're not stars."

"That makes you sympathize? I think that's what's gross about it."

"But it might not be. It might be because he wants somebody to be normal with. Like somebody who's totally on his side who he can, like, talk about baseball with. Somebody who's pretty in a normal way."

"What? Are you nuts? She was a fat girl sucking his dick!"

Laura settled for edible oil creamers. She took a handful, along with a pocketful of sugars and a striped stir stick.

***

The day they brought their father home, the plumbing in the bathroom backed up. Sewage came out of the bathtub drain, water seeped into the chenille tapestry their mother had put up around the window. The sight of it made Laura's heart pound.

During the eight days that Laura stayed there, she slept in the bedroom of her girlhood, sharing the bed with Anna Lee. She and Anna Lee had slept close together in the same bed until Laura was fifteen and Anna Lee thirteen. Even when they got separate beds, they sometimes crept in together and cuddled. Now they lay separate even in grief.

They talked, though. The night before their father died, they talked until four in the morning. Anna Lee talked about her six-year-old, Peter, an anxious, overweight child with a genius I.Q. The kid couldn't make friends; he fought all the time and was often beaten. He'd set his room on fire twice. She was talking about a psychiatrist she had taken him to see. In the light from the window, Laura could see her sister's eyelashes raising and lowering with each hard, dry blink. She could smell the lotion Anna Lee used on her face and neck. The psychiatrist had put Peter on a waiting list to go to a special school in Montana, a farm school with llamas the children could care for and ride on.

After Anna Lee stopped talking, there was a long silence. Laura could feel her sister's body become fractionally softer and more open, relaxing and concentrating at the same time. Maybe she was thinking of Peter, how he might get better, how he might grow happy and strong. Laura had met the child. He'd frowned at her and looked down at the broken toy in his hand, but there was curiosity in his mien, and he was quick to look up again. He was already fat and already bright; he seemed too sad and too angry for such a young child.

"I had a strange thought about Daddy," she said.

Anna Lee didn't answer, but Laura could feel her become alert. In the scant window light, Laura could sense that the muscles around Anna Lee's eyes had tightened. She knew she should stop, but she didn't. "It was more a picture in my head," she continued. "It was a picture of a vagina that somebody was slashing with a knife. Daddy wasn't in the picture, but—"

"Oh Christ, Laura." Anna Lee put her hands over her face and turned away, "Just stop. Why don't you just stop?"

"But I didn't mean it to be—"

"He's not your enemy now," said Anna Lee. "He's dying."

Her voice was raw and hard; she thrust it at Laura like a stick. Laura pictured her sister at twelve, yelling at some mean boys who'd cornered a cat. She felt loyalty and love. "I'm sorry," she said. Her mouth frowned, a weak, spasmodic grimace in the dark. "I'm sorry."

Anna Lee reached back and patted Laura's stomach with her fingers and half her palm. Then she withdrew into her private curl.

Laura lay awake through the night.

Anna Lee moved and scratched herself and spoke in urgent, slurred monosyllables. Laura thought of their mother, alone upstairs in the heavy sleep brought on by barbiturates. Tomorrow she would be at the stove, boiling water for Jell-O in case her husband would eat it. She didn't really believe he was dying. She knew it, but she didn't believe it.

Carefully, Laura got out of bed. She walked through the dark house until she came to her father's room. She heard him breathing before her eyes adjusted to the light. His breath was like a worn moth feebly beating against a surface. She sat in the armchair beside his bed. The electric clock said it was five-thirty. A passing car on the street filled the room with a yawning sweep of light. The wallpaper was yellow flowers. Great Aunt's old dead clock sat on the dresser. Great Aunt was her father's aunt who had raised him with her sister. Two widowed aunts and a little boy with no father. Laura could see the boy standing in the parlor, all his new life coursing through his small, stout legs and trunk. In his head was a new solar system, crackling with light as he created the planets, the novas, the sun and the moon and the stars. "Look!" he cried. "Look!" The dutiful aunts, busy with housekeeping and food, didn't see. The more he tried to show, the more they wouldn't see. The boy hesitated, and with his uncertainty his system began to break. Thrown off its trajectory, the sun became erratic, and the planets went cold. The stars burned fiercely in the cold dark, but the aunts didn't notice that, either.

Another car went by. Her father muttered and made wet noises with his mouth. She imagined him saying, "When I was broken, then they loved me."

"No wonder you hated them," said Laura softly. "No wonder."

***

Behind the reception desk there were two radios playing different stations for each secretary. One played frenetic electronic songs, the other formula love songs, and both ran together in a gross hash of sorrow and desire. This happened every afternoon by around one. Faith, who worked behind the desk, said it was easy to separate them, to just concentrate on the one you wanted. But Laura always heard both of them jabbering every time she walked by the desk.

"Martha Dillon?" She spoke the words to the waiting room. A shabby middle-aged man eyed her querulously. A red-haired middle-aged woman put down her magazine and approached Laura with a mild, obedient air. Martha was in for a physical, so Laura had to give her a preliminary before the doctor examined her. First, they stopped at the scale outside the office door; Martha took off her loafers, her socks, and her sweater, to shave off some extra ounces. A lot of women did that, and it always seemed stupid to Laura. "Five four, a hundred and twenty-six pounds," she said loudly.

"Shit," muttered Martha.

"Look at the bright side," said Laura. "You didn't gain since last time."

Martha didn't reply but Laura sensed an annoyed little buzz from her. She was still buzzing slightly as she sat in the office; even though she was small and placid, it struck Laura that she gave off a little buzz all the time. She was forty-three years old, but her face was unlined and her eyes were wide and receptive, like a much younger person's. Her hair was obviously dyed, the way a teen-ager would do it. You could still tell she was middle-aged, though.

She didn't smoke, she exercised three times a week, she drank twice a week, wine with dinner. She was single. Her aunt had diabetes, and her mother had ovarian cancer. She had never had an operation or been hospitalized. Her periods were regular. She had never had any sexual partners. Laura blinked.

"Never?"

"No," said Martha. "Never." She looked at Laura as if she were watching for a reaction, and maybe holding back a smile.

Her blood pressure was excellent. Her pulse rate was average. Laura handled her wrist and arm with unusual care. A forty-three-year-old virgin. It was like looking at an ancient, sacred artifact, a primitive icon with its face rubbed off. It had no function or beauty, but it still felt powerful when you touched it. Laura pictured Martha walking around with a tiny red flame in the pit of her body, protecting it with her fat and muscle.

Laura felt tense as she watched the doctor examine Martha, especially when he did the gynecological exam. She noticed that Martha gripped her paper gown in the fingers of one hand when the doctor sat between her legs. He had to tell her to open her legs wider three times. She lay with her head sharply turned so that she stared at a corner of the ceiling. There was a light sweat on her forehead.

When she changed back into her clothes, though, she moved as if she were in a women's locker room. She got up from the table and took off the paper gown before the doctor was even out of the room. Laura stared at her. Martha suddenly looked right at her and smiled as if she'd won something.

"She's probably really religious, or maybe she's crazy." That's what Beatrice, the secretary, thought. "In this day and age? She was probably molested when she was little."

"I don't know," said Laura. "I respected it."

Beatrice shrugged. "Well, you know, everybody has the right." She lowered her dark, heavy lashes and continued her graceful movements at her desk.

Laura imagined her father looking at the middle-aged virgin and then looking away with an embarrassed smile on his face. He might think about protecting her, about waving at her from across the street, saying "Hi, how are you," sending protection with his words. He could protect her and still keep walking, smiling to himself with embarrassed tenderness. He would have a feeling of honor and frailty, but there would be something repulsive in it, too, because she wasn't a pretty young girl. Laura remembered a minor incident in a novel she had read by a French writer, in which a teen-age boy knocked an old nun off a bridge. Her habit was heavy and so she drowned, and the writer wondered, with a stupid sort of meanness, Laura thought, whether the nun had felt shocked to have her vagina touched by cold water. She remembered a recent news story about a man who had kidnapped a little girl so that he could tie her to a tree and set a fire at the foot of the tree. Then he went to his house to watch her burn through binoculars until the police came.

Instead of going back to the waiting room, she went to the public bathroom and leaned against the small windowsill with her head in her hands. She was forty; she tried to imagine what it would be like to be a virgin. She imagined walking through the supermarket, encased in an invisible membrane that was fluid but also impenetrable, her eyes wide and staring like a doll's. Then she imagined her virginity like a strong muscle between her legs, making all her other muscles strong, making everything in her more alive, all the way up through her brains and into her bones.

She lifted her head and looked out the small window. She saw green grass and the tops of trees, cylindrical apartment buildings, and traffic. She had not wanted her virginity. She'd had to lose it with three separate people; it had been stubborn and hard to break.

She brushed the dust and particles from the windowsill off her elbows. "I was a rebellious girl," she said, "and I went in a stupid direction."

She thought of the Narcotics Anonymous meetings she had attended some years ago. People had talked about the things that had happened to them, the things they had done on drugs. Nothing had been too degrading or too pathetic or too dull. Laura had talked about trying to lose her virginity. Her friend Danielle had told a story about how she'd let a disgusting fat guy she hated try to shove a can of root beer up her vagina because, he'd suggested, they might be able to fill cans with heroin and smuggle them.

Laura smiled a little. After the meeting, she'd asked Danielle, "Who tried to stick it in, you or him?"

"Oh," said Danielle, "we both tried." They laughed.

Such grotesque humility, she thought. Such strange comfort. She remembered the paper plates of cookies, the pot of coffee on the low table in the back of the room at N.A. She loved standing back there with Danielle, eating windmill cookies and smoking. Laura looked at herself in the bathroom mirror. "A stupid girl," she said to her reflection. Well, she thought, but who could blame her?

When Laura was still a teen-ager, her mother had asked what it had been like for her to lose her virginity. She wanted to know if the experience had been "special." They had been watching TV together. It was late and the living room was dark. Laura was startled by the question. Her mother looked straight ahead while she asked it, but Laura could see her expression was unhappy. "Was it someone you loved?" she asked.

"Yes," said Laura. "Yes, it was."

"I'm glad," said her mother. She still looked straight ahead. "I wanted you to have that." It seemed that she knew Laura was lying and that the lie was O.K. with her.

Virginity was supposed to be honorable, but who would want honor like that?

She went back to the waiting room and got the grouchy middle-aged man. He didn't bother to take off his shoes when she weighed him. He was there, he said, only because his wife had made him come. He had taken off work and shot the whole day. "My wife loves going to the doctor," he said. "She had all those mammograms and she lost her breast anyway. Most of it."

"Well, but it's good to come in," said Laura. "Even if it doesn't always work. You know that. Your wife's just caring about you."

He gave a conciliatory little snort. With his shirt off, he was big and flabby, but he carried it as if he liked it. His blood pressure was much too high. As she worked, Laura let her touch linger on him longer than was necessary, because she wanted to soothe him. She felt him respond to her touch; the response was like an animal turning its head to look at her, then looking away again. She thought he liked it, though.

When the man was gone, she asked Dr. Phillips if she could go outside on her break. He usually didn't like her to do that, because she was always a little late getting back when she went out, but he was trying to be extra nice since her father died. "O.K.," he said, "but watch the time." He turned and strode down the hall, habitually bristling like a small dog with a dominant nature.

Outside the heat was horrible. She started sweating right away, probably ruining her uniform for the next day. Still, she was glad to be out of the building. The clinic was situated between a busy main street and a run-down slow street occupied by an old wig shop, a children's karate gym, and a large ill-kept park where aging homeless men sat around. She decided to walk a few blocks down the park street. She liked the trees, and she was friendly with a few of the men, who sometimes wished her good afternoon.

She walked and an old song played in her head. It was the kind of old song that sounded innocent and dirty at the same time. The music was simple and shallow except for one deep spot where it was like somebody's pants were getting pulled down. "You got nothing to hide and everybody knows it's true. Too bad, little girl, it's all over for you." The singer laughed and the music laughed, too, laughter spangled with pleasure and contempt.

Laura had loved the song; she had loved the thought of its being all over and everybody knowing. A lot of other people must've loved it, too; it had been a very popular song. She remembered walking down the hall in high school wearing tight clothes; boys had laughed and grabbed their crotches. They all said she'd sucked their dicks, but she'd really only screwed one of them. It didn't matter. When her father found out, he yelled and hit her.

"Was it someone special?" asked her mother. "Was it someone you loved?"

She stopped at a curb for traffic. Her body was alive with feelings that were strong but that seemed broken or incomplete, and she felt too weak to hold them.

A car pulled up beside her, throwing off motor heat. The car was full of loud teen-age boys. The driver, a Hispanic boy of about eighteen, wanted to make a right turn but he was blocked by a stalled car in front of him and cars next to him. He was banging his horn and yelling out the window; his anger was hot and all over the place. Laura stared at him. His delicate beauty was almost too bright-lit by his youth and maleness. He had so much light that it burned him up inside and made him dark. He yelled and pounded the horn, trying to spew it out, but still it surged through him. It was like he was at war, like he could kill and kill, without any understanding in his mind or heart. In a real war, Laura thought, he would rush into danger before the other men and be called a hero. Her thought folded over unexpectedly, and she pictured him as a baby with his small mouth on his mother's breast. She pictured his fierce nature deep inside him, like dark, beautiful seeds feeding off his mother's milk, off the feel of her hand on his skull. She thought of him now with a girl; he would kiss her too hard and be rough, wanting her to feel what he had inside him, wanting to show it to her.

He turned in his seat to shout something to the other boys in the car, then turned forward again to put his head out the window to curse the other cars. He turned again and saw Laura staring at him. Their eyes met. She thought of her father showing his aunts the stars and all the planets. You are good, she thought. What you have is good. The boy dropped his eyes in confusion. There was a yell from the back seat. The stalled car leapt forward. The boy snapped around, hit the gas, and was off.

Laura crossed the street. She thought, I told him he was good. I told him with my eyes and he heard me. She flinched under a second of embarrassment—to think that she could give that guy anything he might want! But then she thought of the middle-aged virgin jumping off the examining table and smiling as if she'd won something, and she felt O.K. again.

She walked up the block sweating, and grateful without knowing why. Again, she pictured the middle-aged virgin, this time at home, doing her meticulous toilet, rubbing her feet with softening cream. She pictured herself at home, curled on the couch, watching TV and eating ice cream out of the carton. She pictured the men in her dream, fighting. She pictured herself kneeling down beside the handsome man. She would pass her hand over his broken skull and make an impenetrable membrane grow over his exposed brain. The membrane would be transparent, and you would be able to see his brain glowing inside it like magic stones. But you could never cut it or harm it. She pictured her father, young and strong, smiling at her, the planets all around him.

Deep in the park, she saw the homeless men moving about, their figures nearly obscured by overgrown grass and trees. For a moment she strained to see them more clearly, then gave up. It was time to go back; she was late. ★

LIONEL GARCIA

Lionel Garcia has published four novels and three collections of short stories. Most of his writing deals with the South Texas brush country where he grew up, but he has some stories set in Houston as well. Garcia graduated from Texas A&M with a degree in veterinary medicine in 1965, and he is a practicing vet in Seabrook. This story is from his TCU Press collection *The Day They Took My Uncle*.

From *The Day They Took My Uncle*: The Emergency Room

THE ORDERLY SLID THE WINDOW OPEN AND peeked out from the receptionist's office into the huge waiting room full of people. The lady knitting had been there since morning. She was dressed in a faded black blouse with white buttons and a pale blue skirt with pleats all around the waistband. She wore her hair up in a bun and had wire-rimmed glasses. She had moved only a few places, sometimes giving over her place to someone else. The thought struck him that she must be there for the air conditioning. He had seen her eating her lunch at midday. At three she had taken some more food out of her hemp bag and had spread it on her lap to eat. From a large thermos bottle she had poured an endless supply of coffee. This would have been her *merienda*. She would leave as soon as the evening cooled the air outside. But then he saw her move up one place and he noticed that she put her foot up, above her head, to rest it on the back of the seat in front of her. The foot was bandaged with a bath towel. This brought up the possibility she was injured and the orderly was wrong. She smiled at the man next to her but he was not in any mood to smile. Someone had hit him on the right side of the face and it had swollen so that his eye, as big as an orange, had closed. The orderly tried to estimate the size of the crowd but when he couldn't, when he saw that the people stretched out in the hallway and beyond what he could see, he thought himself a fool trying to find an answer when there was clearly none. The noise—voices, the rustling of bodies, the coughing, sobs, moans, children crying, children shouting, children playing, the steady siren scream of ambulances coming and going—all served to make him feel hopeless, that the night would not end. It would not. From experience, these were the things that have no end. The lady knitting would have no end. She or someone like her would be there tomorrow in the same faded clothes. A symbol of waiting. He would have to turn his back and leave knowing that it had not ended, the misery and pain and subjugation had not ended. He would simply walk off at the end of his shift and he would not see it until the next day. And then he would be told of what had happened when he had not been there, not because someone wanted him to know or that he was interested after all the years but in telling him that person vented the emotions that had built up during the late-night shift, a release of feelings which one cannot keep pent up. He would be sure to listen but he did not care anymore. He did not hear anymore. There were no more feelings in him to care about. He closed the sliding window to keep away from the crowd. Inside the receptionist's office he felt a relief from not seeing the people stacked waiting.

Nurse Johnson came into the office and handed him the list of patients. She asked him to call out the next name. He stepped out and yelled, at the top of his voice, "¿Señora Beltrán? ¿Señora Beltrán?"

No one stepped forward. The orderly was looking at the row of people at the front where the patient would most likely be waiting. He said, again, "¿Señora Beltrán?"

He heard a man's voice from the hallway say, "Esa se fué. Se cansó de tanto esperar."

A black man came forward to the door and said, "Talk English man. We ain't in Mexico."

"She gone," the man said. "She tire of waiting. She said she go home to have baby."

Some wiseguy in the audience said, "She got pregnant here, man. She waited for nine months and she couldn't see no doctor."

"Everyone has to wait their turn," the orderly reminded them, stepping back into the refuge of the office. He was about to leave when he heard the urgent knocking on the receptionist's window. Grudgingly he went over and slid it open to find the small young man, his wife and two children. The man carried a child buried in a blanket. He seemed confused. The woman, very docile and subdued, could not bear to look him in the eye. The two children with them hid behind their mother's skirt.

He heard the words from the father and it stunned him. *"La niña. Parece que está muerta,"* he said.

"Un ratito, por favor," the orderly said. He closed the window and sat down. He looked at the time clock. He should have punched out thirty seconds ago. The doctor came in and sat down at the computer and put in some data and leaned back.

"Aren't you leaving?" the doctor said.

"Yes," he said. "Before I leave you should know that there's a dead child."

"Dead child? Where?"

"Right outside the window," the orderly said. "They just walked in. The father is carrying the child. There's a mother and two children with him."

"Are you sure the child is dead?" the doctor said. He could see through the frosted glass the silhouette of the man and the child in his arms and the woman.

"No," the orderly replied, "but that's what he said."

"I'm stacked," the doctor said. "I've got people in every damn room. Some have two people. I wish the relatives would stay home. Why do they have to bring all the family? Like it was an outing."

"Poor people enjoy each other's pain," the orderly said.

"I don't want to see the child," the doctor said. "There's three other doctors tonight. Give it to one of them. Or send it to the morgue. Let pathology handle it. If the kid is dead there's no sense in my seeing it."

"I've got to go. My shift is over. You get someone to handle it."

"Johnson can handle it. She'll be free soon. She speaks Spanish."

"Then give it to Johnson. Let her see the child to make sure it's dead and then you can sign the death certificate."

"I'm not signing shit," the doctor said. "What if they killed the child? Where would that put me?"

The knock on the window was urgent. The orderly went over and slid the opaque glass open. It was the same young man. He wanted to know how much longer it would be to tell him if the child was dead.

"*Nada mas de un ratito,*" the order informed him and closed the window. "He wants someone to see the child."

"On your way out look for Johnson. Tell her to take care of it."

"What good would that do? You're not going to sign the death certificate."

"Listen, Joe, I can't sign the death certificate without an autopsy. I won't touch it. I can't afford one more mistake. I'll get canned. You know Barkley is after me. All I need is for this child to have been murdered and I sign the death certificate and Barkley finds out I screwed up and I'm gone."

"What about Dr. Rodriguez? Let Rodriguez handle it."

"I'd rather Johnson handle it."

"They'll trust Rodriguez. They won't trust Johnson."

"I've got Rodriguez in Room Three with a gunshot. He's sewing him up."

"Dr. Martinez."

"Martinez is in Four with a stab wound sewing him up. All the nurses are tied up. Johnson is going to be free in a moment."

"I'm leaving. My shift is up. I've got to get out of here. I've got to get away and get some fresh air. I can't take much more of this."

"You're quitting for good?"

"I'm thinking about it."

"And your retirement? You wouldn't give that up, would you?"

"I'm saying I'm thinking about it."

"Seriously?"

"Seriously. Doc, I can't take it anymore."

"And the dead child? You're going to leave the man standing there?"

"I'm off, I tell you. It's your baby. You said Johnson would take care of it."

"Joe, please. Do me a favor. You're right. They won't trust Johnson. They'll trust you. You're the best here."

"Yeah, but I'm not a doctor."

"Who cares? Just stay an extra ten minutes. Put them in my office. Check the baby out. For all we know it's not dead."

"I guess I can stay ten more minutes. I can take this for ten more minutes."

"I'll make it up to you, Joe."

"You always say that but you never do. You're a con artist, you know that?"

"I know that. Put the family in my office. Take a look at the child. Make sure it's dead. Explain the procedure. . . . You know that. What am I telling you for?"

The orderly went and slid open the window. He said, *"Venganse por esa puerta, por favor."*

The man took the infant cradled in the blanket and went to his left and opened the door leading into the hallway. The mother had the two children by the hands and she led them behind her husband. The orderly had come out of the receptionist's office and was waiting for them in the hallway.

"Siganme, por favor," he said and the man followed him down the hallway.

The orderly stopped at the doctor's office and turned the handle on the door and let himself in first. The light was on. At the back of the small office was the desk. He asked the family to come in and they all crowded in.

"Ponga la niña en el escritorio," he told the man.

The man placed the child on top of the desk. The orderly unwrapped the child slowly, hoping the child would move, hoping he could see the child breathe. As he unfolded the blanket covering the child he could see the pallid, morbid skin color. He felt the child as he continued to unwrap it. He felt the coldness, the stillness. By the time he exposed the little face he knew the child was dead. Its little mouth was open, its jaw slack, the eyes were partially open and dry and vacant. He had seen death many times and this was it.

"¿Está muerta?" the mother asked, leaning over the body.

The orderly could not see her two children hiding behind her skirt. *"Sí,"* he answered. *"Sí. Está muerta. ¿Cuando se murió?"*

The man said, *"Pues hace unas cuantas horas. Había estado muy enferma. La llevamos con el doctor pero dijo que no era nada. Le dió una medicina y se la dimos y eso fué todo."*

The woman said, *"Ayer se puso mejor. Parecía que se había aliviado. Tomó leche."*

"Pero la depuso," the man said.

"¿Qué vamos hacer?" the woman asked.

The realization of the child's death was beginning to get to her. She began to cry and to stroke the child's head. *"Era tan buena,"* she said. *"Nunca los dió trabajo. Nunca lloró. Nunca se quejó. Fué muy linda mi niña."*

The orderly looked through the files in the desk and found the death certificate form. He sat down and placed the form into the typewriter. *"¿Qué edad tenía la niña?*

The man looked at the woman for help. She said, *"Tenía tres años y cinco meses. Apenas comenzó a hablar bien."*

The man said, *"Tenía tiempo de que no comía bien. Se ponía la comida en la voca y no la mascaba."*

"¿Me puede decir el día que nació?" the orderly asked.

"Nació el 30 de enero, mil novecientos noventa," the woman said. She turned around and took the children by the arm and brought them in front of her. The children leaned against her thighs and took her skirt and tried to wrap themselves in it.

"¿Cómo se llamaba la niña?"

"Beatrice. María Beatrice."

"¿Apellido?"

"Iturbe," the man said.

"¿Y sus nombres?"

"Faustino y Yolanda Iturbe."

"¿Su dirección?"

The man said, *"Dale la dirección."*

The woman took out a piece of paper from her purse and gave it to the orderly. After he had copied their address he asked, *"¿Y de donde son ustedes originalmente?"*

"De Guanajuato," the man said.

The woman said, *"Dios quisiera que estuvieramos ahí ahorita. Con nuestra familia."*

"*¿Y nadie le pegó a esta niña? ¿Nadie la atropello?*"

"*No señor,*" the man replied.

The woman said, "*Ni siquiera le atocamos un cabello a esta niña. A ninguno de nuestros niños se les pega.*"

"*Muy bien.*"

The orderly stepped out leaving the family with the dead child in the office. He spotted the doctor in one of the emergency rooms. The doctor was sewing up a black man who had been stabbed repeatedly in the back. In the room with the black man were several of his friends who had brought him in. The man was face down on the table, conscious, and talking to the doctor. He said, "So this motherfucker came at me with this little knife and I laughed at him. Shit! He cut my ass up in little pieces. I never saw the motherfucker before. Did you all get his name?"

The other blacks in the room shook their head. "No way," one of them said. "That little motherfucker was so fast we didn't know what he was doing. Bam. Bam. He got on your ass like flies on shit and the motherfucker was gone before we could axe him who he was."

"Like the Lone Ranger," said another one of his friends. "All the motherfucker left behind was your ass all cut up."

"That's for sure," said another partner. "That's that motherfucker's silver bullet."

"That's what you get for acting the foo'."

The man turned around to face his friends and said, "I was not acting the foo'. He was."

"Hell, Estrus," one of his friends said, "you act the foo' all the time."

"No time do I act the foo'."

The orderly asked the doctor to come out to the hallway. "Is the child dead?" the doctor asked.

"Yes. A little girl. Three years and some months. No visible signs of trauma. I asked them and they claim they had gone to a doctor and he put her on medicine and told them to go home. The child looked like it got better but then it got worse and died. They claim never to have hit her. They have never hit any of their children."

"But how can we be sure?"

"You can't. You take their word for it. What else can you do?"

"We can do an autopsy."

"Why not sign the death certificate? Have the desk call the funeral home? Let them pick up the body and let the poor family go?"

"I can't, Joe. You know I can't."

"You said you'd make it up to me. I'm asking you. Let them go. They're clean."

"How can you be sure?"

"I've been doing this for years, doc. I know. Let them go."

"I can't, Joe. It's my ass. I can't afford one more mistake. Barkley will nail me. I just can't do it. I'll make it up to you some other way but not on this one."

"Okay. You tell me exactly what you want me to do."

"Tell them we need an autopsy. They have to leave the body here. The morgue will call them when the body is ready to be picked up. The way we usually do it, Joe. That's not too hard to do, is it?"

"You're the boss."

"Good. Just tell them what they need to do."

"And if they don't agree?"

"Tell them we call the police. Homicide. They wouldn't want that. "

"You're going to call Homicide on this? Are you crazy?"

"No, I'm not crazy, Joe. I'm just covering my ass, that's all."

"Doc, how long have you been here?"

"Too fucking long. Why?"

"This is a child we're talking about here. Do you think that the parents—from Mexico, Catholics who believe God is coming and resurrecting us all from the grave—are going to agree to have their baby cut up and that they're going to bury only a shell of the baby? Do you think they will agree to that?"

"I don't care. We need an autopsy. I won't sign the death certificate without an autopsy."

"I'll get Dr. Rodriguez to sign it."

"Good. Let him do it. I won't."

The orderly took off down the hallway in search of Dr. Rodriguez. He found the doctor in an emergency room with a gunshot victim. He could not sign the certificate. It was not his case.

The orderly found Dr. Martinez in another emergency room sewing up a stab wound. He refused to sign the death certificate.

The other doctor on duty that night, Dr. Day, was busy with the outpatients and he would not sign the death certificate either.

The orderly returned to the office. The family was standing around the desk praying for the dead child.

He said, *"Se requiere una autopsia. ¿Saben lo que significa?"*

"Pues no."

"Tenemos que llevar el cuerpo con un patólogo para que él nos diga de que murió la niña. Sin una autopsia, no se puede firmar el certificado de muerte."

"¿Y qué es lo que le hacen a la niña?"

"Tienen que abrir el cuerpo para inspectar los órganos. El cerebro. El corazón. El hígado. Los riñones. Todo el cuerpo para ver de que murió."

The man said, *"No. Nosotros no queremos eso. Queremos llevarnos a la niña para enterrarla."*

"No se puede. En este país no se puede enterrar un cuerpo sin un certificado de muerte."

"¿No la podemos enterrar en el fondo del solar?"

"No. No se puede. Es encontra de la ley. Tenemos que tener una autopsia."

"Pues yo no quiero eso. Que la corten."

The woman, crying over the baby, had picked up the conversation. She said, *"Ay, Diós mío, no. Que no la corten a la pobrecita. Mi angelita."*

The orderly checked the clock on the wall. He was thirty minutes past his shift. He would be in the car and almost home by now. He left the family in the office and went to look for the doctor. He found him in Exam Room Fifteen, trying to stop a woman from crying. Her son was on a gurney, dead. He had been shot in the forehead. Another gang shooting in Mexican town. He had been the perfect son, she cried, but he had to join the gang in order to survive from day to day. She cried out, "Do you understand that he had to be in the gang, if not they would kill him?" She tried to hang on to the orderly, tried to cry her plight to him when he came in, but the orderly managed to get away from her. The orderly stepped out and the doctor followed.

"Well?" the doctor said.

"They won't go for an autopsy," the orderly said. "I told you. Not on a child. The parents won't allow it. You've got to sign the death certificate."

"Joe? Joe? I won't sign it. How many times do I have to tell you? "

"I'm desperate, doc. I need to get out of here before I go crazy. Before I blow up. I mean it. I can't take it anymore. Now, you've got one more chance coming, don't you? Barkley gave you one more chance, didn't he?"

"What are you talking about?"

"I'm calling in my chips then."

"I told you I'd make it up to you somehow but not now, Joe. This could be what does me in. I can't take the chance."

"Then I'm turning you in to Barkley."

"Are you serious, Joe? What for?"

"I'm in charge of drug inventory, right?"

"Yeah."

"We're missing methamphetamines. We're missing a lot of them. And I know you are the one taking them. Hell, maybe you're selling them."

"Joe, you can't prove that."

"I may not be able to prove it in court but if I go to Barkley and tell him I think it's you he'll believe me. That will be enough. You are out of here, doc. You're out of control."

"Don't do this to me, Joe."

"Now, I can cover methamphetamines and you can too. It's easy to keep robbing one bottle to put in another. But I know you're on them, doc."

"You sonofabitch. You're threatening me over this? Why is this so important to you? You've lost control, Joe. Go on home. I'll handle this now. I don't need your services any longer. You're fucking nuts. You know that?"

"You're calling homicide."

"Yes. I'm calling homicide."

"I'm not leaving then. You're crazy, you know that?"

"I'm crazy, Joe. You're crazy. That's why we're here. Do you think a sane man would do this?"

The dead man's extended family could be seen in the hallway coming toward them. The women were wailing. The men had stern looks on their faces, looks of revenge. There would be more killings. The doctor and the orderly got out of the way and let the family pass into the room. When they saw the body the wailing began in earnest. The men, for some reason, to show their anger, began to beat on the walls with their fists. The sound carried through the hallway like the marching beat of death.

The orderly went back to the office hoping that he could convince the family to have an autopsy done on the child. They would not agree.

The orderly said, finally, *"Entonces el doctor le tiene que hablar a la policía."*

"Diós mío," the woman said, *"Porqué. ¿Porqué la policía?"*

The man said, *"No hemos hecho nada. Se murió la niña en los brazos de su madre."*

"El doctor no va a firmar el certificado de muerte sin una autopsia."

Then came the answer the orderly had dreaded.

The man said, speaking for the family, *"Entonces no queremos el cuerpo de la niña. Ustedes se pueden quedar con el cuerpo."*

The orderly said, *"No queremos el cuerpo nosotros tampoco. Haber que puedo hacer con el doctor."*

"Le agradecemos mucho, señor."

The orderly found the doctor embroiled in the family fight over the gang death of the young man. He was trying to be heard but the family had so much anger that the orderly feared for the doctor's safety. He went back to the receptionist's office and called Security. Two officers arrived in moments and he escorted them to Room Fifteen where the argument was still going. Security was able to quiet the family and they sat in the room with the body and began to pray the Rosary. The doctor was out in the hallway with the orderly.

The orderly said, "Can't you understand what it must be like to be in a strange country and have your child die?"

"No one invited them here," the doctor said. "They come on their own. You take your chances. And don't you think it's worse for them where they come from? Why do you think they're here?"

"They don't want the child."

"What do you mean, they don't want the child?"

"The body. They don't want the body if we're going to mutilate it."

"We're not going to mutilate it, Joe. It's just an autopsy. They won't be able to tell the difference."

"I can't convince them, doc. If the child is cut that's mutilation to them. If we do an autopsy they don't want the body."

"Tell them I'm calling homicide."

"Okay. I'll tell them but they won't understand."

"I don't care if they understand or not. We're in a war zone here, Joe. I've farted around with them too long as it is. People are dying all over."

"Tell me about it. I've been doing this for twenty years. Every year it gets worse."

"Just hold them and call homicide."

"It's your show."

"Thank you, Joe."

"Don't mention it."

"You're not pissed off, are you? You're not turning me in, are you?"

"No. I'm not turning you in. God only knows who would replace you."

"Now you're talking sense, Joe. It could be worse. I could be worse."

By the time the orderly arrived at the office the family was gone. The orderly took the death certificate off the typewriter, tore it into pieces and threw it into the wastebasket.

As the family walked back to the Metro bus stop in the early morning drizzle, small brown raindrops barely pelting the worn out sidewalk in front of Hermann Hospital, the mother struggled behind, crying softly, not wanting to attract attention from the crowd in the streets, her two children following behind holding on to her skirt. She noticed through her tears that her small, frail husband—carrying the dead child buried in the blanket—had lost weight, that the denims he had bought at Fiesta Supermarket were too large and long for him, the waist gathered and puckered around him and she noticed for the first time that in his haste he had missed the belt loops in the back. A police car, its siren wailing, shot past them toward the hospital.

_____

454

At that hour the heavy early morning Houston traffic was beginning to shake the streets and foul the air. Trucks shooting off gray leaden puffs of exhaust and loaded with workers passed them at the bus stop, the men shouting obscenities at the waiting crowd. With the morning downdraft pressing heavily against the city, the air smelled acrid, horribly pungent and unbreathable, as if a giant had eaten sulfur and batteries and was belching on the city. ★

ANTONYA NELSON

Antonya Nelson is the author of three novels and six collections of stories. Her work has appeared in *The New Yorker, Esquire, Harper's, Redbook*, and in many other magazines, and her books have been *New York Times* Notable Books of 1992, 1996, 1998, and 2000. In 2000 Nelson was also named by *The New Yorker* as one of the "twenty young fiction writers for the new millennium." This story originally appeared in *The New Yorker* and was collected in *Some Fun*. Nelson teaches creative writing at the University of Houston.

Eminent Domain

WHAT CAUGHT PAOLO'S ATTENTION WAS the smile, teeth extravagantly white and large, orthodontically flawless. Expensive maintenance in the mouth of a homeless girl. Around the smile was a pale, animated face, and around that a corona of wild purple hair. The owner of this gleeful mouth was drunk, her flame of a head swaying on the thin stick of her body, lit at nine in the morning on the front stoop of a condemned Baptist church.

This neighborhood was called "transitional." The church was being destroyed to accommodate a new freeway, and a ramp jutted raggedly into the sky above it, a road to nowhere: eminent domain. Paolo drove past it on his way to the theatre for rehearsals. Every day, the girl balanced on the church steps, surrounded by a shifting group of men. Always the only female, and, as a result, the center of a kind of stunned, stoned, possessive attention. The group surveyed the street, drinking from brown-paper bags, leaning on bundles, panhandling with plastic cups, laughing too loudly, ready to attack anyone who made the mistake of approaching their girl. Some wore hospital wristbands. They adopted dogs and took better care of them than they did of themselves. They, too, were strays—unclaimed, uncollared, trotting purposefully through parking lots or along sidewalks, jauntily dodging danger, their only objective the next meal or drink and a place to lie down. When inspired, the group catcalled in the direction of traffic—provoked by an angry driver, a hand gesture or a shout, the look of fear or disgust on an elderly face, or the mere fact of a particularly ostentatious vehicle, like a Humvee or a Bentley. Other times, they collected aluminum cans in shopping carts. You'd see them paired off on recycling day, scrounging through the green bins left curbside. They were everywhere, like squirrels, Paolo thought, with routines, like mailmen. You could grow so accustomed to their presence that you stopped seeing them.

But Paolo felt he knew the girl. Her animation most likely had to do with being the only female and therefore the source of a kinetic sexual friction, not only among the men in her circle but among the men in the cars passing, and the ones wearing hard hats and safety vests, operating the raucous city equipment, erecting the freeway. She presided in the manner of a stripper before a paying audience. Still, Paolo stared with what he knew to be special interest, drawn by something about her that he alone perceived.

Then one day he knew what it was. He squealed to a halt in traffic. The street people looked over at the source of the sound with the lazy blinking regard of lizards. And there, showcased among them, was Bobby Gunn's daughter. Sophie Gunn. A Houston River Oaks Country Club girl. Débutante, she should be, by now. Through the steamy window of his convertible Paolo took her in, the furthest thing from a débutante he could imagine, and she gazed upon him with a taunting expression that said she was high, protected, superior. Her glance said, *You fear me. You may even envy me*. Then her smile faltered. She stepped backward. Now she understood that she knew him—that he had ties to her past, that he might leap from his car and reveal her origins, reveal to her companions the fact that she was merely slumming, while they had no other options. Was that it—simply threat, exposure both here and to her parents? She and Paolo held the gaze, across traffic, through the windshield, as if time had gelled.

Then it jerked forward; horns blared all around him. Houston drivers were patient, to a point—their Southern manners, maybe the languor that humidity encouraged—and then they became just as surly as their counterparts in New York. He hadn't been a driver in New York, and his skills were still rudimentary. He sometimes forgot that he was in charge of the car and drifted, foot ambivalent on the pedals. He lurched away now, suspecting that Sophie Gunn, having been recognized, wouldn't hold court on the steps tomorrow.

***

Paolo was having a sort of secret affair with a patron of the arts who was forty-four, ten years older than him. "Sort of," because it seemed that most people knew about it. Her husband, a heart surgeon, had been charged in a recent scandal at the hospital—a dull scandal having to do with billing, rather than botched surgery or drug trafficking—the details of which he'd kept from his wife. (It was the intern mistress, his new confidante, who would have to appear in court, and in the pages of the *Chronicle*, implicated.) Mary Annie was the name of the surgeon's wife, who had now filed for divorce. She referred to herself as "well preserved" which meant that she had streaked-blond hair and tennis-ball arm muscles, minimal wrinkles, and a snappy fashion sense. She'd grown up on a ranch in West Texas, where her larger-than-life father had pampered her in a peculiar way. In addition to the typical female functions, she had been expected to cultivate another set of assets: a bawdy, tolerant sense of humor, a whiskey voice, the ability to give the distinct and disarming impression that she knew your weaknesses and forgave you for them in advance. Intelligent by nature, she'd been a horse handler, a tea drinker, a student of nursing, and was now curious about the creative arts. But she was cautious in love, having been wounded by her husband, that coward, that man whom her father had enthusiastically offered to come shoot dead. Texans—they were a breed apart.

Paolo had been seated near Mary Annie at one of what he'd dubbed the Rubber Chicken Events. They came with the visiting-artist territory— fund-raising dinners with tables full of benefactors there to meet the talent. How many had he attended in his two years as actor-in-residence? For these affairs, he fortified himself with Scotch. Mary Annie had been sitting across from Paolo; when he was asked how he prepared for his roles as, well, such *low-lifes* (his calling was malfeasance, Iago the role he was rehearsing now), she had smiled into her plate. "Assholes are easy," he'd responded. The dowagers and their husbands liked to be scandalized—it was part of what they bought, for a thousand dollars a plate. But the flinch in Mary Annie's face brought Paolo up short; he hadn't truly meant to offend.

"Allow me," he said to her afterward, on the edge of the club portico, where they were waiting for their cars. Gallantly, he held his umbrella over her. She forgave him gracefully, leaning in too close, a woman accustomed to a man's attention, and in need of it. Later, slowly, they'd become true intimates—not when she'd undressed for him, for the first time, in a hotel room, or when they'd kissed achingly in her driveway, but when, on the telephone this month, she'd confessed that she was puzzling over the problem of her daughter's pregnancy. She didn't want to be called Granny or Nana or any other fossilizing term of endearment. Then Paolo knew he'd genuinely been let in.

***

On the phone with Mary Annie, Paolo did not mention the girl on the church steps. Already he'd decided.

He might have first met Sophie Gunn at Mary Annie's house. At a function there—the girl brought along in a cotillion dance dress with a corsage, or perhaps the reluctant teen in an outfit of chains and denim. Whatever she'd been then, she had shed it now.

"You could give me a ride," Sophie had said to him there at the curb, after which she'd coughed ferociously, making a fist and hacking into it. He'd parked in front of the church and she'd stepped forward automatically, the representative of her crew, a pack of cigarettes squashed suggestively behind her metal-studded belt. He was glad to see that she hadn't been scared away by his recognition of her the day before. It was a sunny February afternoon; he had the top down, sunglasses on.

"Beg pardon?"

She repeated her request, pantomiming, pointing at him, then back at herself.

Knowing who she was, he should have delivered her straight to her parents' house. But he had never seen himself as a savior. He was an observer at best, a bad influence or an attractive nuisance at worst. A stringer-along. An actor, for God's sake—hungry for the disreputable, never denying the dark impulses.

"Get in," he told her.

He took her to a Taco Cabana and bought her beans and rice and guacamole. She was a vegetarian, which made Paolo laugh. She joined him; it was as if the same silly slogans ran through their minds: *Sleep in the street, don't eat meat. Smoke pot, not pigs.* She still had her wits about her. How long would they last? She knew every customer at the restaurant and greeted them all extravagantly. She was indulged—the neighborhood had not yet turned its gentrifying back on her ilk. And she had not yet acquired the look of a derelict. Her skin was intact, mostly clean, exposed with utter randomness, her clothes held on with safety pins and zippers, tiny diamond in her nostril, rings in her brow, ears, and lip, ball bearing through the tongue. She wore a rivet-studded bracelet that Paolo was alarmed to recognize as a cock ring, and combat boots, which would probably never go out of style in certain contexts. Every few days, she told Paolo, she went to a high-school friend's house to watch television, take a shower, sit on a sofa. "And dye my hair," she added thoughtfully. The color was eggplant, tipped in jet black. Her vanity about it interested Paolo; some product had been used to make it flare up rather than lie limp. He stared for a long time at her beautifully smooth arms until he realized that she must have shaved them, and recently, to achieve the look.

He needed to know if she was eighteen yet—the wholeness of the number signified something—but she wouldn't say. He pretended not to know instantly what that meant.

Without asking, without promising, they struck a kind of bargain—the kind made between people who will eventually sleep together, whose business is mostly of the subterranean, unspoken variety—that he would not tell her parents where she was. Her father, Bobby Gunn, who had slid out of several investment and oil businesses just before they toppled, was the minorest of minor players in the latest rash of financial scandals. "Wily," Sophie said. "Daddy," she called him. Either it was an affectation (and it was charming) or, as a Southerner, she was unaware of the word's perverse disharmony. "Daddy," she said, as in "Daddy once called the police and had me arrested for pawning Mama's jewelry." She'd summoned the police to come get him, too; he'd beaten her when she set fire to the playroom—extinguished the blaze with the garden hose, then whipped her unrepentant grinning face with the metal nozzle. They went tit for tat in that household, apparently.

All Paolo could recall was Bobby Gunn's habit of muttering to himself. He'd tucked it away as a curiosity for future use in a character study. The under-your-breath aside, the meanness most people kept to themselves. "Fuck you," Sophie, too, had said, sotto voce, instead of "Thank you," as a girl her own age wearing a Taco Cabana paper hat disdainfully took her order.

"I used to Magic Marker 'I want to die' on my arms during tests if I hadn't studied. *Bada bing*—down to the counsellor's office," Sophie told him. She was providing him with tips for a kind of survival. She was entertaining him. She was trying to convey the personality that was uniquely her own—brattiness, joy, jokes, willfulness. The need to shock. "When I was a baby, I would bang my head on the floor until they gave me what I wanted." Paolo noted how tidily she ate, etiquette lessons still coursing through her system like the blood of a feline, fastidious and sexy.

"Didn't you use to ride horses?" Paolo said suddenly, an image returning to him like a forgotten dream.

"Yep," she responded. Bobby Gunn's daughter had been wearing jodhpurs when he met her. She'd stepped into a living-room party when all those present were lulled by liquor into a dreamy observation of her garments, the strange and striking uniform, part English Regency, part Vegas showgirl, the boots, the helmet, and—especially—the crop. She'd been teen-age, scornful, eyebrows arched, lips twitching as if to hold back a derisive snort. She'd had a knowing-ness, a skepticism—a fringe-factor affiliation that Paolo shared—remarkable enough to allow him to recognize her otherwise unrecognizable self on the steps of the torched Baptist church. Without it, he wouldn't have been able to unearth her in that smile. He wouldn't have found himself thinking about her in the circle of men, the liquid movement of her hips and hands.

"Aren't you supposed to be in school?" Stupid, stupid, stupid, he instantly berated himself. But she wasn't listening. She was expanding her eyes as if to hypnotize him.

461

She leaned across the lunch debris. "What would you pay me to suck you off?"

"What?"

"Not what, how much? *Cuánto?*"

"I wouldn't, at any price." Paolo hated the heat that suffused his face, the repulsion that accompanied it. Hadn't he just been considering her flesh in full possession of unclean thoughts? Her confidence wasn't complete, he told himself; she was trying on vulgarity, rather than genuinely inhabiting it. "But I'll lend you money."

"But I can't pay you back, so I have to do something for it. I have to earn it."

"It can be a long-term loan. In ten years, it'll come due."

"I'll be dead," she said breezily. "Daddy says that all debts are forgiven in death." She took twenty dollars. "I won't buy drugs," she promised, bored, anticipating his next stupid statement. She withdrew a foil-wrapped stick of chewing gum from the pocket of her jeans and poked it into her mouth. When Paolo delivered her to a tattoo parlor a mile away, she gave him a kiss on the cheek that left a small minty tingle.

***

He didn't see her for a week, although he looked. Had his twenty dollars bought her oblivion? Then there she was, outside the Starbucks he sometimes frequented. He locked his convertible with his usual qualms; anyone with a knife—screwdriver, ballpoint pen, sharp fingernail—could hack through the roof.

"What are you up to?" he asked nonchalantly, hugely relieved to see her.

"You can't believe how nervous people get when you walk into their place of business carrying one of these." She brandished a red plastic gasoline container like a lunchbox.

"Well, yes," Paolo agreed.

Over coffee—she ordered a large sweet beverage full of cream and caramel, a kid's concept of coffee, consumed with a spoon—she proposed a few favors that he might perform for her. Her cohorts in the world of the disenfranchised, while often fun and generally supportive, couldn't render all required aid. Listening, Paolo was already justifying his attraction to her. He would save her, he told himself as he nodded along. Surely he was better for her than the boys she was currently hanging around with. Boys? Men. More adept at the traditional manly functions than Paolo was. Fighters, hunters, gatherers—after a fashion. Addicts, scroungers, streetwise. Paolo wouldn't last a day in that odd cosmos. He was a pampered dilettante, supported by the gifts of women who were bored and eager for a cause. Sophie could be his cause as he was theirs. He wasn't so different from those do-gooders, he thought, discreetly nudging the gasoline container beneath the table. He was old enough to be her father, more or less. But only if he'd fathered her when he was in high school, he told himself. And that helped.

"This is a school day, right?" she asked suddenly.

"Thursday," he said. "No, Wednesday."

She sent him into her private school to clean out her locker, abandoned several months ago but still full of stuff.

"My parents are afraid to disenroll me," Sophie explained. "It's too hard to get back in—you sign up for this shithole, like, in utero—so instead they just put me *on leave.*" She pronounced the last words like a phrase in French.

The woman at the attendance desk did not blanch; she sent Paolo with a box and a prissy aide, who made a point of looking away when the locker door swung open to reveal its decoration of broken mirrors and slashed photographs, everything held in place with duct tape. Paolo had the feeling that much of what he removed from the locker did not actually belong to Sophie.

He was sweating by the time it was over, unnerved in a specifically immature way. This was the business of adolescence. What was he thinking? An alarm was sounding, he believed, alerting all parents and law-abiding citizens.

He could hear his stereo, practically see the little car throbbing, as he hustled across the parking lot. Sophie snapped the radio off before he could complain, greeting him with "No one in that building has ever set foot in a public school." And, anticipating his next remark, she added, "Including the janitor."

"Nuh-uh."

"Uh-huh," she hummed confidently. Her locker made her seem more deeply disturbed than Paolo had thought. She was a liar, a thief, a beautiful, broken, fathomless girl. She had acne in her eyebrows, which were still blond. When he handed over the locker's contents, she immediately began to separate the salable from the personal.

"Tell me your name," she said as they drove away from the scene of the crime.

"Paul," he said automatically, reverting to the lie. He was legitimately Paolo, but as a child in Milwaukee he'd adopted Paul for use in school and on the street. His mother had given him his name; from her he'd also acquired the habit of crossing his fingers, knocking on wood, making wishes, and looking for portents. On his forehead was the same worried V, entrenched between the eyes. The night his mother died, he'd seen not only a star in the smeary Houston sky but a falling one.

"You're cool, Paul," Sophie Gunn said, thanking him. At the church steps, she took her box of goods and waved goodbye.

Like a kind of church functionary, he'd fed her, he'd listened without judgment, he'd given her money. What more could he do?

At home, in his guesthouse apartment, he took advantage of the rare sunny afternoon to lie outside and tan, gauging his moral temperature. Would he have attached himself to a runaway boy? To an ugly girl? What did he have in mind? Below, in the back yard of the main house, a pool shimmered. Once it had been for swimming, but not anymore. It had been altered by its current owners, Paolo's hosts, who had filled it with concrete except for the top eighteen inches or so: a giant shallow pool that attracted clouds of mosquitoes and wandering rodents. The atmosphere was insidious, suggestive. He drank beer as the sky turned city pink.

His hosts, Clem and Sheila, were also patrons of the arts; his quarters came to him free of charge. Yet there was a cost—his privacy. A steep price, actually, all things considered. But not one he'd thought much about until he had something to hide. He assessed it now as he acknowledged his desire to bring Sophie here, to give her a place to sleep for the night. His thinking took him no further than seeing her safely on his futon, beneath a spare bedsheet, wearing a pair of his soft shorts. He understood that from now on he would be the owner of a small gnawing anxiety with her name attached to it—an irritation that only her living presence would soothe.

In a little while, his hosts would be home from work, standing on their deck, waving at him with drinks in their hands, the way they did every evening—beaming at their pet.

***

It seemed wise to fill her Ritalin prescription for her, picking it up from the safety of the Walgreen's drivethrough, his eyes skidding wildly for spies in the parking lot. Her plan charged her twenty dollars a month for her supply. It kept her from losing focus, she told him. It interacted well with cigarettes, marijuana, alcohol. Not so well with cocaine or Ecstasy. He took this information in without expression. "And I can always sell a few of them," she added. "Some people think it's a trip."

On a weekly basis he delivered her to therapy, in a building without windows. The office was for the indigent; there wasn't even a parking lot beside it, just an open door and a steady stream of runaways and the homeless, people who endured an hour of questions in order to recline on a padded chaise in refrigerated air. Sophie enjoyed her doctor, an idealistic young man who had run away himself and suffered a kind of free-floating angst having to do with entitlement and disillusion. Outside, sweating in his car, Paolo had several less than noble thoughts on the topic of Sophie's therapy. For instance, was the doctor attracted to her? And, if so, was Sophie mutually inclined? Was Paolo perhaps a subject of conversation? He didn't inquire; she didn't reveal.

He, like the therapist, was careful never to seem like a probing parent, never to scold her for being high, for endangering herself, for eluding her mother and father. If she weren't doing those very things—if she were still a senior at St. James High, living in her wallpapered girlhood bedroom, preparing now for the prom—he wouldn't be with her at all. There would be no virtue in seducing her as her parents' child, only reproach and judgment, banishment. Instead, he enjoyed the luxury of being better than the alternative—those filthy men who slept in the bayou and ate out of Dumpsters. The oddest of them actually had horns—a stump on each side of his forehead, surgically installed. A man whose ambition was to become a troll. Paolo was preferable, by far, to him; at least, this was the ongoing imaginary argument he made to Sophie's parents.

Whenever they parted, she kissed him. First it had been on the cheek; now it was on the mouth. What, he asked himself, would her tongue stud feel like, slipped between his teeth?

During rehearsals, he imagined her observing him from the depths of the dark auditorium, her funky shoes hoisted onto the seat in front of her, the bullshit-detecting gaze levelled his way, and he found himself performing for her skeptical expectation, working to prove himself to her. "You were on fire," his director said, praising him, and Paolo, still spellbound by the thought of Sophie, waved the compliment away.

Her name came up by accident with Mary Annie. Paolo's blood surged—in his face, his heart, his groin. They were vacuuming Mary Annie's S.U.V. at a self-service car wash, sucking up the Irish-setter hair. Above the noise of the suction, she mentioned that the Gunns had been through three different private investigators before deciding that Sophie must have left the city. She and the Gunns were social acquaintances, on many of the same boards, and members of the same country club. The older Gunn daughter had gone to school with Mary Annie's girl, Meredith. The families weren't close, but the gossip of their lives circulated through the ranks. There was a lot of support in the system. Mary Annie was stretched across the carpeted cargo cabin, jamming the nozzle of the machine into the crevices, when she said, "I really feel for the Gunns. These kids are like terrorists. They hold their families hostage, basically. They make threats, they break negotiating promises, they aren't afraid of the occasional suicide bombing. Tell me how they're different from the other people we've declared terrorists."

Paolo had no answer. Mary Annie supplied her own, sighing as the machine abruptly ceased. "We love them," she said. "That's the problem." Her eyes were moist Her own daughter, the one who was due to deliver Mary Annie's first grandchild in three months, had been a wild girl. She'd had to go survive in a camp in Utah for a few weeks, detoxing on a clifftop, rappelling and rafting and eating nuts and berries around a campfire with a bunch of other druggies. The cost of such restoration was astronomical. "If they could find Sophie, they could take her there. You can even pay someone to transport her," Mary Annie said.

"Sounds harsh," Paolo said.

She blinked up at him, slamming the hatchback door of the S.U.V. "Teenagers steal years off your life," she said. "The stress gave me an esophageal disorder. I still can't use ziplock bags without thinking of Mere's backpack full of them."

"But she came through O.K.," Paolo said, nearly pleading. "She's fine, right? Husband? Baby?"

Mary Annie used two cupped hands to push back her hair and reattach a silver barrette held between her teeth. "Maybe. But my marriage started to go downhill because Tad and I couldn't agree on what to do about her during those years. We took out all our anger at Meredith on each other. We went at it like tigers. It's terrible to care for someone more than she cares for herself."

Mary Annie's words, these last ones, ran like a banner through Paolo's mind. He did not think he'd felt that way before, and it alarmed him to realize that it might be true of his affection for Sophie.

***

"Did you know that your mom and dad hired private eyes?" he asked the girl later.

This news surprised her, which was gratifying. Very little surprised her. "How hard could it be?" she asked. "Here I am."

"The point is they're looking."

"They're doing a piss-poor job," she said, spreading her arms on the church steps. "Anyone who wants can see me."

But that wasn't quite the case; she didn't look like her old self. His recognition of her hadn't been the same as a parent's. What they were looking for was dated, buried deep.

Paolo bought her a cell phone, because she'd thrown hers away after the battery had run down; also, her parents had known the number and filled the voice mail. He purchased two chargers and kept one in his car cigarette lighter for her to use as they cruised the sultry city in the comfort of air-conditioning and stereo sound. A few times, Paolo panicked because the phone was on his plan, a cheaper alternative but an implicating one, should, say, the unit be found on her dead body. He tried hard not to imagine her body dead, dead instead of slouched in his passenger seat, taking calls in a savage secret fashion.

He fed her. He compromised, buying her cigarettes but not liquor. He considered it progress when she allowed him to see her on a weekend night, because that was when the clubs were busiest, when the kids she knew from St. James sneaked out into the dark. Paolo had once looked forward to weekends, but not anymore. All the worst things happened then. The weekends were when Mary Annie's soon-to-be ex-husband was most likely to be pulled from sleep for an emergency transplant; the organ donors died then, on weekends and during holidays. One family's tragedy led to another's miracle; they might meet in heart-wrenching scenes in the hospital lounges and waiting rooms. Less and less often, Paolo took Mary Annie up on her offer for company during those nights when her husband was called away. As he sat with her—at restaurants, concerts, movies, between the sheets of her very comfortable bed—he resented Sophie's power. And why had he given it to her, anyway? The girl had ruined Paolo's nascent love for Mary Annie, eclipsed her elder easily, without even trying.

"Hey, tough girl, don't you worry about getting busted?" Paolo said peevishly as Sophie lit a small metal pipe in his front seat. She never asked permission. "And, if not for yourself, at least think of me, the adult driver." He hated to feel so threatened by rule-makers. What had become of his own question-authority, fuck-you attitude?

"I was already arrested," she said, as if the event were like a baptism or an inoculation, singular and prophylactic, thereby making her exempt. "Dude, it's so funny." She'd been caught smoking hash in the bayou one night. The cop had cuffed her and dragged her to the downtown station, where he threw her in a cell. She phoned home and reached her father, who, on his outraged way across town, was himself stopped for D.U.I. and resisting arrest. He wasn't allowed to drive her home, so her mother had to be called. But her mother was too sedated on pills to answer the phone, and her father was too embarrassed to call one of his friends, so they ended up calling a cousin, Mina. "Mina's a total fuckup, so we figured she wouldn't tell the rest of the family. It was our secret, me and Daddy's. We didn't fight for a while after that," Sophie finished a little nostalgically.

"That's some family you've got there," Paolo said, as she abruptly opened the passenger window and rapped the pipe on the exterior of the car, where Paolo would later find a ding. Instead of dropping her off in front of the church, he suggested a long ride around the city's loop. Sophie took the opportunity to curl up against the headrest and take a nap, her hands in fists at her chin. Mouth partially open, eyes closed, she could have been ten or twelve years old, an ordinary pretty child. That she so wholly trusted him made Paolo afraid; what if he was not who he—and, presumably, she—believed he was?

***

In April, when "Othello" opened, he gave Sophie a ticket. Like a high-school boy, he waited for her to materialize in the audience, in the seat he'd designated—to be for real where he'd installed her in his imagination for months. And, as he had been in high school, where high hopes wage war with low expectations, he was simultaneously disappointed and validated: no girl, no adulation, no fantasy fulfilled.

It was hard not to be churlish, then, a week later, when he received her desperate call. She phoned him from a McDonald's on Westheimer. "I feel hot," she said—not passionately but listlessly. When he picked her up, her forehead burned beneath his wrist, though he had no notion what he was checking for—it was just another of his mother's gestures. In the driveway of the guesthouse, he ascertained the absence of Clem and Sheila before hurrying Sophie up the rickety steps, following her lurching bottom, the painful pinch of her flesh as it met her metal belt. Once indoors, he drew the shades and opened the oven door to provide mood lighting, hiding inside his own home. She lay on the futon with a wet compress on her head, three aspirin and a slug of whiskey for her cold symptoms, bare dirty feet splayed.

"I can't sleep," she said. "It's been two days, and I just can't fucking sleep!"

"What did you take?" Paolo asked.

"Nothing," she claimed. But later revised—a few unknown things, not much, nothing new, that was for sure, and far less than usual. He was afraid to ask her to change her clothing, though it didn't smell fresh; the sheets wouldn't conform to the bed, slipping off under her twitching need to be constantly re-aligned. At the sink he took a hammer to a bundle of ice cubes, turning them into something palatable and cool for her, shards of slippery water passed from his trembling hand to her pink tongue. He thrilled sickeningly as she closed her lips around his fingers. He promised himself that if she showed just one sign of hallucination or seizure he'd rush her to the E.R.

"My mind is racing," she said. "I just can't relax." The fact that despite her exhaustion she could not let go of consciousness made her cry. Paolo knew the feeling. He sat beside her on the futon.

"When I was young," he said, remembering it as he spoke, "my mother used to do this thing." He cleared his throat, lifted his voice, trying on his mother's cigarette-tinged steadiness, her words like a rich note sustained on a saxophone. "Imagine lying in a field," he began. "A field of grass, the ground below your head and hands, and the sky above. A little wind, the sound of"—he improvised—"wind chimes." (Sheila's were tinkling faintly from the yard.) "You think you're relaxed, lying in your field, but not yet you aren't. Squeeze your toes, squeeze and squeeze, and then let them go, just let them go. They might feel like they want to float. . . ." The ankles, the thighs, the hip bones, the clavicle. Up the body he went, from toes to knees to ribs to face. Paolo's breathing slowed as he took Sophie through the incantation. He had been his mother's youngest child, her only boy, his three older sisters wild girls who disappeared laughing into the night, leaving Paolo and their worried mother to wait for them at home. When he couldn't sleep, when his vivid imagination plagued him, waking nightmares flashing before his closed eyes in a fearsome beating pattern, he called for his mother, who sat beside him and summoned the field of grass, the easy breeze, drifting clouds, sunshine, sleep.

"Whattarya, Yoga Man?" Sophie said, a smile in her voice, but she obeyed his commands to clench and release, seize and relinquish. Calm overtook them both. The oven light flickered. A distant siren cried. And, finally, she slept, her fists as usual near her chin, her limbs still randomly twitching, the drugs firing and ricocheting inside her, despite her essential absence. Paolo breathed as deeply as his guest, more peaceful than he'd been in months. Either it was the certainty of her safety, here with him behind the locked guesthouse door, or it was his dead mother's sudden presence.

"Let him have it," she said later, from inside a dream. "He can have it, I don't want it." She followed through with a dismissive swipe of her hand, which flopped off the futon and onto the floor.

While he waited for morning—for light, for the disappearance of fever, for whatever shift toward optimism was going to occur—he turned the radio to a jazz station and watched the shimmering pool beneath his window. When Clem and Sheila came home, their lights went on, turning the house into a doll house, its bulbs flaring and extinguishing, revealing their ritual movements, the absent-minded passage through doors and halls, objects shifted from one room to another, keys, mail, laundry, a glass of water, the ascent from downstairs to up. Would his life ever resemble that life? House, pool, wife, routine? This guesthouse had been designed for visits from their children, those eventual adults, for the implicitly promised grandchildren.

When Sophie rolled to the far side of the futon and fell into a heavier, unromantic sleep, Paolo shut the oven door, lowered the radio's volume to a vague hum, and removed his outer layer of clothes. Wearing boxer shorts and a T-shirt, he carefully positioned himself beside her. Her back was turned to him, her hand now on her hip. He rested his head beside her pillow, shaping himself to complement her shape, breathing in the complicated odor of her head—hair product, smoke, sweat, something metallic, perhaps from her various piercing hardware. He lay for a long time inching his hand toward hers, finally covering it, as it made a fist in his grip. She arched herself backward against him automatically, her reflex one of welcome rather than repulsion, an attraction to the source of heat. And for a second Paolo, reacting without thinking, pressed his instant erection along the seam of her pants, its tip creased painfully by her studded belt. If he'd closed his eyes and let himself pretend, he could have followed through, could have told himself that she'd done much more with many worse, and later she most likely wouldn't even remember. Instead, he turned over, planting a friendly backside against hers. His eyes were wide and he was aware of blinking them, yet soon enough he returned to the grassy field they both inhabited, watching the clouds and drifting with her by his side.

***

In the morning, she was gone. He could have dreamed the evening, for all the evidence he had of it. After trying her cell phone—"Hey, muthafucka, leemee a messsssssage"—he drove to the church, but it was an act of hope rather than reason. Now he was like her parents, he thought, seeking her at a disadvantage, lagging two steps behind, berating himself for having let her slip, literally, through his fingers.

"Where's our friend?" he shouted to the troll, who did a kind of "You talking to me?" routine before he limped reluctantly to Paolo's vehicle and scowled in at him. "Our friend Sophie," Paolo clarified. The man's forehead sprouted two inch-high protrusions, each of which, though bluish in color, clearly had veins of blood circulating just under the tight thin skin. "Wow," Paolo added, unable not to comment. Without thinking, he touched his own forehead. Though Sophie had patiently told him the names of all her comrades, Paolo had instead assigned them nicknames—the troll, the rooster, the slag heap, Mr. Natural. Others were moving slowly toward his car. If they decided that it was he, Paolo, who was responsible for Sophie's disappearance, what might they do to him?

"Fuck off, man," the rooster said. He was older than Paolo had realized, a tense man with a bright-orange Mohawk razored straight up the middle of his head. Tattoos crawled up from his shirt collar. When he walked along Montrose, he swung a car antenna in front of him as if bushwhacking. He and the troll and half a dozen others had now virtually surrounded Paolo's little convertible. Someone put an anchoring foot on the rear bumper, creating an ominous sag.

"How's it going?" Paolo said to the group, looking for allies. "You guys seen Sophie? Purple hair?"

"Last we saw, she was with you, Miata," someone said. So they had named him, too. Well, it was only fair. The rooster reached into his pocket, and Paolo flinched, fearing a gun or a knife. Instead, he pulled out a cell phone. "You the one calling?" Paolo stared at Sophie's phone. " 'Cause she asked me to take her calls." He put the little device to his cheek. "Hold, please."

"Where is she?" Paolo asked. But none of them were saying. He felt as if he'd been sent back to elementary school, to a circle of taunting children who did not play by grownups' rules. If he got out of the car and grabbed for the phone, they would toss it among themselves. Abruptly he popped the car into gear, shooting out from under the foot on his bumper.

Why this urgency, he asked himself, shifting to third, then fourth gear. Before, he'd gone days and weeks without seeing her. Yet he felt that he had to share with her one important fact: *I didn't do anything*, he would say. *I was good. Nothing happened.*

***

A few weeks later, at the end of Paolo's time in Houston, late one night after the last of his going-away parties, she called him and said, slurring, "Hey, I'm in jail." His had been the only number stored in her cell phone—he'd programmed it himself when he bought it. While it was in the hands of the gang, he'd received a few accidental calls, shouting and singing and odd bits of street noise coming over the line.

He dressed among the boxes that held his belongings. But, before he left the apartment, she phoned again, to tell him that she'd been mistaken: hospital, not jail.

She'd been picked up riding the bus, passed out and in possession of some controlled substances that had poured from her pockets. After she'd ridden the route twice, the bus driver had delivered her to the downtown station, where she'd been thrown into a cell before fully waking. She'd refused to tell them who she was. Her school photo, Paolo assumed, the one her parents had submitted to the cops when she ran away, looked nothing like her.

Someone or something—a fight, a fall—had knocked out one of her top front teeth. Her eyebrow had bled, probably because a ring had been torn from it, but the amount of blood, its flow over her face, had made her captors nervous enough to send her to the emergency room rather than keep her at the jail. And this is where Paolo drove, at four-thirty in the humid May morning, to retrieve her.

"Paul," she said. "You aren't wearing gloves."

In the grim green light of the basement hallway, he looked at his bands, as if he'd forgotten what was or wasn't on them. "Why would I be wearing gloves?"

"The others did." In addition to her slur, she had a vague lisp. Her inability to stand up frightened him. The orderlies found nothing new or interesting in their situation; Paolo was allowed to sit beside her in the busy hallway as paperwork was undertaken. She wore two thin hospital gowns and an I.D. bracelet that named her Jane Doe.

"You have to say who you are," he told her.

"No."

"Then I will. Sophie Gunn," he told a passing uniformed cop. "She's a runaway."

Just like that, he saw, he had joined the other side, turned into an adult. He hadn't felt such relief since a visit to a church confession box, twenty years earlier.

"I'm eighteen," she lisped. "On May 1st, I was eighteen. May Queen," she added, smiling raggedly.

The cop waited for the two of them to get their stories straight. Being eighteen meant that the parents wouldn't be notified but that the possession charge would be transferred from juvenile to regular court. And then if she wasn't indigent there was this emergency-room bill to reconcile.

Sophie started to gag. Both men shifted away instantly; she covered her mouth and staggered toward the women's room. Paolo and the cop watched her disappear behind the door. "Her father's Bobby Gunn," Paolo said. "I'll phone him if you can't."

"If she's eighteen, she doesn't need her daddy."

In the end, it was Mary Annie whom Paolo phoned. The Gunns, naturally, were not listed. She answered unsurprised—she was expecting a call from the hospital, to tell her that her grandchild had been born.

"It's me," Paolo said. "I'm with Sophie Gunn." His explanation was brief, uninspired, suspect, no doubt, but he was too tired to embellish, too close to leaving Houston to really care what Mary Annie thought of him. Maybe that was another grown-up trait—not caring. She found the Gunns' phone number and wished him luck. It took a lot of rings to rouse them. Their expectation of hearing from their daughter had apparently waned.

"'Wha'?" her father, the mumbler, said.

"I've got your daughter," Paolo said. "She's with me."

But this wasn't true, after all. For she had not returned to her seat beside Paolo after running to the rest room. The officer came back, a sheaf of papers in hand, calling her name as he passed through the hallway of the bleeding and bandaged. "Gunn," he said, in time to his heavy echoing footsteps, "Gunn. Gunn. Gunn?"

***

There was a time, earlier in the strange relationship that Paolo had with Sophie Gunn, when he should have given her up, turned her in, ended his role in a questionable business. This was at one of the ubiquitous fund-raisers, not a Rubber Chicken (sit-down) dinner but a cheese-cube, stuffed-mushroom (stand up) affair. At this party, Paolo was paying careful attention to the Gunns— Mrs. Gunn, whose smile clearly pained her, its hollowness owing no doubt to her anxiety about her daughter, and Bobby, who had a talent for attracting people in a circle around him. The others leaned in, scowling, to make out his murmuring anecdotes. Paolo found a place on the edge of the crowd, listening, holding a wineglass like a mask before his face. Bobby Gunn, having reached a few too many times for the champagne that floated by on the caterers' trays and not often enough for the hors d'oeuvres also circulating, was discussing his missing daughter. In the gathering of glamorously dressed friends, parents themselves of teen-agers and young marrieds, he told the story his heartbreak: the all-star-equestrian, straight-A-student daughter who ran away, got into drugs, was lost to him on the streets. Paolo flushed, longing for the strength either to walk away or to confess.

"Teen-age girls are the canaries in the coal mine," one of the party guests posited. "We think they're so hard to live with, and yet just think how hard it must be to *be* them."

"Just think," another listener agreed drolly, a former beauty in late middle age. What she wouldn't do, Paolo thought, to be seventeen again.

"It's the boys who drive up your car insurance," a father said. "Still, they're easier than the girls."

Such was the conventional wisdom concerning delinquency, youth: the wildness that hadn't yet been harnessed, the bad habits still blatant, the obsessions and addictions that might in the future be channeled, put to good, or at least profitable, use. Paolo distinctly felt his place in both worlds, the young and the old, and yet felt committed to belonging to neither. Now the crowd began offering its own evidence. Teen-age girls: This one had stolen her grandmother's silver. That one had driven a car into the swimming pool. Another had left the children she was babysitting to go to the liquor store with her boyfriend. Or she'd let the children watch as she screwed the boyfriend, sex ed in the family room. She'd leaped off a roof. She'd run naked through the mall. She'd set up an Internet porn site featuring herself and her sisters. She'd said to her mother, each and every day, "Die, you psycho cunt!" These girls. They were presented like poker hands, each one upping the ante.

But Bobby Gunn raised his voice above the general din. His story was not over.

Apparently he was offering advice—solace? warning?—to one of the circle of listeners, a newcomer, the father of an eleven-year-old girl, who was just now entering this rocky terrain. The man had bowed his head, and Bobby Gunn reached out a hand to pat his shoulder. "You've done all you can do," he said with certainty. "Sometimes it just comes down to luck. We got unlucky with ours. The worst thing you can imagine just keeps getting worse. You find yourself doing and saying the most unlikely things." And now he related, in his increasingly choked voice, the rest of the story. His daughter had not only disappeared; she had been incarcerated. While there, in psychiatric care, she'd hanged herself.

Paolo gasped, his heart seized, his body believing the story even as his mind swiftly contradicted it. *What?* Sophie had been lounging on her stoop that very morning, no better than yesterday, true, but certainly no worse. Incarceration?

Why, he must mean the hash-smoking incident, with his own D.U.I. to complicate the matter. Was Gunn using Sophie to elicit pity? And how, exactly, did he think he could get away with it? These people had been babysitting and hiring and marrying and nominating and showering and cuckolding and roasting and eulogizing one another for generations; anyone other than the newcomer in the small circle would immediately recognize this as a lie.

"Laurel," Bobby Gunn said then, swilling the last of his drink. The circle of friends bowed their heads. And in the time it took to inhale a single breath Paolo remembered that there had been another daughter. Sophie's older sister. His mind stumbled into chaotic synch with his heart.

This was what should have forced him to end his secret life with Sophie. To retrieve his silly car from the valet service and drive three miles east to the scary rubble of the transitional side of town and pull the girl out of it, drag her by force, by the nape of her neck, into this clubhouse. It should have impelled him to act. But it didn't.

***

Paolo had been back in New York for almost a year when he heard about Sophie's marriage. Mary Annie sent him the *Chronicle* picture of the girl and her fiancé, the two of them no different from any of the other photographed couples, sitting in an arbor in the usual costumes, his hands on her shoulders. Paolo didn't spot her when he first scanned the page, looking for that trademark smile. But the unremarkability of the image was, of course, what made it remarkable. Her hair—could it be a wig? Surely all the king's hairdressers wouldn't have been able to tame that nest of singed straw and dye, or grow it out so hastily to the blond coif she now wore. There were no visible punctures in her eyebrows or nose or the tops of her ears. Airbrushing? Or had she simply healed that quickly? Credit the resilience of youth? He stared at the photo, oblivious of the fiancé, whose hands bore no tattoos, whose brown hair swept over a forehead that might still be spotted with pimples but certainly didn't sprout horns. That person was inconsequential to Paolo. And Paolo realized that he himself was as inconsequential to Sophie as any other Houstonian who happened to page through the Lifestyle section that Sunday morning.

Then Paolo gazed into Sophie's clear, smart eyes until he finally saw what he had missed: this girl had prevailed. Her triumph was in the tilt of her chin, in the provocative parting of her lips, behind which lay the promise of that stunning naughty smile, the knocked-out tooth that would, of course, have been repaired.

All along he'd misunderstood the role she was playing, the drama she was enacting. The story he'd been constructing for himself when he was with her— that intense period during which he wasn't turning her in to her parents or to the authorities, the extent of what he'd considered his moral quandary and journey—had been another story altogether; Sophie had been fashioning it for herself and for her mother and her father, for their well-intentioned, grieving friends, for her own friends still in school, and, most significantly, for the memory of her sister. *I have survived*, she had concluded the tale—the victor. Paolo wondered if others understood the amazing and unlikely thing Sophie had done, the treacherous gauntlet she'd run and come through intact.

This same newspaper had announced the arrival of Mary Annie's first grandchild early the summer before, a little girl, named something fanciful and trendily ridiculous, something that her parents, particularly her mother, Meredith, former dope dealer and hell-raiser, hoped and prayed would suit her as she emerged into the world. ★

FOR FURTHER READING

THE ONES THAT GOT AWAY

This anthology is not encyclopedic. There's no way that it could be, or should be. Readers will probably peruse the table of contents and say *I wonder why he left out X?* If X is *Blood and Money*, then I suppose it's a fair question. But in fact important pieces got left out for lots of reasons. In many cases I couldn't get the reprint rights. And in other cases, there was just too much to choose from. Reprint rights can get expensive. Still, I'm not going to be asking "why isn't more written about Houston" any time soon.

Gaping holes in the Houston bibliography do exist. It's hard to explain why a city of Houston's stature is the subject of so few general histories. Other than David McComb's *Houston, A History* and Marguerite Johnston's *Houston: The Unknown City 1836–1946*, there's not much out there. I'm pretty sure that if Jesse Jones or Roy Hofheinz had been from New York, they would have been the subjects of standard biographies, and, in the case of Hofheinz, a musical. After all, Judge Hofheinz really did become the Phantom of the Astrodome (see David Kaplan's "Let it Rain").

But let me turn now from literature that doesn't exist, to that which does, but which I didn't include here.

I'll start with the good news. Literarily, 2009 was a good year for Houston. Tracy Daugherty wrote an extremely well received biography of Donald Barthelme, and in the process rendered Houston quite vividly. And Attica Locke's *Black Water Rising* attracted more national attention than any Houston-based novel has in some time. Houstonian Gwendolyn Zepeda also published the well-received *Houston, We Have a Problema*. Bryan Burroughs' *The Big Rich*, which looked back at the era of the Texas oilman, discussed at length legendary Houston names, such as Roy Cullen. Most improbably, a play titled *Enron* was among the sensations of last year's London theater season, though it did bomb on Broadway.

Looking forward, substantial biographies of Dominque de Menil and Ima Hogg are currently in the works.

Native son Thomas Thompson's *Blood and Money* is the best known of the omitted titles. Rather than that widely known work, I was hoping to include an excerpt from *Hearts*, Thompson's non-fiction saga about the Texas Medical Center and the rivalry between Denton Cooley and Michael DeBakey, but I ultimately couldn't track down the rights.

I also hoped to include the chapter on the Shamrock Hotel from George Fuermann's *Houston, Land of the Big Rich*, and also the chapter from Edna Ferber's *Giant* in which she gave a fictionalized account of the hotel's notorious opening night party; I'll also point readers to the Aaron Latham *Esquire* article "Urban Cowboy," and to *New Yorker* articles on the openings of both the Astrodome and of Foley's Department Store downtown. Interested readers can find the latter, and numerous other Houston pieces, on the CD collection the magazine issued a few years ago. You can also go *National Geographic's* website to read the very interesting article by Mimi Swartz on the taming of the wild Houston spirit.

As for fiction, the city may not have its signature novel. And it may well be that the city now has so many facets that no novel could do it justice. But there are a lot of titles out there. Here's an incomplete list:

David Appelfield's 1987 novel *Once Removed* deals with Holocaust survivors living in Houston. (You may be unfamiliar with the title, but don't cry for Appelfield. He now lives in and writes about Paris.)

Suzanne Morris' *Wives and Mistresses* follows the fortunes of two competing Houston families. Robert Cohen set part of his *The Here and Now* in the Texas Medical Center. Lionel Garcia's *A Shroud in the Family* deals with a young Latino who is diagnosed as having no personality. Paula Webb's *Domestic Life* was noted for its depiction of a "wild child" young girl, but it is also an insider's look at the world of the Menils. Gail Donohue Storey set a pair of novels about a librarian's search for happiness, *The Lord's Hotel* and *God's Country Club*, in a very eccentric Houston.

Laura Furman set some short stories and a moody crime novel, *The Shadow Line*, in Houston. Her novella *The Glass House* is considered to be a thinly veiled portrait of the Menils, but it is set in the Northeast. Iranian author Farnoosh Moshiri's *Against Gravity* is largely set in Houston.

Former University of Houston professor Mary Robinson's *Substraction* is a bleakly funny evocation of Houston's weirdness.

Patricia Page's *Hope's Cadillac* explores Houston's version of the late-60s counterculture, while J. Miller's *Surviving Joy* is set here during the Depression. Ralph Ditman's *Allen's Landing* is a Michner-esque retelling of the city's founding. David Lindsey's crime novels featuring Houston-based detective Stuart Haydon include *Absence of Light*, *The Color of Night* among others.

On the subject of crime writing, Walter Mosley's famed fictional detective, "Easy" Rawlins is from the Fifth Ward. *Gone Fishin'* tells the story of how Easy left Houston for good.

Before he became *Newsweek's* book critic, native son Walter Clemons wrote a Prix de Rome-winning story collection, *The Poison Tree and Other Stories*, with several of the stories set in Houston. Native Houstonian Katherine Center's *The Bright Side of Disaster* took a humorous look at young motherhood. At least one of Frederick Barthelme's numerous novels is set in Houston: *Natural Selection*. Kathleen Cambor's *The Book of Mercy* is partly set in the world of Houston medicine.

The memoir wave of recent decades includes a significant Houston title: Robert Leleux's *The Memoirs of a Beautiful Boy*.

Playwright Horton Foote's *The Trip to Bountiful* is largely set in Houston, as is his lesser-known one-act *Land of the Astronauts* (and other plays). A chapter in his memoir *Farewell: a Memoir of a Texas Childhood* recalls Foote's frequent boyhood trips from Wharton to Houston.

A chapter from Dan Rather's memoir *The Camera Never Blinks* describes his Huck Finn-like boyhood of swimming and catching turtles in Buffalo Bayou, while a chapter from George Foreman's *By George* (co-written with Joel Engel) recalls his early days as the meanest man on the mean streets of the Fifth Ward.

And, though several of the pieces collected here are critical of Houston, I didn't include any that are outright attacks on the "Houston way." But critiques such as Randall Patterson's *New York Times Magazine* article "Houston Does Not Believe in Tears" were plentiful after the Enron debacle. Native son Benjamin Moser, recently a finalist for the National Book Critics Circle Award for his biography of Brazilian writer Clarice Lispector, really let Houston have it in an American Scholar essay, "Houston and History." His critique of Houston's lack of a historical sense was so biting that I used it in a fund-raising letter for this project.

Finally, the most surprising discovery I've made about "literary Houston" was this: between 1928 and 1932 Houston had its own *New Yorker*-inspired weekly magazine, *The Gargoyle*. Its deco illustrations and sophisticated writing gave me a very different picture of Jazz Age Houston than any I'd previously had. In fact, I'm not sure I'd ever combined the words "Jazz Age" and "Houston" before. Bound sets are available in the Texas Room of the Julia Ideson Library, the University of Houston Special Collections, and perhaps elsewhere.

ACKNOWLEDGMENTS

Assembling this anthology has been a long-term labor of love, one which I began while hanging out in Houston libraries, ostensibly working on other projects. I'd like to thank Judy Alter, former director of TCU Press, whose "yes" allowed me to bring my daydreamed project to publication.

I also thank TCU Press editor Susan R. Petty for patiently guiding the book toward its final form, and offering encouragement along the way.

I am also grateful to Teresa Demchak, Marilyn Oshman, Marion Barthelme, and Stella Lillicrop for their backing, which allowed me to put together what I hope is a collection worthy of the city it represents.

I offer special thanks to the board and staff of the Brown Foundation. This anthology would be very much the poorer without their support.

I'd like to thank the many writers, publishers, and heirs who freely shared their writing about Houston. Without them this anthology really wouldn't have been possible.

Finally, my wife Susanne has supported me in more ways than I can easily explain. I'm very grateful.

PERMISSIONS

Crouch, Stanley. From "Blues in the Capital of Capitalism," *Village Voice* August 12-18, 1981. Copyright © 1981 by Stanley Crouch. Reprinted with permission of the author.

Cunxin, Li. "Defection," from *Mao's Last Dancer* by Li Cunxin. Copyright © 2004 by Qingdao Investments Pty Ltd. Used by permission of G.P. Putnam's Sons, a division of Penguin Group (USA) Inc.

Daugherty, Tracy. "Almost Barcelona," *Gettysburg Review*. Copyright © 1995 by Tracy Daugherty. Used with permission of the author.

de Beauvoir, Simone. *America Day by Day*. University of California Press, 1999. Permission granted by University of California Press.

de la Peña, José Enrique. *With Santa Anna in Texas: A Personal Narrative*. College Station: Texas A & M Press, 1975. Translated by Carmen Perry. Translation copyright © 1975 by Carmen Perry. Reprinted with permission of the publisher.

Diaz, Tony. "A Night at the Opera." Copyright © 2009 by Tony Diaz. www.nuestrapalabra .org. Permission granted by the author.

Doody, Terrence. "Immanent Domains." *Cite* Spring 2004. Copyright © 2004 by Terrence Doody. Reprinted with permission of the author.

Doty, Mark. "Southern Comfort," *Smithsonian Magazine*, October 2008. Copyright © 2008 by Mark Doty. Reprinted with permission from the author.

Gaitskill, Mary. "An Old Virgin." (Originally published as "A Dream of Men.") *The New Yorker*, November 23, 1998. Reprinted by permission of the author.

Garcia, Lionel. "The Emergency Room." *The Day They Took My Uncle and Other Stories*. Copyright © 2001. Reprinted with permission of the author.

Garreau, Joel. From *Edge City*. Doubleday & Co., 1991. Copyright © 1991 by Joel Garreau. Used by permission of Doubleday, a division of Random House, Inc.

Gray, Lisa. "Revolution in Chrome," *Houston Press* July 6, 2000. Reprinted with permission.

Guerard, Albert J. *The Touch of Time: Myth, Memory and the Self*. Palo Alto: Stanford Alumni Association, 1980. Reprinted with permission of Collot Guerard.

Guerard, Albert L. *Personal Equation*. New York: W.W. Norton & Co., 1948. Reprinted with permission of Collot Guerard.

Hardin, Stephen L. From *Texian Iliad: A Military History of the Texas Revolution, 1835-1836*. Illustrated by Gary S. Zaboly. Austin: University of Texas Press. Copyright © 1994. Reprinted by permission of the University of Texas Press.

Hardin, Stephen L. From *Texian Macabre: The Melancholy Tale of a Hanging in Early Houston*. Abilene: State House Press, 2007. Reprinted with permission of State House Press.

Hardy, Robert Earl. *A Deeper Blue: The Life and Music of Townes Van Zandt*. Denton: University of North Texas Press. Copyright © 2008 by Robert Earl Hardy. Reprinted with the permission of University of North Texas Press.

Harrigan, Stephen. "Between Heaven and Earth," *Texas Monthly* April 2003. Reprinted with permission.

Harvey, Douglas Pegues. From "Il Duomo," *Texas Architect*. May/June 1990. Copyright © 1990 by the Texas Society of Architects/AIA. Reprinted with permission.

Hirsch, Edward. "Apostrophe," *Earthly Measures*. New York: Alfred A. Knopf, 2004. Copyright © 2004 by Edward Hirsch. Reprinted with permission of the author.

Hoagland, Tony. "Because It Is Houston." Copyright © 2009 by Tony Hoagland. Printed with permission of the author.

Horne, Jed. From *Breach of Faith: Hurricane Katrina and the Near Death of a Great American City*. New York: Random House, Inc. Copyright © 2006 by Jed Horne. Used by permission of Random House, Inc.

Jackson, James Thomas. "Ned Bobkoff and Me," From *Waiting in Line at the Drugstore*. Ed. June Acosta. Denton: University of North Texas Press, 1993. Used with permission of the University of North Texas Press.

Jordan, Barbara and Shelby Hearon. *Barbara Jordan: A Self Portrait*. Doubleday & Co., Inc. © 1978, 1979. Reprinted by permission of The Wendy Weil Agency, Inc.

Kaplan, David. "Let It Rain," *Cite*. Summer 1986. Reprinted with permission of the author.

Keats, John and Thomas Thompson. From *Howard Hughes*. Copyright © 1966 by Random House, Inc. Used by permission of Random House, Inc.

Kreneck, Thomas. *Mexican-American Odyssey: Felix Tijerina, Entrepreneur and Civic Leader, 1905-1965*. College Station: Texas A&M University Press, Copyright © 2001 by the Center for Mexican American Studies, University of Houston.

Levy, Rich. "Main Street, Dusk." Copyright © 2000 by Rich Levy. Used with permission of the author.

Lewis, Grover. From *Splendor in the Short Grass: The Grover Lewis Reader*, edited by Jan Reid and W.K. Stratton, Copyright © 2005. Reprinted by permission of the University of Texas Press.

Lopate, Phillip. "Houston Hide and Seek," from *Against Joie de Vivre: Personal Essays*. New York: Poseidon Press, 1989. Copyright © 1989 by Phillip Lopate. Reprinted with permission of The Wendy Weil Agency.

Mailer, Norman. *Of a Fire on the Moon*. Boston: Little, Brown and Co., 1969. Reprinted with permission of the Norman Mailer Estate.

McLean, Bethany and Peter Elkind, *The Smartest Guys in the Room*. Copyright © 2003 by Fortune, a division of Time, Inc. Used by permission of Portfolio, an imprint of Penguin Group (USA) Inc.

McMurtry, Larry. From *Some Can Whistle*. Copyright © 1989 by Larry McMurtry. Reprinted with permission of the author.

Mencken, H.L. *Thirty-five Years of Newspaper Work: A Memoir*. Baltimore: Johns Hopkins University Press, 1994. Reprinted with permission of the publisher.

Miller, Vassar. "Pilgrim, Perplexed" copyright © 1963 and "Whitewash of Houston" copyright © 1984. *If I Had Wheels or Love*. Dallas: SMU Press, 1991. Reprinted with permission of SMU Press.

Morris, Jan. "Boomtown." Copyright © 1981 by Jan Morris. Reprint permission granted by A P Watt Ltd. on behalf of Jan Morris.

Nelson, Antonya. "Emininent Domain," *The New Yorker*, January 26, 2004. Reprinted with permission of the author.

Olmsted, Frederick Law. *A Journey Through Texas: Or a Saddle-Trip on the Southwestern Frontier*. New York: Dix, Edwards, 1857. Reprinted by University of Nebraska Press 2004. Introduction Copyright © 2004 by Witold Rybcznski.

Patoski, Joe Nick. From *Willie Nelson*. Little, Brown and Co., 2008. Copyright © by Joe Nick Patoski. By permission of Little, Brown & Company.

Phillips, Robert. "Gene" and "Fester." Copyright © 2010 by Robert Phillips. Published with permission of the author.

Porter, William Syndey (O. Henry.) "A Sporting Interest." *Postscripts*. N.Y.: Harper & Brothers, 1923.

Rifenburgh, Daniel. "El Vendedor," *Advent*. London: Waywiser Press. 2002. Copyright © 2002 by Daniel Rifenburgh. Reprinted with permission of the author.

Roussel, Hubert. *The Houston Symphony Orchestra, 1913-1971*. Austin: University of Texas Press, 1972. Reprinted with permission of Peter Roussel.

Serpas, Martha. "Sunrise," *The Dirty Side of the Storm*. New York: W. W. Norton, 2007. Copyright © 2007 by Martha Serpas. Used by permission of W. W. Norton & Company, Inc.

Sjolander, John. "Cedar Bayou" and "Eileen and I," *Salt of the Earth and Sea*. Dallas: P. L. Turner Co., 1928.

Swartz, Mimi and Sherron Watkins. *Power Failure: The Inside Story of the Collapse of Enron*. New York: Doubleday, 2003. Copyright © by Mimi Swartz. Used by permission of Doubleday, a division of Random House, Inc.

Sweet, Alexander. From *Through Texas on a Mexican Mustang*. 1882.

Thomas, Larry D. "Buffalo Bayou." Copyright © 2009 by Larry D. Thomas. Reprinted with permission of the author.

Thomas, Lorenzo. "Liquid City." Copyright © 1984 by Lorenzo Thomas. Reprinted with permission of Aldon Nielsen and Cecilio Thomas, literary executors for Lorenzo Thomas.

Walsh, Robb. "Guess Who's Cooking Your Dinner?" *Houston Press* December 20, 2007. Reprinted with permission.

William, George G. *The Blind Bull*. New York: Abelard Press, 1952. Reprinted with permission of Stephen G. Williams.

INDEX